Francis Preston Blair

Francis Preston Blair

by
Elbert B. Smith

THE FREE PRESS
A Division of Macmillan Publishing Co., Inc.
NEW YORK

Collier Macmillan Publishers
LONDON

THE FREE PRESS
A Division of Macmillan Publishing Co., Inc.
866 Third Avenue, New York, N.Y.   10022

Collier Macmillan Canada, Ltd.

Library of Congress Catalog Card Number: 79–7580

Printed in the United States of America

printing number

1 2 3 4 5 6 7 8 9 10

Library of Congress Cataloging in Publication Data

Smith, Elbert B
    Francis Preston Blair.

    Includes bibliographical references and index.
    1. Blair, Francis Preston, 1791–1876.
2. Blair family.   3. United States—Politics and
government—1815–1861.   4. United States—Politics
and government—1849–1877.   5. Politicians—United
States—Biography.
E415.9.B633S64   973.5′092′4   [B]   79–7580
ISBN 0–02–929510–6

TO E. BROOKE LEE
because he remembers Lizzie

Contents

Acknowledgments

M Y interest in Blair was first stimulated by Avery Craven, an incomparable teacher. The Social Science Research Council contributed generous research grants, and the University of Maryland provided both grants and a teaching program highly conducive to research. Elizabeth Blair Lee's grandson, E. Brooke Lee, sat at her feet and heard much. His stories and career shed much light on the character of his progenitors. The late Kelly Smither, who held Blair's old clerkship in Kentucky, led me to the ancient court records still tied with ribbons as Blair and his predecessors had left them. At the Kentucky Historical Society, Frances Coleman and G. Glenn Clift were equally helpful. Among many gracious librarians, Alexander Clark, the curator at Princeton University, deserves special mention, and the university microfilmed hundreds of letters for a reduced fee. Kathleen Hall Nicholas spent many hours helping decipher the microfilms. Colleagues David Grimstead, George Callcott, and Emory Evans read a section critically. Graduate students Mark Steinitz and Carolyn Hoffman assisted directly, while Tom Emmerson, Parker Bogue, Tom Johnson, and Mary Kehoe added to my knowledge of the period. Other helpers include Carol Kennedy, Patricia Warren, Dorothy Lukens, Vera Blenkiron, Karen Norman, Gertrude Apple, Jennifer Johnson, Ann Morgan, and my daughter-in-law Jean P. Smith. For the Free Press, Amy Litt read the manuscript with a microscope and won more of our arguments than she lost. Every author should be so fortunate. Editors Colin Jones and Kitty Moore also made valuable suggestions.

And finally, words cannot express my continuing debt to my wife Jean.

Introduction

DURING the early 1870s an ancient couple on horseback occasionally passed along the street and road stretching from the White House into the green hills of nearby Maryland. The old man was skeleton thin. His wife still enjoyed the athletic figure of younger years. They usually wore dark clothes with the cut of an earlier generation, and both still rode straight in the saddle. They were easily identifiable from a distance as Mr. and Mrs. Francis Preston Blair of Silver Spring plantation, and they had been riding together for sixty years.

The old man was prone to exaggerate the value of his crops, but Silver Spring was a delightful place to live. It was a restful retreat just six miles from the tensions of the city, and at least six American presidents had enjoyed the cool shade of Blair's porch and trees. One of the Blairs' descendants still has the well-preserved outhouse that presumably served their needs.

"Old Blair's" rides into Washington no longer set the politicians and newsmen buzzing with speculation over his next move. The White House of Andrew Jackson and Martin Van Buren had been almost a second home for Blair, and he had been almost equally welcome when the occupants were Abraham Lincoln and Andrew Johnson. He had boldly advised and occasionally reprimanded all of them, and his stamp was clearly imprinted on many of their policies. The days, however, when Blair would carry a pail of milk to the White House before he and "Old Hickory" Jackson got down to the serious business of planning national policy were long since gone. His son Montgomery and his daughter Elizabeth Lee still owned the two old family houses, square and stolid, joined together across the street from the White House, but for the Blairs the few hundred yards separating the Blair–Lee houses from the White House of Ulysses S. Grant were a wide gap. General Francis P. (Frank) Blair, Jr., and Grant had faced the Confederate guns together at Vicksburg and Chattanooga, but this was no longer relevant. Grant the general had been a close friend, but Grant the president was a political enemy.

Blair's life had coincided with the development of the American political system, and he had done much to shape its practical structure. In turn, his career personified the uniqueness of the American democratic experience. He had never held an elected office or delivered an important speech. He had spent much of his life in straitened economic circumstances, and even his maximum level of prosperity could be classed only as comfortable. He had edited an important political newspaper, but for only fifteen years. His name was known to every American interested in politics, however, and friend and foe alike considered him a mover and shaker in national affairs. In private life he was the meekest and mildest of men, but four presidents—Jackson, Van Buren, Lincoln, and Johnson—had all been accused of submitting to his domination.

Naturally enough, the verdict on his character and achievements was far from unanimous. "Of all the acquaintances I made at Washington," wrote former president Martin Van Buren to Blair, "there had not been one in whose honor and purity, nor in the sincerity and disinterestedness of whose friendship I had more confidence than I have placed in yours." According to Abraham Lincoln's close friend Ward Lamon, "between Francis P. Blair and Mr. Lincoln there existed from the first to last a confidential relationship as close as that maintained by Mr. Lincoln with any other man. To Mr. Blair he almost habitually revealed himself upon delicate and grave subjects more freely than to any other. When he had conceived an important but difficult plan, he was almost certain, before giving it practical form, to try it by the touchstone of Mr. Blair's fertile and acute mind." Secretary of the Navy Gideon Welles believed that Blair more than any other single person was most responsible for Lincoln's decision to reinforce Fort Sumter. "The Blairs," said Lincoln himself, "are . . . strong tenacious men, having some peculiarities, among them the energy with which their feuds are carried on." The New York editor and politician Thurlow Weed took a slightly different view: "If Old Blair had lived in the days of our first parents, the presence of the serpent would have been superfluous. If, at a later period, he had been 'one of the twelve,' there would have been no question into whose pocket the 'thirty pieces' would have dropped."

Blair was no longer concerned with Thurlow Weed. He was not pleased with the state of national affairs, but he knew that his own time of battle had passed. He was also richly endowed with blessings that sometimes make old age the best part of life. He had enjoyed a momentous past, and he could look to the future of his progeny with immense hope. He was sentimental and much given to memories, and as he walked and rode among familiar scenes there was much to relive. Marked for an early death by lung hemorrhages and general frailty, he had once prayed in agony that he might live to reach forty and educate his children. He had doubled this allotment, and had long since assured his late friend, Martin Van Buren, that he would live on in the lives of his brilliant grandchildren and thereby attain immortality in this world as well as in the next.

At thirty Blair had been bankrupt, heavily in debt, and clearly doomed to obscurity. At forty, the age to which he had aspired, he had stood at the right hand of President Andrew Jackson. He had loved and served Old Hickory well, and had thereby become a national figure in his own right. As the Democratic party's national political editor, he had dramatized the egalitarian ideals of Jacksonian democracy for a generation of vigorous, imaginative, and acquisitive Americans. He had helped to determine the policies of Presidents Jackson and Van Buren, and he had defended their every act with the rhetoric of high democratic principle.

In the years between Van Buren and Lincoln, the democracy that Blair glorified had inflicted him with grave disappointments. Struggles among politicians, sections, and interest groups had become entangled with the great moral issue of slavery. Blair's opposition to the annexation of Texas and the expansion of the South's "peculiar institution" had made him an outcast in the Democratic party he had helped to create. He had fought back, however. His identification with the late Andrew Jackson had enabled him to serve as a bridge over which hundreds of thousands of Democrats could pass into the new Republican party without feeling disloyal to their memories of Old Hickory.

Against the recommendations of the army's commander-in-chief and most of Lincoln's cabinet, the slaveholding Free-Soiler Blair had insisted that the president must emulate Andrew Jackson and stand firm against South Carolina. The year 1861 was not 1833, however, and this time most of the South had united behind South Carolina. The Civil War had come, and the Blairs had done their duty. One son had served with distinction in Lincoln's cabinet. Another had saved Missouri for the Union and had fought heroically from Vicksburg to Savannah as a Union general. A son-in-law had commanded the Union's North Atlantic blockade and squadrons on the western rivers. The Blairs had given Lincoln devoted friendship and loyal support. Their efforts had occasionally been more ardent than wise, and more often accepted than rewarded, but they had shared and rejoiced in the achievement of Lincoln's most cherished goals. As Lincoln lay dead, Blair's daughter Elizabeth Lee had nursed Mary Lincoln through the first dark weeks of her bereavement.

True to their southern heritage and still Democrats at heart, the Blairs had opposed radical reconstruction. Like most Americans, they could not accept the full implications of their own most cherished democratic ideals. Frank Blair had been the Democratic candidate for vice-president in 1868 on a conservative platform. In theory, the Blairs had lost this struggle, but the policies they had feared were already proving to be more form than substance. The North was no more ready to enforce the laws designed to elevate the former slaves than the South was to obey them. Radicals and conservatives alike were now concerned primarily with the new economic developments of the "Great Barbecue" and the "Gilded Age."

Francis Preston Blair and his Eliza had traveled a long road since their marriage sixty years earlier in the governor's mansion in the little frontier capital of Frankfort, Kentucky. They and their beloved American Union had been infants together, and their developing problems, failures, achievements, joys, and heartbreaks had paralleled those of the young nation itself. Their lives were almost finished, but they had lived to see the threat of disunion and the curse of slavery finally destroyed in the flames of a civil war. If they were not entirely satisfied with the results, they could at least share the consolation described by Walt Whitman: "the prophetic vision, the job of being toss'd in the brave turmoil of these times . . . with the proud consciousness that amid whatever clouds, seductions, or heart-wearying postponements, we have never deserted, never despair'd, never abandoned the faith." No historian would argue that they were invariably wise and free from error, but few would question the importance of their story to any one seeking to understand the first eighty years of America's national history.

Francis Preston Blair

Chapter 1

The Beginning

FRANCIS Preston Blair, called Preston by friends, always remembered his mother with deep affection, but no record remains of specific events in the life of Elizabeth Smith Blair and her young children. For Preston his father's struggles with debt remained always a painful memory, but they did not prevent his developing an unusually sunny temperament. The Blair home was filled with warmth and love, and the outside world offered excitement, adventure, and beauty.[1]

The Blair family lived on the edge of poverty, but enjoyed the prestige of a distinguished heritage. Samuel and John Blair, brothers and Scotch-Irish descendants of various fighting Blairs in early British history, had come to America in the mid-eighteenth century; Samuel became a great evangelist who could stir the religious emotions of large audiences to a roaring heat, and his younger brother, John, also a frontier evangelist, eventually occupied a chair of theology and the vice-presidency of the college at Princeton.

Both Samuel and John took time from their ardent pursuit of righteousness to father large families. Samuel, Jr., became one of Virginia's great churchmen and educators. Two of John's twelve children, John Durbarrow and James, also went to Virginia at an early age. John Durbarrow Blair became principal of Washington Henry Academy, founded a classical school at Richmond, became known as one of the "Two Parsons" of Virginia, and was an intimate friend of George Washington and John Marshall. James Blair, however, departed from the practice if not from the faith of his fathers. At Princeton he studied law instead

I

of theology. In Virginia he subsequently practiced with minor success, and he was elected to the state legislative assembly.

In Virginia, James Blair married into another Scotch-Irish family, as well known for military prowess and material success as his own was in the work of the Lord. General John Preston of Smithfield, Virginia, headed one of the state's dynasties. His grandson, General Francis Preston, was a hero at the Battle of King's Mountain. William C. Preston, son of General Francis Preston, became a noted senator from South Carolina. Prestons were thoroughly intermarried with McDowells, Breckinridges, Floyds, and other pillars of Virginia aristocracy. Susan Preston, daughter of General Francis Preston, married her cousin, Governor James McDowell, and their daughter Elizabeth married Senator Thomas Hart Benton of Missouri. Ann Preston, daughter of General John Preston, married Colonel Francis Smith.

Elizabeth Smith, the eldest daughter of Colonel Francis and Ann Preston Smith, became the patient and loving wife of the fledgling attorney James Blair. Her parents moved to Kentucky in the early 1790s, and James Blair, perhaps through her persuasion, followed with his family shortly thereafter.[2]

Membership in the Preston-Smith clan brought James Blair prestige and an occasional minor inheritance. It also carried demands for a worldly success that he could never attain. In 1796 James became attorney general for the state of Kentucky, but the duties were entirely advisory and the annual salary was only $400. The procrastination that his son always remembered as the curse of James Blair's life leads to the inescapable conclusion that James found his profession distasteful. He was well versed in the law, but lacked the aggressiveness and the taste for violent controversy required for success at the bar in a land where out-of-court settlements often meant gouging of eyes, biting of noses, and duels with knife and gun. In early Kentucky men took what they could and got what they took. Rich lands, excellent water transportation, conflicting land claims and perpetual litigation, fluctuations of the currency, swarms of wildcat banks, and the honest speculation made possible by the steady growth of the population, offered rich opportunities to farmers, lawyers, businessmen, and speculators alike. James Blair, however, could never grasp his share. He supported his family in the style demanded by their social position, but the effort meant a bitter and endless struggle against ever-mounting debts. Between 1798 and 1819, James Blair was sued no less than forty-five times for amounts totaling more than $7,000, and most of the suits ended in judgments against him. These included personal notes, a few store bills, and occasional items such as $81 owed a tutor for tuition and books for Blair's two sons.[3]

Despite his troubles, however, James Blair was a useful citizen. He and his partner, Harry Toulmin, revised and published the first written compilation of the laws of Kentucky.[4] His long tenure as attorney general indicated that numerous governors found his legal advice acceptable. For many years he was trustee of the Transylvania Seminary of higher learning, and he was an elder in his church. He was a loving and much-loved husband and father, and was never without a large collection of friends ready to lend him money and endorse his notes.

James Blair fell behind his in-laws in wealth, but he did produce his share of new clan members. There were seven children. Francis Preston, named for the general, was born at Abingdon, Virginia, on April 12, 1791. William Preston Smith Blair arrived in 1796, Susannah Trigg in 1798, and Eliza Jane in 1804. Three other sons died in infancy.

Young Preston Blair was an imaginative, perceptive youth with a keen eye for color and pattern, and Franklin county, Kentucky was a paradise abounding with the gifts of nature. The limestone bluffs surrounding Frankfort were lined with green forests splashed with the hues of dogwood and redbud in the spring and blazing with autumn colors in the fall. The deer and bear that had drawn Daniel Boone like a magnet into the region only a few years earlier were still plentiful. The meandering Kentucky River and its shaded little tributary, Benson's Creek, met at Frankfort, and provided a storehouse of fish for those able to catch them. The young Blair had his own gun and dog, and enjoyed a lifelong reputation for expert markmanship. His fame and fortune would ultimately rest upon urban pursuits, but the world of woods, fields, and yeomen farmers always remained his ideal of life as it should be lived.

Preston Blair grew into a skinny, homely young man of average height. His sharp, angular features were carved on the front of a large head whose weight appeared tilted toward the rear, and his only physical attraction was a pair of steady, clear blue eyes. Various observers thought him consumptive in appearance, and his early death was freely predicted. This physical ugliness was offset, however, by great personal charm derived from a genuinely warm interest in other people of every variety. He was, indeed, highly gifted in the art of giving and inspiring personal affection. His life would be filled with deep and abiding friendships, which were often required to stand the test of bitter political differences as well as long separations and the passage of time. Women particularly, of all ages, found him a confidant and friend to whom they could pour out their hearts without fear of misunderstanding or ridicule. His wide range of associations led his family and friends to consider him a democrat long before such a title had become fashionable or even respectable.

This compassionate nature blended easily with the powerful Calvinist heritage of the Blairs. The good Calvinist proved his election to the Kingdom of God by helping to improve the world of men. James Blair had learned this at the feet of his eloquent father and uncle, and his children received the message early. From his earliest manhood, Preston Blair's personal ambitions and fortunes had to compete with an endless concern for public affairs. Like most people, he identified the public interest with his own welfare and emotional leanings whenever possible, but his long life would be studded with conspicuous examples of personal sacrifice for the sake of principle.

The young man was not, however, a candidate for sainthood. His capacity for tolerance and forbearance was matched by a spirit of intense partisanship and a spectacular taste for bitter controversy when he considered a worthy cause in danger. He was to maintain close personal friendships with numerous political enemies, but his utter detestation for a few others would be deep and abiding. The God of John Calvin and of the Blairs was a God of stern justice, and Preston Blair found forgiveness hard for those whom he came to consider willful instruments of evil.

Books and education were necessities for the Blair family, and young Preston had the best available. He became well versed in the Bible, the classics, and history, and he read widely all his life. At nineteen he rode thirty-six miles to Lexington to enroll at Transylvania University, a little college headed by the Reverend James Blythe, an early Presbyterian leader in Kentucky. Its founder, George Nicholas, was violently anti-Federalist, and the little school left a strong Jeffersonian mark on many of its students. In 1810, when Blair enrolled, the school counted eighteen grammar and thirty-nine scientific students. The subjects ranged from elementary reading and writing to the study of law, a subject that Henry Clay himself taught briefly at the school. Blair studied moral philosophy, logic, criticism, and belles lettres, as well as the law that he hoped to follow as a profession. He graduated with honors in 1811.[5]

The twenty-year-old lawyer returned home immediately to help his father draw up for Kentucky a blistering indictment against the Bank of the United States. The Bank's charter was not renewed in Congress, however, and the controversy was soon dead. In crowded taverns, public squares, and courthouse halls, another subject was pushing the Bank out of the public mind. Kentucky newspapers and politicians were beating the drums for a war with Great Britain to eliminate the Indians and their alleged Canadian sponsors by driving the British out of Canada forever.

The young "war hawks" from Kentucky, Tennessee, Ohio, Louisiana, and the western regions of the old seaboard states had captured control of Congress. They were determined to punish Great Britain for its depredations against New England shipping, and if in the process they conquered Canada, so much the better. The New England preference for peace and profits in spite of occasional losses did not deter the war hawks. The westerners had convinced themselves that every Indian attack was British-inspired. They were now prepared to wipe British and Indians alike from the American continent to make it safe for those selected by the Almighty for its exploitation. Henry Clay sounded the tocsin by assuring the United States Senate that the Kentucky militia could conquer Canada unassisted if given the authority to march.

The irascible Canadians defeated their liberators, Kentuckians included, in the War of 1812, but Kentucky did produce some heroes. Richard M. Johnson supposedly killed the great Shawnee chief Tecumseh in a hand-to-hand combat and thereby won the fame that later made him vice-president of the United States. George Madison, Preston Blair's redoubtable uncle by marriage, left his post as state auditor and rode away as a major of volunteers. Madison returned covered with wounds and glory, and was rewarded with election to the governorship in 1816, even though he was already at the point of death when the votes were cast.

Madison had helped finance Preston Blair's education at Transylvania, and the younger man eagerly enlisted to fight at his uncle's side. Blair, however, was not destined for military glory. At Vincennes, Indiana, he was prostrated by a terrible hemorrhage of the lungs and was sent home more dead than alive.[6] It was all a bitter disappointment, but compensations waited back in Frankfort. Like many young men in all wars, Preston Blair had taken a bride before marching away to meet the enemy.

The new Mrs. Blair had come to Frankfort in 1810 with her stepfather, a doughty old frontier hero who had just been elected governor of Kentucky. General Charles Scott had fought the British in the Revolution, and he had helped "Mad Anthony" Wayne kill Indians at Fallen Timbers, Ohio, in 1794. He had no doubt that Britain must be driven out of North America. He helped promote the War of 1812, and he was an ideal governor for launching the Kentucky war effort. For the young men of Frankfort the governor offered still another excitement in 1812. He had two lovely, extremely marriageable stepdaughters: Eliza Violet Gist, aged eighteen, and her sister, Maria Cecil, aged fifteen.

The girls had a unique heritage. Their grandfather, Christopher Gist, had guided George Washington on his first expedition across the Alleghenies and had established the first English settlement west of the mountains. He was also guide to General Edward Braddock on the ill-fated march against Fort Duquesne. With remarkable success Christopher Gist had enlisted Indians on the side of the English against the French, and emerged as an authentic frontier giant. His son, Colonel Nathaniel Gist, followed in the family tradition by roaming the uncharted West, serving as Indian agent, fighting Indians and French alike, and becoming a hero of both the French and Indian War and the American Revolution.

Family history relates that Colonel Nathaniel Gist, while trading among the Indians, "formed a temporary alliance with a Cherokee maiden and became the father of the famous chief Sequoyah,"[7] who often used the name George Guess or Gist. Sequoyah wrote the Cherokee alphabet that helped his tribe become the most civilized and cultured of Indians, and he is still honored by the mighty California redwood trees bearing his name.

After almost a lifetime of roaming and fighting, Nathaniel Gist at the age of fifty took his military reward of more than 17,000 acres in land grants, sold off a large portion, and settled down to the life of an aristocratic planter. In 1783 he married Judith Cary Bell, whose uncle, Archibald Cary, had presented Thomas Jefferson's bill of rights to the Virginia House of Burgesses. Judith was thirty-three, but the somewhat mature newlyweds were soon producing children with surprising regularity. Their seventh, Eliza Violet, was born in 1794.

After enduring eleven years of tranquillity in Virginia, Colonel Gist again succumbed to his lifelong urge to travel. In 1794 he moved his large tribe of children and slaves to a beautiful 4,000-acre plantation in Bourbon County, Kentucky. The new home, which he and Judith called Canewood, was his final resting place. Their eighth child, Maria, was born in 1797, but the sixty-four-year-old father died shortly before she arrived.

Judith Gist, then forty-seven, remained a widow for ten years before finding another man cut from the same heroic cloth as her late husband. She married General Scott in 1807, and with the younger girls accompanied him to Frankfort in the following year.

The beauty, wealth, and background of the Gist daughters gave them a wide choice of Kentucky manhood, but apparently both fell in love with the scrawny son of the improvident attorney general. The young man himself chose Eliza Violet, by then a womanly eighteen, but he continued to receive long, affectionate letters from the younger Maria for many years thereafter.

From the standpoint of family prestige it was an adequate match, but the rugged old titans in the governor's mansion took no pride in a son-in-law of such delicate constitution. Obviously he would die young, and the governor warned Eliza that she would be a widow in six months if she insisted upon the marriage. Eliza was a woman in love and quickly answered that she would rather be Preston Blair's widow than any other man's wife. The wedding took place at the governor's mansion on July 21, 1812. The timing of General Scott's prediction was inaccurate. Eliza became a widow but not for another sixty-four years.

It was a marriage without a single visible flaw. Eliza Blair was passionate, strong-willed, fearless, and supremely self-confident. She was also brilliant and well educated, and shared her husband's profound interest in public affairs. Above all, she adored her husband, and rarely failed to communicate her feeling that he was the wisest and noblest of men. Throughout his long, varied, and often bitterly controversial career, she was an equal partner. In return, Blair understood his wife's need for self-expression and personal achievement, and he knew the value of the prize he had won. He gladly shared with her every aspect of his life, and drew heavily upon her for strength, courage, judgment, and wisdom. The sensitive understanding that underlay Blair's attractiveness to women was not common among the men of 1812. It was invisible to Charles and Judith Scott, but immediately obvious to their more perceptive daughters.

In 1818 Maria Gist and her mother took a steamboat tour to New Orleans. Maria found the scenery, people, and social life fascinating, but reported in long colorful letters to Blair that the men were rather boring. On the return trip, however, she met twenty-seven-year-old Benjamin Gratz, member of a prominent Jewish family from Philadelphia. (Rebecca Gratz, Benjamin's beautiful sister, inspired the character Rebecca created by Sir Walter Scott in *Ivanhoe.*) Ben Gratz married Maria and settled down in Louisville to become one of Kentucky's leading citizens. Throughout his ninety-two years Ben combined an almost saintly generosity in dealing with friends and relatives with shrewd business acumen. Instead of resenting his wife's affection for her brother-in-law, Ben soon came to share it. Blair was already a vehement Jeffersonian democrat, while Gratz in the War of 1812 had served as a lieutenant in the Washington Guards, an organization which boasted that no democrat could join it. Despite frequent political differences, however, Blair and Gratz were dear friends for more than fifty years.

In 1812, the eighteen-year-old Eliza became a superb ally in Blair's struggle for life. Her presence, her cooking, and her old family lung remedy (various herbs in a base of honey and whiskey) were all highly effective.

This narrow brush with death and the ever-haunting possibility of a recurrence probably increased the young man's tenderness toward his wife, children, and friends. He thought himself living on borrowed time and prayed that he might reach forty and get the regularly arriving children educated. The illness also changed his plans for a career. His lungs could not be risked on the prolonged oratory demanded by a successful practice of the law, and although he was later admitted to the bar he never attempted to practice.

Thus, after his recovery, Blair found a modest substitute for a legal career. He became circuit court clerk in Franklin County and held the post for eighteen years. The annual salary was only $40, but the various duties carried a schedule of fees that usually averaged about $2,000 per year. The fees connected with trials were usually profitable, but the loser in a suit was always assessed with the costs, and already Blair himself was often a defendant because of inability to pay his debts. So many of his fee bills remained unpaid that in some years the clerk received less than half of his rightful income. Blair was soon engaged in numerous real estate speculations and trades, however, and could occasionally use fee bills to pay his debts to creditors who in turn owed money to Blair's fee-bill debtors.

Nathaniel Gist had died intestate, and the division of his property was a long, involved process. The Gists were highly agreeable with each other, however, and exchanged lands and property freely in efforts to attain mutual satisfaction. The Blairs received 750 acres in Logan County and eventually accepted $1,500 from Benjamin Gratz for their share of Canewood, although earlier considerations from Gratz were also involved. They also received money from part of the Gist land in Maryland. Their exact legacy is impossible to determine, but it was considerable.[8]

Real estate speculation was a universal sport in early Kentucky, and Blair had a gambling spirit. In Franklin County alone during the years 1812–1820, Preston and Eliza Blair sold three farms and one lot for a total of $12,381, while buying twelve city lots for $13,980 and four parcels of land totaling 403.5 acres for $14,676.50. In August 1814, after an appraisal of each place by three neutral friends, they swapped a country place called Bellefont to Richard T. Taylor for a brick house and lot.[9]

Blair's favorite property was a beautiful 130-acre farm at the mouth of Benson's Creek. It became the family home, and although his crops and cows were only an avocation, they provided at least some economic support and gave the master extra time in the healthful open air.

In 1821 the county built a circuit court clerk's office on Blair's lot at the corner of Broadway and Lewis streets in Frankfort. Presumably the clerk then collected rent for the property on which his own office stood. In 1816 Blair had paid taxes on 127 acres, two slaves, and three sets of town lots, valued at $11,720. In 1818 his tax list included 650 acres in Logan County, and totaled $18,100. In 1819 he was listed with no property at all, but by 1820 the assessment was back up to $8,500. It was clearly a period of affluence for the Preston Blair family.[10]

Indeed, the years of young adulthood were filled with golden days for Preston and Eliza Blair. The miracle of his ever-improving health was followed by the arrival of handsome children. Montgomery was born in 1813, Juliet in 1814, Laura in 1816, Elizabeth in 1818, James in 1819, and Francis Preston, Jr., in 1821. The deaths of baby Juliet in 1816 and three-year-old Laura in 1819 caused great sorrow, but the loss of only two in six was an achievement in the days when medical treatments were often worse than the diseases. Blair loved all children and worshipped his own. In return no parents ever received more respect and love from their own children than did Blair and Eliza. To the end of their days, Blair's sons regarded their father as the noblest and wisest of all men, and deferred to his judgment in almost all matters. With their parents as an example, the children also grew up with extremely unselfish attitudes toward each other. From its beginning, the Francis Preston Blair family was a clan united by strong feelings of love, trust, and pride.

Chapter 2

Struggle

THE Kentucky of Blair's early adult years was bursting with energy and growth. Vigorous and acquisitive people were working at a breakneck pace to create farms, industries, towns, and cities where only a few short years earlier the Indians and the great hunter Daniel Boone had enjoyed a lonely paradise. Between 1810 and 1820 the population grew from 406,511 to 564,644, with more than 500,000 people living on farms or in village settlements. More than forty steamboats, most of them Kentucky-owned, made the great Ohio and Mississippi rivers a regular highway between Louisville and New Orleans. By 1812 Kentuckians were driving 800,000 hogs a year eastward along the trails across the mountains. By 1816 the Hope Distillery Company of Louisville was producing 1,500 gallons of whiskey a day, and Louisville boasted five tobacco factories, one steam engine factory, a candle and soap factory, a steam flour mill, and a sugar refinery. Land around Lexington sold for $100 to $200 per acre, and one lot in the smaller town of Louisville sold for $30,000. Most Kentuckians felt they were in disrepute unless they were involved in at least one speculative venture.[1]

This prosperity was common to most of the American West, but the builders of the new America also shared a problem. The meager supply of foreign coins and the primitive system of frontier barter did not provide enough capital and credit for greedy, imaginative people struggling to convert their natural heritage into wealth as soon as possible.

Before the Civil War, America's paper money came from privately owned banks, which circulated notes supposed to be immediately redeemable in gold or silver. The government-chartered Bank of the United States, supported by the national treasury, redeemed its notes promptly, and the notes from some of the larger cities and state banks were almost equally sound. Most of the money, however, came from smaller banks, whose notes usually exceeded their specie resources and depended primarily for value upon the willingness of the federal government to accept them in payment for public lands. The free and successful circulation of such notes for long periods of time was a tribute to American self-confidence. It also illustrated the American tradition of ignoring supposedly sound economic principles when seeking practical solutions to immediate problems.

In 1816 the Second Bank of the United States was chartered. Like the first, it held the national treasury, which it could use for banking purposes. Since the local bank notes spent for public lands eventually reached the Bank of the United States, this bank could put the weaker local banks out of business by immediately presenting their notes for payment in gold or silver. Even though the bank's branches at Louisville and Lexington brought needed sound capital into Kentucky, the net effect was to reduce the total amount of paper money in circulation. Until late 1818, however, the Bank followed lenient policies and contributed greatly to the Kentucky boom in land sales and business expansion.

The Kentucky legislature had already chartered the Bank of Kentucky in 1806. In 1815 its capital stock was expanded to $3 million, and its branches were increased to thirteen. In 1818, by popular demand, the legislature created forty new independent banks, capitalized at almost $8,500,000 and authorized to issue notes up to three times their capital. Kentucky now had enough currency and credit if the Bank of the United States and the people could be induced to keep using the notes without inquiring too closely into their specie value.

By the end of 1818, however, almost all western banks were in trouble. Kentucky speculators had put their state banks heavily in debt to the national bank by exchanging vast quantities of state bank notes for national bank notes at a discount. When a drought and crop failures brought hard times in the East, the national bank demanded payment in specie for $2,690,760 owed by Kentucky banks. The state banks promptly brought pressure on their individual debtors, and the ebullient Kentuckians were soon mired in the slough of debt and depression. By the middle of 1819 neither the national bank nor business firms would accept Bank of Kentucky notes, and the independent banks, now called "the forty thieves," would not even accept one another's notes. Overnight, Kentucky became a sullen land of business failures, foreclosures, unemployment, poverty, and bitter lawsuits among former friends.

Francis Preston Blair expected to profit from the inevitable progress of Kentucky and America. Like everyone else, he borrowed money to invest in land and city lots, and generously endorsed the notes of friends borrowing for the same purposes. Refusal to sign a friend's note was an imputation of dishonor that few men in early Kentucky saw fit to make. Though already in financial difficulty, Blair in 1820 joined with friends in borrowing $14,800 on three separate notes from the Bank of the United States. Blair eventually paid $2,000 on the second note, but the three notes accumulated enough interest to total $20,744 by 1830.[2] Blair always insisted that he received none of the money, but simply lent his name to others who were in trouble because of the panic. None of his cosigners ever questioned this version.

The panic years 1818–1821 left Blair with an ultimate debt of at least $38,232. As an original debtor he was sued thirteen times and as an endorser for friends he was sued six times. The judgments against him totaled $17,488.60, in addition to the $20,744 owed the Bank of the United States. At least $28,000 of this debt resulted from his generous endorsement of friends.[3] It was all a terrible burden for a man with four young children, a proud wife accustomed to wealth, and an outspoken mother-in-law always ready to point out his deficiencies.

As the suits for debt backed up in the Franklin court, its clerk worked long hours and accumulated fee bills by the thousands of dollars, but most of them were uncollectible. Three times Blair sued deputy sheriffs and constables for fee bills given out for collection but neither paid nor returned. At least it was a convenient post for a man so often in court anyhow. Over and over he signed orders to the sheriff to "Take Francis P. Blair if he be found within your bailiwick, and him safely keep, so that you

have his body before the Judge of our Franklin Circuit Court."
In 1825 Blair settled most of his out-of-bank debts by borrowing $1,500 with John J. Crittenden, John Harvie, and Ben
Gratz, all political opponents, as security. In 1830 he still owed
these three men $1,000, and deeded his residence, five lots, and
1,050 acres inherited through Eliza to them to secure this debt.
This property, of course, remained in Blair's hands safe from the
efforts of less friendly creditors.[4]

In 1818 Blair's tax assessment had been $18,000. It was
$9,500 in 1820, $6,500 in 1824, $2,000 in 1826, and only $800
in 1829, although it was back to $2,500 in 1830.[5]

Collectable fee bills and pay for certain legal tasks supported
his family, but maintaining their usual comfort occasionally required emergency loans. Happily, John J. Crittenden's strong
disagreements with Blair on political matters never interfered
with his affection or generosity. In 1826 Blair had to borrow from
Crittenden because Eliza, while visiting relatives, had written of a
need for "some articles of clothing without which her situation"
would be "delicate and unpleasant." [6] Eliza's mother, who remained immune to Blair's charm, made occasional contributions,
but she usually made Ben Gratz the trustee. In 1827 Mrs. Scott
gave Eliza "in consideration of the love and affection which I
bear said Eliza . . . a Black cow & calf, a red cow & her yearling
Heifer called gentle, a pied cow (June) & yearling Heifer, a
red & white faced Cow and a sound chesnut sorrel colt . . . .
The said property to be for the use of the said Eliza and not
subject to the control of her Husband or any other person except
the said Trustee." [7] The Blair milk supply, at least, would be free
from the capricious judgment of the local courts.

Like most Americans, Francis Preston Blair viewed the world
as an eternal struggle between good and evil. To him the financial
blight that had befallen himself, his friends, his state, and his
country was an unnatural malignancy to be resisted and overcome. The inevitable progress of a rich land had been halted, and
he knew there must be a cause and a solution. For Blair and many
of his fellows, the most obvious explanation was the Bank of the
United States, in their eyes a monster designed to benefit eastern
aristocrats by impoverishing the West. And the equally obvious

instruments for combating this menace were the state and federal governments.

Defeating the Bank and the creditors profiting from its sins would require a new brand of politics. To save their property from foreclosure and to salvage enough capital for a new start, the debtors would have to get relief legislation from their state governments. Kentucky had already granted the ballot to all white males, and those in trouble would now try to convince the expanded electorate that the fate of the debtors was the cause of common humanity against the interests of the selfish and lordly rich. Reducing the financial issues to democracy versus aristocracy was a gross oversimplification, but enough of this pattern existed to inspire democrats and aristocrats alike to greater efforts.

In 1819 the Kentucky legislature moved quickly to protect its indebted citizens. Debt imprisonment was forbidden, forced sales were delayed for a year, and if a plaintiff refused payment in Bank of Kentucky notes the defendant could replevy his property for two years.

When the Bank of Kentucky suspended payments in 1820, the legislature showed even more imagination. It created the Bank of the Commonwealth for the sole purpose of bailing out worthy debtors. The bank's twenty-year charter provided a president and twelve directors to be chosen by the legislature, with the main bank at Frankfort and a branch in each judicial district. It could make loans on mortgage security, and its notes were to be legal tender for all debts. The president and directors could borrow up to $2,000, but all others were limited to $1,000. Borrowers had to take an oath that they would use the money to pay debts or buy local goods for reexportation. The bank could issue $3 million in notes, backed by funds from certain state land sales, the income from Bank of Kentucky stock, and the unexpended balances in the state treasury at the end of each year. These were weak supports. The $7,000 appropriated for books, paper, and plates for printing notes was the Commonwealth Bank's only real capital. The able and dedicated John J. Crittenden was elected president, and his devoted friend and classmate Preston Blair became a director.

In January 1821 Blair rode off to Philadelphia to get notes for the bank. Frozen rain had made Ohio a veritable "Iceland,"

and he reached Columbus with a lame horse and a painful tooth-ache. There he took pride in the assemblage of lawyers gathered to hear his friend Henry Clay plead a case, and shared their chagrin when the judge postponed the hearing.

After four days the toothache gave way to a renewed spirit of adventure. The bank notes must have a design worthy of their noble purpose, and the young emissary expressed some original ideas in a letter to Crittenden. He would put "Minerva, the Goddess of Wisdom, art, & arms," on all notes above a dollar. On the $100 notes she would appear "in all her habiliments of war" with a "glorious" army in the background. "On the $50 notes She should be seen . . . extending her influence to the arts . . . On the $20 notes she might be seen inspiring Commerce —on the tens, legislature—on the fives literature." The $1 notes would show only the palladium. Literature would be the lowest "not because least worthy, but because it is less likely to obtain much of our commonwealth money to cherish it." If this "*heathen-ish*" design was unacceptable, Blair warned, he would substitute "the christian parable of the prodigal son in the different stages of his progress." The young man would "set off in high snuff on $100's and pass through the eventful scenes in his life . . . till he returns to his father's house in wretchedness & rags on the one dollar denomination." [8]

Crittenden's answer awaited Blair at Philadelphia. He approved of Minerva and had no taste for the Prodigal: "Wicked wits" might say "that the Bank itself was well represented by the Prodigal." Crittenden also instructed his friend to bring back the first million dollars personally and exercise great caution in having the remainder forwarded.[9]

In Philadelphia Blair enjoyed a delightful visit with the wealthy and sophisticated relatives of Ben Gratz. He enjoyed several trips to the theater and convinced Rebecca Gratz that Eliza must truly be a paragon of beauty and virtue. He also received a welcome letter from Eliza. "You would have been very cruel," she wrote, "to threaten me as you did in your letter from Cincinnati if you had not known I have a sufficient stock of vanity to prevent my believing one word of what you say about forgetting me & your children. . . . Our children are very well & very little trouble. . . . I anticipate much pleasure &

amusement from your account of things beyond the blue mountains. . . . I have no fears about my approaching confinement, but I do not find writing a pleasant employment as stooping over the table hurts me." [10]

A few weeks later Blair and his eagerly awaited million-dollar package arrived back in Frankfort just in time. The Bank of Kentucky had already begun 275 suits to collect $887,154 in Franklin County alone—an average of $400 per person in the county. Within a year the new bank had loaned $2,400,000 and had issued more than $2,300,000 in Blair's Minerva-engraved notes. Its total specie was $2,633. None of this conformed to any known principles of sound finance, but the Commonwealth notes held remarkably firm. Originally worth 70 percent in specie, they dropped to 62½ percent by March 1822, and to 50 percent by May. In January 1823, however, the bank was able to burn $1,398,924, and the remaining notes rose to 66⅔ percent by October 1825. By 1830 they were almost at par value. Blair remained a director of the bank until 1830, and in 1829 and again in 1830 he was elected its president. Under his management, the bank burned another $300,000 worth of notes.[11]

Smaller debtors by the thousands saved their homes and household goods with Commonwealth notes and then gradually repaid the bank as Kentucky exports and investment opportunities began to draw in money again from the outside. By the end of 1829 the real estate foreclosures of the bank and all its branches totaled only $58,728. Since the general price level had declined sharply, and since most debts had been contracted in inflated currency, the creditors paid with Commonwealth notes lost very little except the right to profit enormously from mortgage foreclosures. Kentuckians had again demonstrated the American habit of ignoring orthodox theory in situations requiring effective imaginations.

In 1821, however, creditors who remembered the continental currency of the Revolution were certain that their debts were being wiped out by the Commonwealth notes and the relief laws. The debtors controlled the legislature until the end of 1825, but the creditors found strength in the courts. In 1822 two Kentucky judges declared certain relief laws unconstitutional. Then the United States Supreme Court invalidated the Kentucky law restricting debt sales, and ruled that no such law could apply to judgments rendered in federal courts. The state court of appeals joined in by upholding the anti-relief decisions of the lower courts. The legislature fought back by trying to oust various judges, but the relief party could never muster the two-thirds majority necessary for removal.[12]

The most important newspaper on the relief side was the *Argus of Western America*, published in Frankfort by Amos Kendall. Kendall was a Yankee schoolteacher from Massachusettes by way of Dartmouth College. His first year in Kentucky was spent tutoring the children of Henry Clay, but he soon left this pleasant assignment to become a political editor. By 1820 he was editor and chief owner of the *Argus*. Two years older than Blair, Kendall suffered the same poor health, and was also destined to bear this cross for eighty years. Kendall was a strange mixture of passionate idealism and monumental self-righteousness, mixed in equal parts with shrewd opportunism and concern for his own personal fortunes. He invariably considered opponents greedy, immoral, dishonest, corrupt, treasonable, or worse. His occasional shifts of allegiance were always justified by the comforting knowledge that his erstwhile friends had gone from good to bad.

Kendall and Blair became early allies and friends in the relief and court battles. Blair shared some of Kendall's self-righteousness, but in Blair the trait was tempered with a humility lacking in Kendall and a capacity for personal affection strong enough to transcend political disagreements.

Kendall's barbed editorials were often supplemented by the writings of others on the right side of the great questions, and Preston Blair soon became a regular contributor. The *Argus* saw no hope for the Christian who would "take one set of principles to church and another to his court house. To one place he goes with *Father forgive my debts or trespasses* as I forgive my debtors . . .' To the other he goes with his bond in his hand, ready to take the life's blood of his debtors with the cry of 'justice and honesty' in his mouth."[13]

Throughout the spring and summer of 1824 the *Argus* ran a long series of articles by "Patrick Henry," then by "Philo-Patrick Henry" when "Patrick" left town, and finally by the original

"Patrick" upon his return. Kendall and Blair were apparently the authors, and their language was worthy of their pseudonym. The United States Bank, they wrote, was seeking *"unrestrained control of all the monied concerns of the American people and to hold the purse strings of the nation and of every individual in the community,"*[14] and the Kentucky courts were deliberately promoting this evil scheme. In late March Kendall was beaten by a street crowd for refusing to divulge the identity of Philo-Patrick Henry. The *Argus* then charged that a corrupted minority was plotting to maintain its ill-gotten gains by violence.

In 1824 General Joseph Desha, the relief candidate for governor, received a 63 percent majority, and his party accepted this as a mandate against the court of appeals. In the new legislature, a select committee reminded the judges that mankind had been "permitted by a *retrospective act* of divine remedial legislation, to *replevvy* the debt which he had incurred by a violation of the law" in the garden of Eden. Surely the judges would admit that God's *"retroactive replevin* law was . . . a glorious *relief law* . . . graciously followed by *relief* enactions, up through that still more glorious *relief measure,* the incarnation, passion, and resurrection of our blessed Redeemer, to the present day."[15]

Obviously judges who would not follow the divine example should be expelled, but a two-thirds vote was necessary and the legislature counted only sixty-nine votes for removal against thirty-nine for retaining the judges. The relief leaders charged that creditors had bribed some of the legislators pledged to removal, and they soon found another solution. The legislature simply repealed all of the acts establishing the court of appeals in the first place, and then passed new laws creating an entirely new court. This program required only a simple majority. There would now be four judges rather than three, and their salaries would be $2,000 in Commonwealth notes rather than the $1,500 paid the former judges.

It was a clear-cut case of democracy versus constitutionalism, although the reliefers argued long but unconvincingly that the statute law rather than the constitution had created the court of appeals. An angry minority in the legislature proclaimed that "against this sort of tyranny our fathers protested in the Declaration of Independence . . . they fought, and bled, and con-

quered; and against it, those of their sons who cherish their principles, will ever protest." [16]

When Blair's friends Clay and Crittenden opposed the New
Court, he parted company with them, although Eliza was reluctant to oppose the charming Clay. The clerkship of the New
Court, with a much higher and presumably more collectible set
of fees than that of the circuit court, was offered first to Achilles
Sneed, a wealthy old gentleman who was already clerk of the existing court of appeals. Despite Blair's urging, however, Sneed
refused. The position was then given to Blair, and Crittenden,
an opponent of the entire business, signed his security bond. At
this point Eliza found it "extremely amiable . . . to acquiesce
as a wife in the opinions of her husband," and Henry Clay lost a
vassal. She had "felt so severely the oppression of debt and the
humiliation of poverty," her husband wrote Clay, "that to invite
her to take sides with a party whose success must renew those
ills, will be something like inviting an unfortunate person delivered from the rack to make another experiment with its powers."[17]

On January 28, 1825, the Old Court judges declared the New
Court to be unconstitutional. Unconvinced, the New Court met
for business and found a hundred suits pending, but the Old
Court clerk, Achilles Sneed, refused to surrender the records.
Sneed's friend and rival clerk, Preston Blair, wrote him a cour-
teous letter demanding the records. Sneed's refusal was equally
friendly.

Blair was a man of action. He simply pried a shutter off
Sneed's office window, and soon all available court records had
been officially transferred. The Old Court ruled Blair in contempt for seizing the records, while the New Court had Sneed
arrested for refusing to surrender them in the first place. Crittenden, who was Blair's security, served as attorney for Sneed,
who was fined $33.33, which he never paid. Blair ignored the
Old Court, and indeed made a second journey of confiscation to
Sneed's office while the latter was engaged before the New Court.
The grand jury of Franklin County indicted the New Court
from chief justice to tipstaff for trespass upon Sneed's office, and
excited meetings all over Kentucky either endorsed or violently
denounced Blair's conduct. Grand juries in several counties in-

dicted him, and feelings ran so high that one New Court judge began wearing pistols to prayer meeting.[18]

The circuit courts rode the fence by sending cases on appeal to both Old and New Courts, and the New Court decided a total of seventy-eight cases in 1825. In the fall elections, however, the self-appointed spokesmen for democracy got a jolt. The Old Court party won the House of Representatives 62–38, and the New Court majority in the Senate was cut to 21–17.

There were various reasons for this. In 1824–1825, 4,000 mules and more than $1,250,000 worth of hogs walked to market through the mountain gaps and turnpike gates leading out of Kentucky, and the number of debtors decreased proportionately. The new voters in the rising population, furthermore, were rarely debtors. Also the legislature had raised taxes, people resented the high salaries of the New Court judges, and Governor Desha's son had just committed a cold-blooded murder. More and more Kentuckians were turning to the judgment of popular leaders like Henry Clay and John Crittenden.

Tensions continued high. Several Old Court men became desperately ill after a celebration, and it was seriously charged that New Court men had diluted their whiskey with emetic tartar. In mixing their brew, the unidentified villains had apparently judged the human tolerance for tartar and whiskey accurately, because no one died. One newspaper announced an obituary for the New Court. It had died of a "constitutional malformation . . . being illegitimate in its conception; preternatural in its birth; and rikety [*sic*] in its form and habit." It would be buried in a grave long since dug by "the friends of the constitution, of social, civil, and political order." Various enumerated leaders, including Blair, would be the chief mourners.[19]

The stunned Blair retreated to the Gist estate at Canewood to reconsider his position "aloof from public commotion." Writing Henry Clay, he suggested a compromise in which all judges would resign and be replaced by a new court of judges from both of the contending sides. He had never seen "a political contest productive of so much ill feeling. It not only made men entertain the worst opinion of each other, but in a great degree made them deserve the mutual abhorrence." His own newly exalted position would soon end, and rather than "shrink to the dimensions of a circuit court clerk" he might seek his fortune in some new area.[20]

The new legislature met in a bitter atmosphere. Just before the election of a house speaker, the New Court candidate, Solomon Sharp, was murdered by one Jeroboam Beauchamp, and his opponent was elected without opposition. Sharp's friends blamed the political campaign, but his enemies had a different version. Patrick Darby of the Frankfort *Constitutional Advocate* wrote that Sharp in past years had seduced one Ann Cook, who later married the twenty-one-year-old Beauchamp when she was already forty. According to Darby, Sharp, threatened with blackmail, had gathered documents for smearing the good name of Mrs. Beauchamp, and this was why Beauchamp killed Sharp. Other enemies of Sharp spread the word that Beauchamp had nursed a longtime hatred because Sharp had failed to deliver money and property promised him for marrying the lady in the first place. Darby insisted that Mrs. Sharp was concealing the pertinent documents to help the relief party convince the public that Sharp was a political martyr.

In a full-page reply in the *Argus* Mrs. Sharp denied the existence of any such documents and insisted that the hatreds caused by the election had been responsible for her husband's death. Indeed, she believed that Darby himself had deliberately stirred Beauchamp's anger, and she accused Darby of visiting her house just before the murder to get the plan of the house for Beauchamp. Darby hated her husband because of a lawsuit, she wrote, and even though Darby had denied knowing Beauchamp, there was absolute proof that they had been seen together.

Darby repeated his charges and declared that Mrs. Sharp's reply had been written by Preston Blair. Blair answered in the *Argus* that Mrs. Sharp, surrounded by her grieving little orphans, had written the story entirely by herself to defend her beloved husband against the attacks of Darby. "Is affliction and grief," Blair asked, "no protection for a defenceless woman, who has been bereft of her dearest earthly comforts? Shall she, when kneeling before the throne of her God, pouring out the sorrows of an almost broken heart, be reviled as guilty of prevarication and falsehood, by an apostate from all religion? Forbid it, Heaven. Forbid it, all that is just, generous, humane in the bosom of Kentucky's brave sons." [21]

Beauchamp was sentenced to hang on July 12, 1826. During their farewell visit the Beauchamps stabbed each other by mutual consent. Mrs. Beauchamp died almost immediately, but her husband's wounds did not interfere with his execution a few minutes later. In his final statement, Beauchamp exonerated Darby of any complicity, but accused him of perjury at the trial. Darby finally gained a nominal judgment for libel against Mrs. Sharp, but dropped the suit when she appealed to a higher court. Robert Penn Warren would later retell the story in a dramatic novel, *World Enough and Time*.

Blair offered to surrender his clerkship as part of a compromise, but would not accept a total defeat as long as the New Court law remained unrepealed. The House passed a resolution directing the sergeant of the Old Court to regain the records. Blair answered by securing eighteen muskets from the local arsenal through the courtesy of militia commander Edward Bibb. Volunteers took turns guarding Blair's office with loaded muskets and bayonets fixed and the embattled clerk warned that intruders would be fired upon. Sergeant Taylor of the Old Court led a determined band of invaders toward the fortress, but fortunately Speaker of the House Robertson persuaded them to turn back.[22]

The *Argus* parodied the entire business with alleged extracts from London newspapers:

A civil war is raging in Kentucky. . . . fire was set to the capitol in which the Legislative body was sitting and the whole city laid in ashes. Most of the members . . . perished in the flames. This atrocious act was done by the Frankfort Guards, a regiment of ferocious Cuiraissers, [sic] commanded by one Col. Bigg. This band of Jacobins has gone so far as to make preparations . . . to blow up the river . . . on which Frankfort stood. . . . but the river took the alarm and at the latest date was running for the Ohio and has probably escaped.

Col. Bigg's Cuiraissers are a most Cossack looking set of men, fully nine feet eight inches tall with mustaches a foot long. They are mounted on Alligators which are caught in the Kentucky River and . . . are fed upon young Negroes and Indians, of whom they eat at least two a day.[23]

In November 1825 Blair was invited to abandon an obviously losing cause and cast his lot with Clay and those destined to control the future in Kentucky politics. Ben Gratz asked Clay for

a federal appointment for Blair, but the struggling clerk assured
Clay that the request was "wholly unbidden and unexpected."
No Washington appointment to which he was equal was equal to
his needs, he wrote Clay, and he would never abandon his party
"if they were disposed to acquiesce in public sentiment as I understood it." He was, however, considering Florida as a place to
which he might emigrate. The territory offered economic opportunities and the climate might benefit his health.[24]

Partisanship did not interfere with Blair's personal loyalties.
By January 1826 the United States Supreme Court justice
Charles Todd was dying, and Blair strongly urged Clay to seek
the place for Crittenden. Judge John Boyle of the Old Court
and Judge Robert Trimble of the New Court both wanted the
appointment, but Blair assured Clay that Crittenden was superior
to both and that on the whole he preferred Boyle to Trimble.[25]
Meanwhile, Blair was publicly attacking Crittenden and the Old
Court judges, including Boyle, almost daily.

Reminding Clay of his own Missouri Compromise, Blair
urged him to support the court compromise effort. Neither side,
wrote Blair, could break Clay's hold on the people "unless by the
violence of party conflict in the state struggles one party should
be induced to hold out a hand to old Jackson & assume the military cockade to wage the war more successfully." The warning
was prophetic.[26]

The New Court's efforts to compromise were the struggles
of a sinking ship. In 1826 the elections were again clouded by
extraneous issues. The Sharp murder was no longer an excitement, but Governor Desha had saved his son from the gallows
with a pardon after the young man's conviction and sentence.
This quite-natural act was denounced everywhere as a thwarting
of justice. On Election Day the New Court party was routed in
both houses of the legislature. Over the governor's veto the new
lawmakers promptly abolished the New Court and paid the Old
Court judges their back salaries. The House even voted to recover the salaries of the New Court officials, but the Senate declined to go this far.

At this point, Clerk Blair surrendered the records, and Kentucky justice resumed its normal course. Unable to collect the
fees from his New Court services, the newly defrocked clerk con-

tinued to dream of Florida. Henry Clay thought it was a good idea, and Eliza, speaking in the accents of Christopher and Nathaniel Gist, was certain they could not be "worsted." Leaving, however, would mean the loss of Blair's beloved little Benson's Creek farm and other properties to creditors. Also, the return of general prosperity made his circuit court fees more collectible even if less numerous, and his work for the *Argus* was earning small sums. And finally, his friends were ready for a new round in the political battle.

The so-called aristocrats and conservatives had captured Kentucky, but a new presidential election would come in 1828. Kentucky conservatives were irrevocably committed to the reelection of John Quincy Adams, but the hero of New Orleans who had bested Adams in the popular vote in 1824 would clearly have much more than an even chance for victory. It was only natural that the relief party of Kentucky should rally behind Andrew Jackson and seek to rebuild its political fortunes through the power exerted from Washington.

After opposing Jackson in 1824, Francis P. Blair and Amos Kendall by the end of 1826 had seen the light. The election of Jackson to the presidency with their well-publicized assistance was their best hope to recover from an ignominious defeat. Also, he was the only alternative to a continuation of policies they honestly opposed for reasons of principle as well as self-interest. They now saw their erstwhile candidate, Adams, as the lackey of aristocrats, the United States Bank, anti-reliefers, and hardhearted creditors, and they believed that their former great friend, Henry Clay, had been infected in like manner by ambition and association. Clearly the America of Thomas Jefferson had to be saved from such as these, and obviously the great instrument at hand for this noble purpose was Old Hickory Jackson, whose previously noted grave faults were now rapidly fading in the sunlight of his availability as a political Moses. The Promised Land of a victorious national election beckoned dead ahead.

Chapter 3

Old Hickory

The Hickory is a tall, graceful tree, indigenous to America. . . . It yields gracefully to the gale of spring, and bows in whispers to the breath of autumn, but when the storms of winter invade the forest, it presents its recoiling strength to the blast, and saves its frailer neighbors from the fury of the storm. It grows on the poorest ridges as well as in the richest valleys, and furnishes to all classes a most delicious delicacy. . . . Indeed the rough coated mail clad American nut is everywhere welcome, except at the proud feasts of the lordly aristocracy, where foreign luxuries have vitiated the taste, and banished it as rank and rustic fare, fit only for the swinish multitude.

—The *Argus*, December 12, 1827

FROM 1815 to 1824 an era of good feelings existed in American national politics. The War of 1812 had destroyed the Federalist party as such, and the tariff of 1816 and the reestablishment of Alexander Hamilton's United States Bank in 1817 by the agrarian party of Thomas Jefferson completed the erasure of existing party lines.

By 1824, however, America was a land of sections. The old southeastern world of tobacco, rice, cotton, and slavery was suffering from depleted soils and western competition. The frustrated planters found their villain in an increasingly paternalistic federal government that threatened to spend their tax money on internal improvements in other sections and that protected northern industries with a tariff. To many southerners the tariff now meant unfair prices for goods they had to buy in northern markets and lower prices abroad for their own crops in nations affected by American duties. By 1824 the planters were glorifying states' rights and dreaming of a federal government marked by inactivity and frugality. Their candidates for the White House were

John C. Calhoun and William H. Crawford, but Crawford was eliminated by illness before the balloting.

In the Northeast the industrial revolution was well underway in a region already accustomed to a commercial economy. New Englanders wanted tariffs to protect their young industries and internal improvements to open up the expanding markets and increased supply of raw materials in the growing West. A strong central government able and willing to provide protection and services was the goal of leaders like John Quincy Adams and Daniel Webster. New York, New Jersey, and Pennsylvania also felt a need for tariffs, but the forces of agriculture in these states were still powerful. Martin Van Buren of New York was a Jeffersonian agrarian as well as a hero of the growing class of city laborers. The Northeast also needed a strong banking and currency system to provide capital and credit for its expanding economy. The United States Bank's mother branch was in Philadelphia, and the Bank was supported by most of the region, although it received no love from rival banks in New York City. In 1824 this area put its faith in John Quincy Adams.

In the vast, dynamic West, stretching from the Appalachians to Wisconsin territory, Missouri, and Louisiana, hardworking acquisitive, imaginative Americans were pushing Indians ever westward and changing wildernesses into farms, villages, towns, and cities. The westerners wanted free or cheap land; roads, bridges, and canals at federal expense; low taxes; tariffs on their own products and free trade in the products they must buy; and all of the paper money for liquid credit and capital they could get, whether sound or unsound, as long as it could be used to buy and develop land and property. The frontier process had bred into them a mystical faith in progress and an elevated view of their own contribution to it. They were on the whole a suspicious lot, ready to see the evil hand of eastern conspirators, speculators, bankers, and politicians behind any failure to get what they wanted. Westerners were firmly for states' rights except in cases where they expected free land, federal internal improvements, federal removal of Indians, and various other services. The panic of 1819 had left a bitter hatred for the United States Bank, and the section in 1824 had an immensely available presidential candidate who hated all banks with a monumental passion.

General Andrew Jackson had won the only great victory in the War of 1812, and the fact that the war had ended several days before the battle did not dim the luster of his achievement. The dominant ethnic strain in the American West of 1824 was Scotch-Irish, and Old Hickory had shown a magnificent talent for killing Englishmen. This alone was worth a multitude of votes.

In 1824 Kentucky had a split personality. Most of its people had come from Virginia, and the easily transplanted laissez-faire agrarian attitudes of the Old South remained strong in a state still predominantly rural. However, Kentucky was also only two decades from its frontier stage, and its people believed with the usual western fervor in the usual western principles. And finally, the northern rim of Kentucky had become an industrial and commercial region, sending vast quantities of whiskey, meat products, and hemp up and down the Ohio River toward Pittsburgh in one direction and New Orleans in the other. Small wonder that Henry Clay, a farmer as well as a lawyer, sought national influence by advocating an "American System" of tariffs to build up American industries; federal roads, bridges, and canals by which American farmers could reach ready markets for their products and in turn become customers for the new industries; and a national bank to supply the whole with a sound, expanding paper currency. As a presidential candidate in 1824, Clay had a wide but thinly spread following.

When the votes were counted in 1824, Andrew Jackson had won a plurality but no candidate had a majority. When the House of Representatives had to settle the issue, Clay threw his influence to John Quincy Adams, who had finished second. Adams thereby became president and then appointed Clay secretary of state. The choice was logical in each case. Adams shared Clay's economic philosophy. Adams and Clay, along with Albert Gallatin, had negotiated the treaty ending the War of 1812. Gallatin's son had complained that during the negotiations the puritanical Adams' early bedtime and rising and Clay's all-night poker parties and late sleeping hours had kept the two men apart most of the time, but Adams had seen enough to know that Clay was a skilled diplomat.

The election of Adams, however, was a slap in the face to the rising forces of American democracy. New state constitutions establishing universal white manhood suffrage were the order of the day, and the ideals of Jefferson had attained a vogue perhaps not equaled again until the twentieth century. The hero of New Orleans had received the most votes, and by the rules of the new democracy he should have been elected president. The appointment of Clay only added fuel to the fire. The similarity of the Clay–Adams economic policies to those of the long-defunct Federalist party of the antidemocratic aristocracy completed the identification. The ideals of democracy, the popularity of a national hero, and the antipathies of those who opposed Adams personally, objected to Adams' policies, or hated the aristocracy in general could now be used to create a coalition political party such as America had not yet seen. Its members could at least agree on the advantages of political victory and upon their affection for Andrew Jackson. The lack of unanimous agreement among them on anything else meant only that the American political party system had come of age.

The chief directors of the Jackson movement in Kentucky were the late joiners, Amos Kendall and Francis P. Blair. For years the *Argus* had damned Andrew Jackson and deified Henry Clay. In January 1825 Kendall had borrowed $1,500 from Clay and two years later the debt remained unpaid. In 1827 this obligation was met by a loan from Jackson party funds administered by Martin Van Buren, and some historians have concluded that Van Buren thereby bought himself an editor. The political stakes in Kentucky and the issues involved, however, were probably more important factors in Kendall's conversion.

Kendall abandoned Clay with no sign of regret, but for Blair the separation was difficult. "You say it gives you pain to part with me in politics," he wrote Clay in November 1827. "What must my regret be, to lose both you and Crittenden in whom my pride, my partiality and every political wish centered. My affectionate regard will always attend you both. . . . I do not question that you are activated by the purest patriotism." [1]

In December 1826 the *Argus* claimed that a Jackson in the White House in 1814 would have prevented the burning of the Capitol by the British. Indeed, Jackson's claims to the presidency were "similar to those of Washington," and exceeded "in merit those of *John Q. Adams* as those of Washington did those of *John Adams*." Clay, however, said the *Argus,* need not and would not fall with Adams if he would shine by his own light, but if Clay should ever "underrate himself so far as to lean on another's broken arm for support, we shall regret it, but we cannot save him." [2]

If Adams was not yet a broken arm in Kentucky, the *Argus* was prepared to make him one. It soon found Adams guilty of every conceivable sin, including the Panama Conference, the tariff of abominations, extravagance, corruption, and the false assumption of the office in the first place. In childhood Adams had been "educated in the principles of the British constitution." He had opposed Tom Paine's *Rights of Man.* He had gone to Europe at the age of eleven and "received most of his education in royal courts and the society of nobles." He had abused Jefferson, opposed the Louisiana Purchase, tried to betray the West at the peace conference at Ghent, and finally abandoned the Federalist party without, however, abandoning any of its principles. In the words of a toast reported from a Democratic meeting at Boston: "*The marriage of Adams with Democracy*—a fashionable match of convenience—the Parties never having been seen together since the Honey Moon. (Accompanied by the tune 'A Frog he would a Wooing go.')" The *Argus* also scathed Adams for allowing a cabinet officer (Clay) to challenge a senator (John Randolph) to a duel for words spoken in debate "under the sacred guaranty of the constitution." Randolph had denounced the alliance between "the Puritan and the Blackleg," and the "Blackleg" Clay had demanded a duel, in which the two men missed twice and then embraced as friends. And last but not least, the *Argus* complained, Adams had persecuted "faithful, well-tried, and patriotic republican printers," while rewarding those who were "subservient": The *New Hampshire Patriot,* the *Eastern Argus,* and the Frankfort *Argus* had been "deprived of government patronage for exposing fearlessly the abuses committed by Mr. Adams." [3]

In turn the Clay–Adams press charged that Kendall had supported Adams until he had been sold to Jackson as the highest bidder. Kendall hotly denied this and insisted that Clay had offered him a State Department clerkship, which he had rejected because of unwillingness to support Adams. Clay pointed out later that he had indeed offered Kendall a $1,000 clerkship, which Kendall had refused because the salary was not $1,500, and Clay had the correspondence to prove his version.[4]

Kendall then printed a series of public letters charging that two of Clay's closest friends had stated openly in 1824 that the election of Adams would make Clay secretary of state. The friends were soon identified as Blair and Crittenden, and Kendall insisted that Blair had first made the statement after a letter from Clay in January 1824.[5]

Blair was much embarrassed. In 1824 at Clay's request he had urged friends to write letters supporting Adams to their Kentucky congressmen, and he had argued that this would help Clay. Also, even though Clay's letter had offered various other reasons for supporting Adams, it had stated: "My friends entertain the belief that their kind wishes towards me will, in the end, be more likely to be accomplished by so bestowing their votes." Blair was now wholeheartedly for Jackson against Clay and Adams, but was unwilling to take full advantage of Clay's former confidence. He assured Clay that he had not showed the letter to Kendall and had not shared in this particular anti-Clay effort. "I am grateful," he wrote Clay, "that you recognize the possibility of a determined political opposition existing in combination with feelings of the utmost kindness & esteem for the object of it." Blair also remembered that Clay had told him before Congress met in 1824 that he intended to vote for Adams, and he offered Clay full permission to publish this fact along with his own acknowledgment of it.[6]

Clay's friends in the Kentucky senate made their hero's position still worse by holding a formal investigation of the election of 1824. They passed a resolution exonerating Clay, but the debate served only to give the affair nationwide publicity. Newspapers everywhere followed the proceedings, and a rash of editorials and speeches denounced the "whitewash." The Kentucky senate ordered Blair to appear and testify, but he flatly refused to be sworn on the grounds that the senate had no right to pry into anyone's personal correspondence.

Describing these events to Clay, Blair again advised him to ignore the charge. Personally, said Blair, he had never seen any criminality in Kentucky representatives determining who Adams' counsellors would be before casting their votes. "The public would never have considered such a care of the western interest by the western members a corrupt bargain but for *the mystery* that was hung round it." Hoping that Clay would not do so, Blair gave him full permission to publish any of his letters.[7]

When pressed by friends for copies of the letters, the harassed Clay answered that his correspondence with Blair was "characterized by a freedom of language which is occasionally admissible in private . . . but which would not be decorous towards the public." Like Blair he would not sacrifice a principle necessary for "social confidence and intercourse," and would not "on the defiance of a profligate editor, be the first to set a mischievous example."[8]

The *Argus's* attacks upon Clay and Adams were matched by its newly found enthusiasm for Andrew Jackson. For months Kendall and Blair published weekly sketches of the life of Jackson. They skillfully turned to Jackson's advantage the opposition's cruel stories about the marriage of Andrew and Rachel Jackson. Indeed, the Jackson party's attacks on Adams were much less vicious than the shafts aimed at poor Rachel and the well-circulated "black-coffin" handbills commemorating Jackson's alleged murder victims. The *Argus* answered these charges with spirit, and the names of its editors were soon known to a grateful Andrew Jackson.

Whatever the influence of the *Argus*, Andrew Jackson carried Kentucky by a substantial margin, although the vote for the legislature was almost a standoff. Amos Kendall promptly rushed off to Washington to assist the friends of the president-elect in choosing his counsellors, while a compromise atmosphere settled over Frankort. The legislature elected a Jacksonian, George Bibb, senator; Clay's friend Jeptha Dudley, president of the Bank of Kentucky; and Francis Preston Blair president of the rival Bank of the Commonwealth. Blair's new salary was $1,000, and he apparently had little difficulty exercising the duties of a banker while writing for the *Argus* from his well-worn clerk's desk in the courthouse. The tide of fortune had begun to turn.

Andrew Jackson was the first American president chosen by a great mass of ordinary voters not screened by property-owning qualification. His supporters included southern planters, wealthy agrarians in the Middle states, many small farmers everywhere, various social reform and intellectual groups in New England, most of the more recently arrived European immigrants, segments of the infinitesimal but growing labor movement, and the great majority of people, whatever their station, in the expanding West. A wealthy Tennessee planter who had once gone bankrupt in land and other speculations, Jackson was now an enemy of the tempter banks and of the paper money that had been their instrument. In his native state he had opposed the coming of democracy as related to matters like voting, legal justice, taxes, and land policy. He was highly adaptable, however, and had no difficulty in identifying himself with the great democratic forces that had made him president. A self-made aristocrat, he was for the first time in his life required to view the American situation in its entirety, and he would soon believe passionately in a Jeffersonian democracy of farmers, laborers, and mechanics, as opposed to the growing new aristocracy of industry, commerce, and finance.

In 1829 Jackson came to Washington filled with pain and sadness. His ailments included splitting headaches, a hacking cough, bleeding lungs, and occasional twinges from the lead souvenirs carried in his chest and arm since a duel with a detractor of his wife and a brawl with the Benton brothers. He had killed Charles Dickinson in the duel, and had then walked from the field with Dickinson's bullet lodged next to his heart. He was now sixty-one and in desperate health, but an unimpaired iron will and unconquerable spirit in the face of opposition would keep him alive and fighting for seventeen more years. Indeed, a few months of uninterrupted peace might have been fatal to Jackson, because the recent death of his wife had destroyed much of his reason for living. The simple-hearted, saintly Rachel had never wanted to be anything but a good wife, and the shock of the vile stories circulated by political enemies had turned a chronic ailment into a fatal illness. Jackson considered John Quincy Adams, Henry Clay, and their followers no better than murderers, and the opportunity to frustrate them gave him a major reason for clinging to life.

There was also dissension in the new president's own ranks. Vice-President John C. Calhoun of South Carolina had been virtually promised the succession when the Jackson managers were persuading him to accept second place on their ticket rather than enter the lists against Jackson and Adams. General Duff Green, editor of the *United States Telegraph*, was ostensibly the public voice of the administration, but his chief concern was preparing the way for Calhoun to become president. By the middle of 1830, General Green was spreading the word that Calhoun's pretensions could not wait another six years. Calhoun's supporters in the cabinet were the secretaries of the treasury and the navy, and the attorney general.

Calhoun's chief rival, Secretary of State Martin Van Buren of New York, was backed by young Secretary of War John Eaton and Postmaster General William T. Barry, the recently defeated gubernatorial candidate from Kentucky. Van Buren was a keen judge of men. He was also patient and loyal, and he soon realized that if Andrew Jackson chose to live another eight years or longer, there would be no new president in 1832.

The rivalry soon erupted in a bizarre situation. Secretary Eaton had recently married the beautiful and ambitious Peggy O'Neill Timberlake, the widow of a young naval officer who had allegedly committed suicide because of shortages in his accounts. A close friend of the lady for several years, young Senator Eaton had helped her father financially and had rescued her husband from at least one earlier misadventure. Peggy had become engaged to Lieutenant Timberlake the first day she met him, and later had made no effort to hide her friendliness toward the handsome Eaton. These facts made her vulnerable to the gossip of various ladies who might have found her good looks insufferable under the best of circumstances. Also, not a few matrons may have been angry that Eaton had found Peggy preferable to their own daughters. Soon Amos Kendall was writing Blair that gossip that the Eatons had shared a premarital bed was "rife among the ladies, many of whom . . . are no better than they should be." [9] The aristocratic Mrs. Calhoun and most of the cabinet wives chose to ostracize Mrs. Eaton socially, and there was apparently an effort to use Eaton's personal situation as an excuse for driving him from the cabinet. This was an unwise decision for the friends of Calhoun.

Andrew Jackson had long brooded over his inability to save

Rachel from the cruel traducers of helpless womankind, and in Peggy Eaton he immediately found a substitute for Rachel. With a roar of anger he went to her defense, and the affair ultimately brought the resignation of every member of the cabinet except Barry. Martin Van Buren had an incalculable advantage in all of this. He was a widower, and without fear of a wife's disapproval he could help the fair lady in and out of her carriage, happily attend her parties, and join his fellow widower, Andrew Jackson, in long talks about the wickedness of gossiping female tongues.

When certain friends discovered also that Calhoun as secretary of war in 1819 had urged a court-martial for Jackson after Old Hickory's invasion of Florida, the break between president and vice-president was complete, and Calhoun's chance for the presidency was sidetracked forever. All of this meant that by 1830 Andrew Jackson was still looking for friends he could trust, and his supporters had become convinced that his true friends did not include General Duff Green and the *United States Telegraph*. In faraway Frankfort, Kentucky, the heavily indebted clerk, bank president, and part-time editor Francis Preston Blair was kept informed of these events by Kentucky's self-appointed ambassador to the White House, Amos Kendall.

On March 5, 1829, Kendall reported to Blair his impressions of the sublime inaugural of Andrew Jackson. The roaring crowds, the stirring military music, the great speech, and the supreme moment when the president threw open the doors of the White House to the common people—these memories would live in his heart forever. Kendall could not get near the front door of the White House, but "like hundreds of others" he "lept in at the window of an adjoining room." One incident reminded Kendall of the "ominous flight of birds." When the general left his lodgings before the inaugural, "the sky was overcast with dark clouds. . . . just as the General was entering the avenue after the inauguration, bright sunshine was resting on the president's house where he was going. At the same time, the smoke of the city was borne by the southerly winds in the direction of Porter's house where Mr. Adams had taken refuge, and almost concealed it from view." It was indeed an exhilarating moment for the disciples of Jackson.[10]

Kendall could press his case at the White House for federal

officeholders from Kentucky with a powerful argument. Henry Clay would surely be the opposition candidate in 1832. How better defeat Clay than use the federal offices to strengthen the Jacksonians in Clay's own state? Those who would save Kentucky from Clay, Kendall wrote Blair, would create "irresistible claims on the administration which shall succeed General Jackson" and would be able to "command anything they may desire." Kendall believed the successor would be Van Buren, Calhoun, or Supreme Court Judge John McLean, and he advised Blair that "we must stay clear and support Jackson and the successor most likely to succeed when the time comes." Kendall shrewdly rejected an opportunity to join Duff Green and the party newspaper because he was certain Green would ruin himself within two years. Van Buren and Louis McLane, secretary of the treasury, offered Kendall chief clerkships, while Calhoun promised an auditorship. Kendall prefered the auditorship, which would enable him to answer only to Jackson and to choose his own favorite from among the aspirants to the succession later.[11]

By April 8, 1829, Blair and the *Argus* could print a lecture on virtue from Amos Kendall: "Men may learn wisdom from the past. Who were more unjustly villified than Barry, Bibb, Moore and myself? . . . we were defeated; denunciation and proscription were to pursue us until we were crushed. . . . What has Heaven done? So disposed of events as to make Barry Post Master General, Bibb a Senator, Moore a foreign Minister, and myself a mere humble auditor." For Blair, Kendall had advice for supplementing the divine assistance. The political managers in Kentucky's congressional districts should be replaced with county superintendents directly responsible to a central committee that Blair should organize. To keep Democratic correspondence safe from prying eyes, the Frankfort and Louisville post offices must be entrusted to "honest and true men." Indeed, there should be a change in "every office in the state which has been recently prostituted to aid in the electioneering contest." For these efforts Blair would be rewarded. "I have not yet determined," wrote Kendall, "what you will be four years hence. . . . I have more confidence in your opinion when you will take time to think, than I have in any man's except my own, and sometimes more than I have in my own." Save Kentucky from

Clay, said Kendall, and you will save the nation. "If the task be difficult, the greater is the honor in accomplishing it. A fig for the fainted [sic] hearted men who are ready to surrender because I leave the state." And for Eliza, Kendall also offered praise and advice: "I believe she is a true friend of her country and I therefore conclude she will soon be as firm a Jackson man as any woman can be." [12]

For the next several months, Blair attacked the Clay party at every opportunity, defended the administration with skill and passion, and worked around the clock organizing the Jackson party for the congressional elections of 1830.

An immediate issue was the new governor's appointment of Old Court men to vacant judgeships, which Blair denounced as a violation of preelection pledges to work for statewide political harmony. The *Argus* and other pro-Jackson papers accused the well-known conservative Robert Wickliffe of slandering the people with the remark "God save us from such a curse as to pay any attention to the opinion of the people in the appointment of Judges of the Court of Appeals."

Wickliffe's son, Charles, using the pseudonym Coriolanus, published a letter denouncing the *Kentucky Gazette* and two unnamed abusers for their attacks upon his father. Colonel A. G. Meriwether, printer for the *Argus,* and a Major Shannon assumed that they were the two unnamed gentlemen. Using the name Dentatus, they challenged Coriolanus to come out from behind his cowardly alias and face the consequences of his libel. The hot-tempered young Wickliffe ordered *Gazette* editor Thomas Benning to reveal the name of Dentatus. When Benning refused and brandished a stick in his defense, Wickliffe shot him dead on the spot.

A grand jury indicted Wickliffe only for manslaughter, and a jury swayed by the eloquence of defense attorneys Henry Clay and John J. Crittenden declared him not guilty. With Blair in the lead, the Jacksonian editors denounced the verdict as a gross miscarriage of justice, and from far-off Washington came the sound of the bugle from Amos Kendall: "Fear not. All must die. Do your duty, and if you bleed for it, remember that your blood will rouse the people to put down the ferocious aristocrats and confirm their liberties. For years I have felt myself prepared for the sacrifice, and I thank God more than man for my preservation."[13]

Blair often used words that cut like a sword, and his lifelong immunity from duel challenges remains something of a mystery. One version has it that his life was insured by a fearsome reputation as a hunter and a crack shot with both rifle and pistol. He was credited with killing deer in full flight, and friends preparing for duels sometimes came to him for instructions in marksmanship. Also, his pistols were regarded as superior weapons, and were occasionally borrowed by friends preparing for the field of honor. This reputation probably had at least some effect. Numerous contemporaries were compelled to shoot or be shot for language often more temperate than Blair's daily editorial output.

The Wickliffe affair ultimately moved on to further tragedy. George J. Trotter succeeded Benning at the *Gazette*, and promptly began "lacerating the feelings" of young Wickliffe. Wickliffe answered with a challenge to Trotter, and the two men fought at a distance of only eight feet. Both missed on the first fire, but Wickliffe demanded a second chance. On the second fire, Wickliffe fell dead.[14]

In Washington, meanwhile, Amos Kendall was happily working at reform so vigorously that the Senate's confirmation of his appointment hung in the balance for almost eighteen months. He secured indictments for fraud against various Adams officials. His predecessor, Tobias Watkins, went to jail, and various others were promptly reformed out of office. Kendall also persuaded Jackson to reduce the shore-duty compensation of all naval officers and order to sea a batch of land-based officers and surgeons who had not been on a ship for twenty years. When a marine paymaster complained of Kendall, Jackson investigated personally, reprimanded the paymaster severely, and put him on the list for reforming as soon as his accounts could be closed.

By May 1830, more than one year after his appointment, the still-unconfirmed Kendall was complaining bitterly that Congress was filled with professed Jacksonians who did not really support the president's programs of reform. Kendall could take comfort, however, in the support of his chief. Jackson's campaign managers had cast the general in the role of an avenging knight who would correct the abuses and corruptions of his predecessor,

and Jackson wore the armor with no doubts as to the righteousness of his cause and the wickedness of his enemies. In Amos
Kendall he found a kindred spirit who could draw the lines of the
plot with oversimplified clarity and who, like himself, was a man
of action. "If those around him do not harmonize," Kendall
wrote Blair, "he will scatter them like a whirlwind." Kendall's
alternative was clear. If rejected by the senators he would start
another newspaper. If unable to "correct them in office," he
would "expose them out."[15]

The Senate ultimately decided that Kendall the auditor
would be more endurable than Kendall the editor, but Green's
obvious allegiance to Calhoun indicated clearly that a new editor
must be found for a newspaper to rival the *Telegraph*. Overtures were first made to the well-known Thomas Ritchie of Virginia, but Ritchie wanted certain financial guarantees that the
would-be sponsors felt unable to meet. Amos Kendall, meanwhile, waited in the background with a candidate of his own.

Blair's efforts in Kentucky had not gone unnoticed in Washington. Kendall had distributed the *Argus* in the right places, and
the *Telegraph* and the *Argus* had often printed each other's editorials. The recent purchaser of Kendall's interest in the *Argus*,
however, was financially unable to pay Blair a salary. Convinced
that without Blair the *Argus* would fail, and hoping for a Washington editor under his own influence, Kendall began promoting
his friend for the new administration editorship. To soothe
Green's fears, Kendall argued that the *Telegraph*'s chances for
the congressional printing would be improved by the creation of
another Jacksonian paper to take the executive patronage. This
transaction, said Kendall, would result in executive pressures for
Green in Congress.[16]

Blair's attacks on the Bank of the United States were the final
straw in winning over Andrew Jackson. By October 1830 Kendall
could make a clear-cut proposition. Blair should come on by mid-
November, and the new paper should be in print by December 1.
The new organ must support a thorough reform in the government and mildly oppose the South Carolina nullifiers. It should
favor a judicious tariff and either national internal improvements
or a distribution of the surplus revenue. It should call for payment of the national debt, for a reduction of the duties on articles

not extensively raised or manufactured in the United States, and for "leaving the States to manage their own affairs without other interference than the safety of the whole imperiously requires." It should oppose the United States Bank. Blair should be under no pledge to Van Buren or anyone else, but stand only as "the friend of General Jackson and his administration, having no further political views other than the support of his principles." Kendall would be "a silent (not altogether silent perhaps) partner." He would "share all its responsibilities, aid in writing, . . . and after allowing Blair enough of the profits for a respectable support, share the balance. " Blair could rely upon $2,000 to $3,000 of Barry's $4,000 to $6,000 patronage. Van Buren would give his influence and most of his patronage. The War and Navy departments, the register, second comptroller, and second and fourth auditors would do likewise. Blair could expect at least $4,000 in government printing business a year, and it might ultimately increase to $10,000 or $15,000. The president's friends would provide a printer, and the president, vice-president, and their friends would exert themselves to provide a circulation.[17]

Kendall's proposition offered a vague basis for giving up a relatively steady $3,000 income and moving a family 600 miles to an unfamiliar city and a job that might well disappear at the first shifting of political winds. Apparently, however, Preston and Eliza Blair did not hesitate. Their responsibilities were only to each other and their children, since Blair's own family was for the moment no longer a burden upon them. His mother and brother had died a few years earlier, his sisters were married, and his father had remarried a fairly well-to-do widow who loved the old man dearly and enjoyed watching him make a career of managing her small estate. There was also the problem of Blair's debts, but perhaps these could be settled without the loss of his Frankfort property.

Benjamin Gratz was a director of the Lexington branch of the Bank of the United States, and through his influence a settlement was soon made with the special bank agent already engaged in settling desperate debts for a fraction of their value. The $1,500 note on which Blair was the initial signer was settled for a $200 note from Gratz plus $37.42 in court fee-bills from Blair.

Also Blair was released as a cosigner on the other two notes, although the initial borrower and the other cosigners remained committed in person and property in each case. Counting ten years of interest the three notes totalled $20,744 in legal obligation, and Blair's sense of relief as the bank agent signed the release can only be imagined. He was still owed several thousand dollars in court fee-bills. These affairs would keep Ben Gratz and other agents busy for several more years, and while the fee bills were never collected except when they could be applied to debts, Blair eventually paid off all of his obligations.[18]

The America of 1830 was a land of progress, optimism, and self-confidence, and the Blairs were children of their time. If they felt any awe at the prospect of moving from a small county clerk's office to a post at the right hand of the president of the United States, it was never apparent. Their travel preparations were eager and happy, and Amos Kendall's descriptions of the life awaiting them were read with delight. Blair, Eliza, and daughter Elizabeth could board respectably in Georgetown for $570 a year, including food, wood, and candles, but the same accommodations in the city would cost $700. Ladies without carriages usually hired hacks at seventy-five cents an hour when visiting at any distance. Eliza would have her choice of society, but Kendall did not think she would "have much taste for that which is called the *very first.*" Keeping a horse would cost more than a hundred dollars, but Blair would need one if he insisted upon hunting. Deer in nearby Virginia were plentiful, and he would find the Potomac full of bass, perch, pike, rock sturgeon, shad, and herring. Kendall suspected, however, that Blair would not "find much time to trouble fish, flesh, or fowl." [19]

On Sunday, November 6, 1830, the Blair entourage got underway by stage for Washington. For the time being the three sons were left at the Gratz home in Lexington, where Montgomery was preparing to enroll at Transylvania. In an exchange not entirely favorable to Ben Gratz, his wife, Maria, accompanied Eliza and Elizabeth just for the ride and a chance to visit Washington. Other hardy travelers joined the party along the way.

It was a long, arduous, but exciting trip along abominable roads through magnificent scenery. Between Lexington and Maysville Blair had to walk eight miles because of a broken carriage spring, and a broken tongue caused further delay at Maysville. After "various councils in which romantic feelings gets the better of hateful prudence," the party decided to take the treacherous but more adventurous route across the Kentucky and Virginia mountains. They forded the Little Sandy River at a place where two people had recently drowned. Twice the horses pulling accompanying carriages ran away. On one occasion the hack carrying Eliza and the children was kept from sliding off the road and down a steep bank only by a quick-thinking driver who leaped out and seized the wheel. After fifteen days of narrow escapes and nightly stops at various rude inns and way stations, they finally reached Charleston, Virginia, where they took "the big stage" with a sigh of relief.[20]

The excitement, however, was not quite over. A few miles from Washington the stage overturned, but only Blair was injured. A gash on top of his head required several stitches and a long patch of court plaster. He arrived in Washington dusty, bloody, worn, and eager to make a good impression. He had hoped for a few hours of rest and refreshment, but friends were waiting to take him directly to the White House. Andrew Jackson wished to see his new editor.

Chapter 4

The Editor

ONE day in November 1830 a skinny man in a badly
wrinkled frock coat was escorted to the White House. His
egg-shaped head was decorated with a long plaster patch, and he
was not exactly a picture of dynamic power and self-confidence.
For weeks the president's friends had been eagerly anticipating
the arrival of a fire-eating Kentucky editor who would carry the
battle of thundering epithets directly to the enemy. "Wait till
Blair comes," had been the hopeful watchword, but now Blair
had arrived, and his mild countenance and insignificant appearance were an immediate disappointment. Major William B.
Lewis, Jackson's robust aide, greeted him with the words "Mr.
Blair, we want stout hearts and sound heads here."

Andrew Jackson, however, had commanded enough fighting
men to know the irrelevance of external appearance as a factor
in determining the stoutness of hearts and heads. Within minutes
the president was unreservedly confiding in his new lieutenant.
The machinations of the nullifiers, the increasing power of the
Bank of the United States, the schemes of the devilish Clay, and
the cabinet combination against the Eatons—each was discussed
in turn. The old man had his friends and enemies properly sorted,
and left Blair no doubts as to who they were. Even Jackson's own
nephew, Andrew Jackson Donelson, must be watched because of
his affinity for the nullifiers. "Let him do what he will," said
Jackson, "I love him. I can't help it. Treat him kindly, but if he
wants to write for your paper, you must look out for him."

The interview lasted until evening, and the hungry newcomer
was both surprised and pleased when the president asked him to
stay for dinner. To his embarrassment, however, an elaborately

dressed company soon gathered for a formal affair. Blair tried to be inconspicuous, but Jackson led his new editor and friend to the head of the table, introduced him with a glowing compliment, and placed him at his own right hand. On this note began Blair's undying love for Andrew Jackson.[1]

Francis P. Blair lived a life of many thrills and happy moments, but nothing ever quite matched the excitement and exhilaration of his days with Andrew Jackson. His love for Jackson was akin to the personal attachment common in the clan struggles of his Scotch ancestors, and for a romantic like Blair the opportunity to serve an authentic hero in a battle for lofty principles was the culmination of every possible ambition. Eliza shared her husband's enthusiasm. Old Hickory combined rugged masculinity with a gentle, courtly attitude toward women and children. Eliza could understand his continued mourning for Rachel and sympathize with his fierce defense of Peggy Eaton. Eliza and her twelve-year-old Elizabeth, usually called Lizzie, gave the sad old man a tender love in which he took much comfort. Lizzie's health was such that her family feared she might not live to adulthood, and in the winter months she frequently spent the night at the White House to avoid the dampness prevalent in the Blairs' quarters.

The new Jackson paper, the *Globe,* was an immediate success. Blair was everything his supporters had hoped for, and soon his fiery editorials were being read all over America. By 1835 it had 17,000 subscribers, and its influence went far beyond its numbers. Democrats bought it for the benefit of state legislatures. People unable to subscribe as individuals took it as partners and in groups. As the Jacksonians used the patronage to build up their grass-roots organizations, subscriptions to the *Globe* became the responsibility of local politicians everywhere. It was the authentic voice of Andrew Jackson—first to know his views on any subject and first to communicate and justify them to the faithful. Ultimately, more than 400 newspapers around the country drew information, arguments, and inspiration from its columns. They regularly exchanged news and editorials with it, and promptly wheeled into line with each change of official policy.

The *Globe* was blessed with several assets: the editor's dynamic literary and political abilities, its influence over those dispensing local federal patronage, its genuinely democratic philosophy in a democratic age, and the magic name of Andrew Jackson. One William Kearney spoke for a multitude when he advised Blair to consider him a subscriber "so long as you support the man that asks nothing but what is right, and will submit to nothing that is radicaly rong [sic]."[2] Among those working hardest to make the *Globe* a financial success were Blair's friends and devoted creditors back in Kentucky.

The government contracts for printing such things as circulars, laws, blank receipts, commissions, labels, Indian treaties, presidential proclamations, passports, statistical tables, and congressional documents came much more slowly. Each session of the House and the Senate elected an official printer to publish its journals and records, and these contracts were quite lucrative. General Green defeated Blair in the election for House printer in 1833, however, and was succeeded in 1835 by the Whig publishers, Joseph Gales and William Seaton, of the *National Intelligencer*. Indeed, the constant struggles of presidents Jackson and Van Buren on Capitol Hill were nowhere more clearly indicated than in the failures of their protégé to win the congressional printing. Although from its beginning the *Globe* trumpeted the political and economic principles of Andrew Jackson as the national conscience of the Democratic party, the party was a coalition of groups and individuals lacking in unity either political or economic. Numerous members agreed with Jackson's attitudes toward banks, paper money, internal improvements, public lands, and tariffs no more fervently than they had endorsed the watchdog activities of his fourth auditor, Amos Kendall. Had he served up less principle and more political cooperation to his own party, Blair might have received vastly more work from Congress. Instead, the *Globe* was destined to receive significant congressional patronage during only four of its fifteen years of life.

Even the *Globe*'s executive patronage did not reach $15,000 until 1834. Although Jackson used personal pressure on cabinet members, contracts with the executive departments were reached only after much haggling and competition with other bidders. Secretary of State Van Buren remained scrupulously neutral, and the *Globe* received no important patronage from his department until 1833, long after Van Buren's resignation. Green, Gales and Seaton, and others were consistently successful in competing with the *Globe,* even though it did good work at prices usually lower than theirs. During the first eleven years of its life, all but a few months under Democratic administrations, the *Globe* received a total of $440,717.52 for government printing, and $179,899.44 of this came during Blair's term as printer to Congress in the years 1840–1841. In contrast, the combination of Thomas Allen, Gales, and Seaton received $216,403.15 in 1837–1838, and Gales and Seaton received $186,788.70 in 1842–1843, all of these sums from Congress alone. The *Globe* never received more than half the amount spent by the government in any given year. Nevertheless, the *Globe* ultimately made Blair a moderately rich man, but several yars of struggle came first. Its paper and supplies were bought on credit, and not until 1832 was Blair able to pay his press foreman the standard wage.[3]

During the first few months, Amos Kendall proposed an arrangement that would leave him free for auditing but also guarantee him a place with the *Globe.* He would accept $800 a year for writing, to be increased by $100 for every 1,000 subscribers above 3,000 added to the list. If he should relinquish political office at any time within six years he would receive half interest in the *Globe* without purchase. If Blair should die within six years without Kendall as a partner, everything would go to Blair's heirs. If Kendall should die within six years, half the *Globe* would go to his heirs. Blair should not sell the *Globe* for six years, but if Kendall did not become a partner within six years the *Globe* would become Blair's exclusive property.[4]

How much of this Blair accepted is not clear, but Kendall's government service went beyond six years. In a case involving a would-be writer for editor Mordecai Noah, Jackson had already objected to having a government official share in a business dealing in government contracts. In December 1831, therefore, Kendall asked Jackson's permission to write for the *Globe* for pay. He informed the president that he had done considerable writing without pay, but now that the paper was self-supporting Blair wanted to pay him for any future work. Kendall would have no formal connection with the paper, but would write occasionally in his spare time. Blair added a postscript praising Kendall's work, and Jackson agreed to the arrangement.[5]

While boarding in Georgetown during his first few months in Washington, Blair became friendly with a Treasury Department clerk named John C. Rives. Rives was a hairy, rough-handed, rock-faced giant of six feet, four inches and two hundred and six pounds, which eventually became two hundred and forty. He had an infectious wit and sense of humor, and a genius for organization and finance. The two men soon found a common interest in hunting and in shooting contests. Forty-five years later Gideon Welles would remember meeting Blair and Rives for the first time when they were returning from a "trial of marksmanship." Senator Isaac Hill of New Hampshire made the introductions and on the way home predicted sorrowfully to Welles that Blair's health would keep him from living more than another two or three years. In March 1832 Rives resigned his government post and became office manager at the *Globe*. Two years later he became a full partner, and he spent most of a long life managing the financial affairs of the Blair family as well as those of the *Globe*.

John Rives joined the Gist sisters, Ben Gratz, John Crittenden, Andrew Jackson, and the many others captivated by the character and spirit of Francis P. Blair. Rives and Blair shared the *Globe* office for seventeen years, and Rives continued thereafter as the Blair family's private banker after buying Blair's interest on a long-term basis. Rives remembered in 1855 that no angry word had ever passed between them, and not even an angry thought, "except when we both kept dairies he used to intercept the butter wagons on the road, which furnished us with butter, and buy it for the use of his own family. . . . we did think a little hard of him for doing so, as we told him when we commenced the farming and dairy business, six miles from him, that our only object in settling so far from him, was not to come into competition with him in purchasing produce for home consumption." [6] This was a joke well understood by two men for whom exaggerated boasting about their respective farms had long since become an avocation. In Blair's rich treasury of close friends, Rives may well have been the brightest jewel in the vault. Rives loved the Blairs as his own, and his energy and talents left Blair entirely free for the editorial and political tasks that had become his chosen profession.

Eliza, too, found a new career. She assumed responsibility for the foreign news, human interest news, and special features, which included short stories, poetry, book reviews, letters from diplomats and foreign travelers, brief anecdotes, riddles, and other similar items. American diplomats abroad who aspired to impress the public with their problems and observations usually wrote directly to Eliza. There were stories like "The Patriot's Grave," "The Sleepless Woman," "The Seaman's Grave," and "Haidee: A Tale of the South," as well as poems like "To a Butterfly Resting on a Skull." Eliza was also an advocate of women's rights, and on one occasion she published a blistering review of James Boaden's life of the British actress Dorothy Jordan. The book emphasized the lady's loves, illegitimate children, and other sins, and the *Globe* printed several letters in refutation. Indeed, said the *Globe*, "the whole range of biography does not furnish so contemptible a production . . . through which we have waded in vain with the charitable hope of discovering some passages that would justify us in according to the author an incidental good word . . . no one living can make a spirited subject as dull as Mr. Boaden." [7]

Established primarily as a political instrument, the *Globe* was also a highly readable newspaper. Marriages, deaths, suicides, murders, duels, robberies, lawsuits, trials, civic events, foreign revolutions and politics, exploring expeditions, earthquakes, fires, bizarre events, and accidents on steamboats, railways, and stages were duly recorded and often described. Readers might learn that "by divine permission the Rev. Mr. JAMES will preach . . . next Sabbath morning at 11 o'clock," or receive the perhaps more exciting news that at the National Theatre "HERR CLINE" would "go through an entirely new performance on the ELASTIC CHORD, in which he will perform astonishing feats of activity, concluding with a pictorial display of the contending passions of the human heart." Some could appreciate the news that the "CATHOLIC TOTAL ABSTINENCE ASSOCIATION" would meet on Sunday, "after which the pledge will be administered by the Rev. Pastor," while others might have preferred the announcement that first prize in the next "UNION LOTTERY" for the benefit of "Internal improvement in Alexandria, D.C.—State Treasury, Delaware College, and Common Schools in the State of Delaware—Useful Manufactures in the State of South Carolina—Green and Pulaski Monuments in the city of Savannah, and State of Georgia—and Public Institutions in the State of Louisiana and Kentucky" would be $50,000. The total amount in prizes was $912,912. "CLARK'S OLD ESTABLISHED LUCKY OFFICE" in Baltimore—"where have been sold PRIZES! PRIZES! in Dollars, MILLIONS of Millions!"— made no claims to such public spirit. In October 1835 readers learned of the "ARRIVAL EXTRAORDINARY" of "THE ETHIOPIAN SERENADERS whose astonishing performances have attracted crowded houses in New York, Boston, Philadelphia, and Baltimore," to perform with "Songs, Duets, Trios, Quartets, Glees, Choruses, Conundrums, &c., accompanying themselves with the Accordion, Banjo, Congo Tambourine, Bone Castenets, Tongs and Triangles, &c.," for "25 cents, under 10 half price." [8]

The *Globe* also printed at least one story by a promising young Englishman named Charles Dickens, and discussed books like that of Major Sir Grenville Temple's *Travel in North Africa*. Attention was given to "THE DAUGHTER'S OWN BOOK, or Practical Hints from a Father to His Daughter," and long excerpts were reprinted from Richard Henry Dana's *Two Years Before the Mast* and William H. Prescott's classics on the Spanish conquests of Mexico and Peru. One daring article reprinted from a New York magazine, entitled "Domestic Manners of the French" concluded that "if our ladies would add to their pretty faces the French fashions of manner and dress, they would be altogether irresistible." On another occasion Eliza advised "THE LADIES" that "the Journal of Health strongly recommends simple soap and water as the best wash for preserving the complexion, instead of the thousand varieties of cosmetic lotions, which are much used." Advocating better wages for women in factories, she argued that any society could best be measured by the status of its women. [9]

A few years later, when Dickens visited America and wrote harsh criticisms of everything he saw, Blair explained that the famous novelist obviously had never recovered from the seasickness incurred on the journey over. That America's faults would be exaggerated by "the horrors of the morbid imagination of this writer of fictions, familiar with the most depraved, disgusting, and shocking aspect of society in England, and made painfully sensitive by the long endured nausea which attended him to our shores" was "not at all surprising." Obviously, Blair added, Dickens could not have enjoyed seeing "Africans dressed in fine broadcloth, fat, sleek, and saucy, cracking their own hack whips and their jokes . . . in the broad avenues of the American capital, when he had been accustomed to see, at home, fine specimens of his own blood—men and women—fair-haired, blue-eyed Saxons—sneaking from door to door, begging crumbs and rags." [10]

The *Globe* must have gleaned at least $50 per day from private advertisers. There were schedules for stage, steamship, and railroad lines; prospectuses for other newspapers and magazines; offers of personal services; vivid descriptions of books, clothing, and luxury items; advertisements for runaway slaves and announcements of slave sales; appeals for the return of lost or strayed cows, horses, and pets; and universal claims for almost every conceivable kind of medical remedy. Horse dealers could learn that the stallion "INDUSTRY" would perform at his usual stand for the rate of $15 per single leap. Some readers could take comfort from the description of "FRANK'S SPECIFIC COMPOUND, an immediate and certain cure for the Gonorrhoea, Gleets, and all kinds of analogous diseases," while the less desperate could prefer "REV. I. COVERT'S BALM OF LIFE," guaranteed to cure "dypepsia, [and] all pulmonary diseases and serve as an excellent household physic," or Dr. A. Fitch's Indian Vegetable Elixir, which after curing various diseases would also "leave a most delightful flow of the animal spirits after its operation." An apparatus "for the excitation of Galvanic Electricity in the system" was "a sure cure for constipation, vertigo, painful sensations in the head, flatulence or wind, unnatural distention of the abdomen or stomach, attended with hardness, *some of the affections* of the liver and spine—and in some cases difficulty in breathing, falling of the womb, diseases of the vagina and hemmorhoids, or piles." "COMPOUND TINCTURE OF CREOSOTE" was a standard treatment for teeth and gums, and even stammering could be cured at "DR. COMSTOCK'S VOCAL GYMNASIUM AND LYCEUM FOR ELOCUTION." Another public-spirited item urged people to subscribe at one dollar per head to a project for regularly watering Pennsylvania Avenue to keep down the dust. This would protect the wares along the street and be "not only a source of profit to the merchant, but of pleasure to the pedestrian."

Blair would send copies of the *Globe* to John Crittenden and Ben Gratz with expressions of pious hope that they would find Eliza's page as interesting as they were certain to find his obnoxious. To Crittenden once he added: "*Although I love you I can not love your faults.* Yours in everything politics excepted." [11]

Crittenden answered: "Tell Mrs. Blair that I read the aforesaid paper with more punctuality than could have been expected—I do not profit much by it, as the Editor seems to be a great partisan, and wonderfully given to praising Old Hickory overmuch. I once liked that old gentleman very well myself, and indeed I bear him no malice now tho he has raised a wall of partition between us." [12]

Ben Gratz described the paper as a "Globule," bordering on the insane in its political philosophy, but he was much pleased by its financial success. "From what I see of you politically," he wrote Blair, "I should think all was deranged and that the 'aid Eliza affords you to build up your establishment' was counteracted by yourself. . . . I would not recur to your editorial course, as in it I see nothing to commend, were it not for the allusions made in your letters to the aristocrats, menacing the safety of the republic, and which by the substitution of the word, Democrat, which I always dispised [*sic*], would portray your party most emphatically." [13] Gratz spent many long hours collecting Blair's rents, worrying over the condition of Blair's property, struggling with Blair's accounts receivable as opposed to debts payable, and hoping that the *Globe* would get his favorite brother-in-law out of debt without doing too much damage to the forces of law, orderly finance, and political conservatism.

From its beginning the *Globe* spoke directly for Andrew Jackson and his agrarian principles. This meant warfare not only with the opposition party but also with various individuals and factions within Jackson's own party. Indeed, the "true" followers in the Jackson "Kitchen Cabinet"—like Thomas Hart Benton, James K. Polk, Churchill C. Cambreleng, Van Buren, Blair, and Kendall—were an embattled minority on many of the economic questions of the day. They preached the right of ordinary men everywhere to acquire and accumulate more of the riches of a developing and expanding America, although they were opposed to the concept of a paternalistic government that would take positive action to speed up the developing and expanding. Many nominal Democrats were happy to take political shelter under the great hickory tree that was Andrew Jackson, but flatly rejected most of his specific policies.

The *Globe* was not dedicated to party unity. "We do not belong to that class of men," said the paper, "who . . . hourra for Jackson . . . without making an effort to produce those reforms which he recommends." What this meant was spelled out in the first issue on December 7, 1830. At the masthead was the motto destined to remain there for the paper's life: "*The world is governed too much.*" The only legitimate object of the government, said the *Globe,* was "*to protect men in the pursuit of happiness.*" Without this protection "the weak would be the victims of the strong, and the world would be full of violence and crime." Men did not establish government, however, "to *direct,* much less to *force* them into the road to happiness," which Blair defined as "the free indulgence of their opinions, the unrestrained exercise of their religious rights, the choice of their pursuits and the disposition of their property according to their own will." If government, however, should tax the poor "to create monopolies in the rich," or use "its unnecessary and oppressive executions to buy over sections of the country to the support of particular men, at the same time accumulating to itself undue influence and power," it would be "attempting to govern too much." In *Globe* language, Americans must choose either "a *pure* government, confined to its proper duties, protecting all in their favorite pursuits, exacting from the people only the necessary means of their own support, and returning all surplusage to the States, or a scene of widespread abuse, corruption, injustice, murmuring, and possible insurrection, civil war, and disunion." [14]

The possibility that a strong government might take positive action to protect and elevate the poorer classes apparently did not occur to Blair and his fellow Jacksonians. It was part of the natural order of their America and their universe that if the government made the nation's public lands and natural resources equally available to all, the common people would automatically find prosperity, security, and maximum liberty. Their ideal

America, composed of independent yeoman farmers and small tradesmen developing a land of limitless resources, was democratic by its very nature, and they would keep it so by preventing the development of a government strong enough to change it.

America's greatest danger, said the *Globe* in editorial after editorial, was the possibility that wealthy aristocrats might use the government's great power to increase their own privileges, thwart the ambitions of the less fortunate, and create a permanent native aristocracy. To allow lawyers to monopolize all the offices and favor the monied "capitalists as their allies" would produce in America "the divisions between the *governors* and *governed,* which exists throughout Europe and the repugnance between the interest of the two classes which naturally arises from the separation." [15]

In *Globe* language, Henry Clay's American System of a national bank, national debt, tariffs, and federal internal improvements was clearly an attempt to push America down this fatal path; but standing with drawn sword to turn the government back to its original purpose stood

> Andrew Jackson, the "Hero of New Orleans," at the head of the American people, grasping the glorious standard of *"E. Pluribus Unum,"* protecting our rights abroad, fostering our interests at home, and viewing with an eye as unblenching as his country's eagle's, the gathering array of hostile force . . . a moral spectacle, sublime without a parallel in the history of Republics . . . unmoved as the White Mountains of the Granite State . . . too deep in the people's affections to be undermined. The storms of faction beat around him unheeded. The cloud rests upon him but a moment and leaves him more bright than before, towering in the sunshine of spotless honor and eternal truth.[16]

Within this framework Blair fought the battle for the reelection of Old Hickory.

The *Globe* editor soon abandoned any reluctance to attack his old friend Clay. The American System, he wrote, probably originated as a copy of Napoleon's Continental System, and it should be remembered that Napoleon "lost between two and three hundred thousand men . . . and finally got himself exiled to the Rock of St. Helena, by his Continental System." The *Globe* happily resolved the disagreement between two biographers over the profession of Clay's father. This gentleman, said the *Globe*, was first a dancing master, but had "turned a somerset" and become a Baptist preacher when a religious revival had made dancing unfashionable in Virginia. The son had shown "equal versatility of genius," but had reversed the good example. "The father turned from a *bad* to a *good* calling. The son went from *good* to *bad*." When admirers presented Clay with an American-manufactured carving knife as a testimony of respect, Blair found the gift most fitting. "What . . . could be more appropriate than the presentation of such an important item . . . to a man whose whole time is spent at public dinners? Distinguished military men are generally presented with *swords*—distinguished gormandizers with *carving knives*."[17] Clay was pictured almost daily as a gambler and rake, and as a paid Bank attorney who had bartered his soul to political ambition.

Jackson's opponents, naturally enough, considered his practice of "reforming" employees by dismissing them in favor of his own supporters as a new "spoils system" that would destroy the efficiency of the public service. The *Globe*, however, had a different version. After citing long lists of employees by political affiliation to show that the number of removals had been greatly exaggerated, Blair defended the policy. If long government service should be rewarded with further tenure, he wrote, then legitimacy and hereditary monarchy were the only proper forms of government. According to the Jackson philosophy, no man had the

> right to office and no man should be in office too long. It is the natural tendency of office to corrupt. We might appeal to most men who have the expenditure of public money . . . to say, whether they were not more precise and tenacious when they entered office than they are now. They think some things right which they then thought wrong, and look without sensation upon claims at which their nice sense of right formerly revolted. This indicates no depravity; it is the natural course of things, which will exist until man becomes perfect.[18]

Obviously, Jackson was engaging only in the noble task of preserving the morality of the former employees. And when a federal judge in Florida protested publicly in the *Telegraph* because he was not reappointed, the *Globe* preached a lesson:

> The Lordlings of America and the Lords of Europe are exactly alike. Touch their offices and their sinecures, their pensions and their places, deprive them of the means of living upon the labor of the people, and they denounce the democrat that does it as a tyrant and a robber! . . . Mr. Breckenridge has the same opportunity to earn his living as any other citizen . . . thousands of freemen . . . have more cause to complain that they *never had an office,* than he has to complain that he *has lost one which he long enjoyed.*[19]

While defending Jackson's removal policies, Blair also praised the achievements of the new men in office. Navy Secretary Levi Woodbury issued an order that any sailor who refused his daily allotment of grog could accept six cents instead. Blair hailed this as a great moral revolution in the navy, and boasted that more than half the men were accepting it.[20]

From its beginning the *Globe* extended the welcoming hand of the Democratic party to the immigrants daily pouring into America. The new Americans did not find everyone friendly, but the *Globe* reprinted an essay describing prejudice as like

> a misty morning in October; a man goes forth . . . and he sees at the summit of a neighboring hill a figure, apparently of gigantic stature, for such the imperfect medium through which he is viewed would make him appear; he goes forward a few steps, and the figure advances towards him; the size lessens as they approach; they draw still nearer, and the extraordinary appearance is gradually, but sensibly diminished; at last they meet, and perhaps the person he had taken for a *monster* proves to be his own brother.[21]

Blair also took prompt advantage of anti-immigrant statements in opposing papers. Answering the *New York American,* Blair defended the concept of the United States as "the asylum of the oppressed":

> This benign policy has drawn to it the arts and manufactures, the capital and labor, of foreign countries, with an immense population from Europe. Besides the national strength thus derived, the value of property of every species to native owners, is rapidly enhanced by the influx of strangers. . . .

It is this horror of poor men, who, by our institutions, are made instantly the equals of our would-be nobility, which has called forth the Anti-American denunciation from the misnamed "American" of New York. Doubtless he would make Mr. Clay's *American System* operate on emigrants and drive them back by weightier taxes here.[22]

The *Globe* denied a *Richmond Whig* story that Jackson had been born in Ireland, but took

pleasure in admitting that Gen. Jackson is of immediate Irish descent. Ireland is the birthplace of heroes and patriots, who have given lustre to the cause of liberty in both hemispheres. Her genius has added the greatest glory to the arms and literature of England, and has participated in all the high achievements of our own country. A native American may therefore feel proud that he can trace his lineage to an Island, renowned for all the high qualities which enoble human nature.[23]

Irish voters in the New York and Boston slums understood this message, and their descendants have rarely forgotten it. Other immigrant groups were equally attracted by such sentiments.

Blair also allowed neither the Irish nor Scotch-Irish to forget Jackson's great victory over the English at New Orleans. In January 1831 the *Globe* assumed the task of making January 8, the anniversary of the battle, a national occasion second only to July 4. For weeks the *Globe* reprinted the proceedings from celebrations around the country, replete with toasts like "*The heads of Departments*—a bright constellation of stars revolving round a refulgent sun" and "*Massachussetts*—Always wrong except when she is right, but never contented without she has the chief seat in the synagogue."[24] Throughout its life the *Globe* always treated January 8 as a national holiday, and its editor continued to organize January 8 celebrations for many years thereafter.

One issue on which Jackson did command a congressional majority was his program for removing the southern Indians to new areas west of the Mississippi. Opposition on humanitarian and legal grounds, however, was loud even if weak, and Jackson's opponents exploited this feeling wherever possible. The *Globe* answered by reviewing for months the earlier Indian policies of each New England state to show the inconsistency of New

Englanders now defending the Indians. The famous Massachusetts divine, Cotton Mather, had compared the Indians to wild beasts obstructing God's chosen people, and his descriptions of the Indians' treatment by New Englanders gave Blair powerful ammunition. These "political religionists," said the *Globe*, after ruthlessly exterminating their own Indians were damning Jackson's humane efforts to remove them from harm's reach. The Indians had to be moved, because "who can arrest the march of our population to the West! HE only, who can thrust out his arm and arrest the sun in its course." When Chief Justice John Marshall and the Supreme Court ruled in favor of the rights of the Cherokee Indians in Georgia, Jackson made no effort to enforce the decisions, and the *Globe* defended Georgia. Indeed, the "Red Allies" of the Clay party became a favorite *Globe* theme. By 1832 Blair was warning that the Cherokees expected the election of Clay as president to establish their tribe *"in independence and nationality* in the heart of Georgia! !" [25]

In the sectional alignment the *Globe* sought primarily to isolate New England as the chief source of opposition to Jackson. Blair opposed the "excessive" tariff advocated by Clay, but accepted the idea of a judicious tariff, defined as a "system of protection to those interests necessary to the defense and independence of the nation." Coincidentally, "the mineral products and the fabrics of Pennsylvania" were "precisely those . . . essential to these objects." The *Globe* also expressed great satisfaction that the liberal spirit which had led Kentucky to abolish imprisonment for debt was finally being extended to New York, Maryland, and Massachussetts. It questioned the motives of Massachussetts, however, in the light of that state's opposition to Benton's program for selling the public lands at low prices and giving away those unsold after a certain number of years. This opposition, said the *Globe*, was admittedly for the purpose of keeping men enslaved in factories. Massachussetts would "release the unfortunate poor from their jails to confine them in workhouses, but would by no means allow them to escape and become cultivators and free holders in the West." [26]

Until February 1831 Blair worked to keep the peace with Calhoun, Green, and the *Telegraph*, and denounced efforts by the Whig paper, the *National Intelligencer*, to promote a quarrel within the Democratic party. Then, however, John C. Calhoun published his correspondence with President Jackson dealing with his antagonism in 1819 toward Jackson's conquest of Florida. The *Telegraph* supported Calhoun, and Blair immediately opened fire for Jackson. Intrigues, said the *Globe,* had been launched at the very beginning of Jackson's administration to make Calhoun the candidate in 1832 whether Jackson should wish to be reelected or not, and the *Telegraph* editor had been a leading promoter. The quarrel between Jackson and Calhoun was private, Blair asserted, and the correspondence should not have been published. Its publication was a "firebrand wantonly thrown into the . . . party," and Calhoun would be responsible for any resulting mischief. The *Globe's* pages were soon filled with editorials and private letters from gentlemen *"of the best political intelligence"* out in the hinterland—all of them denouncing Calhoun and praising Jackson—and Blair was thus able to pronounce that Calhoun's publications were "scarcely a ripple upon the great ocean of public opinion. Mr. Calhoun falls upon its surface, sinks and is forgotten." [27]

Blair quickly recognized, however, the possibility of a new alliance between Calhoun and Clay. Public meetings in South Carolina were endorsing Calhoun's principle that a state could nullify a law it considered unconstitutional, and the issue had been dramatized in 1830 by the Webster-Hayne debate. On February 12, 1831, Blair charged that an excessive tariff was equally important to Clay and the "Southern ultras," who would not accept "the repeal of the whole revenue system, unless accompanied with the concession of the right of nullification—a right which is to enable certain men, who, like Caesar, would rather reign in a village, than be second in Rome, to rule the whole union." A common interest in the tariff question would probably "bring the *ultra politicians,* who advocate the opposite extremes of the question, to act together, however widely they may differ theoretically." It would be "a grand coalition of the GRAND AMERICAN SYSTEM AND THE GRAND NULLIFICATION SYSTEM, *with the Telegraph for its organ."*

In April 1831 the "Little Magician," Martin Van Buren, resigned from the cabinet to enable Jackson to demand the resignations of the other cabinet members. This brought the long-smoldering Peggy Eaton affair to a climax. The ex–secretary of war, Major Eaton, invited some of his ex-colleagues to support their remarks about his wife on the dueling ground, but the invitations went unaccepted. Soon the *Globe* was printing an angry exchange of letters on the subject between Eaton and former treasury secretary Samuel D. Ingham, and damning the *Telegraph* for publicizing the slanders against Peggy. In the end the *Globe* cited the quarrels as proof that the former cabinet was incompatible, and turned the entire affair into praise for Jackson's matchless judgment in deciding to reorganize his cabinet.[28]

Van Buren was rewarded with an appointment as minister to Britain. Several weeks after he had reached the post, however, the Senate, with Vice-President Calhoun casting the deciding vote, rejected the appointment. Blair agreed with Senator Benton that the rejection would make Van Buren the next vice-president, and the *Globe* proceeded to make the New Yorker into a national martyr. Senators Gabriel Moore of Alabama and George Poindexter of Mississippi, both elected as Jackson men, voted against Van Buren, and Blair promptly denounced both as traitors. Poindexter was a quarrelsome man with a reputation for being dangerous, but when he charged Blair with vilification and slander Blair denied that he "had ever employed epithets sufficiently strong to characterize" the conduct of a man "fast sinking to the depths from which his pretended friendship for Gen. JACKSON drew him." [29] At this point the *Globe* editor began carrying a small pistol in his umbrella.

Chapter 5

Victory

It was not his nature to be "savage or ferocious," but he thought his duty to the party sometimes—yea, oftentimes—required that he should use the tomahawk and the scalping knife and he did. It gave him pain to do so. Often, when he was about attacking a man whom he respected personally, but abhorred politically, he said to us, "it gives me pain to attack that man. . . .

Those whom he considered "not worthy of his steel," he committed to our tender mercies, to squeeze to death by damning him "with faint praise." . . . Our backward defense to a man was almost as fatal as Blair's Toledo blade, which was rarely in the scabbard for seventeen years, and was so frequently thrust into someone, that the blood rarely dried on it. He often expected to be called to account for what he wrote, and made up his mind to settle it, if deemed necessary, in a desperate way. In one case with a desperate man, who wrote to him that he would challenge him if he did not take back a charge made, he . . . reiterated the charge, and the man acknowledged that he had been guilty as charged. . . . That man afterwards fell in a duel fought with another.

Both his leaders and followers were written with a lead pencil, after night, in a great hurry, and we had to keep two boys to run to him for copy. We have known him to send one of the boys after the other to overtake him and get the last word on the last sheet sent off. . . .

He does not care for money. Several times, while we were partners, we attempted to tell him how we were getting along in money matters, and he as often replied that he did not desire to know, and changed the subject.[1]

THUS John Rives later remembered the *Globe* and its editor during their best days.

By early 1832 the *Globe* had clearly marked and labeled

Jackson's great enemies in the coming election: Clay and the United States Bank, which threatened democracy; and Calhoun and nullification, which threatened the Union.

Since its brief period of corruption and the unwise promotion of the boom preceding the panic of 1819, the Bank had been a valuable public servant. Its vast power over the American economy had not been abused, and it had provided a growing nation with a stable currency. After 1828, however, the suave, self-confident, and able Bank president, Nicholas Biddle, had become somewhat reckless. Between 1828 and 1832 Western loans were increased to over one-half of the Bank's total, and immediate demand liabilities were increased by $12,340,000, while specie resources for meeting them rose by only $1,572,000. Also, bills of domestic exchange, which were in effect loans on expected crops, were issued freely by the western branches until the total loans in 1832 doubled those of 1828. Despite the surface prosperity and the popular confidence in the Bank's notes, specie was leaving the country, and Biddle was seeking help from the English banking house of Baring Brothers. Every western branch was burdened with permanent debts, and in 1831 the Bank began to retrench by contracting its western loans. This, however, only increased the flood of angry complaints from westerners who remembered 1819. Acquisitive frontiersmen engaged in developing America wanted credit and capital, and saw only that the Bank was not providing money as fast as they wished to borrow it. They also resented the Bank's restrictions on paper-money issues of state and other local banks, and were quick to suspect that money was being taken away from them to enrich the aristocratic speculators of the Eastern cities.[2]

In the Northeast the Bank was generally popular, although certain New York banks resented its monopoly privileges and competition. Also, the social reformers and leaders of the growing labor movement had come to hate the Bank as the fountain of the paper-money system. Following the teachings of William Gouge, they blamed paper money for fluctuations of the economy that all too often brought lowered wages and unemployment, and occasionally caused the payment of wages in depreciated paper currency.

In the South as in the Northeast, the Bank enjoyed widespread support, but there remained a powerful residue of leaders and followers who shared the agrarian economic principles of John Taylor, Nathaniel Macon, and John Randolph. Their ideal was a simple, frugal government that spent money only for defense, kept tariffs and taxes at a minimum, and granted no artificial privileges or favors to anyone. To this group the Bank was the agent of those promoting a national debt, high tariffs, and the supremacy of the industrial Northeast.

Those who felt directly or indirectly menaced by the Bank in their personal fortunes could also muster powerful arguments based upon principle. The Bank controlled the currency and credit of the United States, yet Biddle allowed no dissent from fellow directors and insisted that the Bank was responsible to neither the government nor the people. The Bank could determine life or death for state and local banks, it could cause prosperity or depression for the country, and it could easily strengthen the economic power of any group or section at the expense of the others. These powers had been exercised responsibly since 1819, but the Bank's capacity for harm if mismanaged was clearly inconsistent with the Jacksonian philosophy of equal economic opportunity.

For many Americans, also, the Bank symbolized the passing of a way of life that they were reluctant to lose and the coming of a new America that stirred vague feelings of guilt even when it made them richer. America traditionally was a society of self-sufficient, industrious citizens who worked for what they received and received what they earned. By the 1830s, however, the nation had already become a land of speculation, unearned increment, financial manipulation, usurious lending, industrial and business investment, and other practices that made possible the accumulation of great wealth by those who might not even give lip service to the ancient virtues of hard work, thrift, and concern for one's neighbor. It was also becoming a land of tension, insecurity, and competitive struggle among classes, groups, and sections. For those who still dreamed of holding the older, purer America back from the point of no return, the Bank was the symbol of all the wickedness and evils of the new age.[3]

For Francis Preston Blair the Bank was all of these things. As the great tempter it had led him and his Kentucky friends to risk their fortunes and reputations in the scramble for greater wealth through speculation. The Bank had then become the powerful opponent of relief legislation and liberal court decisions designed to alleviate the sufferings of those caught in the catastrophe that Blair blamed upon the Bank's own evildoing and mistakes. It was the scapegoat for his own ten years of bitter struggle—the monster still in the business of corrupting men, changing the pure character of the America of the founding fathers, and opposing Andrew Jackson, the last great champion of preserving America as it should be. Blair had once triumphantly carried a million dollars in Commonwealth Bank paper currency into Kentucky, but he was now prepared to advocate a hard-money system and attack the Bank as a source of inflation and dangerous speculation.

The Bank's great enemy in the Senate was Thomas Hart Benton of Missouri. Physically large, egotistical, and sometimes overbearing, but able, hardworking, and well informed, the Missourian had a reputation for temper and violence equal to that of Jackson himself. In 1813 Benton and his younger brother had engaged Jackson and three friends in a furious gun-and-knife battle, and had left Old Hickory lying badly wounded in the street. By 1831, however, Benton and Jackson had long since become close friends again. Transplanted to Missouri from North Carolina by way of Tennessee, Benton was a curious blend of the Old South and the ebullient young West. In one breath he could predict a future America of 160 million people stretching from ocean to ocean, and in the next call for the elimination of the paper-money system. To Benton the Bank was the great "Whore of Babylon" stripping both the South and the West for the benefit of the Northeast, and he was the knight self-appointed for the mission of slaying the monster. Benton had also long since come to regard America as a great worldwide experiment in democracy and freedom, which for the sake of all mankind must not be allowed to fail. Like Blair, he acquired at an early period a thorough detestation for John C. Calhoun and a fear that the Carolinian's ideas might destroy the Union.[4]

Mrs. Benton, the former Elizabeth McDowell, was the granddaughter of General John Preston and was therefore a cousin of Francis P. Blair. The Bentons and Blairs soon became close friends. The families visited back and forth, and the children were happy playmates. In later years after the passing of Old Hickory, Blair would bestow much of his own special brand of affection and loyalty upon Benton.

In 1831 most Americans probably considered the United States Bank an acceptable institution. The country was prosperous, and the notes and credit resources of the Bank were apparently the soundest in the young nation's history. Two-thirds of the press supported it, and many nominal Jackson followers were Bank adherents. The Bank's charter did not expire until 1836, but petitions and memorials urging a re-charter were already pouring into Congress. By 1831 Biddle was quietly negotiating with Secretary of the Treasury McLane, and Major Lewis had assured Biddle that Jackson would not oppose a re-charter.

Lewis should have known better. The *Globe* had been attacking the Bank since its first issue, and on February 2, 1831, Senator Benton repeated all previous attacks against the Bank and added a few new charges in a roaring Senate speech that lasted several hours. In Benton's words, the Bank was "a system of centralism, hostile to the federative principle of our Union, encroaching upon the wealth and power of the States, and . . . designed to aggravate the inequality of fortunes; to make the rich richer, and the poor poorer; to multiply nabobs and paupers; and to deepen and widen the gulf which separates Dives from Lazarus." [5] Blair happily broadcast thousands of copies of the speech to citizens from Maine to Florida, and continued with daily indictments in the *Globe*. Indeed, the *Globe*'s attacks probably helped push Biddle, Clay, and Webster into a fateful decision.

Since the Bank's charter was valid until 1836, prudence should have suggested a delay in requesting a charter until Andrew Jackson would no longer be a candidate for reelection. Clay and Webster, however, failed to reckon with the role played in American politics by personal appeal unrelated to specific issues. Clay had been nominated to oppose Jackson in the coming election, and a rallying point was needed. The Bank had a clear-cut majority in Congress, and Clay and Webster, therefore, persuaded Biddle to call for a renewal of the charter in 1832. Acceptance by Jackson, they reasoned, would weaken him in the West and South, whereas a veto of such a well-accepted agent of financial stability might well destroy him almost everywhere. The plan was logical, but Andrew Jackson's hold on the hearts and minds of most Americans had little to do with logic.

In Congress the Bank bill began its long but inevitable path to victory. Benton in the Senate and James K. Polk in the House fought a delaying action by introducing amendment after amendment, each of which required many hours of debate. The *Globe* dutifully printed the speeches and distributed the more powerful ones in pamphlet form. It had a strong case against the Bank's use of financial influence. The Bank had long given drafts for salaries of congressmen payable at distant points without charging the usual exchange fee; it often paid congressmen before their salaries were due; and it had made large loans to certain prominent lawmakers. John Watmough in the House and Webster in the Senate were on the Bank's payroll as attorneys, and the Bank's highly placed debtors included George McDuffie, Samuel Smith, Richard M. Johnson, and the redoubtable Davy Crockett, who had left the wild frontier to become a Bank and tariff Whig. Clay had been paid well by the Bank for important legal services in the past, although he had no financial interest in its fortunes by 1832. His former speeches against the Bank, however, could be cited with devastating effect to show his change of mind after receiving money from the Bank. Biddle had also recently made large loans to several prominent editors, including Green, James Watson Webb, Mordecai Noah, Gales and Seaton, and Robert Walsh, and Blair took great delight in citing the facts and figures.

The final vote on the Bank indicated a wide variation in sectional opinion. In the Senate, where the Bank won by 28–20, six states—New Hampshire, New Jersey, Kentucky, Mississippi, Illinois, and Missouri—had a senator on each side. The rest of New England, Pennsylvania, Delaware, Maryland, and the western states—Ohio, Louisiana, and Indiana—went for the Bank. New York and six remaining southern states completed the opposition. In the House, where the bill passed by 107–86, several states were also closely divided.

The bill revived the ailing president. Rising from his bed of pain, the old soldier sounded the call to battle. Historians have disagreed on the authorship of the final draft of the veto, but every point had already been broadcast through the *Globe* by Benton and Blair. Jackson charged the Bank with monopoly, foreign influence, and the granting of unequal and artificial privilege to those already richer than most, and he announced that each branch of the government had equal power to decide questions of constitutionality. The veto was a powerful assertion of doubtful executive power and a fierce attack upon unfair privilege, but it was not a call to economic radicalism. The charge that the Bank was a bad bargain for the people's government and bestowed unearned wealth and privilege upon a small group of favored stockholders was an argument that a nation of capitalists, large and small, present and expectant, could understand. Foreign investment in the Bank might actually increase the available capital resources of the United States, but the argument that such investment would give aristocratic foreigners undue influence in America struck a chord in the hearts of a patriotic and suspicious people. Jackson had protected his nation from the British soldiers at New Orleans, and he would now save it from the British bankers seeking to infiltrate Philadelphia.

The image of Old Hickory defending the Constitution against all comers—whether congress, the courts, or the foreigners—was a magnificent political theme. The *Globe* found it "difficult to describe in adequate language, the sublimity of the moral spectacle now presented to the American people in the person of Andrew Jackson."

According to the *Globe*, the Bank was warring upon America itself. The founding fathers 'thought they had rescued our country from British thralldom . . . . But we are to be again conquered." A "few hundred rich men in a small European Island" had enslaved their own people, made "all Ireland labor amidst misery and groans," and sought gold in the East Indies "in rivers of Indian blood." Now, charged Blair, the British through their connections with Biddle's Bank, would resubjugate America by "bribing our presses and corrupting our statesmen, poisoning the fountains of public intelligence, and scattering pestilence in storms of interested eloquence." [6]

James Watson Webb and Mordecai Noah of the *New York Courier and Enquirer* had been among the *Globe's* original financial angels, and the *Courier* had once called the Bank "dangerous, *in principle and practice,* to the liberty of the country." In 1832, however, these editors suddenly became Bank converts, and Blair solved the riddle in just a few words. As of January 2, 1832, said the *Globe,* Webb and Noah were indebted to the Bank for $52,975, all loaned in the course of nine months. General Green and the *Telegraph* owed the Bank $20,000, Gales and Seaton owed $52,370, and Robert Walsh of the *National Gazette* owed $6,541.72. Blair conceded, however, that Walsh, unlike others, really did believe in the Bank and supported it without "degradation or infamy." [7]

The other great enemy of Jacksonianism and the *Globe,* the doctrine of nullification and the threat of disunion, was in large part the peculiar brainchild of Vice-President John C. Calhoun. The Carolinian was humorless, intense, noted for a sinless life, and utterly devoid of self-doubt or intellectual humility. A towering self-righteousness made him immune to ideas and facts alike if they collided with his own prior reasoning. A brilliant mind enabled him to go immediately to the heart of the most complex problem, but this talent often led to the oversimplification of issues far less subject to logical analysis than Calhoun made them. Calhoun's diagnoses of southern ills were often harsh, but they were usually easy to understand and emotionally satisfying for those southerners fearful of any threats, real or imagined, to their wealth and power. After his break with Jackson, Calhoun became the statesman of crisis. He and South Carolina—and, he hoped, the South—would stand together against an evil world of unfair tariffs, excessive federal power, Jacksonian tyranny, and Northern enemies of slavery. These were not necessarily the South's real dangers, but they were recognizable, and Calhoun would try to maintain national influence by riding in full armor out to meet them. As historian William Freehling has pointed out in detail, many South Carolinians were afflicted by a paranoia caused only in part by the tariff. [8]

In time Calhoun would identify himself as an opponent of the entire philosophical basis upon which Blair's version of democracy rested. He would argue that the natural-rights idealism of the Declaration of Independence was nonsense, and led only to dangerous economic and class struggles that the South was wisely avoiding through the institution of slavery. In Calhoun's view, no laboring population was either qualified for or entitled to equality. For the moment, however, Blair saw the Carolinian primarily as a thwarted presidential aspirant threatening the Union for the sake of selfish ambition. Calhoun, said the *Globe*, could only survive politically by creating a "SOUTHERN LEAGUE" and making himself its leader. If it succeeded, Calhoun would "occupy high ground as the founder of a Southern confederacy." If a period of successful nullification and anarchy should be followed by a compromise, Calhoun would "come in as one of the high contracting parties." If, however, "nullification should perish in the arms of a little nursing faction in South Carolina, the father of it is undone. South Carolina will disclaim it as a bastard doctrine—the whole South will disclaim it—the whole Union will scout it." Only Clay and his system could save Calhoun and his plans, because only a high tariff could make southerners angry enough to follow Calhoun's "violent course." [9]

Indeed, the *Globe* gave nullification almost as much attention as it did the Bank. In July 1832 Congress passed a tariff that reduced most rates from the 1828 level and eliminated the duty on cheap woolens so repugnant to the South. Most of the states found the new tariff at least tolerable, but South Carolina's leaders continued to threaten nullification, while opposing Jackson for president. The *Globe* praised the new tariff and denounced the nullifiers as unprincipled troublemakers. Jefferson, Madison and a host of other southerners were paraded in turn through the *Globe*'s pages as opponents of nullification and supporters of the Union. Particularly effective was the five column editorial from the *Southern Patriot* by William Drayton. Drayton insisted that the new tariff offered much in the way of conciliation and compromise. A total annual relief of $5,187,078, he insisted, was worth having, and such "*former zealots in the cause of protection*" as Calhoun should stop trying to destroy the great and glorious Union.[10]

Blair was a master of the bandwagon technique, and he filled his pages with reports from other papers and accounts of public meetings throughout the country to show the unanimity of support for Jackson against the Bank and nullification. Blair's editorials and lead stories were the fountain of wisdom and inspiration for some 400 other papers, and no other single agency did so much to create the national image of Andrew Jackson.

Indeed, the *Globe*'s image of the pure, incorruptible, disinterested warrior hero, standing above petty politics and risking everything to defend his people, captured its own creators. The *Globe* organized Jackson's accumulated attitudes and instinctive reactions into a coherent philosophy and a historic role that no one appreciated more than Old Hickory himself. The *Globe* was in fact a mirror into which the president could look each day with ever-increasing satisfaction and determination to justify the image. For their part, Blair, Benton, Van Buren, and others would spend the rest of their own lives trying to live up to their picture of Jackson as the uncompromising champion of righteousness. This would give them much personal satisfaction, but it would contribute nothing to their skill and success as politicians.

Jackson was a magnificent political subject, and when the votes of the presidential election of 1832 were counted it was clear how skillfully the *Globe* had drawn his portrait. Clay carried only Massachusetts, Rhode Island, Connecticut, Delaware, and Kentucky. To the celebrating Jacksonians the victory was a clear-cut popular mandate against the Bank, but the congressional elections did not support this conclusion. Despite Jackson's personal landslide, his party gained only six seats in the House and lost five in the Senate. The rebellion of the anti-tariff southerners was partially responsible for this, but the Bank could probably have passed a re-charter with equal ease in the new Congress. Missouri, the westernmost state, voted overwhelmingly for its heroes, Jackson and Benton, but chose two pro-Bank representatives in the same election. Numerous other states followed in the same pattern. Clearly, the election of 1832 was a personal victory for Andrew Jackson.

John C. Calhoun, Henry Clay, and Nicholas Biddle had lost a battle, but the war was not yet over.

Chapter 6

Days of Triumph

He is about five feet ten inches high, and would be full six feet, if his brain were on the top of his head instead of being in a *poll* behind it. He looks like a skeleton, lacks but little of being one, and weighed last spring, when dressed in full winter clothing, one hundred and seven pounds, all told, about eighty-five of which, we suppose, was bone, and the other twenty-two pounds, made up of gristle, nerve, and brain—flesh he has none. His face is narrow, and of the hatchet kind, according with his meat-axe disposition when writing about his enemies. His complexion is fair, his hair sandy, and his eyes blue—his countenance remarkably mild, so firm that he can look any man in the face steadily, without winking. We thought him very homely until we became well acquainted with him and got used to his looks. But we still think he is as homely as one man in ten thousand, not excepting ourself—as far as he goes. Having less face than most men, he is, of course, not so ugly as many.[1]

—Description of Blair by John C. Rives

T HE reelection of Jackson in 1832 brought Blair to the zenith of his personal power. "Take it to Bla'ar" became Old Hickory's standard answer to questions of executive patronage, and the editor's mail was soon swamped with requests for favors and assistance. Men wanted to be collectors, consuls, registers of deeds, postmasters, land commissioners, surveyors general, Indian agents, port officers, paymasters, pursers, printers, and military cadets, to name a few, and all considered Blair's approval necessary for success. Thomas Barry, a navy gunner, asked Blair for a transfer from the Brooklyn Navy Yard back to his former assignment in Washington. Preparing son Buonaparte for West Point, Andrew Staunton wrote Blair for the information "indispensible" for Buonaparte to know in order to pass the examination. Kentucky friends asked Blair to block the nomination of Crittenden's son to West Point, but this Blair would not do. J. Bledsoe complained that "declaring what I conceive to be interesting and important truths—based on revelation and consistent with reason" and "endeavors to do good for others" were interfering with his financial support. Also, wrote Bledsoe, the "rage for politics" had so overwhelmed his daughter's husband with bad habits that the young man had "become altogether negligent of his first duties as a Parent and a Husband." Only a judgeship in Arkansas could alleviate Bledsoe's condition. Samuel Daviess was certain that "if an office much more lucrative than that of a Judgeship was presented to me I could persuade myself in a short time that my talents were altogether Sufficient however difficult the undertaking might be." Isaac McCord was "desirous to contract for the building [of] the contemplated Bridge over the Potomac." Being "a little modest owing to a portion of Irish blood," William H. Davis asked Blair to inquire about a position he had been promised.[2]

Such attentions might have turned the head of a lesser man, but Blair never did develop any overwhelming love for power merely for its own sake. He was an architect of the game of competitive politics as it came to be played in the days of Jackson, and he enjoyed immensely both the sport and the wielding of influence. He would not, however, sacrifice or even compromise his views or principles for the sake of either personal station or party victory. This may have stemmed in part from his undimmed faith that in a democratic society the ultimate political triumph would always go to the forces of uncompromising righteousness, usually defined as his own view on any question. It was a comforting faith, often useful, but fraught with danger for the politician unable or unwilling to doubt its entire validity. It served the Jacksonians well as long as the matchless vote-getting appeal of Old Hickory was on their side of the scale.

Shortly after the election of November 1832 Francis P. Blair made a routine visit to the White House and was startled by Jackson's face and temper. "The lines in his face were hard drawn, his tones were full of wrath and resentment. . . . Any one would have thought he was planning another great battle." The president had just leaned that the nullification theories of John C. Calhoun were flowering into practical reality.

By December Jackson's fury had settled to an icy calm. In his annual message to Congress he proudly announced the imminent extinction of the national debt. This, he said, would make possible the limiting of protective tariffs to those items necessary for national defense and the sale of public lands at bare minimum prices. Grimly, however, he announced two problems. First, the United States Bank had been guilty of deception in its handling of a national debt payment, and Congress should investigate its soundness as a keeper of the public monies. Second, a certain state was threatening to defy the laws and break up the Union. He would handle the situation himself, but would ask Congress for assistance if he found it necessary.

Through the *Telegraph* and other papers, Calhoun had warned throughout the election campaign that Jackson's reelection would "subvert the very foundations of liberty and corrupt this government into . . . the most odious and profligate despotism." In reality Jackson and his "corrupt politicians" were the South's best hope for a low tariff, and the Democratic party would defend southern values consistently until 1860, but Calhoun saw no paradox. He believed that his interests and Southern interests were synonymous, and that his own fall from power was a mortal blow against the South. Despite the efforts of Joel Poinsett and other South Carolina unionists, Calhoun's personal influence was decisive in the state elections. The nullifiers won South Carolina, declared the tariff unconstitutional, and passed laws ordering citizens and officials to resist its collection.

Announced as a blow against the tariff, nullification served a practical role more like that of a St. Bernard helping a mountaineer lost in the snow. The tariff of 1832 was much lower than that of 1828, and circumstances pointed clearly to a further significant reduction in 1833 through normal processes. The national debt was almost paid, the treasury was overflowing, the administration was anti-tariff in principle, and the elections of 1832 indicated that the Congress scheduled for December 1833 would have a low-tariff majority. Clay and his fellow high-tariff senators feared the worst, but the nullification crisis came to their rescue.

The nullifiers found Andrew Jackson an indomitable enemy and a superb rallying point for the forces of nationalism. Five days before announcing the crisis to Congress he had already sent troops and a fleet of warships to Charleston Harbor. Poinsett sent a request for "grenades and small rockets . . . excellent weapons in a street fight," and they were soon on their way. On December 10 the old president issued a stirring proclamation condemning South Carolina's absurd and unjustified threat to "the rich inheritence bequeathed by our fathers."

Numerous Jacksonians, including Van Buren and Benton, were fearful that the president's bluntness might provoke a major disaster. They advised caution, but Francis P. Blair offered nothing but fiery encouragement. *Globe* readers were quickly reminded that Blair had been predicting just such an event throughout the campaign. Calhoun and his friends were out *"to dissolve the Union, peaceably if they can, forcibly if they must."* The nullifiers knew, said the *Globe,* that payment of the national debt would soon make the tariff unnecessary, and that the newly elected Congress would concur with Jackson "in removing every pretext for complaint on the score of the Tariff." The Nullification Ordinance was "passed to anticipate and prevent the healing of the divisions in our country—to keep up a contest among the States, and to satisfy the selfish purposes of ambitious leaders." If Americans needed any lectures on the blessings of the Union, the *Globe* was ready with a full supply. "What is it," asked Blair,

> that preserves perpetual peace between twenty-four rival and sovereign States? What is it that makes one little army and one little Navy adequate to the protection of twenty-four independent nations? What is it which has enabled us to pay off our war debts by duties on imports alone, and bring into the Treasury, money beyond our wants? Why is it, that while all petty States and great nations have difficulty in finding objects of taxation capable of yielding a revenue equal to their necessities, we are at a loss what to do with the superabundant contents of our Treasury, and are embarrassed . . . in determining what shall not be taxed? What sends forth intelligence from the center of our country to its far extremes almost with the rapidity of the sun's rays? What secures to us free intercourse and free trade between the several States? What has created new States and cleared them of a savage population? What makes us respected by civilized nations and protects our commerce from the depredations of pirates and barbarians? What secures our exports from taxation, erects lighthouses, improves harbors, and builds fortifications? What preserves the inviolability of contracts, and furnishes us with an uniform currency in coined gold and silver?—What, in fine, guarantees the inde-

pendence of our States and secures the liberty of our people, civil and religious?[3]

What true American would endanger such blessings merely to further the ambitions of John C. Calhoun? *Globe* readers were soon being treated to vivid accounts of patriotic anti-nullification meetings and to reprinted editorials attacking nullification from almost every part of the nation except South Carolina.

The *Globe* also publicized a "SECRET HISTORY OF NULLIFI-CATION," reprinted from the *New York Advocate and Journal.* One Thomas Hulme had reported a conversation with a British leader who argued that if Britain were not so perplexed with its own problems, it could quickly stop American economic progress despite America's inexhaustible resources and wealth. How? "By convincing the South that the tariff was oppressing them, offering them trade concessions and encouraging them to revolt. . . . *in less than five years we would produce a separation of the Union.*" For those Americans prone to see Perfidious Albion lurking in the shadows of every catastrophe, the secret history had a frightening appeal.[4]

With Jackson's intentions unmistakable, the administration moved quickly to head off any serious defection of its low-tariff supporters. In the House a bill reducing the rates was introduced and apparently had a chance for success. Henry Clay, however, quickly thwarted this effort with a compromise of his own that was much more satisfactory to the tariff interests. Clay would reduce the tariff gradually over a ten-year period to a maximum of 20 percent by 1842, with the bulk of the reductions to come near the end of the period. The administration bill would have been better for the agrarian South, but Calhoun could not endure the prospect of a Jackson victory in southern eyes. In a late-night conference, at which Calhoun was also warned of Jackson's threat to apply a rope to his neck if secession should actually occur, the friends of Clay persuaded the Carolinian to accept the compromise. The bill restored the 50 percent duty on coarse woolen cloth worn primarily by slaves, and a last-second amendment provided for evaluations at the American port of entry. This would add transportation and handling costs to the taxable value of dutiable products. Calhoun complained bitterly, but he and his friends swallowed the amendment to save the bill.

The new tariff and a bill authorizing Jackson to use force to collect it passed on the same day. South Carolina repealed the ordinance against the former tariff, but passed another one nullifying the Force Bill, which was of course already dead because of the state's acceptance of the new tariff. All sides claimed victory, but the hero of the hour was Andrew Jackson. He had saved the Union, the compromise was a bad bargain for the South, and the *Globe* was determined that everyone should know it. Hailing Jackson as the savior of America, the *Globe* also stressed his unsuccessful efforts to get the tariff reduced. The nullifiers, wrote Blair, would claim a victory, and would never confess that "if they had waited until the coming of the new Congress they would have obtained the same gradual reduction of the tariff unclogged by the hard conditions imposed by Mr. Clay, *in the cash duties— the home valuation—and the increase of the duty on coarse woolens.*" As for constitutional principle, Blair doubted "whether in the private interview in which Mr. Clay disposed of Mr. Calhoun's constitutional scruples, a word was uttered in relation to the Constitution." And Blair offered a final prophetic warning. Nullification had ended, "but the project of a Southern league and separation" had not been abandoned. "To gain time and support, Mr. Calhoun had patched up a truce with Mr. Clay, and accepted terms which would have been scorned, if proposed by the Head of the Government." Most alarming, Blair warned, the nullifiers were now trying to stir up the fears of the southern slaveholders "by attacking the Colonization and abolition societies which have existed for years without hurting anyone." [5]

Francis P. Blair never forgot the way in which Andrew Jackson saved the Union with both peace and honor by direct and forceful action in 1833. Twenty-eight years later he would not allow Abraham Lincoln to forget it either.

During the crisis the *U.S. Telegraph* had defended Calhoun and his doctines, and warned that the "Bloody bill" authorizing Jackson to use force would "*sink forever the liberty, the peace and the prosperity of the country.*" After passing the Force Bill, however, the Senate elected *Telegraph* editor Duff Green their printer. "What a comment this," said the *Globe,* "upon the Senators who elected him printer. . . . In this *viva voce* vote they expressed the will of their constituents against nullification. In their *private ballot* they consulted the wishes of Mr. Clay, and supported nullification in the person of Mr. Calhoun's printer. Such are the under currents of intrigue." [6]

In the House Blair made an all-out race for the printing, but after leading for eleven ballots he lost to Gales and Seaton on the fourteenth. This was a bitter disappointment to Blair and the administration. In March the *Globe* printed the names of the Jackson men who had voted for Blair and commented: "We have received several letters from different States, enquiring whether particular members of Congress, elected as friends of the administration, 'voted for the Editor of the Globe, as Printer to the House?' " In reply the editor could only say that ninety-five Jacksonians and five from the opposition had assured him of their vote, but only ninety-five votes had been cast on the final ballot. [7] The whereabouts of the lost five would have to remain in doubt. The Congress that had bowed to Andrew Jackson in the matter of nullification had now reasserted its independence in the choice of its printers. And perhaps editor Blair had begun to realize that wholehearted devotion to only one segment of his party had its perils as well as advantages.

The disappointment was alleviated slightly by an unsolicited and apparently unexpected letter from New Orleans containing $1,000 from ten citizens "in testimony of the high consideration entertained for the Editor of the Globe, and to enable him to support 'those true Democratic and American feelings proclaimed and acted on by our illustrious Chief.' " Old Hickory had a satisfying explanation for the gift. "These friends of mine," he said, "mean to pay back through you the thousand dollar fine imposed on me at New Orleans." The letter was marked confidential, but Jackson thought the writers' names should be published. By mid-June 1833 John Rives was in New York arranging for the delivery and installation of a Napier press for $3,125. [8]

In February 1833, when nullification was still the topic of the hour, editor Blair startled some friends with a vehement announcement that "the damned bank [of the United States] ought to be put down, and the only effectual way of doing it was to take from it the whole of the public money; if it were allowed to retain that money it would undoubtedly be re-chartered." The ever-cautious Major Lewis asked how possession of the public money could aid the Bank in gaining re-charter. Blair exploded:

"By corrupting the members of Congress; it would have the *means* of buying up half the members, and would do it unless the public funds were taken from it." Lewis chided Blair for lack of confidence in the integrity of congressmen, but Blair was unmoved. "He would not trust them any more than he would Biddle and the other officers of the bank, and he would not trust either further than he could throw a bull by the tail." Lewis argued that Jackson would never remove the deposits and that Van Buren certainly would not approve. Blair disagreed on both counts, and rushed off to check with Van Buren. An hour later the editor returned crestfallen. Van Buren considered such a move both "injudicious and impolitic." [9]

The idea of removing the deposits had already been mentioned in November 1832, when the cabinet discussed the Bank's mishandling of the national debt. The government had ordered the Bank to pay on July 1, 1832, some $6,500,000 in 3 percent bonds held by foreign investors. Because of its expanded business and commitments, the Bank could not raise the money, and Biddle asked if the Bank could pay the interest to the government and delay payment of the principal. Jackson agreed. The Treasury then decided to pay off the 3 percent bonds entirely with payments in October and the following January. In October, however, Biddle made a private arrangement whereby the foreign investors left their money in the United States for another year and the Bank assumed direct responsibility for interest payments to the bondholders. Baring Brothers in England was among the large foreign investors, and this firm was also directed to buy up as much of the debt as possible from smaller holders at a price not to exceed $91 per $100. Meanwhile, of course, the government funds originally earmarked for payment of the debt had been loaned out by the Bank at rates considerably in excess of 3 percent. The Bank's charter forbade it to purchase any public debt, and the entire arrangement clearly interfered with the goverment's plan to pay off the debt. At best Biddle was guilty of extreme foolishness, and at worst of considerable wrongdoing.

In response to Jackson's remarks about the Bank to Congress in December 1832, the House Committee on Ways and Means brought in two reports on March 1, the day before adjournment. The five-page majority report declared the Bank sound. The

184-page minority report submitted by James K. Polk was a fierce indictment, much of it exaggerated, but some of it worthy of careful attention. Several western branches of the Bank were in serious difficulty, the Bank had evaded the order to pay the debt, its expenditures for printing and propaganda had increased enormously, and it was continuing its lenient loans to newspaper editors and congressmen. Celebrating the adjournment with various forms of liquid refreshment, the House members had no time for Polk's massive document, and passed a resolution based upon the shorter report of the majority.

The sober Jackson and his editor had long since digested the Polk arguments, but only Roger B. Taney in the cabinet was willing to support a removal. Secretary of the Treasury McLane, whose approval was necessary, produced a ninety-one-page opinion in favor of leaving the deposits alone until a new Bank could be created to receive them. McLane was soon promoted to the State Department, although his successor, William Duane, shared his Bank views.

The issue was temporarily sidetracked while Jackson went on a two-month vacation tour of Pennsylvania, New York, and New England. The old man's lungs bled and his head ached, but he clearly enjoyed the booming salutes, stirring music, and immense throngs who flocked to see their hero in every city. He even paused at Harvard long enough to receive an honorary doctorate, which infuriated alumnus John Quincy Adams. Doggedly Jackson ignored his ailments and moved on from city to city, but at Concord, New Hampshire, he collapsed entirely, and almost at the point of death, had to be returned to Washington.

Jackson's companions on the tour had argued long and hard for leaving the deposits alone, but the *Globe* in Washington was already advocating their removal. Back in the atmosphere of controversy, the president's health revived. He demanded from Duane an agreement either to remove the deposits or resign. With this step taken, the Blair and Jackson families departed with several carriageloads of Jackson nieces and nephews and Blair offspring for a seaside vacation at the Rip Raps in Virginia.

Jackson and Blair were weak-lunged but iron-willed. In Virginia they enjoyed long happy days in the sun and surf with the children and equally happy evenings discussing their common enemies. The omnipresent Major Lewis continued to urge caution, but Blair beat down his arguments with language that Lewis considered "highly unpleasant, and in some degree offensive." Lewis reminded Blair of his defeat in the Kentucky court struggle, where in trying to push the enemy to the wall Blair had *"lost all,"* but the president and his editor were immune to discouragement. A deluge of letters urging him to leave the deposits alone only strengthened Old Hickory's resolve. To Jackson they were just another proof of the Bank's ability to buy and command influence. "Mr. Blair," he said, "Providence may change me but it is not in the power of a man to do it."

Meanwhile, Amos Kendall was touring America from bank to bank in search of sound substitutes for the vaults of Nicholas Biddle. At first some state banks were unwilling to accept the deposits because of a paralyzing fear that an aroused Biddle might retaliate with a ruinous tightening of credit. By August 11, however, the redoubtable Amos reported that more than enough banks would be ready when the time came.[10]

Untroubled by the timid, Jackson and Blair drafted a fiery proclamation announcing and justifying the removal. Revived, restored, and ready for battle, they were back in Washington by August 25.

At the *Globe,* meanwhile, John Rives, who looked the part, had been playing the role of John the Baptist, preparing the way for what was to come. Why not remove the deposits, asked Rives? Their possession by the state banks would not produce distress, and if the United States Bank did so, it would be *"in mere wantoness."* The Bank would "distress its debtors *merely to show its power and prove itself the heartless tyrant,* verifying the worst that had been said of it." Kendall, warned Rives, had been

seen to get in a stage for Baltimore, taking with him a *large black trunk.* He looked charitable, but his intent may be wicked. The Editor of the Globe left here for the South, two days before, with baggage enough to last a man his life time—he took the whole of his family.

Put all these strange circumstances together, and it bodes the owners of the U. S. Bank stock, who purchased at 50 percent, advance, no good.

A *Globe* employee promptly assured Mrs. Blair in a joking letter that he had no responsibility for the "allusion . . . made to her and the children as constituting 'baggage of the editor!'" [11]

The *Charleston Mercury* warned the secretary of the treasury not to remove the deposits, while the Philadelphia *United States Gazette* expressed its certainty that the noble secretary would never stoop to such a deed. "So," announced Rives in the *Globe,* "if the Secretary *do not* remove the deposits he is to be GLORIFIED. It is thus the Bank employs nullifiers to *bully* and *batter,* and sets its minions to *fawn* and *flatter.*"[12] Soon *Globe* readers were being inundated with the usual rash of editorials from other papers, each calling for prompt removal of the deposits.

Meanwhile, unhappy news along with further encouragement against the Bank came from Kentucky. The veteran Jacksonian Thomas P. Moore was defeated for the Senate, but drew consolation from Blair's plans. "Once cripple the old whore & lessen her ability to bribe," wrote Moore, "the aristocracy will be down here in six months. Her money has been lavished . . . & at least 5000 active men . . . have been sustained by it for years. Once *convince* them that the Bank cannot be rechartered & they will desert in droves." [13]

Blair promptly forwarded Moore's news to the wavering Van Buren. The Bank, he wrote, had crushed the Democrats in Kentucky and if unchecked would do so everywhere: "We can only meet the Elephants of the enemy, by tying blazing torches to the horns of our own bullocks, & driving them in amongst them." The cautious Van Buren must have shuddered at Blair's final declaration. Jackson's plan was "that of Cortez, who burnt his ships on the shore when he marched on to Mexico. Our doubtful friends should have no ships to flee to—no hope but in the success of the Administration." [14]

On September 23 the *Globe* carried Jackson's proclamation in six and one-half columns, along with several more columns of praise. Because of the Bank's misconduct and misuse of funds for propaganda purposes, wrote Blair, it would receive no more public money after October 1. Routine government expenses would soon strip the Bank of deposits. The ships had been burned, and there could be no turning back. Van Buren, Lewis, McLane, and the other doubters swallowed their fears and loyally but timidly joined the fight. En route to Washington from Virginia, Thomas Hart Benton read the announcement and "felt an emotion of the moral sublime at beholding such an instance of civil heroism." The *Boston Post* compared the act to Christ expelling the money changers from the temple and offered an epitaph for the Bank: "BIDDLE, DIDDLED, AND UNDONE." [15] Within a month the *Globe* had reprinted editorials from more than forty other papers supporting the removal. Enemies often charged that Blair had sent out canned editorials for other papers to publish and then reprinted his own material under the name of the other paper. Thus Blair stood indicted as America's first national press service. The *Globe* also began immediately to document the charges made in Jackson's proclamation. Column after column of figures citing the amounts spent by the Bank on propaganda, and the ever-growing list of editors and congressmen receiving Bank loans, again marched and countermarched through the pages of the *Globe.*

Blair's pen was indeed a Toledo blade without restraint. "If the *Telegraph* is the most honest newspaper of all the Bank journals," said the *Globe*, "if Duff Green is the most incorruptible of all the editors in the service of this Corporation, what a pack they must be indeed! . . . this self-same Green . . . was one of the most violent opponents of the Bank . . . until his mouth was shut by a loan of TWENTY THOUSAND dollars." After receiving $52,000, the *New York Courier and Enquirer* had "lost all coherency in its ravings." Gales and Seaton of the *Intelligencer* had been "*foisted* upon the present Congress, by the Bank and the fraud of some of its partisans" for deemphasizing the evidence of the House majority report condemning the Bank. The Bank-supporting *Quarterly Review* of Philadelphia, in proposing to restrict the vote to native-born citizens, was clearly "trying to throw the Government entirely into the hands of the few." [16]

Even a pro-Bank, anti-Jackson picnic at Philadelphia was

a scene of revelry and rapacity . . . never before witnessed since the worshippers of the rosy god cried "Io Bacche" on the mountains. The bank worshippers seized the meats from the hands of the cooks and waiters, drenching them in their own gravy. Here a lusty banky brandished a round of beef over his head, and there ran another with a ham . . . pursued, like a well-known quadruped with a nubbin of corn in his mouth, by a long train of followers. . . . Here ran one with a pitcher of foaming ale, and there another with a bucket brimful of wine, while mother earth drank more than her children . . . the speakers of the day, unheard and unheeded, wasted the fragrance of their eloquence upon "the desert air."

By such entertainments, wrote Blair, the people of Rome had been corrupted, and the path opened for the corrupting Caesars. The Bank's object was to "corrupt the American people, deprive them of their independence, and deliver them, a race of slaves, disfranchised and degraded, over to the government of an arrogant Bank, and its usurping Caesars in the Senate!" [17]

On November 28, The *Globe* issued an ominous warning. Clearly Biddle's purpose was to create a money shortage under the pretext of paying out the deposits, although almost twice the amount of the government demands had already been called in. Simultaneously, an alarm would "be raised through the Bank press, of universal scarcity" to persuade "monied men and monied institutions to hoard their cash, and make them contribute to the object of the Bank." The plan was to create economic distress "designed to operate like the torture of the rack upon the people, and compel them to resign their rights—their principles—their power over their own government, into the hands of those who work the engine, which has hitherto controlled the currency of the United States."

Blair's analysis was essentially correct. Biddle had decided to create a financial crisis and blame the consequent suffering upon the illegal removal of the deposits. He was certain that public pressures would compel Jackson to change course. By suddenly reducing loans, notes, and credit, the Bank produced a panic in every area where a business could not operate without credit. Commodity prices fell, stock values collapsed, businesses failed by the dozens, wages declined, and unemployment increased rapidly. If, as Biddle wrote, "nothing but the evidence of suffering abroad" would spur Congress to action, then suffering there would be.

Up to this point the Bank had been a valuable public servant, and most of the Jacksonian criticisms had rested upon the fears of what might happen rather than what had happened. The tactics of 1834, however, proved the worst of the Jacksonian charges against the Bank, and ensured that no such institution would ever be created again. Perhaps Biddle did not intend the crisis to be so painful and last so long, but he met unexpected resistance. He had made a fatal error in assuming that his opponents really were unprincipled, popularity-seeking politicians, interested only in winning votes and staying in power. Whatever the validity of their economic principles, Jackson, Benton, Blair, Kendall, Taney, Polk, and their followers were men of steel who would have fought the Bank in the face of certain disaster.

Congress was soon assailed with memorials and petitions decorated with more than a hundred thousand signatures from a multitude of well-organized mass meetings demanding restoration of the deposits to save the country. Also, dozens of delegations poured into Washington to lobby and present their memorials personally. In Congress Clay, Calhoun, and Webster launched a seven-month battle. Day after day they pictured Jackson as a mad Caesar deliberately seeking to destroy the republic to satisfy his personal ambitions.

In return, Jackson's congressional supporters and the Democratic newspapers spearheaded by the *Globe* were unmovable. In Blair's view, the fate of the republic was at stake, and the unconquerable spirit of Andrew Jackson was the indispensible barrier to the extinction of American democracy. The Jacksonians received a bonanza on March 28, 1834, when the Senate passed Clay's resolutions denouncing Jackson for dangerous, lawless, and unconstitutional behavior. This personal attack on Old Hickory created an issue that transcended policy and struck where he was strongest—in the hearts of his fellow countrymen everywhere. Thomas Hart Benton immediately announced that he would never rest until the Senate by its own action "expunged" the censure from the official record. The *Globe* joined Benton in this battle, and Benton's speeches, printed and supplemented in the *Globe*, soon made the "expunging" resolution an issue in state politics destined to unseat several senators.

A rumor started that Jackson was using the army as a personal bodyguard. The *Globe* answered this by quoting an elderly Mrs. Gadsby, who had told friends that "the General did not want the aid of the army. She had recruited a volunteer corps of Lady veterans, that would protect him with broomsticks." A few days later Jackson and Blair were conferring when several frightened administration congressmen came to report the expected arrival of a Baltimore mob that had threatened to camp at the Capitol until the deposits were restored. Jackson gave them full reassurance: "He would in person meet them at the head of Mrs. Gadsby's corps of old women armed with broomsticks, at Bladensburg & drive them back." The congressmen should inform their friends that "in the case Biddle's mob ever showed themselves around the capitol to threaten the Houses, they should see the Ring Leaders hanging as high as Haman about the square." Afterwards, Jackson lay on a sofa discussing the situation with Blair. Suddenly he rose and took from the top of a wardrobe a coronet of eagle feathers surrendered to him many years before by a defeated Indian chief. Donning this "royal cap," Old Hickory shook his head till the feathers rattled, laughed heartily at his appearance in a mirror, and speculated: "I think these fellows would not like to meet me at Bladensburg in this war equipment." For the delighted Blair it was a never-to-be-forgotten scene.[18]

In March 1834 Richmond editor John H. Pleasants attacked Old Hickory in language Blair considered revolutionary, and the *Globe* described Pleasants as "bankrupt in every particular." Pleasants demanded a public retraction and implied that a refusal would lead to a serious confrontation. Blair and Rives interpreted this as a threat of a duel, but Blair would not quail. He replied that he had meant only that Pleasants would lose nothing from a revolution, "being bankrupt in politics and (as I had heard) in property. . . . My opinion of the political condition of yourself and all depending on the hopeless interests of the party with which you identify yourself, is not likely to undergo a change." Pleasants chose to interpret this as a denial of any reflection upon his personal character, and assured Blair that he too abhorred revolution. Later Pleasants was killed in a duel with Thomas Ritchie, Jr.[19]

In the end, the business community itself decided not to perish in Mr. Biddle's hopeless battle against the government. Such former supporters as Hezekiah Niles, the venerable Albert

Gallatin, and James G. King concluded that Biddle had gone too far and threatened him with public exposure. Biddle finally accepted defeat with outward grace, and with one simple order opened the floodgates of prosperity. By the end of July 1834 money was growing plentiful, and an incipient boom was well underway. The Jacksonians had again defeated their favorite enemy.

In July 1834 Old Hickory left the battlefield to his lieutenants and made the long, wearying journey by coach back home to Nashville. The Blairs moved into the White House as caretaker guests. Jackson's long letter to the Blairs finally arrived on August 18 and brought great relief to friends who had feared the journey might be too much for the old man's shattered constitution. Blair immediately wrote Jackson that he and Lewis had been returning from a visit when they "met Eliza walking as active as Emily on the Race Course, and smirking with" Jackson's "letter in her hand, which she had just got from the Post Office. She had travelled a half mile to spread the good news" indicated by the handwriting. They returned to the White House, drank Jackson's health in "Ice Sangree, notwithstanding the cholera," and wished that he might not return to take possession of their "*high life above stairs*" until the ice formed as thick in a local ditch as it was in the sangree.[20] Jackson well understood this sentiment as a hope that he would enjoy a prolonged vacation from the cares of office, the steaming Washington weather, and such minor annoyances as White House bedbugs.

The battle for the deposits was the major triumph celebrated by Jackson and the Blairs in 1834, but the Jacksonians also won another sweet if short-lived victory by passing much of Thomas Hart Benton's hard-money program.

Jackson and his inner circle had long blamed the indiscriminate issue of paper money for every boom-or-bust cycle. In this view paper money aided the speculator and gambler, caused price and credit fluctuations that injured small farmers, small businessmen, and great planters alike, and enabled employers to cheat employees with wages paid in depreciated bank notes. The most dramatic and emotional arguments against paper money were those of "Old Bullion" Benton; the most scholarly arguments came from William M. Gouge, a Philadelphia editor and economist. Blair himself sent Gouge a detailed account of the bank and court wars in Kentucky for use in writing his classic treatise, *A Short History of Paper Money and Banking in the United States*.

Benton had long crusaded for changing the gold ratio from the underevaluation of 15:1 to the more realistic 16:1, and in June 1834 his bill finally passed Congress. Between October 1833 and December 1836 the coin supply increased from $30 million to $73 million. Gold, said the *Globe*, would now be diffused "in defiance of bank power . . . and spread across the country, and become the familiar inmate of every industrious man's pocket." Laborers and farmers everywhere would now have sound money, and would certainly "sustain the statesman and hero who gives *gold* to his country and *lead* to his enemies." [21]

The end of Biddle's Bank did indeed coincide with an increase of gold in people's pockets, but the gold ran a poor second to the onrush of paper money released from every state and wildcat bank no longer under the heavy hand of the Bank of the United States. By 1837 some $149 million in paper was generating and lubricating the wheels of economic expansion. The recent panic quickly gave way to a great speculative boom in farmland, real estate, industry, trade, roads, and canals.

Blair fretted angrily over such unsound developments, while increasing his own personal investments, and he correctly predicted that disaster might follow. Complaining in the years 1834–1836, however, was difficult for a Jackson Democrat. Old Hickory stood victorious over his enemies, and editor Blair basked triumphantly in the full rays of his reflected glory.

Chapter 7

Golden Years

DAILY communion with their peerless leader in a victory-spiced atmosphere was not the only source of happiness for Preston and Eliza Blair during their early years in Washington. Back in Kentucky, Ben Gratz and their young son, Montgomery, juggled notes and endorsements, paid a debt here, collected one there, and balanced numerous notes off with Blair's ancient and long-overdue circuit court fee-bills until at last the Blair debts were all paid. It was like a release from prison. Overjoyed by their successes, their longtime friend J. C. Pickett, by now the American Minister to Colombia, warned Blair to avoid speculation and "make Mrs. Blair the Administrator (or administratress), of your financial concerns. Make her your Minister of Finance . . . and you will escape all entanglements." [1] Blair needed no such warnings. He occasionally speculated in real estate with considerable success, but he remained relatively debt free for the rest of his life.

During their first two years in Washington, the Blairs lived in various boardinghouses and hotels, and Blair came to enjoy fancy dinners and parties as a relief from the sparse fare dictated by his limited circumstances. At his first party he learned that a seven o'clock invitation really meant supper at midnight, and that "the great folks" came by degree: "Senators and Representatives . . . about nine; Barry, Eaton, etc., about ten . . . Van Buren and the British minister upon the stroke of eleven." When the "canvas-back ducks, the turkeys without bones, the oysters, and the quail" were finally served, however, he "made them all *quail* before me." The parties were usually crowded because a good host would invite everyone in the city. "They sometimes try to dance," he reported, but it was like "a Kentucky fight when the crowd draws the circle so close that the combatants have no room to use their limbs. They have . . . four and twenty fiddlers . . . trying by dint of loud music to put amateurs in motion. They jump up and down in a hole and nobody sees more of them than their heads." [2]

As the *Globe* prospered the Blair bed and board improved, and the editor no longer needed crowded parties. By 1836 he was ready to buy a home. He was tempted by the elaborate Decatur house on Lafayette Square, but Van Buren warned him against undemocratic ostentation. In October 1836 Surgeon General of the Army Joseph Lovell suddenly died only a few weeks after the death of his wife. The eleven Lovell children were eager to sell the family's two-story brick house across the street from the White House. According to the advertisement, the house had an excellent well, a brick stable and carriage house on the alley, and a "flower and fruit garden tastefully laid out and highly cultivated." On December 6, 1836, the Blairs bought the house that still carries the family name today, even though it became the official guest house for the United States government in 1942. The price was $6,500. There was room for a cow and some horses on the premises, and Blair soon began leaving a pail of milk for Andrew Jackson at the White House door each morning. [3]

Young Montgomery Blair had won the hearts of Ben and Maria Gratz, and he was happy with his schooling at Transylvania. His father and President Jackson, however, thought the boy should go to West Point. Gratz wrote sadly that Montgomery "could withstand Father and Mother but Genl Jacksons vote determined him, he being the God of your idolatry he thought probably it would be best for him to worship at the same shrine." Ben considered Montgomery a "rare boy for his years," but warned that Blair's other sons, James and Frank, had been "wild quite long enough. If their errors are not soon corrected they may become vices." [4]

Montgomery was indeed a rare son. He was puritanical in tastes and habits and devoted to his parents, brothers, and sister. Like his father he possessed a streak of self-righteousness and could be an implacable and intolerant enemy when his favorite beliefs and principles were at stake. He was fearless, tactless, independent of thought, and absolutely outspoken. Compromise, expedient adjustments, and alliances with those he distrusted came hard for Montgomery Blair. From a distance he appeared cold and unfriendly, and he was destined to failure as a vote seeker in the political arena.

Among family and friends, however, Montgomery was a man of great warmth and compassion. He accepted without rancor the obvious fact that mercurial young Frank was his father's favorite, and as the years passed he ultimately made the careful supervision of Frank's interests part of his own filial duties. There is no evidence that he ever quarreled with his brothers or sister or ever gave his parents a moment of concern for his conduct. With those he loved he was painstakingly thoughtful and patient. "I wish you would write to Grandmother," he wrote his father from Kentucky in January 1831, "for altho she cannot claim your affection she ought to have respect as Mother's parent." To his brothers and sister he was "Gunger" or "Gum." [5]

Making plain his aversion to military life and preference for the law, Montgomery nevertheless acceded to his father's wishes and enrolled at West Point in 1831. From the beginning he considered most of his life there a waste of time. The education, he wrote his father, might help one become a competent soldier, but it had no value for the man who would be a civilian. Senior classmen, he added, lost all initiative once they reached the point where expulsion would be difficult. "You . . . have never seen a real luxuriously lazy man till you have seen some of the first-class men of Uncle Sam's Academy. It is not strange that they can so suddenly give up the habits of industry. . . . these facts . . . are the necessary results of our system, and of every system of military education, & have characterized military men in all times. . . . the graduates of it were well-suited generally to perform the duties expected of them— sleep in peace & fight in war." Cadet Blair was also thankful that he had not enrolled younger because he "should have imbibed morals & contracted habits which my older judgement enabled me to resist in great measure." He had seen promising boys "ruined for life from the blind imprudence of their parents in sending them here unknown & unfriended," and he hoped that no other members of his family would follow in his footsteps. [6]

And as might have been expected, not even the discipline of West Point could save Montgomery from the usual Blair habit of getting involved in the affairs of others. He bitterly complained to his father when another cadet was expelled unjustly after being "amply wronged by the Instructor of Tactics." When a highly regarded professor of natural and experimental philosophy resigned, Montgomery urged his father to interfere if a certain "ignorant and vain" mathematics instructor should attempt to "politick" his way into the position. A Lieutenant Bartlett was the choice of the other professors and should get the job. A mathematics instructor, Thomas Warren, also applied to the elder Blair for help when he was placed under arrest for remarks about the school's administration. Whether from Blair's assistance or the justice of his cause, Warren was reinstated.[7]

In the winter and spring of 1835 Montgomery spent two months in the West Point hospital recovering from a serious illness. In 1836, however, Cadet Blair received his diploma and commission. Of his original class of 126 only 45 graduated, and he was one of the favored handful designated as honor students. This, however, left him unimpressed. Among those dismissed for demerits, he wrote his father, were "some of the most talented men of the institution and always western men who have not art enough to escape reports or are too noble to lie themselves out of scrapes as the Yankees generally do. This school is somewhat like a military school of the Spartan Government. It is no harm to do wrong so long as you escape detection." [8]

The young man promptly resigned his commission, but before this could become effective the Seminole Indian War broke out in Florida. No man of honor could resign under such circumstances. Montgomery immediately cancelled his resignation and prepared for action in the Everglades. He also reached another decision. "From this date," he vowed in his notebook on May 30, 1836, "I will leave off the habit of smoking cigars." [9]

Two years younger than Montgomery, the second Blair son, James was less the intellectual and more the adventurer. After much indecision in choosing a profession, James in 1835 was appointed a naval midshipman. In August 1838 an expedition commanded by Captain Charles Wilkes sailed for the South Seas on a three-year voyage that included exploration of Antarctica. James

Blair sailed as a midshipman on the ship *Relief,* but a few months later was transferred to the *Peacock.* The first lieutenant of the *Peacock* was an extraordinarily handsome, hard-eyed young officer named Samuel Phillips Lee, and he and Jim Blair were soon close friends. They shared pleasant adventures in various South American ports as well as much suffering during part of their travels in the Antarctic. It was a fateful expedition for both. James Blair's health never fully recovered from the expedition, and his sister, Elizabeth, never recovered from her first meeting with Samuel Phillips Lee.

It was young Frank Blair, however, who gave the father his moments of greatest hope as well as gravest despair. Frank was a true son of Christopher and Nathaniel Gist. He was brilliant, athletic, fearless, aggressive, passionate, reckless, thoughtless, irresponsible, and utterly spoiled by family and friends alike. His personal magnetism offered promise of the political career only dreamed of by his infinitely more thoughtful older brother, Montgomery.

Preston Blair believed correctly that this son had the capacity to be another Andrew Jackson, and for many years he dreamed of seeing Frank in the White House. There were anxious moments, however. In various Washington private schools Frank was the bane of his teachers. In October 1837 the seventeen-year-old boy enrolled at Yale, but by the following January his father was informed that "the Faculty . . . have considered it expedient that your son should return home . . . his deportment has been such, and he has formed such connections, that it is the opinion of the Faculty, that he would probably do better at some other institution . . . since the time of Mr. Brace's letter he has been concerned . . . in breaking the windows of one of the College tutors." [10]

Perhaps attributing his son's difficulties in part to Yankee peculiarities, Blair despatched him southward to the University of North Carolina. Here the academic climate was even less congenial. On June 21, 1839, the unhappy father was notified that

> since the first day of April, a period of 11 weeks, Mr. F. P. Blair has been absent from prayers 37 times from recitation 32 times and from attendance on divine worship 2 times. . . . His relative graduation of

scholarship in his class is considered tolerable in ancient languages respectable in mathematics. . . .

He is recorded 3 times for irreverence at prayers and 15 times for other improprieties. His general deportment is bad.

. . . at a meeting of the Faculty . . . it was resolved "that it is inexpedient to admit Mr. Francis P. Blair into this institution at the opening of the next session." [11]

Perhaps because of the Blair family's early connections with the institution, the Presbyterian college at Princeton was persuaded to give the errant scholar a further chance. Whether because of a more flexible code at Princeton or increasing maturity of his own, Frank Blair managed to finish the work for a Princeton degree in 1841. Because of a wild party during his final week, however, the faculty refused to let him graduate, and only through the intercession of Professor Joseph Henry, the famous scientist, was he finally granted a degree in 1842.[12]

Like her eldest brother, Elizabeth Blair was a rare example of filial love and obedience. She was delicate in health but lovely in form and face, and like her father, she possessed a resilience and strength rarely visible but always present when needed. From tutors, private schools, and constant association with her father's affairs, she received an education considerably above that of the average American woman in the 1830s. She learned practical politics as well as music and the usual feminine graces. She adored her parents and vigorous brothers, and was usually but not always prepared to defer to their superior judgment. She enjoyed visits to the cultured and sophisticated relatives of Ben Gratz in Philadelphia, and her friendships with other young people were both numerous and constant. "Her errors lie on the side of her affections," wrote Montgomery, "but a more constant heart and more loving nature is not given to man or woman." Elizabeth's health was a constant worry to her father, who convinced himself that she could never withstand the rigors of marriage and would always require the tender care that only he and her mother could provide.

Blair's own father, James, had been shocked to learn that his son had moved to Washington, and only "the tender solicitude of one of the most affectionate and best of women" had restored his spirit. His dismay soon gave way to paternal pride and gratitude for the many favors Blair could now bestow. From time to time Blair would send a barrel of oysters, and when the old man's horse died in 1834 Blair had Ben Gratz get him another one. In 1835 James had a leg amputated, and Blair provided him with a cork substitute of the newest and best quality. The old man died in 1837, and Blair and Gratz helped his stepson attend college and find a good position.

Blair's sisters had both married indigent types like their father, and the brother was equally generous with them and their children. He later sent his favorite nephew, Abram Ward, to college, and he was forever trying to help these relatives buy and keep farms and other property. Ben Gratz, who was usually Blair's agent in such matters, finally insisted that he let his "collateral relatives depend more on their exertions—if you are always helping them they will continue their dependence on you instead of putting their own shoulders to the wheel." [13]

And finally there was Eliza—calm, confident, and still beautiful, carefully watching to make sure Blair got the proper food and exercise, sharing his enthusiasms and antipathies, enjoying the same friends and enemies, making tactful suggestions, and always agreeing with his decisions that she was helping to make.

Chapter 8

The Changing
of the Guard

THE year 1835 dawned auspiciously for Democrats, as even the most unpromising situations and events usually conspired to strengthen the president's hold on the affections of most Americans. Jackson took a firm stand in a dispute with the French over nonpayment of spoilation claims due to American citizens. His enemies accused him of pushing the nation toward war, which enabled the *Globe* to array them all on the side of the French. The best hope for peace, wrote Blair, was to convince the French that Old Hickory meant business, whereas the Whigs were simply encouraging them to violate American rights. Ultimately, the French backed down before a blunt defiance for which Jackson received high praise from his countrymen.[1]

On January 30 a young psychopath named Richard Lawrence fired two pistols point-blank at the chest of President Jackson. The caps fired, but the charges failed to explode. The pistols were later fired through a one-inch plank from six yards away, and a small-arms expert estimated the odds against the misfires at 125,000 to 1. The miraculous escape added further to the popular Jacksonian legend of supernatural invincibility, and the *Globe* attributed it all to divine providence. Blair also assured the horrified but fascinated public that the young man had reached his distraught state of mind from listening to the speeches of Clay, Calhoun, and other assorted presidential enemies. At one point Blair cited affidavits that Lawrence had been seen talking with

Senator George Poindexter, but he later confessed in the *Globe* that the affidavits had proven to be false.[2]

On May 25, 1835, the Democratic party in solemn convention unanimously nominated Martin Van Buren for president and thereby began the longest official political campaign in American history. The early nomination gave the Whigs sixteen months for efforts to destroy Van Buren's reputation, while the *Globe* and its followers received an equal time to develop a popular image for their candidate.

For vice-president the Democrats chose Colonel Richard M. Johnson of Kentucky, who reportedly had slain the great Indian chief Tecumseh at the Battle of the Thames in 1813. Johnson had been badly wounded, and he was a political favorite because of his long fight for laws against debt imprisonment, his attention to the poorer members of society generally, and his thirty years of service to the Democratic party. Unhappily, however, Johnson did have certain handicaps. He had produced two illegitimate daughters by his mulatto housekeeper, and after her death had engaged in further unorthodox domestic arrangements. The *Globe* was never able to do much in defense of Johnson's family habits, but it did angrily deny a charge by the *Boston Post* that the Kentucky hero had been seen betting on horse races in New York. The editor of the *Post*, wrote Blair, had confused Colonel Johnson of Kentucky with Colonel Johnson of Virginia who was doing the betting, a thing the Kentucky Johnson "never did in his life." Indeed, Colonel Johnson of Virginia was a Whig, "one of that profligate editor's own panic associates in politics." [3]

On the surface at least, the head of the ticket posed few problems. "The course of Mr. Van Buren," editorialized the *New York Evening Post*, "has been one of unobtrusive usefulness, not of turbulent injury." Thomas Hart Benton thought Van Buren "inattackable, for the whole volume of his private life contains not a single act which requires explanation, or defence." [4] The first statement, at least, was true. The second ignored the fact that blamelessness often has little to do with immunity from attack.

Van Buren was a political technician with rare skills in the organization and management of public opinion, and a man of democratic sentiments and great personal compassion for the less favored. Indeed, he was probably more of a genuine democrat than his great friend Andrew Jackson. He was also, however, a man of rare sophistication who found intense emotional commitment to his own views hard to come by. Highly intelligent, he remained humble with regard to his own infallibility. He believed with all his heart in the democratic process, and found compromise on specific issues much easier than did his friends Blair, Benton, Jackson, and Kendall. A man of introspection, Van Buren considered this trait a defect in his own character, and under the influence of Jackson he strove mightily to correct it. Under different circumstances Van Buren might have been ideal as both a candiate and a president. Walking in the footsteps of the dynamic old Indian fighter and hero, however, was a different matter.

The Whigs countered with three different candidates: Daniel Webster in the North, Hugh Lawson White of Tennessee in the South, and William Henry Harrison in the West. They hoped each would gain enough electoral votes in his own section to prevent a majority of the total from going to Van Buren. Then, as in 1824, they might combine forces in the House of Representatives to elect another minority president.

The *Globe* promptly denounced the incongruity of a campaign that combined southern nullifiers with Webster, the great advocate of the Union and the high tariff, and with Harrison, who had once joined an abolition society. The Calhoun junta, insisted Blair, was trying to deceive southerners into thinking slavery was in danger when in fact "the diversity of character and occupation in the two sections . . . like that of the sexes" was the bond of their union. Their laboring systems were not in competition even though the southern products could be produced only by slave labor, because the racial differences would keep northern laborers from ever supporting the abolitionists.[5]

The slavery problem, however, had come to stay. In 1835 moderate abolitionists led in large part by Theodore Dwight Weld and reinforced strongly by many Quaker organizations began flooding Congress with petitions for abolition in the District of Columbia. Weld's program called for gradual emancipation to begin immediately through legal and peaceful processes, and a petition campaign for abolition in the only local area constitutionally ruled by Congress was the logical first step. Most members of Congress agreed that such action would violate the spirit if not the letter of the Constitution, and were eager to table the petitions promptly without action. Calhoun, however, insisted that even the tabling of the petitions would be an admission of Congressional power on the subject. His argument against accepting the petitions at all led to a long debate in which the previously discredited abolitionists emerged as the defenders of the sacred right of petition. Calhoun's role of southern defender required a northern antislavery enemy infinitely stronger than it was in 1835. By exaggerating the abolitionist strength and opposing the right of petition, the Carolinian in fact helped create what he professed to oppose.

The *Globe* denounced both abolitionists and nullifiers as dangerous enemies of the Union, but classed the nullifiers as "far more numerous and talented . . . in the use which they make of their rivals in the evil work of disunion." The abolitionists, Blair insisted, were all Whigs: "There is not a single political friend of Martin Van Buren and democracy who is an abolitionist, OR WHOEVER CAN BE AN ABOLITIONIST; because abolition is as much in opposition to the principles of democracy as Nullification, Federalism, Monarchy, or Bankism." [6]

Finally, in a public letter to a North Carolina committee, Van Buren himself condemned the abolitionists as "disturbers of the public peace," whose activities should be "arrested." Van Buren could not agree that Congress lacked the legal power to control slavery in the District of Columbia, but he was certain that this power would have been denied by the founding fathers if they had known the capital would be established in a slaveholding region. If elected, he would be "the inflexible and uncompromising opponent of any attempt on the part of Congress to abolish slavery in the District of Columbia, against the wishes of the slaveholding states." [7]

After much debate the question was settled temporarily by passage of a rule for tabling the petitions immediately without consideration. "We congratulate the country," wrote Blair, "upon the final overthrow of the joint plot of these malcontent confederates to unsettle the Government and disturb the union, by agitating the slave question in Congress." [8] The so-called "gag rule" would become an annual question of debate, however, because neither Calhoun on one side nor ex-president John Quincy

Adams on the other would be willing to accept it as a permanent solution.

The slavery issue was complicated further by southern efforts to get abolition literature barred from the mails. In December 1835 President Jackson himself recommended legislation for this purpose. Earlier, Postmaster General Kendall had written publicly to a New York postmaster that he himself had no legal authority to stop the mailing of incendiary publications, but that he fully supported such action at the local level. The *Globe* added its blessing: "From the bottom of our heart we thank Messrs. Kendall and Gouvereur for the course they have pursued." [9] At the *New York Evening Post*, editor William Leggett, in every way an ardent Jacksonian, took sharp issue with his friends and suggested that Kendall was acting from political motivations rather than conviction. Blair promptly answered publicly that Kendall was entirely sincere and was fully supported by the administration. Leggett cited Washington, Jefferson, Patrick Henry, and John Randolph in support of the rights of the abolitionists, but Blair continued to denounce the abolitionists as dangerous foils of the Calhounites and denied them any place in the Democratic party. For more than a year these bulwarks of the Jacksonian press ceased to correspond, and the resulting emotional trauma may have contributed to a dangerous illness from which Leggett recovered with great difficulty. Proscription of the *Post* by the *Globe* was an important factor in the financial problems that plagued the *Post* until William Cullen Bryant reassumed the editorship in 1837.[10]

Ultimately, after a long and acrimonious debate, a bill to suppress incendiary publications was defeated in the Senate. It went to its third reading, however, on a tie broken in favor of the bill by the vote of Vice-President Van Buren. Northern Whig presses attacked Van Buren for this vote, while the *Globe* insisted that he had opposed the bill as originally submitted by Calhoun, but had supported the later proposition when amendments limited the provisions to deputy postmasters in southern states.[11]

Circumstances everywhere seemed to conspire to throw slavery into the gears of Van Buren's painstakingly forged alliance of 1828 between northern radicals and southern planters. At San Jacinto, Texas, Jackson's old friend, Sam Houston, caught the

Mexican army taking its afternoon siesta and won independence
for Texas before most of the enemy could get aroused. Immediately the American Senate had to consider the question of recognition, and the president had to begin planning for a future
annexation. Jackson, Benton, Van Buren, and Blair all favored a
"go slow" policy until Texas should make a permanent peace
with Mexico, but they also wished an immediate recognition of
the Lone Star State. Abolition leaders promptly denounced the
entire business as a slaveholder's plot for the sole purpose of extending slavery. The *Globe* and Jacksonians like Benton in the
Senate answered that the settlement of Texas and its revolution
had nothing to do with slavery. Calhoun and his followers, however, insisted that the abolitionists were indeed correct—that the
preservation and extension of slavery was a primary reason for
their views that Texas should be annexed as well as recognized.
After an angry debate, the Senate recommended recognition.

Whig papers charged that Jackson's administration had interfered in the affairs of Mexico. The *Globe* denied this and skillfully portrayed the abolitionists and Whigs as friends of Santa
Anna, the villain of the Alamo. With all of its appeals to the
sympathies of most Americans for a liberated Texas, however,
the *Globe* also insisted that strict neutrality must be maintained
in the quarrel between Texas and Mexico. Mexico was a friendly
neighbor producing vast amounts of gold bullion so dear to the
hearts of hard-money advocates. Justice and honor dictated that
no action beyond recognition should be taken in the Texas matter
until peace should be made. Like so many political issues, the
question of Texas did not lend itself easily to a complex, difficult
to explain, middle-of-the-road position, and it would soon become an ever-larger source of discord within the Democratic
party.

Blair was also desperately anxious to keep the Texas issue
separated from the arguments over slavery, although his attitudes
toward the "peculiar institution" were still those of a moderate
southerner. Like most of his contemporaries in both the North
and the South, he considered the slave race inferior, although he
had great respect for those freemen able to overcome the handicaps of slavery and discrimination. He believed firmly that
emancipation would result in a much worse status for the slaves,

who would have to live in a highly prejudiced white society without the protection of their masters. He also feared that the ensuing exploitation of the newly freed blacks would be an even more corrupting experience for the white population than the existing system of slavery had been. Ultimately he would strongly advocate emancipation, but would insist that it be accompanied by colonization for the good of the freedmen themselves. He feared that premature emancipation would cause the slaves to suffer the same fate as the Indians, and he considered the abolitionist efforts of the 1830s to be a burden rather than a service for the slaves, because southern states everywhere were responding with harsher restrictions. Still, however, he saw a ray of hope. "Many [slaves] in the South," he wrote in 1836, "have acquired intelligence, skill, and energy sufficient to pay for their nurture and purchase their freedom. In doing this they show their capacity for self-preservation, and it may be in this way, that, in time, providence may fit them for a better state of being on this continent than they have yet enjoyed." [12]

The most obvious advantage of the Democrats in the coming 1836 election was the exuberant prosperity and economic growth generated by the enormous expansion of the currency after the defeat of the United States Bank. Unchecked by the Bank, which was now contributing to the boom with excessively liberal lending policies, hundreds of state and smaller banks were issuing money in all directions. Supporting the process was the willingness of the federal government to accept the notes in payment for public lands. As a result, land sales had jumped from 4,658,200 acres in 1834 to 20,074,900 acres in 1836, and the paper-money circulation had increased from $82 million on January 1, 1835, to $120 million by December 1836. The Bank of the United States had increased its loans by $2.5 million monthly and its paper circulation by $10 million between December 1834 and July 1835. Unfortunately, however, the prosperity was not a harmonizing influence for the Democratic party.

In February 1835 Blair had been entranced at an enormous banquet when toastmaster Thomas Hart Benton announced that "Andrew Jackson being President, the national debt is paid, and the apparition, so long unseen on earth—a great nation without a

national debt—stands revealed to the astonished vision of a
wondering world." Actually, the payment of the debt was only
part of the story. As money from the land sales poured into the
vaults of the pet banks selected to receive the federal deposits,
they promptly loaned most of it out to investors, while the United
States Treasury records showed a surplus of some $27 million.

Complaining bitterly that so much money should not be at
the disposal of a military tyrant like Andrew Jackson, John C.
Calhoun in 1835 introduced a constitutional amendment to provide for distribution of all federal surpluses among the states. In
the following year, Henry Clay offered a much simpler proposal
to perform the same service by an act of Congress.

The fearful warnings of Calhoun and Clay that Jackson might
use the surplus to create a dictatorship did not frighten the general public at all, but the prospect of getting the money for roads,
canals, bridges, schools, and other improvements was another
matter. If Calhoun and Clay needed the philosophical justification
of protection against Jackson, the average voter, whether Whig
or Democrat, was ready to help spend the money for its own sake.
Most of the Democratic party in Congress as well as throughout
the hinterland had no quarrel with either the economic boom or
the proposition to distribute the surplus.

The editor at the *Globe*, however, along with a hardy few in
Congress led by Benton, saw only disaster in the making. "We
tell the Bank," warned Blair, "that it perceives not the precipice
near which it is already tottering. We tell the community, that
they are resting in security, dreaming only of successful speculations and profitable business . . . when disaster, desolation, and
ruin, is not far off." The distribution plan, charged the *Globe*,
"was primarily a war upon the deposit banks holding the treasury,
with the idea of rechartering the National Bank after proving the
weakness of the pet banks." [13]

As most Democrats fell into line behind the distribution plan,
Blair remained adamant. Day after day for many months, the
Globe printed and praised the arguments of Benton, who staged
a one-man defense of the Treasury in the Senate. The distribution
scheme, insisted Blair, was an aristocratic conspiracy to preserve
the tariff and overtax the people for corrupt purposes. Its advocates were deliberately blocking vital appropriations just to create

a surplus and tempt the members of Congress. Bills totaling $28 million for defense, harbors, national roads, navy yards, lighthouses, beacons, river surveys, marine hospitals, and improvement of navigation had already been introduced, and the *Globe* wanted these essential needs met before the enactment of any corrupting distribution.

To answer critics, the distribution bill was finally amended into a Deposit Act whereby the federal money was to be deposited with the states but be immediately returnable on demand. With only five other senators joining Benton in opposition, the Deposit Act passed overwhelmingly. No more hypocritical piece of legislation ever passed the United States Congress.

Aware that it would pass over his veto, and under pressure from Democrats anyhow, Jackson signed the bill. The *Globe* was soon explaining that the president had signed only because everything making it a grant to the states had been stricken out by amendment. Far less convincing was the *Globe's* effort to excuse the Democrats who had supported the act. These Democrats, said the *Globe,* had voted for it on its face value as a Deposit Act. Only the Whigs had intended "to subvert and misconstrue it into a direct gift to the states for internal improvements."[14]

Whatever the intent, Democrats and Whigs alike promptly spent the first three installments placed in the state treasuries. Before the final payment came due, the national treasury was bankrupt. The United States government still holds an astronomical lien for the principal plus interest against the states existing in 1836.

Various New York papers rejoiced that the Deposit Act would ease the money market, but Blair pointed out correctly that of the $12 million in New York banks $7.5 million would now have to be transferred to other areas. The *Globe's* warnings were prophetic. In many cases the Deposit Act required the transfer of money out of regions where credit and capital were desperately needed into regions where the demand was much less. In almost every case it forced the pet banks to pay the states money that had already been legitimately loaned to investors. Ultimately, most of the pet banks failed, in large part due to the Deposit Act.

In the Senate, meanwhile, Benton and his little band of Jeremiahs worked unsuccessfully for a bill to require hard-money payments for public lands. Other Democrats were terrified by this proposal, but Benton and Blair still had the ear of Andrew Jackson. As soon as Congress adjourned, Old Hickory issued their proposition in the form of an executive order.

A gradual tightening of the money supply over a five-year period might have corrected the inflation without excessive economic trauma. The sudden removal of support from a major portion of the national currency, which, however flimsy in its relation to gold, was serving a productive purpose was another natter. Based on pure motives but catastrophic judgment, the Specie Circular of Jackson, Benton, and Blair destroyed the value of millions of dollars in paper currency at the very moment when the wheat crop had failed, the price of cotton was falling, and for several reasons the flow of European money to America had been reduced to a trickle. The circular only hastened and made certain the result its authors had sworn to prevent.

While the Democrats remained preoccupied with economic issues, by the mid-1830s the Whigs had learned a lesson and had begun efforts to identify their party with the same emotional and psychological forces that had served Jackson. One of their instruments was an alleged homespun philosopher who wrote humorous tales about Andrew Jackson under the pseudonym of Major Jack Downing. The original creator of Major Jack, a journalist named Seba Smith, and Smith's occasional imitator, a New York merchant named Charles A. Davis, were both sophisticated easterners. The stories, written in a strong back-country vernacular, probably did Jackson more good than harm, but the idea of Downing himself being a Whig served to identify that party at least in a small degree with the rural, less educated, more common elements of society.

The other well-known Whig commoner was the wild frontiersman from Tennessee, Davy Crockett, who had quarreled with Jackson and then joined the Whig party of banks and tariffs. Crockett wrote letters for Major Jack's *Downing Gazette*, and was soon provided with a rollicking autobiography by Whig ghostwriters. Inspired by the success of the autobiography, the Whigs also produced a scurrilous biography of Van Buren with Crockett as its formal author. From one city and town to another the Whigs transported their new champion for picturesque speeches against his supposedly more educated and sophisticated Democratic enemies.

The *Globe* generally ignored Major Downing, but maintained a steady fire against "Dainty Davey." Crockett, wrote Blair, had been bought with big loans from the Bank. He had betrayed both Jackson and Tennessee. Even more damning, the *Globe* printed a host of articles and letters from other papers indicating that Davy was being wined and dined throughout the country while charging the people $8 a day for his services in Congress.[15]

Another issue plaguing the Democrats in the election campaign was the war against the Seminole Indians in Florida. The removal of the Creeks and Cherokees westward was successful, but the 1,500-odd Seminoles in the Florida Everglades would not surrender. Ultimately the United States spent more than $20 million and used a total of 60,691 fighting men, of whom 1,500 were killed, without ever accomplishing the basic objective. In 1836 the frustrations caused a quarrel and bitter recriminations between Generals Winfield Scott and Thomas Jesup. Scott was a darling of the Whigs, and the *National Intelligencer* tried to turn the general's troubles into a saga of persecution by the Democratic administration. Jesup, on the other hand, was a close friend of Blair, and the *Globe* took up his defense. Blair, however, did print Scott's letters as well as those of Jesup and argued that the controversy was only a misunderstanding that should not be a political issue at all. Old Hickory promptly ordered Scott recalled and investigated, and the command was given to Jesup. Ultimately, Scott was exonerated of any wrongdoing, and he graciously denied that he had been unfairly treated. In the end, the *Globe* was praising Scott for repudiating the efforts of Whig papers to create a political issue.[16]

The only real threat to Van Buren in the 1836 election was William Henry Harrison, the hero of the less than overwhelming victory against the Indians at Tippecanoe in 1811. Harrison was an authentic frontier soldier who could be skillfully presented as a carbon copy of Andrew Jackson. In a series of long articles, the *Globe* described Tippecanoe as a victory for the soldiers despite inexcusable blunders by General Harrison. The general, said the *Globe*, had selected his campsite on the advice of the Indians, and had admitted later that it was the worst possible place. Then he had been surprised by the Indians' initial attack, and three brave colonels and two captains had been killed needlessly because of this culpable negligence. The *Globe* also blamed Harrison's alleged blunders for the disastrous American defeat at the Raisin River in the War of 1812. Blair's source for the attacks on Harrison was a book by General John Armstrong, who had also served without distinction as secretary of war.[17] Historians still disagree over Harrison's military performances, but he was clearly no Andrew Jackson. Blair's effort to head off a popular identification of the two generals was a shrewd though not entirely successful tactic.

On September 6, 1836, a *Globe* editorial called attention to an advertisement that would run daily until the election. One "JM" was offering to bet $100 on Van Buren in each of the eight new southern and western states; $250 that Harrison, White, and Webster combined would not get more electoral votes than Van Buren in any section; $1,000 that Van Buren would be elected; $250 that Van Buren's electoral vote would double that of Harrison, be three times that of White, and four times that of Webster; and $250 that Van Buren would get twenty-five more electoral votes than the combined total of his opponents. Any takers should inquire at the *Globe*. The ad, wrote Blair, was to show that "not one of the coalition of bankers, betters, and braggers, from one end of the continent to the other, do believe a word of what the whole opposition press is asserting, in regard to the result of the approaching elections."

With Andrew Jackson still on the scene, 1836 was not the year for reckless partisans to accept the challenge of "JM," although Blair suffered a net loss of $300 from a total of $900 bet for him by Thomas Ritchie in Virginia.[18] Van Buren received 170 electoral votes. Harrison got the seventy-three votes of Delaware, Maryland, Kentucky, Vermont, New Jersey, Indiana, and Ohio. Webster carried only Massachusetts, while White carried Tennessee and Georgia. The popular vote of Harrison, however, was surprisingly large, and might have been still larger if the general instead of White had been on the southern ballots. "Old Tippecanoe" would be heard from again. The laboring man's champion and slayer of Tecumseh, Colonel Richard M.

Johnson, apparently ran afoul of middle-class objections to his unorthodox family relationships, and he failed to gain an electoral majority for vice-president. Later, however, he was properly elected by the United States Senate.

In his final message to Congress in December 1836, Andrew Jackson reminded Americans again of their endless blessings but plaintively insisted that the Deposit Act had never been intended as a gift to the states. Instead of distributing surpluses, he said, the taxes and the paper-money speculations creating the surpluses should be eliminated. Above all, he warned, the wild spirit of speculation was threatening the very foundations of the republic.

A majority of the Congress, however, saw Old Hickory's Specie Circular and general deflationary policies as the real threat to prosperity. A bill to rescind the circular passed handily after many weeks of congressional wrangling, but Jackson pocket-vetoed it. The *Globe* fought valiantly for the Specie Circular as the only barrier against national bankruptcy, and made clear its willingness to attack those Democrats who saw the matter differently.

Meanwhile, in the early-morning hours of January 17 the Jacksonians enjoyed their final triumph. On January 12 Thomas Hart Benton delivered his often-repeated oration on the glories of Jackson and the misdeeds of the president's enemies. On January 16 the Missourian had ordered an ample repast of food, wines, and hot coffee for a committee room, and with his supporters thus fortified for an all night session he began a debate on expunging the 1834 resolution of censure against Andrew Jackson. Although the hour grew late, every effort to adjourn was defeated as the expungers traveled back and forth in small groups to the banquet table, while always leaving enough senators on the Senate floor to protect the cause. One at a time Calhoun, Clay, and Webster delivered diatribes against this "ruthless violation of a sacred instrument." A few senators sent for firearms, but no violence developed. Finally, amid wild excitement, the Senate voted 24–21 in favor of expunging. As gallery partisans hissed and cheered, the clerk drew black lines through the sentences condemning Jackson.

On January 20 the *Globe* had the last word on "THE LIFE,

TRIAL, AND EXECUTION OF A CERTAIN PREAMBLE AND RESOLU-
TION" against Andrew Jackson. It had claimed many paternal
ancestors, but the community had generally agreed that "the
Bank of the United States was its mother. This lady . . . did
not openly avow which of her many gallants had the honor of
its paternity." Though defended ably by "those whose gallantries
with the mother taught many to believe that they were not ungrateful for past favors," it had been found guilty: "It exhibited
many writhings, contortions, and dying agonies, for a long time
after the appearance of breathing had ceased. Its friends and phy-
sicians mourned in sackcloth and ashes. . . . Funeral services were
performed . . . by the Rev. Nicholas Biddle, and it was finally
buried in the vaults of the defunct Bank." [19]

A few weeks later the *Globe* reported the farewell of Jackson
and the inauguration of Van Buren. More than a mile of paved
avenue was thronged with eager, happy citizens, as a "soft spring
snow . . . lost in the warm day, its touch of water, and, in vir-
gin purity, reflected from the surrounding hills the cheering light
and benignity of the Heavens." Behind infantry, cavalry, and a
great band playing martial music, Jackson and his successor rode
to the Capitol in a beautiful phaeton made from the wood of the
frigate *Constitution* and presented to him by the Democrats of
New York City. Jackson, Van Buren, and Chief Justice Taney,
"all three hated and persecuted by the money power, stood in
honor and glory before their countrymen." Sixteen of the senators
who had traduced them "were not present," but "had been gradually expelled by the force of public opinion." Blair was glad,
however, that Clay and Webster were present and looking
happy. But he noted that "there was one . . . reprobate spirit
that could not bear to look upon the bright and auspicious day;
and it was a pleasure to all that the face of *Cataline* [Calhoun]
was not seen on the occasion." [20]

Jackson's farewell address was a final warning against all
the old enemies—banks, paper money, speculation, corruption,
and false prophets of disunion. Echoing a view expressed by the
Globe since the earliest threat of nullification, Old Hickory denounced "systematic efforts publicly to sow the seeds of discord
between different parts of the United States and to place party
divisions directly upon geographical distinctions; to excite the

South against the *North* and the *North* against the *South,* and to force into the controversy . . . topics upon which it is impossible that a large portion of the Union can ever speak without strong emotion." Let the Union once divide, he warned, and "the controversies which are now debated and settled in the halls of legislation will then be tried in fields of battle and determined by the sword."

In turn, Van Buren, like President Herbert Hoover a century later, hailed the United States as "an aggregate of human prosperity not elsewhere to be found." Echoing Jackson's plea for sectional harmony, the new president promised to be "the inflexible and uncompromising opponent of every attempt on the part of Congress to abolish slavery in the District of Columbia against the wishes of the slaveholding states, and also with a determination equally decided to resist the interference with it in the states where it exists." [21]

More than a century later historians would still be debating the meaning and significance of the stewardship of Andrew Jackson, and the contemporary judgment of his administration's chief ideologue and phrasemaker is therefore worth noting. In the agrarian-liberal, laissez-faire, states' rights doctrines expounded many years before by John Taylor of Caroline County, Virginia, Blair found a complete philosophical justification for all of his idol's policies. "You will find," he later wrote Jackson after publishing a Taylor pamphlet in the *Globe,* "how perfectly all the steps you took while at the head of the Govt. were calculated to restore the principles of the Revolution and to counteract the schemes which Hamilton engrafted on our Institutions under the power and sanction of Washington's great name." [22]

Obviously, a biographer cannot fully grasp the innermost thoughts of his subject, but he can speculate on Blair's possible reactions to the various interpretations of the Jacksonian period by several modern historians. He would have been both delighted and puzzled by Arthur Schlesinger, Jr.'s *Age of Jackson.* Recognizing the talents of a brilliant fellow polemicist, he would have reveled in Schlesinger's oversimplification of the conflict between democrats and aristocrats. However, the editor whose masthead proclaimed that "THE WORLD IS GOVERNED TOO MUCH" would have questioned Schlesinger's comparison of the Jacksonian administration with the New Deal of Franklin Roosevelt. He might have also wondered why Schlesinger failed to notice that most of Jackson's closest followers were either slaveholders or defenders of slavery, while the abolitionists were often Whigs. Schlesinger's chapter on the southern dilemma in having to choose between a Democratic party of states' rights and dangerous libertarian ideology as opposed to a Whig party advocating federal supremacy while standing safe and conservative on slavery would have mystified Blair. Blair would have admitted freely that Jackson's leading subordinates were indeed men of position and property, and he would have wondered why so much effort on the part of so many historians was necessary to discover and prove it. Unlike Lee Benson,[23] Bray Hammond, and numerous others, however, he would have seen nothing inconsistent between this and the old general's posture as the prophet and defender of the true democracy. Frank Gatell's work[24] showing that after the Bank struggle most wealthy New Yorkers were in fact Whigs would have confirmed one of Blair's deepest convictions. He would also have been pleased by the evidence of Benson and Ronald Formisano[25] that various newer immigrant groups usually voted Democratic, because recruiting them was one of the *Globe*'s most consistent goals. He would probably have questioned Benson's designation of New York as a test case for the nation, since numerous politicians even at this early date recognized that New York politics had never been and would never be typical of any other state. He would also have been disturbed by the implication of Benson, Formisano, and a long line of earlier historians that the Whigs were the humorless, straightlaced party of grim propriety and stern morality. The Whigs, after all, were led by Clay, a notorious gambler and womanizer as well as a brilliant wit, and Daniel Webster, whose propensity for hard liquor was recognized both on and off the Senate floor. The party that glorified "Dainty Davey" Crockett and Major Jack Downing was hardly lacking in bawdy humor.

Blair would have probably agreed with Richard McCormick, Glyndon Van Deusen,[26] and others that the political parties were far more alike than different, but he had built a career on the differences, and he would never have admitted that the specific issues dividing the parties in presidential election years were unimportant to the lives of most Americans. Blair would certainly have applauded Richard Hofstadter's view[27] that the Jacksonians were aspiring new capitalists trying to break the stranglehold of an earlier wealthy generation and its descendants on the nation's opportunities for acquisition. Blair had a mystical faith in America's destiny to expand its population, territory, and wealth, but his concern for an equitable distribution of the new riches made him blind to the advantages of Clay's programs for increasing the size of the treasure. His Kentucky experiences left him extremely cautious, but with the trusted John Rives making the decisions, Blair did not hesitate to invest in any speculation that offered a profit. He remained a pious opponent, however, of speculators who were dependent upon government action for the success of their ventures.

Blair would have agreed fully with John Ward's explanations[28] for the personal popularity of Andrew Jackson, but unlike Ward he would have insisted that Jackson really was everything the public thought him to be, and he would have quarreled but little if at all with the popular standards of taste and judgment that made the old general such an invincible political asset. Perhaps in Marvin Meyers' *The Jacksonian Persuasion* Blair would have recognized himself most clearly. He felt a powerful sentimental attachment to the simpler rural values of his youth, and he probably was genuinely torn between his desire for economic progress both personal and national and his fear of the new values and national habits the new commercial and industrial revolution was certain to bring. The Bank of the United States was a highly available scapegoat for the new catalogue of sins being created by progress, and Blair and others probably did find much solace in their war against it.

Blair would have admired Robert Remini's understanding[29] of the political process, and he might have been disturbed rather than angered by the doubts cast on the unselfish purity of his motives. He would have agreed with Charles Sellers[30] that the southern Whigs were capitalists and businessmen—he was forever condemning their support of the Bank—and would also have included numerous southern Democrats in their ranks. He would have appreciated Peter Temin's argument[31] that Jackson's policies did not cause the boom-and-bust cycle of the 1830s, but he would have questioned Temin's contention that the Bank and the Whigs had almost nothing to do with it either. He would have respected Edward Pessen's willingness to let opposing viewpoints speak for themselves, and he would have admired Pessen's research in the nonpolitical aspects of the period.[32]

Obviously, the period named after Andrew Jackson was marked by strong paradoxes often illustrated in the life of Francis P. Blair. Vigorous technological and economic progress was accompanied by the spread of an enlightened political ideology totally inconsistent with human slavery, but the loudest voices in the glorification of democracy were often identified with or at least ready to defend the South's peculiar institution. Clearly motivated to a considerable degree by self-interest, men and parties struggled for wealth and power without conscious hypocrisy in the name of unselfish and noble principles, while grossly exaggerating both their opponents' misdeeds and their own virtues. The net result, however, was a steadily if slowly improving society trying to catch up with its own ever more lofty ideals. Unfortunately, this process would soon be hopelessly ensnarled with a problem it could not digest—the quarrel over slavery.

Chapter 9

Van Buren and the Jacksonian Aftermath

THE inauguration of Van Buren was a joyous triumph for Jackson and Blair, but a great many other Americans were far less happy. On February 10 a mob of hungry people had broken open 600 barrels of flour and more than 1,000 bushels of wheat in a New York warehouse. As women carried the flour and wheat home in aprons, sacks, and pans, the crowd overwhelmed the police and threw snowballs at the mayor when he begged for order. At a second warehouse troops quelled the invaders. Several of those arrested and sentenced probably considered the warm jail and prison food an undisguised blessing. In early April ninety-eight New York business houses went bankrupt, and city lots that had sold for $480 fell to $50. On May 9 all New York banks suspended specie payments. The situation was soon being duplicated in cities and towns all over America. The economic machinery had temporarily stripped its gears.

The argument that re-chartering the United States Bank in 1832 might have prevented the catastrophe has some logic, but it presupposes that the disastrous policies Nicholas Biddle actually did follow after 1834 would have been different if the Bank had not lost its government privileges. Biddle in fact stands convicted of either innocent but serious misjudgment or deliberate wrongdoing. Various factors produced the panic of 1837, but the Bank's easy credit and paper-money expansion did its share in creating the psychological atmosphere that tempted many smaller banks to follow suit. The deposit banks favored by Jackson succumbed to overwhelming temptations, but did nothing illegal and might have weathered the ensuing storm but for the distribution act.

Blair, Benton, and the little group who risked their popularity and defied their own party in the futile attempt to protect the deposit banks from the Deposit Act were sound in their judgment. Jackson's Specie Circular was a much too painful and dangerous remedy, but even without the circular, the land bubble would have burst eventually, and possibly with an even greater disruption of normal economic processes.

In the sophisticated atmosphere of the late twentieth century an important school of thought stresses the ideological similarity of American political parties in earlier days and attributes their differences entirely to conflicts of personal interest.[1] Since both parties were devoted to capitalism and private enterprise, goes the argument, they were in principle like Tweedle Dee and Tweedle Dum, and their contests were of minor significance in determining the American future.

The American nation obviously did have the basic economic strength to withstand the abuses and cures of its political parties and leaders. The bedraggled mother scooping up flour left on the streets by the New York mob in 1837, however, would have drawn only small comfort from the knowledge that she would soon be forgotten and that her suffering would have but little impact upon the long-range development of her country. The economic collapse of 1837 was in fact a major event in American history, and the political differences that helped to cause it were both real and significant.

The effort by Jackson and his friends to turn America back to the simpler and purer laissez-faire society of Thomas Jefferson ran counter to every technological force in America, but it clearly set them apart from their Whig opponents, and it was related to a much more defensible objective. The Bank had in fact demonstrated that it could arbitrarily adopt policies dangerous to the livelihood of large numbers of innocent people. The question of whether or not it should be restored and continued was a political issue of genuine magnitude for the American future.

Had Nicholas Biddle not triggered the panic of 1834, not contributed large loans and favors to editors and members of Congress, not helped stimulate the excessive speculation of 1835–

1837, and not bankrupted the successor United States Bank of Pennsylvania by 1842, the chances for the eventual re-chartering of another United States Bank would have been excellent. That Biddle did do these things, however, illustrated sharply the folly of placing the national financial system in the hands of an unregulated and uncontrolled private corporation.

The Bank was in fact the potential nucleus for a financial oligarchy whose relative power was certain to expand as the growth of the nation brought more and more revenues into the national treasury. Historian Marvin Meyers has brilliantly described it as a scapegoat symbol of the wickedness of a new age, which everyone was prepared to enjoy but which also brought guilty nostalgia for the lost innocence of a simpler day.[2] Perhaps the Bank was such a symbol, but it was also a great deal more. It was a banking and currency system certain to prove inadequate, while its power to cause national damage in a struggle for its self-preservation was very likely to grow in proportion to its inadequacy. Modern defenders have argued that the Bank's existence might have prevented the financial corruption and the private banking behemoths that developed in the Gilded Age following the Civil War. It is more likely that a national but privately managed bank blessed with the national treasury would have become involved in the Great Barbecue of the post–Civil War years in ways even more dangerous to the public welfare and the American system of political democracy.

At least one able historian has compared the United States Bank of Nicholas Biddle with the Federal Reserve System, and has seen the adoption of the latter as a vindication of the former.[3] The differences, however, are more striking. Federal Reserve banks do not earn profits for stockholders and officers and do not lobby, provide lawmakers and editors with unusual loans and subsidies, or sharply inflate or deflate the national currency arbitrarily. The directors cannot speculate with the banks' funds. They cannot, even in theory, enrich one section of the country at the expense of another. They are ruled by a varied board of seven persons appointed by the president with the consent of the Senate, and are subjected to many regulations and controls from which the earlier United States Bank was entirely free.

In 1836 Pennsylvania chartered the United States Bank as

a state bank. In 1837, when the panic forced the banks to suspend specie payments, most major banks felt a moral duty to retrench and resume payments as soon as possible. Biddle, however, saw quite correctly that resumption would continue the deflationary trend when the expansion of credit facilities was desperately needed. When the venerable Albert Gallatin led the New York banks toward resumption, Biddle used his full influence in the opposite direction. Even with a valid position, however, Biddle appealed to partisanship by arguing that a successful resumption with the Specie Circular still in operation would prove Jackson's case against the banks and exonerate him from responsibility for the depression. In effect Biddle was offering to exchange specie resumption for a congressional repeal of the circular.

In May 1838 the New York banks, assisted by the Bank of England, resumed specie payments, Van Buren's Independent Treasury bill was again defeated in Congress, and the Specie Circular was repealed. By the fall of 1838 banks everywhere had resumed payments, and Biddle was riding a crest of triumph. In February 1839 he was Van Buren's dinner guest at the White House.

Meanwhile, however, Biddle had already begun policies that would destroy both the Bank and himself by 1842. In the words of a historian friendly to Biddle, he

> had no realization or suspicion of what was developing. The policies included prodigal loans on stocks, especially to officers and directors of the bank, heavy investments in corporate stocks and speculative bonds, and purchases of cotton and other agricultural commodities for export. The cotton transactions were undertaken in the emergency of 1837 as a means of sustaining domestic commodity prices and providing European exchange. They succeeded initially, but once begun they were hard to stop, and they produced loss, litigation, and recrimination that was probably more damaging to Biddle himself than to the bank.[4]

In January 1842 Biddle and several associates were arrested and placed under $10,000 bail on charges that they had "conspired to cheat and defraud the bank by obtaining large advances upon shipment of cotton to Europe" and "by the unlawful receipt and expenditure of large sums of money." A court ruled 3–2 that no fraud had been committed. Soon stockholders filed another suit asking that the same group be required to account for another $400,000. The court ultimately ruled that information that might tend to incriminate could not be demanded. Biddle, however, had already died. Earlier he had paid a stockholders' demand for $320,000, using Texas bonds that were accepted at more than their face value.

Biddle's most ardent modern defender has argued strongly that his disastrous efforts to acquire and hold enough cotton to drive up the price in European markets were motivated entirely by a patriotic desire to restore American money balances abroad and rejuvenate the national economy. This view is probably correct, but it does not change the fact that the policies destroyed the Bank and injured its stockholders. The contingent argument that Biddle failed because the rest of the world would not abide by his superior judgment[5] indicates only that he was woefully blind to the power of the prevailing financial ideology of his time. The obvious fact that America needed a governmental system of central banking like the Federal Reserve System does not at all mean that the nation needed the United States Bank of Nicholas Biddle or any other system that gave one man so many opportunities to make so many catastrophic mistakes. The anti-Bank rhetoric of Blair and the *Globe* was grossly exaggerated, but it was not without truth. Jackson, Van Buren, and Benton believed fervently everything they said about the Bank, and if they were mistaken in degree and in their estimate of Biddle's motives, the great banker himself was in large part responsible.

Jackson's deflationary hard-money principles were utterly useless in a nation crying for liquid capital and credit to stop the momentary spiral of economic contraction, low prices, and unemployment. Blaming it all on the banks and the previous inflation, however, Van Buren and his friends sought to inoculate against the future before curing the present. They were determined to take the government funds entirely out of the banking and currency system by keeping the national revenues in an Independent Treasury. Clay, Webster, and the Whigs believed that this would deny the government its obvious role and responsibility as a national agent of economic progress. The Jacksonians, however, were certain that it would restore the federal government to its proper limited role as envisioned by the founding fathers. Despite Democratic majorities, however, the Independent Treasury was defeated by at least one house in Congress each year until 1840, when Van Buren at long last signed it on a note of short-lived triumph.[6]

Preserving the Specie Circular, blaming the United States Bank for the depression, purifying the nation with an Independent Treasury, and keeping the public reminded of the glorious image of Jackson were the great objects of Blair and the *Globe* during the Van Buren administration. On the economic issues, Blair's major problem was keeping dissident Democrats in line. For eight years Democratic leaders had agreed unanimously on the importance of public loyalty to Andrew Jackson as a method of winning elections, but they had often agreed on little else. Now, however, the invincible old general was gone. Even Chief Justice Taney advised strongly against the Independent Treasury, and editor Thomas Ritchie of the *Richmond Enquirer,* the Democratic party's major southern paper, publicly shared this view. Two prominent Jacksonian senators, William C. Rives of Virginia and Nathaniel P. Talmadge of New York, began organizing a movement within the party to block the measure. Virgil Maxcy, Jackson's first solicitor of the Treasury, wrote Whig industrialist Abbott Lawrence a confidential letter offering his cooperation and urging eastern efforts against the Specie Circular.[7]

Aware that only the Jackson–Benton–Van Buren version of economic policy would be presented in the *Globe,* the Democrats who favored keeping the government's funds in the state banks established their own newspaper. "If the Globe has an *exclusive* patent right to be the organ of the *executive,*" wrote editor Thomas Allen in the first issue of the new *Madisonian,* "perhaps he will allow us to be the organ of the Republicans in the *legislative* department." The *Madisonian* would not "levy war upon 800 Banks with 800,000 allies."

The new alignments on financial policy, however, did help end the estrangement between the *Globe* and the *New York Evening Post,* whose editors mirrored the anti-Bank attitudes of the Locofoco workingmen's faction of the New York Democrats. William Leggett, who had disagreed so sharply with Blair over abolition literature, wrote that editor William Cullen Bryant was in every way cooperating with the regular party machinery in New York. He hoped Blair would make a statement in the *Globe* to allay the earlier impression that the *Post* was out of favor with the official Democratic paper. Blair promptly complied. Leggett, meanwhile, carried his genuine and deeply felt radicalism to Cleveland and the new *Plain Dealer*. The *Post* was in financial straits and needed the *Globe*'s friendship, but their restored unity of purpose was entirely genuine. Leggett's health ultimately failed, and he died just prior to departure for a diplomatic post in Havana.[8]

Blair and Jackson were never happier than when they felt surrounded by traitors and enemies, and the postal service enabled them to continue sharing this experience. Day after day the old general tottered the mile to his front gate to receive Blair's almost indecipherable communiqués from the battle and spend the next several hours scrawling out his own equally illegible replies. The *Globe* had lost valuable friends in Virginia, wrote Blair, by attacking Alexander Stevenson, the American minister to England, for publicly opposing Jackson's Specie Circular, but if Jackson approved, it would solace him for the friends lost in Virginia. Eliza, meanwhile, had sighed for Jackson like a lost father, carrying his letter "in her bosom for some days until I got possession of it and put it in an old family pocket-book. . . . She has now transferred her love to the Cow, has her stabled and curried like a race Horse, and I do not know but she may follow the Egyptian superstition, which turned the Bull Apis, into a divinity." [9]

The general approved. If Stevenson had advocated allowing Biddle and the Barings to manage the United States currency, it was Blair's duty to "lay his apostacy bare and naked before the public. . . . *I say, lay on, temporize not, it is always injurious.*" Jackson was certain that "only the specie circular had saved the country from total Bankruptcy." With sentimentality matching that of Blair, the old man promised to raise Eliza a "real short horned cow," but he would give it to her only after they had come for a visit. His little niece knew that Mrs. Blair would not forget her and her brother Andrew "because she cut off a lock of each of their hair, and she is shure she never will forget Mrs. B because she looks at the shawl every day that Mrs. Blair gave her." [10]

In May the *Nashville Banner* published a story from the *Intelligencer* by way of the *New York Star* that a draft of Jackson's for $6,000 had been protested, and that the ex-president was liable for $300,000 because he had loaned his name to a relative involved in land speculations. Jackson's angry words smoldered on the page as he avowed to Blair: "I have endorsed no one, have no connection with the bank, banking companys or companys of land speculators, or individual Speculators in Land, Cotton, or anything else." Blair must quickly "contradict the lies of Joe Gales, Webb and Noah, who . . . send their falsehoods all over the country in hopes that those who read their vile and repeated slanders may never see the contradiction." Calhoun had made a similar charge in the last session of Congress, and Jackson saw the Carolinian's hand also in this new attack. [11]

On September 1 Congress convened in special session to deal with the financial crisis, and five days later Jackson sent his editor an unneeded warning. The *Madisonian* was "a *viper*, in the hypocritical disguise of friend, to the administration, and . . . intended to sting it, by dividing the republicans, and to undermine, and destroy you." [12]

Three days later Blair reported that the viper had indeed struck. A combination of Whigs and paper-money Democrats had awarded the congressional printing to the *Madisonian*, even though it had no equipment and would have to do the actual work on the presses of the Whig *Intelligencer*. Democratic Senators Rives and Talmadge had worked all summer to line up some twenty Democrats behind the new press. Unhappily, mourned Blair, the banks had "our Editors and Statesmen or their Brothers or sons in their debt, and the result is that their politics take the color of the corporation that feeds them." His real grief was for the *Globe*'s office hands, both men and women, who would have to be discharged because of the loss of the government contracts [13]

The new administration soon found its Democratic defectors partially replaced by a new set of allies— the followers of John C. Calhoun. For six years Calhoun had worked with Clay, Webster, and the Whigs against the southern slaveholding planter Jackson, even though Old Hickory had advocated most of the economic policies he supposedly supported. In 1837, with Jackson replaced by the far more libertarian New Yorker, Van Buren, Calhoun quickly and easily returned to the Democratic fold. "I go," the Carolinian wrote a friend, "against the chartering of a United States bank, or any connection with Biddle's or any other bank." [14] Soon Calhoun was allied with Benton in an effort to stop the payment of the final installment due under the Deposit Act to the states, and he was also debating for the Independent Treasury. Clay responded with taunting denunciations, and the Jacksonians watched with grim satisfaction as the two erstwhile allies swapped insults and argued over who had really won the tariff contest of 1833.

On October 1 Blair reported to Jackson that Benton and three other senators had dined at his house that day. They had drunk Jackson's health "as the man of this century, whose principles were destined to put down the new form in which tyranny has appeared under 'The Paper Dynasty.' " The speeches of Benton and others, including Calhoun, had put the enemy to flight. "Who would have expected," marveled Blair, "in six months after you retired from the Presidency to hear Calhoun speaking of you as *that great and remarkable man.*' " [15]

Jackson was unimpressed by the news of Calhoun, and Blair quickly agreed. Calhoun, Blair wrote, would "probably keep on his mask, until some other opportunity to betray his party should occur, but that he will betray it at some time, is to my mind certain. There is treachery in the man. . . . I shall mind your hint about Cataline. He may be trusted, as you trusted the Pirates at New Orleans." [16]

In his battle report to Jackson in February 1838, Blair added almost as an afterthought that Eliza had been thrown from a horse and had broken her arm above the elbow. Despite his objections she was determined to "ride the rascal again, whom she petted into the spirit of kicking up his heels and throwing her off in two heats." Five weeks later the arm was taken out of a sling, but she was not yet "able to take the reins . . . and make good her promise of conquering the unruly horse. She is very proud of him as he behaved so well in your constitutional triumphal car on the last inaugural day." [17]

Perhaps Blair sensed instinctively that a few weeks of uninterrupted peace might have killed his old chief years before. "I have regained more strength in the last three days than in weeks before," wrote Jackson as he read Blair's account of the debates. "I now hope to live to see the Government divorced, *a mensa* and *thora,* from all Banks." [18]

The delighted editor answered with a hope that Jackson would live to become "the most beloved of all our Octogenarian Chiefs." Every day,he assured the general, proved "the Wisdom and patriotism of the great reform you originated." Biddle's recent policies would "ere long make every Patriot in this land and those of every future age bless the man whom providence raised up to deliver in the crisis of its fate this continent set apart as the abode of freedom." [19]

Meanwhile, Blair had assumed the pleasant task of promoting the first two volumes of George Bancroft's *History of the United States* with numerous excerpts and laudatory articles from foreign as well as domestic periodicals. He expected the work to "make its way triumphantly wherever the English language is read." Bancroft, a New England aristocrat converted to the religion of democracy, had reached the end of the colonial period in his multivolume study, and almost every line was a vote for Jackson. Braving the social scorn of Boston to become one of what Richard Hildreth called "the uncircumcized Phillistines," Bancroft had been rewarded with various positions of leadership in the Democratic party. In January 1838 he became collector of the Port of Boston. His monumental history was destined to reach ten volumes without ever arriving at the Jackson administrations.[20]

In 1836 Blair had denounced Calhoun for refusing to allow the petitions for abolition in the District of Columbia to be accepted and tabled without debate. As this question continued through the Van Buren administration, the *Globe* turned its heaviest guns against John Quincy Adams for also refusing to accept the same policy. In January 1838 Calhoun introduced six resolutions that were all adopted by wide margins. In essence, the resolutions averred that the states had entered the Union voluntarily and had retained exclusive control of their domestic institutions, including slavery; that attacks against slavery were unconstitutional; that abolitionist efforts in the District of

Columbia violated the constitutional rights of Maryland and Virginia; and that congressional abolition in any territory where slavery already existed was also unconstitutional. Blair hailed the discussions of these resolutions as "characterized by calmness, dignity, and mutual desire to . . . devise some common means of producing harmonious action, and of avoiding, for the future, the dangers and difficulties which appertain to the decision of this question." [21]

The *Caroline* affair, in which Canadians burned a small American ship and allowed it to float over Niagara Falls, and the Aroostook War in Maine also tested Blair's talents as a popular persuader. The *Caroline,* which was privately owned by American citizens, had been carrying arms to Canadian revolutionaries, and the Maine conflict was a boundary dispute with Canada and Britain. In each case the *Globe* gave eloquent support to Van Buren's policy of firmness tempered by a willingness to be reasonable. Speaking with the voice of the administration, Blair warned American citizens everywhere that the United States government would not support them if they became involved in private controversies with the Canadian government. General Winfield Scott, a well-known Whig, was sent with troops to the Canadian border to ensure that further violence did not erupt, and the *Globe* assured readers that Scott would do everything "that prudence, courage, and sagacity can suggest, to maintain the peace and honor of the country." When peace was restored, Blair showered Scott with praise for the way he had "repressed the spirit of lawless adventure." In a long editorial the *Globe* charged that "the American citizen who endeavors to embarrass . . . the nation's Government, in its intercourse and relations with a friendly foreign nation, commits a fearful crime." [22]

Another problem that Van Buren wisely managed to nurse along without a confrontation was Texas. Public sentiment for annexation was rising, but Van Buren and followers like Blair and Benton remained reluctant to risk a war with Mexico for a plum they believed certain to fall eventually to the United States anyhow. In 1836 the ambitious Texans defined their boundaries to include large parts of four Mexican provinces that had never, either by law or conquest, been part of Texas. This thorny problem, along with the evidence of northern opposition to the idea of adding such a vast new slave territory, kept Van Buren limited to a policy of friendly support and watchful waiting. Already by 1839, however, rumors of British influence in Texas were spreading, and Andrew Jackson as always responded to the distant smell of possible combat. One bottle of the "matchless sanative" had improved his health, he wrote. Another would cure him, "& if a British war should ensue, which god forbid, I will be able to face their army in the field." [23]

In the elections of 1838 the Democrats gained six House seats, but their margin of 124–118 over the Whigs remained slight, and their Senate margin declined by four seats to 28–22. Although the nation had begun to climb out of the slough of depression, the presidential election of 1840 would be anything but certain. Van Buren was a dignified leader and an able administrator, but unlike Jackson he could not keep unruly Democrats united even for the sake of victory. He had contributed very little to the slow but certain economic recovery, and his one important innovation, the Independent Treasury, did not pass until July 1840. The Independent Treasury was probably a mistake at best, but its effects either way would not be seen by Election Day. Van Buren's handling of potential crises with Britain and Mexico was highly responsible and skillful, if not universally popular, but he projected little charisma and no excitement at all.

While Van Buren could never command the hero-worship from Blair that Jackson had inspired, Blair and the New Yorker shared a strong mutual affection and respect. They agreed fully on the agrarian economic policies so many other Democrats had rejected, and Blair must have enjoyed the subconscious realization that he himself was the more aggressive and stubborn of the two. For Eliza, Van Buren was never even a pale shadow of the dynamic Old Hickory, but her husband apparently made no comparisons and accepted Van Buren for his own virtues. As the Democratic party's chief propagandist, Blair would support Van Buren with the same loyalty and dedication he had previously reserved only for Jackson.

Chapter 10

Defeat

IN February 1839 the *Globe* denounced a bill proposed by Blair's old friend Crittenden. Anticipating the much-later Hatch Act, the measure would have forbidden political persuasion by government employees under pain of a $500 fine, disfranchisement, and forfeiture of the right to hold office. Blair insisted that intermeddling by persuasion or discussion was the "political *duty*" of everyone, including officeholders and those denied the vote. Even the "gentler sex, although disfranchised by the tenderness which would not expose them to the rude scenes at the polls" should "employ for what they may consider their own and the country's interests, all the persuasive influence not only of fact and argument . . . but the persuasion of every sentiment and sympathy which the most intimate of family ties beget." [1] Blair really did believe that every American should participate in the political process. He also had seen clearly that the reelection of Martin Van Buren in 1840 would require the hard work of every Democratic officeholder as well as the intimate influence of every disfranchised female willing to support the president.

Like everyone else, Blair expected Henry Clay to be the Whig candidate, and he missed no opportunity to needle his old adversary. In August 1839 the *Globe* was bemoaning the "melancholy spectacle" of Henry Clay, "an aged man . . . perhaps for the last time dragging the wreck of fame, of talent, and of existence, through the heat and dust of a political canvass, only to disgrace the close of a career whose commencement, alas, promised so brightly."

On December 4, however, Blair suddenly found that he had

been shooting at the wrong target. The Whig convention at Harrisburg nominated General William Henry Harrison for president. Somewhat stunned, Blair immediately began denouncing the Whigs for abandoning their only truly great leader. Even the "genius, energy, skill, and indefatigable perseverance of Clay," wrote Blair, could barely hold Whiggery together, while the totally unqualified Harrison was "nothing but the mummy of defunct Federalism."

For once Clay agreed with Blair. "God Damn it! I knew it!" he roared. "My friends are not worth the powder it would take to blow them up." He had led on the first ballot, but Thurlow Weed and Thaddeus Stevens had talked the convention into a unit rule that ended Clay's chances. The nomination had been followed by three solid hours of glowing tributes to Clay, however, and soon Clay, the loyal party man, announced his full support for the ticket.[2]

After nominating Harrison, the Whigs offered no views, promises, or principles, but agreed only to reconvene at Baltimore in May to reaffirm their faith in the candidate. In 1836 Nicholas Biddle's strategy for Harrison had made him the strongest of the Whig candidates, and the Whig leaders had not forgotten it. "Let him say not one single word about his principles," Biddle had directed. Harrison should "say nothing—promise nothing. Let no committee, no convention, no town meeting ever extract from him a single word, about what he thinks now, or what he will do hereafter. Let the use of pen and ink be wholly forbidden as if he were a mad poet in Bedlam."[3]

Harrison's silence gave the Democrats considerable ammunition, but an indiscreet correspondent for the *Baltimore American* provided the Whigs with a theme far stronger than principles and issues. Reportedly, the writer told an angry Clay supporter how to get rid of Harrison: "Give him a barrel of hard cider, and settle a pension of two thousand a year on him, and my word for it, he will sit the remainder of his days in his log cabin by the side of 'sea coal' fire, and study moral philosophy."[4] The Democrats made the initial mistake of reprinting the quotation widely, and the Whigs immediately recognized its advantages. The Democrats, said the Whigs, were sneering at people who lived in log cabins and drank cider, whereas Harrison was the true democrat and representative of the common man. Harrison, in fact, was very well off by the financial standards of 1840. He did not drink hard cider, he was earning over $6,000 anually, his estate was valued at $25,000, and only the north wing of his $10,000 home at North Bend, Ohio, had any logs in it. No amount of repeating these facts, however, could rescue the Democrats from their initial error.

At Baltimore in early May the Democrats renominated Van Buren, but the choice of a vice-president was much more difficult. Vice-President Johnson was the idol of the Locofocos and northern workingmen everywhere, but these were a distinct minority, and the southerners were determined to remove him from the ticket. After all, his election in 1836 had caused enough trouble. Andrew Jackson urged Blair and Van Buren to drop Johnson and nominate James K. Polk of Tennessee, but swinging the northeastern delegates to this viewpoint was difficult. Also, Johnson's alleged feats of heroism in the War of 1812 could be used to counteract the military record of Harrison. In addition to his reputation for having killed Tecumseh in hand-to-hand combat, the vice-president had the scars of five enemy bullets and a shattered hand as evidence of his patriotism. Ultimately, the convention resolved to leave the vice-presidential nomination to the party organization in the various states. Johnson himself acquiesced publicly, but was clearly displeased. Soon the *Globe* was denying charges by the *Intelligencer* that the colonel had been thrown overboard, but the effort required much ingenuity.

In sharp contrast to the Whigs, the Democrats adopted a clear-cut nine-point platform. They were for strict interpretation of the Constitution, minimum government spending, states' rights, the Independent Treasury, and the "liberal principles . . . sanctioned in the Constitution." They were against federal aid for internal improvements, federal assumption of state debts, sectional favoritism, and a National Bank.[5] Assuming that voters would be guided by their reactions to the platform, the Democrats obviously took serious risks by announcing specific goals certain to alienate large numbers of people.

In Baltimore, while the Democrats were quarreling over the vice-presidency, the Whigs convened simultaneously and literally overwhelmed their opponents in competition for local attention. Their activities included a "Grand National Procession," six major addresses, two drownings, one murder, and numerous physical assaults, both given and received. The major speakers, whose disagreements with each other were carefully hidden, included Clay, Webster, William C. Preston of South Carolina, and Henry Wise of Virginia. A three-mile parade featured an "army of banners," eight log cabin floats, Daniel Webster riding in the first barouche, several thousand marchers, and an ample supply of hard cider. The noisy procession took an hour and a quarter to pass by the hall where 248 angry Democrats were trying to nominate a vice-president. As before, the Whig resolutions dealt with no issues whatever, and the delegates spent most of one day voting an assessment of one dollar per delegate for the bereaved family of a member killed in the procession "in the glorious cause of his country," and attending his funeral en masse.[6]

The *Globe* found this spectacle of "LOG CABINS, AND HARD CIDER; BAROUCHES AND WHITE HORSES; GUZZLING AND BOASTING AND BRAGGING" an "insulting display of . . . contempt for popular intelligence." The Whigs, Blair wrote, should have passed resolutions of principle against the administration and sought "by powerful address" to justify their opposition. Instead there had been only a vast assemblage drawn together for no other purpose than "to march through the streets of Baltimore."[7]

The convention, however, had set an irresistible pattern. In the Whig press Harrison was the man of the poor who might have used his many positions of trust to get rich but had refrained from doing so. He was a farmer who earned his livelihood on the soil. He was a soldier in the mold of Washington and Jackson— simple, kindly, honest, and dedicated to his country's welfare. With such a candidate, platforms and principles were irrelevant. In answer to every question related to contemporary issues, the Whig managers and press simply referred to the general's past political record, which was almost as devoid of any clear-cut pattern as his party's 1840 platform.

At the *Globe*, Blair daily attacked the old general as altogether unfit for the presidency. For weeks the editor tried to spread the truth about Harrison's lucrative clerkship, his fine home, his large personal fortune, and his taste for fine wine, which left little room for hard cider. Blair, however, did not go as far as some of his more rabid colleagues. In Ohio it was reported that "all Germans and Irish were to be expelled from the country if Harrison were elected," and Illinois Democrats charged that Harrison's first act of office would be "to sell off all the Irishmen to pay the State debt." The *Globe* also ignored the charges by some Democratic papers that Harrison had once seduced "a young and unprotected female," and that he had propagated "clutches" of halfbreed Winnebagos in his earlier years on the frontier.[8]

Harrison's military career, however, was another matter, and Blair bitterly resented the equating of Harrison with Jackson. The *Globe* insisted that Harrison's mistakes at Tippecanoe had caused many unnecessary deaths. Blair's beloved uncle George Madison, the erstwhile short-lived governor of Kentucky, had blamed Harrison for the American defeat at the Raisin River, and Blair repeated this charge in detail. There had also been ill-feeling between the famous scout George Croghan and Harrison, and Blair appealed to the Irish vote by emphasizing this. At Fort Meigs, wrote Blair, Colonel Croghan had saved Harrison's camp from destruction, but had received from Harrison only "injustice and ingratitude." The ladies of Chillicothe, Ohio, however, had not been deceived. According to the *Globe*, these wise women had prepared a petticoat to present to General Harrison at the time that a sword was presented to Colonel Croghan." And finally, Blair insisted, Harrison's one major victory, the Battle of the Thames, had been won primarily through the advice and battlefield heroism of Colonel Richard M. Johnson. Johnson, said the *Globe*, had "plenty of wounds on his body, *but not a single certificate of bravery in his pockets!*" In contrast, Harrison had "plenty of certificates of bravery in his pocket, but not a *single wound in his body!* Mark the difference between a real hero and a sham hero!" [9]

Blair apparently considered the Irish vote a rich field for cultivation. He linked the Federalists and Whigs with the British on numerous counts. Denouncing the imprisonment of Matthew Lyon, the Irish Congressman from Vermont, under the Alien and Sedition Acts of 1798, the *Globe* pointed out that Van Buren and the Democrats had passed a bill refunding Lyon's

$1,000 fine to his heirs. The Whigs had opposed this restitution. Daniel Webster, continued Blair, had stood silent and unmoved when an Irish convent in Charlestown, Massachusetts, was sacked and burned by a mob. According to Blair, the Whig editor James Watson Webb had exclaimed: "Had I the power I WOULD ERECT A GALLOWS UPON EVERY WHARF IN THE CITY OF NEW YORK, AND HANG EVERY IRISHMAN AS FAST AS THEY COME ON SHORE." And finally, warned the *Globe,* Harrison himself had said: "I RELY FOR MY ELECTION ON THE VOTES OF NATIVE AMERICANS. I CARE NOTHING FOR THE OPINION OF THOSE WHO CAME THREE THOUSAND MILES ACROSS THE WATER." [10]

Another aspect of the campaign was the necessity for Van Buren to mend fences and win new friends in the South if he were to be reelected, and much of the *Globe's* recent kind attention to Calhoun had probably been directed toward this end. Harrison as a young man had once belonged to an abolition society, and day after day the *Globe* emphasized this. The usual debates over the petitions for abolition in the District of Columbia were going on, and the *Globe* made clear the Whig identification with this movement. On February 5, 1840, the *Globe* heaped praise on Calhoun's anti-tariff speech, and expressed sorrow that Webster was not present to hear it and be converted to the views of his early manhood, when he was the advocate "of the agricultural, manufacturing, and commercial classes—not the stock-jobbing, speculating gentry."

In April, a slave ship en route from Washington, D.C., to South Carolina was driven by contrary winds to Bermuda, where the slaves were set free. Calhoun offered resolutions calling for the United States government to insist upon protection for the property of its citizens, and the *Globe* supported his position. The southern Whigs were silent, and numerous northern Whigs refused to vote on the resolutions. The *Globe* taunted them with "trying to please Northern Whiggery, now working to get Abolition votes for HARRISON." [11]

Blair also discovered that in 1821, in the Ohio Senate, Harrison had voted for a bill authorizing sheriffs to sell the services of those imprisoned for debt. Thus Harrison was "willing to *set negroes free, and sell white men into slavery!* !" Furthermore, those suffering this horrible fate had fallen into bondage because

Whig tariff and banking policies had "fixed them fast in the withering grip of poverty." [12]

The Whig *Intelligencer* answered that such charges were false and repulsive, but also chose to explain the legislation. The sale was for only a limited time, and there were similar laws in other regions. Also, selling convicts was better than keeping them confined for life in jail. [13]

Feeling that the Whigs had at last been stung, Blair next revealed that as governor of the Indiana Territory in 1807 Harrison had approved a similar law, which also allowed the punishment of both male and female runaways with thirty-nine stripes "*well* laid on at the public whipping post." American women, said Blair, should ponder this and then let their "husbands, lovers, fathers, and brothers, know what you think of making General Harrison President." [14]

Blair's attack on Harrison's ancient flirtation with abolition was countered by two forces: the nomination of slaveholder John Tyler for vice-president and the infamous case of Lieutenant George Mason Hooe of the United States Navy. In 1839 Lieutenant Hooe had ordered the flogging of several members of his crew, including a thirteen-year-old boy who received 120 lashes with a cat of four cords. Hooe was promptly court-martialed, convicted on several charges, and dismissed from the West India squadron at half pay. Among the numerous witnesses, however, were two Negro seamen, and Hooe appealed the decision on the grounds that Negro testimony had been used against him. After the federal district attorney and the attorney general had both ruled that the Negro testimony had had no bearing on the conviction, President Van Buren, in December 1839, refused to reverse the decision. More than six months later the Whigs suddenly discovered that Van Buren had approved of "Negro evidence against white men." On June 12, 1840, Representative John Minor Botts of Virginia introduced a resolution of inquiry into the case and charged that Van Buren was sanctioning a practice that would destroy the navy, humiliate its officers, and discredit the government. An amended version of this resolution passed the House, and was answered by the administration eleven days later. Meanwhile, according to Blair, the Whigs distributed throughout the South at least a hundred thousand handbills attack-

ing Van Buren for accepting "NEGRO EVIDENCE AGAINST WHITE
MEN." [15]

In the *Globe* Blair showed that the testimony of Negro seamen had always been accepted on board ships without objection
until this case, and that five of the seven white officers who had
tried the case were southerners. Most important, the conviction
had resulted from the undisputed testimony of white men, and
the Negro testimony was irrelevant.[16] The *Intelligencer* praised
Botts for bringing this disgraceful event before the public and
warned of the horrendous results such a precedent might bring.
Military officers would be degraded to the level of the Negro,
and honor and character would be at the mercy of slaves or servants. Van Buren had in fact endorsed "the complete overthrow
of all the distinctions and all the barriers which separate the two
races." [17] Blair answered with logic. "What if a crime were committed by a white officer in the presence of all Negroes?" If
Negroes were to serve, they must be allowed to testify. Otherwise, they should be excluded from the armed services.[18] In short,
debates about this irresponsible Whig tirade against "Negro evidence" occupied a vast amount of printed space, and the Whigs'
arguments probably carried a much stronger emotional impact
than the Democratic charges of Harrison's youthful flirtation with
abolition. Also, the latter was undoubtedly neutralized considerably by the presence of Tyler on the Whig ticket.

Harrison could not avoid the issues entirely. He denied that
he was either a black-cockade Federalist or an abolitionist. He
also insisted that he was not a Bank man and would not sign a
Bank bill unless "it was plain that the revenue of the union could
only be collected and disbursed in the most effectual way by means
of a bank." In the same speech he announced that the abolition
petitions were inconsistent with the theory and spirit of the Constitution and concluded with a vigorous reaffirmation of "the right
of the people to write and speak openly upon all matters of public
policy." [19]

The Seminole War in Florida did not actually involve many
people, but the inability to win the conflict was another mark
against Van Buren. The Whigs attacked the war as a needless
expense and blamed the president for the inability of the American soldiers to catch the Indians. The *Globe* and the Democrats

charged the Whigs with disloyalty to the brave men suffering in the swamps and jungles. When the War Department imported bloodhounds from Cuba for use in Florida, northeastern humanitarians wailed over this frightful cruelty. When the administration insisted that the dogs were for finding the Indians but not for attacking them, and announced that the dogs would henceforth be muzzled, other opponents became angry over this waste of dog-power. To the *Charleston Mercury*, which had denounced Secretary of War Joel Poinsett for the muzzling, the *Globe* replied: "Their virtue is in their nose, not in their teeth." As it turned out, the dogs had been trained exclusively for chasing Negro slaves, and were worse than useless against the Indians. They dragged the soldiers and accompanying caravans of dog food and supplies in circles through the Everglades without ever finding or biting any Indians. The *Globe's* efforts to defend the administration on the issue were almost equally handicapped.[20]

The most devastating broadsides the *Globe* had to absorb and repel, however, were the false charges concerning Van Buren's personal habits. Blair was kept busy denying that Van Buren had opposed the War of 1812, that he was a Catholic, and that he was actually an Irishman who had "sent off immense sums of the public money to Ireland." In the *New York Herald* James Gordon Bennett suggested that there might be some children at Kinderhook with "light hair and small cunning eyes" and no knowledge of their father, but Blair ignored this. Three scurrilous biographies of Van Buren, the most famous being that ascribed to Davy Crockett, also made the rounds. The Crockett book, worst of the three, had a wide following because of Davy's own legendary and largely mythical frontier career, and was written in a crude vernacular easy to remember and retell among those unlikely to read it. To Crockett, Van Buren was "as opposite to General Jackson as dung is to a diamond," and only his whiskers made it possible to distinguish "whether he was man or woman."[21]

In April, a debate over an appropriation to repair and improve the White House enabled Representative Charles Ogle of Pennsylvania, a protégé of Thaddeus Stevens, to deliver a three-day speech that was quickly published in two parts. *On the Regal Splendor of the President's Palace* and *On the Pretended Democracy of Martin Van Buren* were mailed out by the tens of thousands under the congressional franking privilege. Ogle described the White House as a "PALACE *as splendid as that of the Caesars, and as richly adorned as the proudest Asiatic mansion,*" located on grounds that had been rearranged to form several "clever sized hills, every pair . . . designed to resemble . . . AN AMAZON'S BOSOM, with a miniature . . . hillock on its apex, to denote the n—ple." Inside Ogle found "SILK TASSELS, GALLOON, GIMP AND SATIN MEDALLIONS," foreign-made carpets "deep enough for a good locofoco democrat to bury his foot in," and "FRENCH BEDSTEADS," all of which were both an insult to and a discrimination against native American mechanics, weavers, dyers, and manufacturers. In the "Court Banqueting room" Ogle found no hog and hominy, fried meat and gravy, or hard cider, which were "vulgar foods" in the eyes of "*gourmands, French cooks, and locofoco Presidents.*" Instead the table, furnished with "*massive gold plate and French sterling silver services,*" was graced with a seven-course French dinner that would take at least five hours, the normal time "required by Kings and democratic Presidents to masticate a state dinner." And what, asked Ogle, would honest democrats say to Van Buren for wasting public money on "FOREIGN FANNY KEMBLE GREEN FINGER CUPS, in which to wash his pretty tapering, soft, white lilly fingers, after dining on fricandeau de veau and omelette souffle?" In another room, Ogle complained, the president had four $2,400 mirrors so wide and high that he could ride his horse into the room and admire the horse's hooves and his own crown at the same time. And equally vain and wasteful, the president had spent $2 for only one chamber pot, and had actually installed a bathtub in the White House, when all previous presidents had been content with a simple shower bath. In fact, John Quincy Adams had "indulged his aristocratic propensities" each morning by bathing in the Potomac. Van Buren, however, had discovered that "the pleasures of the warm or tepid bath" were "the proper accompaniments of a palace life." In short, Ogle would oppose the $3,665 appropriation for fear it would be spent for a throne and "a *crown, diadem, sceptre, and royal jewels.*" [22]

Blair and his fellow Democrats could neither ignore Ogle nor refute him in language colorful enough to match the speech in repeatability, and the Whig press kept the stories going till the end of the campaign. Thousands of copies were franked out to constituents by members of Congress, and the *Louisville Journal* informed its readers that Van Buren's rage at the Ogle speech had caused him to "actually burst his corset."

Blair complained that Ogle's "low tirade" had cost the Treasury at least $25,000 in the expenses of Congress, and showed conclusively that the speech was a lie from start to finish. In September Blair listed the total spent on the White House by each of its occupants: John Adams, $14,000; Jefferson, $29,000; Madison, $28,000; Monroe, $50,000; John Q. Adams, $20,000; Jackson, $39,000; and Van Buren, only $20,000. All of these expenses—including the disbursements by John Q. Adams of $4.50 for a valve in the water closet and cleaning the pipes, $2.50 for repair of a leak in the water closet, and 37½ cents each for two chamber pots—were obviously entirely necessary. Countering the Ogle stories, however, was like trying to dam up a stream with sand.[23]

Quoting from Ogle's speech the false charge that the administration was costing Americans $4,250.87 per hour and $70.84 per minute, the Whigs warned further that to pay these expenses and reward corrupt officials, the administration was about to impose a direct tax on the people. The census of 1840, according to a widespread Whig rumor, was a plot to gather information to be used in assessing these direct taxes. Blair pointed out in vain that the census questions had been written by Whigs and that the act providing for the census had been introduced by a Whig. Census takers everywhere had many difficulties, and Andrew Jackson later argued that the Democrats lost Tennessee because of the foolish questions asked by the census takers.[24]

The Democrats of 1840 and several generations of historians came to believe that the election of 1840 was settled primarily by foolish trivialities. Many voters, however, may have been instinctively motivated by far more practical considerations. Whatever Harrison's carefully concealed personal principles, the longtime economic goals of Clay, Webster, and the Whig party in general were well known. Perhaps even more important, Van Buren's clear-cut deflationary and laissez-faire program, climaxed by the passage of the bill creating the Independent Treasury on June 30, 1840, coincided with a sharp new dip in the national economy.

The year 1840 did bring the nation its first favorable balance of payments since 1830, but this did not produce higher living standards right away. More obvious to western Americans on the make in 1839–1840, the number of banks fell from 901 to 840, total bank resources declined from $702,382,000 to $657,750,000, and the total money supply fell from $222,171,000 to $189,969,000. However loudly the *Globe* might denounce reports of low prices and economic distress as Whig inventions for misleading the public, the statistics were on the side of the Whigs. Newspaper advertisements offering $3 a barrel for flour if Van Buren were elected and $6 if Harrison should win, and similar disparate prices for numerous other articles, were not exactly fair tactics, but they probably had an impact. The *Globe's* regular flaunting of the financial policies and principles of the administration was an honorable tactic in the best tradition of the democratic ideal that the voting public should have a clear idea of what candidates and parties stand for. Despite Harrison's silence, those voters willing to read had a clear-cut referendum on financial policies. Unhappily for Van Buren and Blair, however, their principles had little appeal for many thousands of voters hungry for credit, liquid capital, and higher prices. Editor James Gordon Bennett was probably correct in his view that while songs and hard cider might affect "loafers without wives, and office seekers without breeches," the low prices touched "a nerve that vibrated to the breast, among all calm thinking, and reflecting men with wives and children."[25]

In the final weeks of the campaign Blair continued to express confidence in the popular wisdom, but, significantly, the *Globe* was not advertising bets on the election. Above all, Blair warned almost daily, Democrats everywhere must look out for fraud in the balloting. Actually, the voting procedures did encourage irregularities. No state yet had the secret ballot, and the argument that the delicate sensibilities of women could not be subjected to the vulgar and violent scenes at polling places was in part justified. The voter asked for his ballot in the midst of angry partisans who threatened as well as cajoled while he was making his final decisions. Also, the voting took place over a two-week period. Ohio and Pennsylvania voted on October 30, eleven other states followed on November 2, and the final twelve made their decisions at various times between November 3 and November 11. The earlier results, naturally enough, tended to create a bandwagon effect, and each party accused the other of taking voters from state to state. Whig pamphlets charged the administration with sending warships from port to port to enable the sailors to vote several times, and compared the "harpies of the Custom houses," the "pirates of the Post Office," and the census takers to the "locusts of Egypt," seeking to "influence, control and overawe the ELECTIONS OF THE PEOPLE."

The *Globe* in turn claimed knowledge of Whig voting frauds in ten states. Blair's great villain in Pennsylvania was Thaddeus Stevens, and his attacks on Stevens began a personal enmity that would continue through the days of southern Reconstruction. Blair was convinced that five hundred "BULLIES" had been shipped to Philadelphia from Baltimore to vote for Harrison. "LOOK TO THE BALLOT BOXES!" the *Globe* warned daily. Several days before the election in New York, James B. Glentworth, the Whig state tobacco commissioner, was imprisoned on sworn testimony that he had imported several loads of repeaters from Philadelphia to vote in Manhattan. At first the New York Whigs insisted that the extra voters were workers hired to lay pipe for the Croton aqueduct. Further documentation, however, led to an admission by Moses Grinnell and others that they had indeed supplied some $4,000 to the workers through Glentworth. They insisted further, however, that they had spent the money to assist in detecting voters imported by the Democrats.[26]

Blair and Van Buren had hoped that this sensational revelation would cause a wave of revulsion among voters everywhere, but the federal district attorney could not prove that the pipelayers had actually voted, and a friendly grand jury refused to indict Glentworth. "The Loco Foco bomb," announced the *Intelligencer*, had "exploded." The impact upon an electorate beset by charges and countercharges on all sides was obviously negligible.

As the election results slowly made their way to Washington, Blair held out hope as long as possible. The sad day finally came, however, when he, daughter Lizzie, and Martin Van Buren, Jr., had to take the unhappy tidings to the president where he was visiting out in the country. At the gate, Blair and young Martin remained reluctant to carry out their mission and momentarily turned their horses back down the main road. As Lizzie hesitantly sat her horse near the gate the kindly president came to the door. "Come on in, my dear," he called, "I saw those cowards ride past the gate and I know that if their news had been good they would have come with you." [27] Van Buren had carried only three southern states: Alabama, Virginia, and South Carolina. He had lost the entire East except for New Hampshire, and had carried only Illinois, Missouri, and Arkansas in the West. The popular vote, however, was very close: 1,275,017 to 1,128,702, and a change of only a few thousand votes in key states would have meant a Van Buren victory instead of a Harrison electoral college landslide.

Van Buren's defeat was not Blair's only concern in 1840. His daughter, Elizabeth, kept family, friends, and doctors convinced that she either had or was on the verge of having tuberculosis, and by October her current physician was insisting that she must go to a warm climate for the winter. Naturally she would have to be accompanied, and the parents finally agreed that her father must be the escort. Blair tried to change the original plan and send Eliza, but Eliza, probably convinced that her husband needed the journey also, firmly demurred. Blair, therefore, sent Ben Gratz a sealed copy of a new will, and father and daughter embarked for Havana at New York on November 5. The election returns were still coming in, but the issue had been settled before they left Washington. Unfortunately a fierce storm, which had Blair feeling at the point of death before the ship even left the narrows, forced a return to the harbor and a delay of several days.

During the waiting period, Blair offered further solace to his defeated friend. He had expected to find the Whigs engaged in wild rejoicing, but instead they looked "like a gang of downcast Devils—Like felons they probably feel that it is not safe to make a great hurrah over their ill acquired fortune." Van Buren's supporters, Blair added, were "too proud of the administration which they have so ardently supported for its purity, wisdom & patriotism, to be humbled by a defeat accomplished through crimes." He regretted being compelled to leave his post, but his daughter's life demanded it, even though her cough was already much better.[28]

Elizabeth Blair did not have tuberculosis or any other ailment serious enough to prevent a long, active, and useful life, but her delicate health kept her loved ones worried to the end of her eighty-eight years. Assuming that the preventive treatments prescribed by doctors and family did not involve some habit or habits that made her a constant victim of the common cold, an amateur diagnostician might well suspect the possibility of an allergy or perhaps a minor glandular problem whose nature a future generation would understand better. She was an expert horsewoman, she could boast on at least one occasion of winning a foot-race against several young competitors, and the life depicted by her letters clearly involved great amounts of energy. Perhaps her sporadic illnesses were partly conditioned by the overpowering personalities of her parents and brothers, who had long since assigned her to an invalid status and appointed themselves to be her loving protectors.

As Francis Preston Blair and his ailing twenty-one-year-old daughter watched New York recede into the distance, he was probably also convinced that he was removing her from an additional menace. At some point in 1839, her dashing brother Jim had brought home from the South Seas an even more handsome friend, Lieutenant Samuel Phillips Lee. Lizzie's habit of writing undated letters makes the chronology difficult to follow, but at least as early as November 1839 Lieutenant Lee was being feted in the Blair home, where the warm hospitality of Mrs. Blair was in marked contrast to the icy civility of her husband. Jim, who was closest in age to Lizzie, delighted in teasing her about his friend, and her immediate response to both the teasing and its subject was quite obvious. The young officer's antecedents were impressive. Although his father, Francis Lightfoot Lee, had succumbed to alcoholism at an early age, his grandfather was Richard Henry Lee, the noted patriot of the Revolutionary period. Blair, however, decided immediately that his darling child was not strong enough to marry anyone, and that in any case she could never be happy with a professional naval officer. Also, despite the distinguished record of the Lee family, this particular member had been sent to sea as a midshipman when he was only thirteen years old and had no financial resources beyond his naval salary. Perhaps, thought Blair, he was interested only in the modest Blair fortune. This suspicion was not very complimentary to Lizzie, and for many months it remained a secret shared only by Blair and his elder son, Montgomery.[29]

Blair was highly satisfied with the rest of his family. Montgomery was happily married to Caroline Buckner, daughter of a prosperous planter, and was preparing to begin a highly successful law career under the eye of Thomas Hart Benton in St. Louis. Ben Gratz was already urging that Blair allow Montgomery to make a thorough investigation of his father's financial affairs and arrange them with an eye to a more secure future. Montgomery in turn was constantly on the lookout for investments that would give Blair "an anchor to windward" if the political skies should darken. Blair was also constantly involved with loans and gifts to his sisters—two of whom had married chronic failures—to various nephews, and to his stepbrother from his father's second marriage. Gratz, who usually managed all such affairs, protested that Blair should let these relatives solve their own problems, but the editor could never forget his own days of poverty and humiliation, and he was invariably generous with both his money and his advice.

Even Frank, Blair's almost incorrigible favorite, was giving evidence of improvement. Writing from Princeton in July 1840, Frank asked for $50 and "a letter from you which shall not be wrung from you by some fresh instance of my misconduct, for altho I cannot boast of having conducted myself this session in a faultless manner—I yet hope it will be considered an improvement on my past life and an earnest of better things." [30]

In due time the devoted father left his charge in Cuba with Mrs. Septimus Meckelhaar, a granddaughter of Thomas Jefferson, and made the long journey home. Whatever the extent of Lizzie's illness, she enjoyed the next few months immensely and finally returned in excellent health and spirits, influenced strongly by word from a friend that Lieutenant Lee was overjoyed by the news of her improved condition.[31]

Chapter 11

The Maverick

BLAIR returned to Washington eager for the struggle that he hoped would vindicate the democratic system by restoring Van Buren to his rightful place in 1844. The journey had produced various rumors, but Rives in the *Globe* had warned their enemies against premature "ecstasies," because he would "be at his post before GENERAL HARRISON declares his principles." [1]

The early weeks of 1841 were spent happily taunting the "log cabin" Whigs for their opposition to Benton's "log cabin" bill designed to grant permanent preemption rights to actual settlers on unsold government lands. When the new president delivered an inaugural address advocating the usual Whig principles, Blair spent days denouncing each policy one by one.

Understandably enough, the Whigs fought back. According to a longstanding practice the outgoing Senate had elected Blair and Rives as printers for the next session. The new Senate, however, refused to honor the contract, even though Blair showed that the printing by the *Madisonian* for two years had cost more than the *Globe* had charged for four. The *Globe,* he pleaded, had already invested $40,000 in equipment and supplies to do the work and by law had been promised the job for at least two years.

Henry Clay, however, was adamant. He would dismiss them "on the ground of infamy of character of the print and the Printer. . . . [The Senate] owed it to the purity of the national character to disconnect themselves at once and forever from these men."

Senator William B. King of Alabama replied that "for kindness of heart, humanity, and exemplary deportment as a private citizen," Blair "could compare proudly with the Senator from Kentucky, or any Senator on this floor." On the following day, Clay, "cheerfully" withdrew "every epithet disparaging to his [Blair's] character," but the *Globe*'s contracts were revoked by a straight party vote of 26–18.[2]

On April 5, 1841, the *Globe*'s daily tirades against the Whigs were interrupted by a black-bordered edition announcing the death of President Harrison. He had caught a severe cold on Inauguration Day, and a steady swarm of office seekers had given him no time to recover. Since Harrison was the first president to die in office, a controversy quickly rose over whether John Tyler was in fact president or merely assuming the duties of the office. While others debated, Tyler took the oath of office and moved into the White House. A later congressional resolution confirmed his judgment, and the pattern for the future was thereby established.

Henry Clay and the Whig Congress soon had many reasons to mourn their fallen leader, because his successor had never supported the Whig party's economic principles. Over the next several months, the Congress passed most of the legislation Clay and Webster had advocated for years. One at a time, however, two tariff bills, the distribution of the funds collected from public land sales, and two long-drawn-out efforts to create a new United States Bank fell victim to presidential vetoes. Tyler did approve the repeal of the Independent Treasury, but his bank vetoes left the Treasury no place but state banks for keeping the national funds. Only an $11 million Treasury deficit finally compelled Tyler to accept a mild tariff considered inadequate by his party.

On the last day of the 1841 session, fifty Whigs met on Capitol Square and officially announced their repudiation of John Tyler. The president was a man without a party, and the *Lexington Intelligencer* spoke for orthodox Whigdom: "If a God-directed thunderbolt were to strike and annihilate the traitor, all would say that Heaven is just."

In September 1841 everyone in Tyler's cabinet except Webster resigned. The secretary of state was negotiating the northeastern boundary dispute with Great Britain and felt that his talents could not be spared. In March 1842 Henry Clay resigned from the Senate as a further protest against Tyler, delivered a dramatic speech of farewell, and returned home to begin running for president in 1844.

This collapse of Whiggery was accompanied by remarkable surface unity among the Democrats as the erstwhile bitter enemies Benton and Calhoun joined forces against Clay's ill-fated program. Calhoun, who had once denounced Jackson's vetoes as unbridled tyranny, now discovered that the veto "was a high conservative power, intended not only to guard . . . the people against the encroachments of Congress, but also the weaker interests of the community against the oppression and plunder, of the stronger . . . a high and salutary power . . . almost incapable of abuse." He had once introduced a distribution program and had supported the United States Bank against Jackson. In August 1841 he denounced both and proclaimed his refusal to believe "that this free, gallant, and enlightened people, are prepared to sink down into base servitude to an odious moneyed power."[3]

The apparent harmony among the Democrats, however, would clearly have difficulty surviving the presidential nominating convention of 1844. An election victory appeared inevitable, and the party had a surfeit of candidates. Blair, Jackson, and Benton, of course, were passionately committed to Martin Van Buren, and Blair had the task of promoting his friend while appearing to remain neutral. Speeches of the other candidates, and particularly those of Calhoun, were highly praised, but every Democrat knew where the *Globe*'s sentiments really lay. In the spring of 1842, the *Globe* carried a running account of Van Buren's triumphant tour of the West and down the rivers to visit Andrew Jackson at the Hermitage, and every speech and cheering crowd was fully reported. In January 1843 conventions for Van Buren, James Buchanan, Lewis Cass, Calhoun, and Richard M. Johnson received extensive coverage, but Blair gave the Van Buren affair the most attention. It occurred, appropriately enough, on January 8, the anniversary of the Battle of New Orleans, and Jackson's long public letter explaining his inability to attend a celebration was filled with praise for Van Buren.

In April and May 1843 Blair left the *Globe* with Rives and Frank, Jr., and made his own long-delayed pilgrimage to Nashville. The paper lost none of its spirit in the hands of the substitute editors. Young Fletcher Webster, son of Daniel, was

appointed secretary of legation for China, and Frank Blair, no
stranger to Washington nightlife, promptly denounced Webster
as a "frequenter of hells," with "nothing but his father's vices
to qualify him for this situation." When Webster's friends
threatened to sue the *Globe* for libel, Frank editorialized that the
paper had the evidence to support its statements. No suit was
filed.[4]

Rives enjoyed being an editor. When one of his editorials
provoked the threat of a duel against Blair, Rives assumed full
credit and added: "We stand six feet four inches and a half in
our stocking feet; weigh 215 pounds neat; can run and go *half
hammond* forty feet. . . . Our true calling, as we now understand it, is 'fighting with our heels.' It would take a wise man to
convince us that nature . . . made so large a mark . . . to
stand up, and be shot at—we may say, shot *into*; for our *least
exposure* is nearly as large as a barndoor, which a coward can
hardly help hitting, if he shuts his eyes." After this disclaimer,
however, Rives invited the challenger to bring with him "the
whole 'Tyler party.' " Rives described Tyler's situation as "the
happiest imaginable . . . he has just enough offices for his
friends, and friends enough for his offices." [5]

Blair, meanwhile, filled the *Globe* with heartwarming letters
from the Hermitage. Jackson had greeted him like a long-lost
son. On Sunday they had attended church, and Jackson had led
the way to the communion table. He had refused to join a church
while in politics, the old man confided, because he feared charges
of hypocrisy, but he had promised Rachel he would join when
his political wars were ended, and the promise had been kept.[6]

In August 1843 Amos Kendall announced in his struggling
new paper, the *Expositor*, that he would support Tyler against Clay
if they should be the candidates, and asked if the *Globe* agreed.
The *Globe*, replied Blair, would support neither. His position
against readmitting Tyler to the Democratic fold had already
been stated: "Injured wives do frequently relent to a repentant
husband, but never when he brings his paramours home with
him." Tyler had "a train of the most notorious political pros-
titues—not to say the veriest bawds—ever known in this or
any other country." Kendall was suffering hard times and desperately wanted the House printing, which, however, was

awarded to Blair. Blair, who was preparing to pay half of a $4,000 security note he had signed for Kendall, was much irritated by his old friend's flirting with the Tyler faction. Kendall later charged bitterly that he had never been sufficiently paid for his role in founding the *Globe,* and he and Blair were never reconciled—to the great consternation of their mutual friends. Rives finally proved that Kendall had received $28,609, and pointed out that the paper became self-supporting only after he himself had bought a half-interest and assumed the management. Kendall ultimately became a rich philanthropist, founded Gallaudet College for the deaf, and served as its first president— thereby reconfirming his faith in the inevitable success of the righteous.[7]

Blair did try to remain neutral on the vice-presidential nomination, and thereby sowed bad seeds for his own future. In January 1844 a two-column letter from "Amicus" argued that Alabama senator William R. King would be a stronger candidate and was more loyal to Van Buren than James K. Polk of Tennessee. A week later, an equally long communication from "A Tennessee Democrat" urged the qualifications of Polk and protested the invidious comparisons made by Amicus. Another lengthy letter for Polk from *"A TENNESSEEAN"* continued the argument, but Amicus was given the final word with a letter insisting that Polk should be rewarded only after he won Tennessee back from Whig control. Both sides had been heard, editorialized Blair, and the *Globe* would print no more on the subject.[8] James K. Polk would later remember only the sentiments of Amicus and identify them with Blair himself.

On February 2, 1844, Blair probably breathed a sigh of relief as he published Calhoun's official withdrawal from the presidential contest. He would abide by the convention decision, wrote Calhoun, but he would not support any candidate who did not publicly oppose abolition and the tariff or who had any friends or backers who did support either of these policies. These conditions, said the *Globe,* would make Van Buren a virtually unanimous choice.

Calhoun's conditions, however, were more stringent than they appeared, because he would design his own test for being pro-slavery. He had already insisted that Texas should be annexed

as evidence of northern goodwill toward the South. To Van
Buren and Blair, however, Texas was a very complex problem.
The Texas boundary as defined by Texas included large parts
of four Mexican provinces that neither by law nor right of conquest had ever been part of the Mexican province of Texas.
Clearly, this boundary would have to be adjusted either by
negotiations or by force. Furthermore, the abolitionists were
still arguing that the Texas revolution was a plot to increase the
territory and political power of slavery in the United States.

Both Jackson and Van Buren as presidents had fully expected
and favored the annexation of Texas, but they had rejected overtures from Texas pending settlement of its conflict with Mexico.
Webster, as Tyler's secretary of state, had taken the same position. In 1842–1843, however, the efforts of Britain to gain influence in Texas brought the issue again into sharp focus. Particularly galling to southerners was the fact that the British chargé
d'affaires in Texas was openly antislavery and had publicly suggested that Britain should offer Texas an enormous loan in return for the abolition of Texas slavery. By the spring of 1844 the
British had recognized the futility of this project, but Sam Houston had shrewdly played a game of arousing fears in the
United States. The idea that annexation might become necessary
to save Texas from Britain was firmly planted in many American
minds.

Congressman Thomas Gilmer of Virginia had published
a dramatic warning that Texas must be saved from the greedy
clutches of England, and in early 1843 Congressman Aaron V.
Brown forwarded this appeal to Andrew Jackson. Senator Robert
J. Walker of Mississippi, deeply involved with Texas bonds
and land warrants, followed with a letter brilliantly designed
to rouse Jackson's phobia against everything British. On March
12, the old man responded by vigorously endorsing immediate
annexation in a letter to Brown. Almost immediately, Gilmer
took the letter to Blair for publication in the *Globe*. For once,
however, Blair had second thoughts about the judgment of his
hero, and he simply declined to publish the letter for almost a
year.[9]

In February 1844, however, Brown took Jackson's letter
back from Blair, and the editor was finally compelled to grapple

with Texas. He and Benton and Van Buren had never doubted that Texas would eventually join the Union as a slave state, but they also saw the dangers of the issue. They did not want a war with Mexico, and they did not want a sectional quarrel between North and South.[10]

Democratic party unity on the Texas issue seemed at least possible, but fate soon intervened. On February 14, 1844, the *Globe* reported the arrival of the magnificent new warship *Princeton*, which had recently beaten the British *Great Western* in a formal race. On February 24, a happy gathering of dignitaries and their families enjoyed a cruise down the Potomac on the *Princeton*, and the guns were fired for entertainment. One of them burst, however, and six people, including Gilmer (by now secretary of the navy) and Secretary of State Abel Upshur, were killed. Six sailors were badly wounded, and Captain Stockton and Senator Benton were less seriously injured. Six days later, President Tyler appointed John C. Calhoun secretary of state.[11]

With Calhoun in direct control of American relations with Texas, Mexico, and Britain, all hope for an annexation acceptable to both North and South disappeared. To the Carolinian, Texas was the ideal opportunity to force a sectional confrontation on the slavery question. If the North refused to accept a Texas treaty based upon a moral defense of slavery, it would only confirm the warnings he had been trumpeting since 1832, If his program also splintered the Democratic party and destroyed the presidential hopes of Martin Van Buren, this result would be a proper punishment for his own rejection.

On March 18 Blair finally sent Van Buren a copy of Jackson's letter to Brown, and explained his own long delay in communicating it. He warned that the document would carry great influence with the Democratic party and added that he "should not be surprised if Mr. Calhoun was to give new features to the contemplated treaty calculated to defeat it for the present & make it a main question for the next canvas. . . . he may seek to introduce stipulations on the negro question colored to make it odious in the north & peculiarly a Southern question." The "craze of *acquisitiveness*," he added, was "very strongly developed in our people especially the Democrats—& they will never rest until they have driven England from our continent & neighboring islands." Unfortunately, as Blair also explained to Van Buren, he was going through this crisis of decision while suffering terribly from an infected ear, a boil on his back, and the extraction of a tooth without modern anesthesia. Only a parcel of leeches behind his ear had given him sufficient composure to write.[12]

On March 20 the *Globe* finally published Jackson's letter calling for annexation of Texas, but for the next three weeks the paper took no editorial position despite numerous queries and pressures. Walker made several vain efforts to show Blair some further secret communications from Jackson, and finally on April 13, he wrote an angry letter warning that the *Globe*'s silence would be "ruinous" to the Democratic party. Walker hoped Blair would inform Jackson that he had done his best to show him the documents, and deplored both Blair's illness and the "irreparable injury" done to the party as well as the country. Blair, however, was determined to risk damage to the party and his own political influence rather than endorse what he considered a dangerous policy.[13]

On April 12 Rives learned that a Texas annexation treaty had been signed. On April 15 an editorial dictated by Blair to Rives finally explained that the editor had for six weeks suffered an illness "so extremely painful as to disable him from thinking, reading, or writing, and . . . from conversation with his friends." The *Globe*, however, would now "earnestly advocate the reannexation of Texas to the Union." Nevertheless, Blair insisted, "it is proper, if possible, that the consent of Mexico should be conciliated to any arrangement we may make with Texas. It is due to our honor, and to our interests."

Blair had expected Calhoun to send his treaty to the Senate on April 15, but the Carolinian instead fulfilled all of the suspicions Blair had expressed to Van Buren on March 18. Instead of minimizing the slavery issue and arguing for Texas as a national acquisition of great value to the whole Union, Calhoun held the treaty another week and finally presented it to the Senate as a project for saving slavery in Texas. The British government had written the late secretary of state a long letter denying any efforts past or future to interfere with slavery in either Texas or the American South. Almost as a conscience-saving afterthought, however, Lord Aberdeen added that "although we shall not desist from those open and honest efforts which we have constantly made for procuring the abolition of slavery throughout the world, we shall neither openly nor secretly resort to any measures which can tend to disturb their [the southern states'] internal tranquillity." Six days after the treaty had been unofficially announced and three days after Blair's editorial indicating that he and Van Buren would support the annexation, Calhoun wrote a long answer to the British letter. Ignoring the bulk of the letter, he accused the British of abolitionist designs on Texas, announced that his treaty was designed to prevent this catastrophe, and concluded with a lengthy essay on the glories of slavery. The letter was released to the press, delivered to the British, and included as a major document accompanying the treaty. On such a basis, no northern senator could vote for the treaty without voting by implication for the moral righteousness of slavery. If northerners would not do this, wrote Calhoun, it could only mean "that the spirit of faction and opposition to the South on the ground of slavery are stronger than the love of country." [14]

Blair immediately concluded that Calhoun had taken these steps just to make it impossible for Van Buren to accept the treaty. On April 26 he was still too sick to write, but the *Globe* tried to minimize the possible damage. Others, it announced, had surmised that Blair's editorial of April 15 had forced Tyler to add arguments that no northern man could accept, but this view was "weak, silly, and ridiculous." Van Buren could "go for Texas without going for, or subscribing to, Mr. Tyler's arguments in favor of slavery. . . . Is there any man out of the mad house, or the white house, who would go against the annexation of Texas because Mr. Tyler has lugged slavery into the question, as a bugbear to keep Mr. Van Buren from going for it? We hope not."

Van Buren, however, stuck to the same position he had always taken, and opposed the treaty primarily because of its ruthless approach to Mexico. He and Clay had submitted letters that were published simultaneously on April 27. Clay emphasized the dangers of sectional conflict and disunion and made his opposition clear. Van Buren was all for annexation, but only when it could be done peacefully. In a war with Mexico, he said, "we could not justify ourselves in the eyes of mankind. . . . It has hitherto been our boast, that, whilst the lust for power, with fraud and violence in its train, has led other and differently constituted governments to aggression and conquest, our movements in these respects have always been regulated to these considerations . . . whether we stand or fall in the estimation of our countrymen, it is always true wisdom, as well as true morality, to hold fast to the truth." He did not believe Texas was seriously threatened by any European power, but if a majority of the American people clearly felt that annexation was being delayed past a danger point, he would follow the popular will as expressed by the Congress.

Benton followed with an even more outspoken letter. Texas, he wrote, was that area defined as such by the Treaty of 1819, and did not include "the capital, and forty towns and villages of New Mexico! now and always as fully under the dominion of the Republic of Mexico as Quebec and all towns and villages of Canada are under the dominion of Great Britain." The annexation could and must be accomplished without an unnecessary "cost in national honor—in foreign war—in ruined commerce—in domestic dissension—in sectional animosities—and in the disturbance of the harmony of the Union and the business of the people." [15]

Shaky at best, Van Buren's hold on the Democratic party in the Northwest and South began to collapse immediately, while Benton was destined for reelection by only a tiny majority in a state where he had ruled supreme for twenty-four years. A more prudent and self-seeking editor might have printed the various statements and taken a position of editorial neutrality with a promise to support the ultimate platform of the party convention. By pleading his role of official editor for all Democrats, Blair might well have come through the brief preconvention period and the election campaign with no serious personal damage. Andrew Jackson, after all, was on the other side, and Blair had never opposed the old man before. Furthermore, he owed no political debts to either Benton or Van Buren, while on March 15 the House of Representatives that had just elected him its printer had voted down by 129–40 a resolution against the annexation of Texas.

Blair and his *Globe,* however, had always portrayed Jackson as an incorruptible hero who disregarded personal consequences and did only what he thought was right, and the editor himself could do no less than live up to the image. His letter to Van Buren on March 18 and his qualified editorial of April 15 showed clearly his agreement with Benton that Calhoun's treaty threatened the Union with a dishonorable war and a dangerous internal conflict. As he later wrote Van Buren, Jackson had "allowed his patriotic ardor about Texas to outrun every other feeling. He confidently believed you would go with him as I did that you would go with me." [16] Blair believed quite correctly that Calhoun had left Mexico no alternative but war to the surrender of territory not part of Texas and had wrapped it in a pro-slavery package that northern politicians could not accept. His painful illness had been as much an excuse as a reason for his delay.

Van Buren and Benton had suddenly become anathema to the South and West, but the *Globe* had only the highest praise for both. Never had the former "presented to the country a production more creditable to his talents, his patriotism, or his character as a statesman." Benton's letter was "that plain, direct, straight forward expression of facts and opinions which the American people have been so long taught to look for from his tongue and his pen." In the Senate Benton took the lead in thunderous speeches against the treaty, while the *Globe* lashed Calhoun with the charge that he had deliberately repulsed the northern states to make ratification of the treaty impossible and foment a new sectional conflict.[17]

The excitement provoked by this and other issues and the pain of illness were not the only concerns at the Blair home in May 1844. Along with the arguments over Texas, Oregon, slavery, disunion, and political nominations, the *Globe* on May 9 carried a brief advertisement for a "wet-nurse, who can produce satisfactory testimonials of character" to "apply at the residence of F. P. Blair opposite the War Department on Pennsylvania Avenue." Montgomery Blair's young wife had died in childbirth on January 11, and the grieving father had brought his small daughter Betty and infant daughter home to their grandparents.

When the Democratic convention opened on May 27, Blair was still under a doctor's care, but the *Globe* had reporters covering the convention. Its editors also anxiously awaited the news filtering in on the newly constructed telegraph wire linking Washington with Baltimore. Only four days earlier its inventor, Samuel B. Morse, had transmitted his famous message, "What hath God wrought?" The line was an experiment by Congress, which, however, refused to buy the invention. Soon Morse would team up with Amos Kendall, whose unique organizational and promotional talents would eventually make both of them immensely rich. For the moment, however, Morse was still wondering if his invention was worth the trouble, Kendall was struggling to avoid bankruptcy, and Blair and Rives were primarily concerned with what had been wrought by Robert J. Walker and other annexationist Democrats.

At the convention Benjamin F. Butler of New York made an impassioned two-hour plea against the adoption of a two-thirds rule, but the unanimous vote of the South plus Michigan, Indiana, Illinois, and Arkansas and a few scattered votes from other states passed the rule by 148–116. When it was clear that Van Buren could not get a two-thirds vote, Butler withdrew his name and cast New York's vote for James K. Polk. The convention ended with paeans of praise for the great statesman Martin Van Buren, but the party's choice for president was Polk, on a platform calling for all of Texas and all of Oregon as soon as possible.

It was a sad time for the Blair family. The editor was still suffering from ailments that might have killed someone with less endurance, and Montgomery's infant daughter died of whooping cough and complications while her father was attending the Baltimore convention. The general misery was only compounded by the fate of Van Buren. Blair hastened to write the New Yorker that "the corrupted intriguers" would ultimately gain only immediate disappointment and lasting anathema & disgrace." [18]

The *Globe*, however, had nothing but praise for Polk, "a man of ability, unquestioned probity, untiring energy and sound judgment." Also, Polk's nomination would give "the old hero of the Hermitage the satisfaction of witnessing the return of his beloved Tennessee to the Democratic fold." Van Buren "would rather see a ray of joy gild the evening of the life of his venerable friend of the Hermitage, than achieve a new triumph for himself." The *Globe*, Blair promised, would support Polk and the Democratic party.[19]

On June 7 Calhoun's Texas treaty, opposed even by 9 of the 20 voting southerners, was rejected by the Senate, 35–16. The dead treaty, exulted the *Globe*, had "an inheritance of constitutional infirmities from its father enough to bring down 'twenty mortal murders on its crown,' " and its extinction would "give birth to a legislative measure which will bring Texas into the Union with flying colors—a measure beginning with conciliation in Mexico, and hence rallying the moral sense of the whole American people in support." [20]

Blair's hoped-for solution was a bill introduced by Benton. It would annex Texas only after negotiation of the boundary dispute with Mexico and would divide Texas into one slave state equal in size to the largest existing state and two approximately equal territories, one slave and one free. This, argued Benton in the Senate and Blair in the *Globe*, would accomplish the inevitable annexation without an unjust war with Mexico or a sectional quarrel that might split the Union. After a furious exchange on the Senate floor with George McDuffie of South Carolina, Benton was greeted with a congratulatory handshake from the ancient Jacksonian enemy John Quincy Adams. The two old men agreed that despite past differences they would spend their remaining years defending the Union. Reading of this aberration, Andrew Jackson needed no further proof of Benton's "derangement," and warned Blair that any further support for Benton would ruin the *Globe*. Still racked with pain, Blair spent many hours writing long letters seeking to explain and justify his friends to their old idol. On June 13, Benton's program was defeated by only five votes on a straight party basis.[21]

Blair dutifully supported Polk. He made Polk's position on Texas sound more similar to his own views than was justified by either the platform or the candidate's own statements, and he carried on a vicious running attack against Clay. In various ways, however, he defied the party's leaders, including Jackson himself. The failure of Calhoun's treaty was a reflection on the official position of the Democratic party, but Blair continued to attack the treaty and rejoice over its defeat. In mid-August a widely heralded

Democratic convention met in Nashville with the ultra-annexa-tionists in charge, and their influence on Jackson was immediately obvious. Jackson considered Benton's bill an insult to Texas and decided that his old friend was deranged by hatred of Calhoun. The only mitigating factor was his suspicion that Benton's brain had been jarred loose by the explosion on the *Princeton*. The Whigs were circulating Benton's speeches by the thousands, and Jackson reproached Blair for printing them. They had "injured the Democratic cause more than all the whiggs." Blair, however, continued to praise Benton's Texas program and print the Mis-sourian's speeches, including one that urged the selection of a northerner for president in 1848.[22] Although Blair did his best to mollify Jackson, whose personal affection for him never waned, he ignored his mentor's opinions, suggestions, and advice.

Equally important, in a close election the support of the Ty-ler–Calhoun faction was vital to Polk. Tyler's friends, in fact, had held their own convention at Baltimore and nominated the incumbent for reelection. If Tyler had remained a candidate, Henry Clay would have been elected. Democratic leaders, includ-ing Jackson and Polk, urged Tyler to withdraw, but the president and his friends insisted that he could not do so honorably as long as he was being attacked in the *Globe*. Blair, however, would not relent. He had evidence that Calhoun was using the patronage of his office to get various Democratic editors to attack Benton, and Robert Barnwell Rhett was insisting daily in *The Spectator* that Texas without the Union was preferable to the Union with-out Texas. Blair would not make peace with those whom he con-sidered both threats to the Union and the architects of a policy cer-tain to cause a war with Mexico. He continued to charge that Calhoun's treaty had hurt rather than helped the cause of an-nexation and he ignored Jackson's blunt admonition to "let Tiler alone." Tyler finally withdrew without any concessions from the *Globe*, because his friends knew that his candidacy would only elect Clay.[23]

Otherwise it was a typical *Globe* campaign. The money, bank-ing, and tariff issues had lost much of their emotional appeal, but the *Globe* repeated most of the ancient clichés about them. The *National Intelligencer* extolled Clay as the candidate of law and order. Blair answered that Clay's life had been "a continued scene of brawls and violence, and disregard of laws the most sacred in the eyes of God and Man." [24] The pure Polk in contrast to the scandalous Clay was the *Globe*'s theme throughout the campaign.

The *Globe* also identified Native Americanism with Whiggery and attacked all such philosophies. Blair denied flatly that Anglo-Saxons were of superior breed, and stressed the contributions of the other stocks composing America. Special praise was given to the Irish and Germans, both of whom had been victims of recent Know Nothing riots in various cities. Native Americanism, wrote Blair, was part of the long-standing Federalist "scheme of placing the government in the hands of the few." [25]

The most dishonest canard against Polk was a story published in Thurlow Weed's *Albany Evening Journal* and allegedly taken from a book by a man named Roorback, who had made a southern tour in 1836. Allegedly, Roorback had met a drove of manacled slaves en route to Louisiana, and forty-three of them carried the brand JKP on their backs. The *Albany Argus* editor demanded to see the book, which in fact had never existed at all. Except for the Polk story, the extract was a verbatim copy from a book by a man named Featherstonhaugh in 1834. Weed ultimately blamed the Roorback forgery on another newspaper. The *Globe* announced that Polk owned no slaves that were not inherited and no slaves that would consent to be sold or emancipated, and had never bought or sold a slave except upon the slave's own entreaty to avoid separation from members of his family or to join someone of another family. Under the circumstances by which Polk owned and cared for his slaves, Polk's slaveholding was "AN HONOR TO HIM." The *Globe* also charged that the oppressive laws enacted against freed Negroes in Washington in 1827 and 1836 had been passed by Whig-dominated city councils, and that every notorious slave trader in Washington was supporting Clay. The *Intelligencer* charged that a Polk and Dallas flag was flying over a slave dealer's pen, and the *Globe* answered that the owner of the pen was a well-known Clay supporter who had raised the flag to get abolitionist votes for Clay. [26]

The Liberty party, unwilling to accept Clay even though its immediate objective was to prevent the annexation of Texas, nominated abolitionist James G. Birney for president. As various

Whigs, including Abraham Lincoln, argued, the Liberty party might have accomplished more of its goals by supporting Clay. Antislavery Whigs like the eloquent but quarrelsome Cassius M. Clay of Kentucky toured the North with long speeches to this effect. The *Globe* quickly pointed out these speeches to the South and warned that Clay's friends were trying to get Birney out of the race so the abolitionists would vote for Clay.[27]

On August 19 came a challenge Blair and Rives could not ignore. A Clay supporter published an offer to make several $250 and $500 bets on states and combinations of states that Clay would carry. "He has nothing to do but put up the money," answered Blair and Rives. On October 1 the *Globe* announced that "John C. Rives bets (for F.P. Blair) Bushrod Taylor that Henry Clay will not receive the electoral vote of Pennsylvania; and $1,000 that he will not be elected President . . . and also $500 that the electors in the several states in favor of James K. Polk will receive more votes . . . than the electors in favor of Henry Clay." Rives also offered to bet large sums on the size of Polk's victory, and promised "to *give* $100 toward paying for the coon pen in this city, called by them [the Whigs] the 'club house,' (the lumber in which, I learn, has not yet been paid for by them), if I shall fail to take up every *responsible* person who may offer to meet my propositions." Blair also bet $10,000 with Messrs. Betts and Cochran of Richmond, Virginia. All of this embarrassed Blair no end, he wrote Jackson, when he sat down to write editorials condemning Clay for being such an inveterate gambler.[28]

Once again Henry Clay was doomed to defeat, but not by any mandate against his position on Texas. He and Birney had a combined popular vote of 1,361,368 to 1,337,243 for Polk. Birney received 15,812 of his 62,300 votes in New York, which Clay lost by only 5,080 votes. If Clay had carried New York he would have been elected by seven electoral votes. In South Carolina, where the electorate was denied a vote for president, the legislature voted for Polk electors, and while presumably the popular vote would have been cast the same way, the margin cannot be guessed. Polk's own home state of Tennessee, supposedly expansionist and aggressive, would soon gain the title of "Volunteer

State" in the Mexican War, but Clay carried it by 124 votes: 60,039 to 59,915. The election of Polk rather than Clay was a fateful decision for the American Union in 1844, but the reasons for the public's choice remain debatable.

On November 28 the *Globe* reported a joyous victory celebration in Washington, with "brass bands, joyful shouts of exulting thousands, the gaily decorated procession of horses and foot, and vehicles and symbols extending nearly a mile along the avenue." Blair was equally happy over the reelection of Benton in Missouri, although his friend's usual overwhelming majority had been cut to a margin of only eight legislative votes. Collecting the $22,000 he and Rives had won on the election was also no small pleasure. He still mourned the fate of Van Buren, however, and continued to praise the New Yorker's unselfish conduct.

There was little time for euphoria. In December 1844 no one yet knew exactly what Polk's policies would be, but the platform had called for immediate annexation. To survive as party editor Blair would have to adopt a Texas formula acceptable to those now ruling the party. On December 10 George McDuffie introduced a joint resolution for annexation under the constitutional right of Congress to admit new states. On the following day Benton introduced his own former bill providing for negotiation with Mexico and a prior territorial compromise on slavery. Meanwhile, Jackson's nephew, Andrew Jackson Donelson, had been appointed chargé d'affaires to Texas. Donelson, Jackson, Benton, and Blair engaged in a series of letters that culminated in an agreement by Benton to support annexation by a joint resolution on the basis of the treaties of 1803 and 1819.

On Christmas Day 1844 Senators Benton, William Haywood, William Allen, and others (probably Benjamin Tappan, Arthur Bagby, and John A. Dix, all of whom had voted with Benton on most Texas questions) dined at the Blair home. Benton was pleased with Jackson's letter urging annexation on the basis of the 1803 treaty, and said "he would rather act on the ground provided by Jefferson . . . than move on the slippery slime of Calhoun & Tyler." Equally important, Donelson had written a letter urging Benton to omit the questions of slavery, the number of states, and the boundaries in his specific proposals. It would be enough, Donelson argued, to specify boundaries as embracing only the territory where Texas maintained actual jurisdiction; the United States could plan to buy the disputed areas later.[29]

On January 6 the *Globe* suggested that the annexation might come as a bill authorizing the president-elect to proceed with differing alternatives at his discretion. On January 25 the House passed a joint resolution for annexation that also declared the new state "subject to the adjustment by this government of all questions of boundary that may arise with other governments" and authorized a division into not more than four states, with those north of the Missouri Compromise line to be free and those south to be free or slave according to the wishes of the inhabitants. Blair praised this resolution with a clear conscience.

On February 5 Benton withdrew his original bill and offered a substitute calling for admission of a fully equal, "proper-sized" Texas state, cession of the remaining Texas territory by agreement between the United States and Texas, and an appropriation of $100,000 to carry out the negotiations. He hoped, said Benton, that the new president would particularly consider the compromise principle between free and slave territories and the provision for peaceful adjustment with Mexico. He would "consider all this as remaining just as fully in the mind of the President as if submitted to him in a bill."

Blair at least thought, whether wishfully or on the basis of reliable information, that Polk had agreed to a modified form of the Benton plan—negotiation with Mexico unless Congress should decide otherwise. Shortly after Polk's arrival in Washington, Blair and Senator William Haywood conferred with Polk and came away convinced that the president-elect would indeed follow the Benton approach in dealing with Mexico. Blair insisted later that they had even discussed the names of possible appointees for the crucial mission of negotiation with Texas and Mexico.[30]

Many senators would have supported either, but neither the Calhoun nor Benton faction would support the plan of the other. Walker, therefore, developed the idea Blair had suggested on January 6. On February 27 Walker proposed Benton's bill as an amendment to the joint resolution and added a preamble giving the president an option between the two. Amid wild rejoicing in an emotion-packed evening session, the bill passed by a scant 27–25 margin as Benton and his friends swung into line.

Fears that the outgoing administration might act during the last three days of its tenure had been voiced by opponents, but McDuffie had assured the Senate the president would have no such audacity. Calhoun, however, would not be denied. He and Tyler ignored the Benton alternative and immediately forwarded the joint resolution to Texas. Mexico would have to surrender the disputed territory or fight for it. Benton would later claim that he and four friends were cheated of their votes by assurances that Polk rather than Tyler would execute the measure and follow his amendment. Blair would later attack Polk for not modifying the action taken by Tyler.

Behind the scenes, meanwhile, decisions fateful for Blair were in process. Polk offered the Treasury Department to Silas Wright and the War Department to Benjamin F. Butler, but these close friends of Van Buren refused. Butler, under pressure from a wife who did not wish to return to Washington, was holding out in hopes of getting the Treasury Department, but before Van Buren could persuade him to accept the offer that had been made, Polk became irritated by the delay and gave the War Department to William Marcy, Van Buren's New York enemy. The Treasury Department went to Robert J. Walker, who had done so much to engineer Polk's nomination. James Buchanan became secretary of state. The Texas question was still far from settled, and Benton and Blair remained serious obstacles to any forcible acquisition of the disputed territory. Walker was eager to destroy this opposition. Buchanan considered Benton a future rival for the presidency, and had long felt that the *Globe* was less than fair in its coverage of his own activities and speeches. Polk had also blamed the *Globe* for inadequate support of his earlier campaigns in Tennessee, and he remembered all too well the letters of "Amicus" questioning his right to the vice-presidential nomination. It was easy for the new president to agree with advisors and friends who insisted that party harmony demanded a new editor. Andrew Jackson pleaded for retention of the *Globe*, but James K. Polk was his own man. Blair would have to be replaced.[31]

Blair should have expected nothing less. In 1844 he had in

fact abandoned his role of party spokesman and performed as a highly responsible journalist. Most of those leading the party, including Jackson, wanted all of Texas as defined by Texas and had no feelings of responsibility toward Mexico. They were unwilling or unable to comprehend the dangers to the Union that a war with Mexico and a sectional conflict over its spoils would bring. By attacking Tyler's treaty and siding with Benton and Van Buren, Blair had defied his party's chosen leaders. He had ignored their pleas to stop attacking Tyler and Calhoun when they were trying to get the president to withdraw and support Polk. Blair had demonstrated beyond a doubt that he could not be trusted to serve as a mere propagandist for the official Democratic platform and leadership, or as an agent for harmonizing their divergent views before the public. From the standpoint of the national welfare he had been both courageous and wise, but he had forfeited his right to serve as official party editor. It was clear also that the Calhoun southern wing of the party could not be reconciled to a continuation of Blair as official editor. What the Blairs dubbed "the chivalry" might have no hope for effective political action except within the party, but they could threaten disruption and disunion. Restoring them to a reunified party was a worthy political objective for the new president if their demands could be kept within reasonable bounds.

The decapitation was accomplished with overt courtesy, but with several incomplete strokes that belied the clear determination of the executioner. Certain friends of the president suggested that the South might be mollified by the addition of Andrew Jackson Donelson as a nominal editor and partner at the *Globe*. Blair and Rives had paid security notes for Donelson, however, and wanted no part of him or any other coeditor. Meanwhile, Polk told Blair that his feelings about the editorship would be indicated by the disposition of his inaugural address. When Rives was given a copy in the presence of the other editors several hours before they received one, Blair assumed that all was forgiven. During the following month, however, Polk indicated a certain restraint in conversations, and the *New York Herald* denied that the *Globe* was the official party organ. Blair then asked Polk for the official list of diplomatic appointments and explained that he wished to publish them as a refutation of the *Herald* article. Polk sent Blair to Secretary of State Buchanan for the list. Buchanan, however, delayed until further consultation with the president. He then furnished the list, but the *Madisonian* and the *Constitution* also published it on the same day with a comment that this would be the policy until the official organ should be chosen. Blair went back to Polk, who again suggested the addition of Donelson to the *Globe*. Blair again refused and thereby insured his dismissal. Polk explained that the party could not be united with Blair as editor. Blair protested that hostility to himself had not created the divisions and cliques: In the last Congress all of the cliques had united to elect him House printer, and all divisions and cliques grew out of aspirations for the presidency. Polk, however, was adamant. He was convinced that Blair was more devoted to Benton than to his administration.[32]

At first Blair and Rives were tempted to stand their ground and continue their paper without the executive or party patronage. They had operated at a reasonable profit for the past four years without executive patronage. Jackson, Van Buren, Benton, and others, however, agreed that such a policy would further divide the party. Blair did not wish to be a troublemaker, and he was genuinely weary from the strains of battle and his various illnesses. Three years earlier he had bought a plantation a few miles north of Washington, and he was eager to give it his full attention.

Thomas Ritchie of the *Richmond Enquirer*, himself $30,000 in debt, was brought to Washington to edit the newspaper. Secretary of the Treasury Walker transferred $50,000 in government money to a bank in Middleton, Pennsylvania, of which Simon Cameron was president. The bank then loaned $35,000 to the managers of the new official paper, to be called the *Washington Union*. The money was used to buy the *Globe* from Blair. For the office building and lot, subscription lists, and enough equipment to publish the paper Blair received $35,000. This did not, however, include the equipment used for the *Congressional Globe*, which remained the only public record of the debates and proceedings of Congress, and this meant that Blair and Rives would continue as competitors for job printing both public and private. Blair also had his new farm, various sound investments in real estate, his house on Pennsylvania

Avenue, and his half of the $22,000 won on Polk's election. In 1842 Rives had invested $100,500 for the two of them in state bonds, most of them from New York. In all, Blair wrote Van Buren, he believed himself to be worth approximately $100,000, in addition to what he had spent establishing his sons in their professions.[33]

Financial independence was pleasant, but the dismissal was a painful blow. While on the surface Blair accepted it with grace, he would not soon forgive James K. Polk, James Buchanan, and the various southerners he held responsible. Jackson, Van Buren, and others wrote glowing public tributes to his long, faithful, and effective service. John L. O'Sullivan requested a picture for a feature article on him in the *Democratic Review* and informed Van Buren that it was "by way of a lump of sugar after a dose of ipecac. If he consents to such an immortalization of his proverbial ugliness, I should be very glad if you would write some personal sketch of him—presuming as I safely may, that it would be a labor of love for you." [34]

Polk offered Blair the mission to Spain, which for one so enamored of travel as Blair must have been a considerable temptation. Rives feared for a time that Mrs. Blair and Elizabeth, "as ambitious of being seen & heard as her mother," might talk him into accepting and taking them abroad. Rives assured Van Buren that he "would rather give Mr. Blair $18,000, than Mr. Blair should go abroad now, under pay of the Genl. Govt." In the end, however, Eliza strongly opposed Blair's receiving anything from Polk, and all such overtures were refused.[35] Montgomery, by now a rising politician in Missouri, also refused a diplomatic post, but he had been appointed judge of the court of common pleas, and he accepted Polk's offer of a considerable share of the Missouri patronage.

The *Globe*'s public farewells were spread over a two-week period while the editors awaited the arrival of Ritchie. On April 14, 1845, Blair announced that the office and equipment had passed into new hands because the editors "in supporting basic principles" had made enemies of some of those who had helped elect the new president. Party success, he wrote, required that all who had contributed to the recent victory should continue to give their support, and a change of editors was therefore necessary. "The *Globe*," he continued, "had its origin in the will of Gen. Jackson, and owes to him and Mr. Van Buren, and their political friends, the success which has attended it through fifteen years of conflict, closed by the late triumph of democracy, which effaced the disaster of 1840." "We have unbounded confidence," Blair assured the public, "in the ability, integrity, and patriotism of the man who is now to preside over the establishment, and shall consider ourselves amply compensated for the sacrifice we are now called on to make, if our anticipations of the continued union and success of the democracy shall be realized by the official journal, under its new name and auspices. We cannot express our gratitude to the democracy, to which we owe everything."

On April 29 the editors thanked the other members of the press for support during the past fifteen years and for their expressions of regret over the paper's demise. On April 30, in the final issue, Rives announced that Blair, having gone to Philadelphia, had left him "forced to the disagreeable duty of closing the eyes, and laying out the departed." With the noblest of motives, Rives concluded, Blair had sold out to avoid division and distraction in the Democratic party.

Thus ended the editorial career of Francis Preston Blair and the newspaper he had founded. The *Globe* had begun as a propaganda instrument for the reelection of Andrew Jackson, and it had faithfully presented the ideas and principles that Old Hickory had found most congenial. It had assumed the role of spokesman for the Democratic party on specific policies, but it had spoken only for the party segment that shared the agrarian principles of Jackson and Blair. In basing its advocacy of Jacksonian policies upon broad, sweeping flights of democratic rhetoric, however, it had done much to popularize the language of democracy and equality. Its excessive partisanship and frequent exaggerations of both the virtues of the Democrats and the wickedness of the Whigs can be faulted, but it provided a valuable balance to the equally fallacious claims and accusations coming from the far more numerous presses of the Whigs.

Ironically enough, after jousting for nearly fifteen years with Democrats who did not share the economic conservatism of Jackson and Van Buren, Blair was finally discharged by James

K. Polk, who had been second to no one in his opposition to banks, paper money, internal improvements, and tariffs, and who would soon make Van Buren's Independent Treasury again a reality. On all such matters Blair would have been the ideal spokesman for Polk as he had been for Jackson.

On the Texas question, however, Blair had risen from party editor to responsible journalist. Living up to the righteous Jacksonian image he himself had helped create, he had defied a majority of his party's leaders, including Jackson himself. He had opposed the annexation before the convention, praised the opponents of the annexation after the convention, and attacked the annexation by implication through his warfare on Tyler and Calhoun throughout the election campaign. By all the standards of American politics he had earned his dismissal, but the demise of the *Globe* at the point where it had become an independent and responsible newspaper was a national loss. American politicians and voters alike desperately needed sources of information and intelligent reasoning unindebted and uncommitted to specific parties and leaders, but in 1845 they were almost nonexistent.

Chapter 12

The Planter

IN April 1845 Ben Gratz congratulated his favorite brother-in-law upon "being relieved from the burden of the Globe." Ben hoped Blair would move west to Kentucky or St Louis, or at least give up the corrupt atmosphere of Washington for Baltimore or Philadelphia. "Take care," he advised, "that those who buy you out, do not swindle you." Blair, however, was far from ready to retire from the great sport of politics. The high compliments tendered by Secretary of State James Buchanan when offering the mission to Spain gave Blair at least some reason to hope that much of his influence had survived the *Globe*. John L. O'Sullivan assured Van Buren that a friend had certain knowledge that Polk personally wished to retain the *Globe* but had been overpowered by demands that he "harmonize" the party.[1]

Others also still thought Blair influential, and the usual pleas for jobs and favors continued to come in. His old friend John J. Crittenden wanted him to save the postmastership at Maysville for James Coburn, a good man, poor, and with thirteen children. Also, their "old friend and country man, Capt. John W. Russell," was en route to Washington, and Blair could not "give aid or assistance to a nobler fellow. . . . It will take, I fear, a great many acts of justice & charity towards the Whigs to atone for the mischief you have done. And as I would be glad to help out in your redemption, I am pleased to have it in my power to present to you an opportunity for some good works." Blair was also somewhat mollified by Polk's cavalier handling of Calhoun, who had hoped to remain as secretary of state. At Jackson's suggestion the president offered the Carolinian the mission to England, "there to combat with Lord Aberdeen the abolition question," but Calhoun angrily refused. By mid-July the pro-Calhoun editor of the *Spectator* and the *Constitution* was complaining that Polk's policy was to "forget his friends and buy up his enemies. Hence Benton, Blair, and the New York regency can command anything." This was a gross exaggeration, but the possibilities of a return to power and influence were so obvious that Blair never once thought of quitting Washington.[2]

An immediately pressing concern was the disposal of his election winnings. Widespread rumors that the ex-editors of the *Globe* had $20,000 to contribute to charitable purposes brought a rash of helpful suggestions from around the country, but Blair had already made a practical decision. On July 4, 1845, Blair and Rives laid the cornerstone of an impressive new building, and exactly a year later it was formally dedicated with the name Jackson Hall. The ceremonies included a parade, the erection of a hickory pole in front, and various notable addresses. Unfortunately, Jackson did not live to see this monument built with Whig money lost to Blair and Rives, but he was fully informed of the plans and could appreciate both the joke and the honor. The three-story brick and granite building included two large basement rooms designed for a restaurant, and two large and elegant rooms on the first floor for rental to merchants. The second and third floors contained public halls forever free to the Democrats and available for a fee when needed for affairs of lesser organizations, with the rents to go to the Democratic party. To the rear of Jackson Hall Blair and Rives erected a large three-story building for a printing office, provided with steam and other modern machinery. Despite Ritchie's angry protest, they remained in the printing business.[3]

Having managed the Blair finances for fourteen years, Rives continued in this role for at least another fifteen. Despite the value of his property and investments, Blair was often short of cash because of a constant readiness to help his children and relatives. "The skeletons of my old check books . . . drive repose from my pillow," he wrote Rives in May 1847. "I am sometimes filled with apprehension that I may end my life as I began it, in pecuniary distresses. If on examination you find my condition, as good as you suggested in our conversations, I shall be happy.

If otherwise, you are the man on whom I must rely to suggest some mode or make some arrangement to retrieve my affairs & give at least an independence to my old age." For the sake of their families, Blair continued, there should be a statement of their concerns while they were both still alive, although "with the feelings we entertain for each other we cannot disagree." Rives made a careful audit and concluded that Blair was indeed affluent and had in fact received and spent some $250,000 over the past fifteen years. By March 1849 Blair's public opposition to slavery was costing the firm dearly in printing contracts, and this produced a difficult decision. The political controversies, Blair wrote Rives, "from which it is not in my nature to retreat threatens to make my position worse for the Globe at the next than it was at the last session. Painful, then, as is our separation, I yield to the necessity of dissolving our partnership." Rives should take the *Globe* printing office and everything connected with it, including Jackson Hall, and estimate its value. Blair would accept whatever Rives offered. While the partnership ostensibly ended at this point, the final contract was not reached until October 25, 1855, when Rives bought Blair's interest for $100,000 plus 7.3 percent annual interest until paid. Between this date and July 9, 1860, Rives paid Blair a total of $123,028.73, and on the latter date Blair actually owed Rives $5,851.39. Another statement of account covering the years from October 25, 1853, to November 13, 1860, showed total drawings of $135,085.26. The statement included hundreds of items such as "Colored boys' wages in full, 7.50," "Mrs. Blair for market money $2.50," "Mrs. Brown for cages $12.00," "St. John's church pew rent 40.00," "railroad freight on threshing machine 11.05," "S. Parker for millinery and toilet articles 82.02," "W. Palmer, Musical instruction for Miss Bettie, 43.00," "Dr. Maynard for dentistry for self & for Mr. and Mrs. FPB. Jr., 310.00," "Ragan for seeding and milking cows 120.75," "F. Coyle's bill for guano 447.62," and "Morrison for Uncle Tom's Cabin 1.00." During the late 1850's Blair loaned out approximately $50,000 at 10 percent interest in St. Louis.[4]

Throughout the entire period until Rives's death in 1864 no harsh word ever passed between Blair and Rives. Though each often quarreled with others, they shared a friendship such as few men know, and Rives named his youngest son Blair. In March 1853 Rives wrote poignantly:

> Dear Sir,
>
> My wife died at 5 o'clock this morning . . . after giving birth to a child prematurely. The child was born dead.
>
> The object of this letter is to ask the favor of you to write a short obituary notice—very short. . . . I would rather that it should fall below her merits, than go beyond them. I think it might be justly said of her that she was a woman of uncommon natural intellect; & you will, perhaps, agree with me in that, when I tell you that she never went to school, except for a short time to a Sunday school.
>
> But I doubt if any more should be said than that she died at the hour above named in the 43rd year of her age having been born on the 3rd July, 1810, leaving myself & seven minor children . . . the youngest three years old to deplore her loss.

During the Civil War Rives gave more than $30,000 to the wives of poor enlistees from the District of Columbia.[5]

In addition to building Jackson Hall, Blair also spent much of 1845 finishing up his new house in the country. According to family legend, Blair selected his plantation site by accident. One day when he and daughter Lizzie were galloping through the woods in the area, Blair's horse threw him off and ran away. When Blair finally overtook his mount after the bridle had caught on some bushes, he discovered nearby a beautiful bubbling spring that appeared to have a silver halo because of the sunlight on the mica in the white sand under the water. The spring and the beautiful surroundings convinced father and daughter alike that this was the place for their long-dreamed-of country home. Blair bought the land in 1842 and finally moved there in 1845. Silver Spring, as Blair named his estate, became a constant gathering place for the high and mighty as well as friends and relatives of every degree. The large mouse-colored, two-story house was furnished for comfort rather than ostentation. Winding paths led to neighboring woods and fields, and a summer pavilion shaped and colored to resemble an acorn stood near the spring. A small white marble statue of a beautiful water nymph was placed in the spring, and a small artificial lake lined with flowers and graced with a small island of honeysuckle added to the beauty of the surroundings. Like Benton, Blair ascribed his long life to cold baths and severe brushings, and his new estate was equipped with a concrete bathhouse supplied by cold spring-water. An ingeniously designed waterwheel supplied power for various tasks such as threshing and grinding grain, washing clothes, and churning.

The farm eventually numbered several hundred acres, and for Blair it was never merely a residence. Corn, wheat, pigs, cattle, dairy products, peaches, and other fruit were produced, although rarely in the great profusion boasted of by the master to his fellow planters Rives and Van Buren. Peaches were apparently the most glittering ornament, and every fall Eliza spent long hours canning and brandying them for shipment in great quantities to distant children, relatives, and friends. On one occasion Blair wrote a work schedule in his usual almost illegible handwriting. After lengthy directions concerning the planting of sugar cane, the building of various walkways, and the erection of a fence for the hogs, he added some plans for the future employment of certain slaves:

> 6.   Albert & Alick must be taken from Mary's control & put under Henry's tutorship—Henry must make them do their work whatever is set them teach them—correct their behavior & in all respects act the part of a parent to them.
> 7.   I have made Henry master of the Quarters where he lives & shall hold him responsible for whatever goes amiss there.
> 8.   I want Montgomery to see Vance & see that Emory is disposed of if he can be bound either for a term of years or absolutely upon such terms as he may think just.
> 9.   I want Susan hired out for a term of years; or if Shoemaker will buy her & agree to keep her & her young child with her husband, I want Montgomery to let him have her at a low price.[6]

For many years only one servant, a slave named Joanna to whom Eliza was deeply devoted, lived in the house. The handful of slaves who did most of the work lived in neatly furnished little buildings by themselves. The slaves enjoyed a maximum of independence, and their chattel status was as much a product of Maryland law as the choice of Blair, who had to sign a bond that he was not bringing them into Maryland for purposes of manumission. On one occasion a female who while drunk tyrannized the other slave women was simply ordered to find herself

another master. In another case, Blair endorsed an $800 note
at the Riggs bank that enabled a free black to buy his own wife and
child. In return the wife was to cook for Rives and the husband
to work for Blair for standard wages until the debt should be
paid. In May 1846 Blair's son James asked the family for slave
Thomas, but was refused because Thomas was so useful to Eliza.
In November 1847 Blair scolded Frank, Jr., sharply for buying
Beverly from Ben Gratz. Frank, soon to become famous as a
Free Soiler and opponent of slavery, wanted Beverly to help rear
his children and produce a servant boy to replace Edward. He
would have preferred Joanna or Phillis, but knew his mother
would not part with them. Two years later, Frank was still inquiring unsuccessfully about the possibility of having Joanna
sent to nurse his children.[7]

Among the friends who shared the hospitality of Silver
Spring as well as the principles of its master, the Bentons and
Van Burens remained closest, with Senator Preston King of New
York perhaps next in line. Montgomery and Frank served their
legal apprenticeships in Benton's St. Louis office, and were like
Old Bullion's own sons. Lizzie Blair and Benton's daughter
Jessie enjoyed a long, intimate relationship, the very strength
of which enhanced the bitterness when it was finally broken.
Lizzie and both Jessie and her sister Nina exchanged long,
friendly letters when apart, and the Bentons and Blairs constantly exchanged visits, occasionally for days at a time, between
Washington and Silver Spring. When seventeen-year-old Jessie
Benton defied her father and eloped with Lieutenant John C.
Frémont, "Father Blair" sided with Jessie and made a strong
contribution to family peace. When Blair was trying to prevent
the marriage of Lizzie to Lieutenant Samuel Phillips Lee, Benton won Lizzie's undying gratitude by his often-expressed regard
for Lee. Benton liked Lee's "good manners—particularly to old
people—a thing left out in the manners of most young people
now a days."[8]

Although Blair rarely saw Van Buren, the two maintained a
steady correspondence as well as frequent exchanges of the
boasted produce of their respective farms. The Van Buren sons
made Silver Spring their home whenever they were in Washington, and the gentle Martin, Jr., a tubercular youth, spent many

winter months with the Blairs to avoid the colder New York climate. When John Van Buren, the ex-president's brilliant but heavy-drinking son, came to Washington in November 1847 to try a Supreme Court case, the anxious father appealed to Blair: "I hope you will try to keep an eye upon him & prevent him from getting into any scrapes or see that if he does he gets out of it without discredit." [9]

"Farmer Blair," wrote Martin Van Buren, Jr., in February 1847, "is ploughing for corn with four mules, & making great scattering with the stumps & stones the latter of which he has much diminished by transferring as a basement to his new carriage road & walls around his cow & pig pen, thereby killing two birds with one stone." [10]

"You have not yet fulfilled your promise," wrote Martin, Sr., a year later, "by sending me the directions through which I am to raise 100 bushels of corn to the acre." [11]

In 1846 Blair, Eliza, and Lizzie went to Newport, Rhode Island, from whence after a few days the parents proceeded to Kinderhook for a long happy visit with Van Buren. At a ball in Newport Eliza was fascinated by a dance she described as "two people hugging as close as possible with nose to nose & getting up on the floor & moving backwards & in the gallop fashion—but with jig time & movement, & in the waltz they did it in a way as to display the stocking bands up nearly to the corsetts & they wear real flesh colored silk drawers just like the fancy elastic style." With Van Buren later, the Blairs attended a great agricultural fair whose exhibits and machinery Blair found almost overwhelming. From Kinderhook they continued to Niagara Falls. "We have looked on the great wonder . . . for two days," Blair wrote Lizzie. "I never saw the sublime & beautiful so enchantingly blended." As might have been expected, John Rives had to send extra money to get the family home. [12]

Blair's move to the countryside also left him free to perpetuate the fame of his beloved mentor with a definitive biography. In his deathbed letter on April 9, 1845, Andrew Jackson left his "papers and reputation" in Blair's keeping, and asked "nothing but what truth will mete to me." His last wish was for Blair's "health and prosperity, and that of all your family, and that you may triumph over all enemies." He had already given Lizzie

Blair the wedding ring of his beloved Rachel. Soon young James Blair was in Nashville collecting the three cedar chests full of papers, which he promised to guard with his life. Catching the Jacksonian spirit at the Hermitage, James suggested that his father should "accidentally" tell Secretary of the Navy George Bancroft that he had no wish to "go Buccaneering & blockading" against the weak Mexicans, but if war came with "bloated old England" he would like to "Paul Jones a little on the Coast of England. . . . Burn, sink & destroy right in the mouth of the English lion." [13] Year after year Blair talked and dreamed of writing the great book that would enshrine Jackson, but somehow the interests of the living always intervened. His conscience on the matter was usually assuaged by the hope that Bancroft would eventually get to the task and by the fact that getting numerous important papers away from Kendall was a never-ending task.

In other ways, however, Blair was true to his trust. He raised the money for the project and served as advisor to the sculptor, Clark Mills, who produced the enormous bronze equestrian statue of Jackson that still decorates Lafayette Square in Washington. The statue was made from metal taken from the cannon Jackson had captured at New Orleans, and although opinion was sharply divided over its artistic merits, Blair thought the dashing figure truly magnificent. Senator Stephen A. Douglas agreed to deliver the address of dedication if Blair would write it, and the ex-editor happily complied with eleven closely packed pages. Jackson, Blair insisted again, had taught his followers to "ask nothing but what is strictly right—submit to nothing that is wrong." The statue would provide "evidence to the World, how harmless is the thunder of Kings, when hurled at the man of iron, whose armor is the patriotism inspired by the Republic." [14]

In 1842 Blair had already brought comfort to Jackson's final days by loaning the general $10,000 secured by a largely undeveloped Mississippi plantation and thirty slaves. Also, less than three weeks before Jackson's death the old man was further relieved when Blair and Rives assumed all of his remaining debts, amounting to $7,000, with the Hermitage as well as the same Mississippi plantation to be the security for both loans. The fear of dying in debt had been a torture for Jackson, and he shed tears of gratitude while taking comfort in the knowledge that his estate was more than ample security for his old friends.[15]

Jackson, however, had not reckoned on the extravagance and incredible mismanagement of his adopted son and heir, Andrew Jackson, Jr. By 1847, Andrew, Jr., deeply in debt, was begging Blair to relinquish his lien on the Mississippi plantation so he could accept an offer to buy it from a local purchaser. Seventeen of the slaves had died of cholera, and the others had been returned to Tennessee. Floods had inundated the plantation, and young Jackson was fearful lest the buyer back out of the sale before Blair's lien could be eliminated as a barrier. By 1855 Andrew, Jr., owed $100,000 in addition to $30,000 owed to Blair and Rives, and only their prior lien on the Hermitage kept it from falling to creditors unconcerned with preserving it as a shrine to Old Hickory. Blair sent his son Frank to Nashville, where he and William B. Lewis arranged a settlement whereby the state of Tennessee bought the Hermitage and 500 acres for $48,000 in state bonds. By then Jackson, Jr., had paid $26,000 for a worthless lead mine after going bankrupt in the iron business. Blair and Rives agreed to relinquish all claim to ten years of interest and accept their original $18,000 principal in state bonds. Lewis advised them further to convey the remainder of the money to someone in trust for Jackson's wife and children. Otherwise, they "might as well throw it into the Potomac." Blair made the offer, but Jackson, Jr., preferred to go his own way. The Hermitage, at least, was saved for posterity.[16]

Blair never wrote the great biography, but for many years he continued to write as the self-proclaimed voice of Jackson "from beyond the grave" in dealing with their mutual enemies from the past and his own newer enemies of the present.

Chapter 13

The Clan

AFTER the deaths of his wife and daughter in 1844, the unhappy Montgomery Blair returned to St. Louis to accept an appointment as judge of the court of common pleas, and "Judge" replaced "Gum" as the family title used by his brothers and sister. Two years later, while on an extended visit with his parents, he fell in love with Mary Elizabeth Woodbury, daughter of Levi Woodbury, the former secretary of the treasury. Indeed he was so filled with romance and unconscious of the world around him that he carried some important letters, including one from Van Buren, around for days before remembering to deliver them to his father. He and "Minna" were married at the bride's home in Portsmouth, New Hampshire, on July 6, 1846. Montgomery's little daughter Betty had already been living with Preston and Eliza Blair, and by mutual consent the grandparents happily adopted her.

For several years Montgomery remained a Benton protégé in St. Louis, where both his law practice and his real estate investments prospered. In 1851, however, his mother and father began urging him to move east and live nearer them in Maryland. Then on October 21, 1851, the elderly parents received a frightening telegram from St. Louis: "Montgomery has had a favorable change but he is very low." Knowing that their son had had a recent illness, the distraught parents immediately began the long journey west by train and riverboat. It was a miserable trip. Eliza felt that she had done wrong to leave Betty behind, but on the Mississippi she met a family who had left New Orleans with five children and had lost four of them to scarlet fever and other ailments. While sharing their grief, Eliza could proceed with a clearer conscience about leaving Betty.

Five days after her parents had left Lizzie received an astonishing telegram from Montgomery himself: "Your dispatch surprised us. We are all well." Two days later the weary and anxious parents learned the same happy truth. The original telegram had concerned another Montgomery and had been delivered to the Blairs by mistake. Once in St. Louis, the Blairs had a happy three-week visit with their children and grandchildren and persuaded Montgomery to move back to Washington and Maryland. The nation's capital would enhance his professional opportunities, and his parents would have at least one son nearby. Frank and his family begged Eliza to spend the winter with them. Informed of this, Lizzie commented, "They might as well invite the Rocky Mountains to step over the Atlantic," and she was right. On November 24, the older Blairs were home at Silver Spring. Soon Montgomery and his family were living in the Blair House on Pennsylvania Avenue.[1]

Meanwhile, Blair had long since lost his battle to keep Lizzie from becoming a navy wife. Her four-year courtship with Phillips Lee was a mixture of bliss and despair for both parties. Lee's first proposal in November 1839 was left unanswered pending the resolution of her health crisis, which lasted until the spring of 1841. The young officer's occasional tours of duty and visits in Washington were spent with Lizzie taking long walks and attending the usual social affairs such as balls, parties, and river cruises, although because of her health her strict father forbade her to go out at night more than once a week. "I am so glad you are back again," she wrote to Lee on one occasion. "Come up dear Phillips just as soon as you please. Father has gone to the country and I know not where we shall drive."

"What color of Japonica? (white or red) will you have for your hair tomorrow," he wrote when permission from her father to attend a ball was still doubtful. "I shall send flowers, to look at, to give away, if you stay home, or to wear if you go."

In late 1841, despite the opposition of her parents, Lizzie finally agreed to a spring wedding pending the approval of her dear elder brother, but to her great disappointment Montgomery sided strongly with their parents. They would love her best, he argued, and besides he had learned that Lee had previously courted another young lady with "a comfortable patrimony & a far less engaging person." Eliza burned Montgomery's letter and ordered her daughter to say nothing about it to Lee, but Lizzie, all innocence and jealous curiosity, communicated its verbatim contents to her swain and added: I put the ugly rich woman in from the 'meanness' of the charge & from a womanly curiosity to know who she is. Mother says I do it from a secret delight in knowing she is ugly." Thus began some twenty-five years of ill-feeling between Phillips Lee and Montgomery Blair that was probably increased rather than lessened by the success of the eventual marriage.

Months followed in which Lee's pride and Lizzie's devotion to her family were in constant conflict. "What a blow these *others* have aimed at me *through you*," wrote Lee. "What an argument they use? Who have been more decided in all their feelings, and have been more abused therefor, than Col. Benton & your own father? What two men are such admirable natures in domestic life?" Occasionally the harsh words of a proud, insulted, and angry man left Lizzie crushed with humiliation, but they were always followed by tender regrets. "You can make me what you please," he wrote, "only afford me the opportunity to cultivate the kind, & remove the other feelings you have for me. . . . To wed, live with, & love you, to watch over your pillow & caress you, to nurse you in sickness, to share all your joys, & your sorrows if any you have,—in a word to devote myself to you—these, & such as these are the thoughts and wishes which animate the heart long more yours than mine."

In January 1843 the frustrated suitor forced a showdown, which brought about a temporary break but accomplished its purpose. "I thank you sincerely," wrote Lizzie, "for the package of letters which you returned to me on Tuesday. . . . I now send you all the letters I have ever received from you. I also enclose a thimble & pencil. . . . You have my best wishes for your happiness & welfare."

A few weeks later Francis P. Blair received a brief note: "Sir, I am again engaged to your daughter & I now ask the consent of her parents to our marriage. I have the honor to be, sir, very respectfully, Your obedient servant, S. P. Lee." [2]

They were married on April 27, 1843, and the wedding was followed by Francis P. Blair's letter of confession and penitence. "I am activated by the strongest affection," he wrote to Lizzie. "I cannot bring myself to resign my rights in you to any one & to confess a truth I never saw the man I was willing you should marry." He would contribute as far as he could to her "future enjoyment of life & to make amends for the clouds which I have cast over it for the last four years." He hoped she would make his house their home whenever her husband's duty permitted them to reside in Washington, and he added, "The coldness and distance I have observed towards him was intended to repress the feelings he indulged for you—leading to a result my judgment did not sanction. If hereafter they are as constant & as kind as they have . . . been . . . I shall give him gratitude in proportion to the kindness he shows you." [3]

It was an ideal marriage for the Blair family. Most of Lee's career was spent either at sea or in the Washington area, and Lizzie consequently never really left home except for relatively short periods. In November 1846 Lee calculated that since their marriage his wife had resided at her father's home for twenty months and he himself had lived there for twelve months. He did not like the sense of obligation, and announced that he would henceforth provide them a separate home in Washington. The family objections at Silver Spring, however, were overwhelming, and Lizzie's sad pleas were finally irresistible. He could not remove her from Silver Spring fully, she wrote, and a quarrel between him and her mother would break her heart. She could not leave her home because "you are a wanderer— & will necessarily leave me utterly desolate in your absence." Instead, he should be like herself a child to her "dear, good parents." The doctors, furthermore, had warned that excessive excitement was bad for her health. Satisfied that he had done his best against impossible odds, Lee surrendered. Finally, in 1859, he built an excellent brick house joined by a common wall to the Blair residence on Pennsylvania Avenue. By this time the elder Blairs had given their side of the double building to Montgomery and Eliza was barely on speaking terms with Montgomery's wife. The Lee house in effect became a second residence for the elder Blairs—an arrangement that Lee accepted with obvious satisfaction.[4]

Year after year Lizzie poured out her heart daily in long letters that kept her husband up to date on family matters, local events, and national politics as seen through the eyes of her father, brothers, and the Bentons and Frémonts. When she was not tending to her flock of more than a hundred chickens or teaching young Betty music, French, and other subjects, she was serving as a director of the Washington Orphanage Asylum or working until the early morning hours as her father's secretary and scribe for the long public letters, pamphlets, and ghosted speeches that kept him constantly busy. She was also both participant and spectator at the innumerable political meetings and councils going on at Silver Spring. Childless for many years, she took great delight in the affections of her nephews and nieces, who, attracted by the farm's pleasures as well as by her indulgence, would beg "Aunt Lizzie" to keep them permanently and would occasionally hide when their parents came for them.

Phil Lee was an almost equally faithful correspondent, and a spirit of deep affection was rarely missing from their letters. There was an occasional lapse, such as when Lizzie ingenuously repeated her father's remark that he did not want Lee's brother's family inheriting any of his estate since there were plenty of Blairs around. The conversation had started when she refused her father's offer of $10,000—the stake given her brothers—and asked instead for a permanent right to live at home and a promise of equal treatment in the matter of inheritance. Naturally enough the proud young officer sent a furious disavowal and did not write again for several days until the obvious misery in her pleading letters caused him to relent.[5]

Since most of his salary went home, Lee may have been somewhat miffed in 1854 when his urgent request for money brought a regretful answer from Lizzie that she had loaned it all to her father, who could not repay her at the moment because Rives was absent at Cape May for reasons of health. Also, he may not have fully appreciated her instructions on how his shipboard table should be arranged, her frequent admonitions not to eat too much, and her relayed advice from his father-in-law on which books would improve his professional abilities. No man, however, could have felt more secure in the love of his wife, and he was probably the best-informed officer in the United States Navy as to the happenings within the social and political inner circles of the national capital.

Lizzie's inheritance problem, if it ever existed, was solved in 1857 when after fourteen years of embarrassing childlessness she produced handsome young Francis Preston Blair Lee. Francis P. Blair adored all of his grandchildren, but living on the premises gave young Blair Lee an obvious edge in the grandfather's heart. Rebecca Gratz thought young Blair extraordinarily handsome, and marveled that at the age of two he was the size of most five-year-old children.[6]

Closest to Lizzie and Phil, of course, was brother James, who had brought them together in the first place. Though badly frozen on one occasion and apparently the victim of physical stresses from which he never fully recovered, James had regaled his family with long, descriptive letters about his adventures with the Wilkes expedition in the South Seas, and had returned home full of ambition and energy.

In October 1843, in Philadelphia, James Blair proposed unsuccessfully to beautiful and talented Mary Boswell, a Gist in-law adopted by Ben Gratz. Undaunted, he was accepted later on the same day by Elizabeth Guillon, daughter of a Philadelphia physician. Mary may have preferred the more sophisticated and wilder Frank Blair, who in turn became furious at her for not accepting his brother. James professed undying adoration for Miss Guillon and announced that the wedding would take place before his return to sea, but he insisted also upon his father's approval.

Eliza and Lizzie, aware of Jim's erstwhile love for Mary Boswell, promptly intervened. Francis P. Blair, with his womenfolk at his elbow, reminded his son that he was of age and required no permission, but refused to approve a hasty marriage that might prove unhappy to both parties. In letters to both James and the young lady's mother, Blair urged a postponement. By this time in a rage, James Blair informed his parents that no law "military, civil, or natural" could make him leave Philadelphia before his marriage. His mother was equally adamant. "Say to him," she instructed her daughter, "that none of my sons shall bully me (& the lioness spoke) into doing or approving of a wrong & if he is not man or gentleman enough to follow faithfully his honorable profession the sooner he gets to the [indecipherable] the better." Ultimately, "Uncle Jo and Aunt Becky" Gratz arranged with Dr. Guillon to postpone the marriage until Jim's return from sea. Rebecca Gratz reported that the young man looked "greatly relieved." [7]

Shortly afterward, Mrs. Guillon ended the affair with an angry letter to Francis P. Blair. She herself had tried to discourage the match, she wrote, but had been moved by the obvious affection of the young lovers for each other. When James showed her his father's letter, however, this had ended all disputes. She would not permit her daughter to intrude unwanted into any family. "By mistake" John Rives opened the mother's final letter to Blair, read it, and added the notation: "I thought while opening it, that it might be on the subject it turns out to be, & was almost as anxious as you can be to see it." [8]

Frank Blair, meanwhile, wrote a letter denouncing his entire family in harsh language for not trying to help Jim marry his lady love, and called Mary Boswell so many violent names that Lizzie burned the letter without even finishing it. Ultimately, with Lizzie in attendance and with Henry Clay giving the bride away, Mary married Elisha Riggs of the famous banking family. Eliza Blair later served as assistant midwife and godmother to Mary's first child.

James Blair quickly recovered from his heartbreak. By January 1844 he was in Buenos Aires "riding 20–30 miles a day and dancing every evening in the home of some native Don, where there was usually to be found a fine collection of native Spanish blackeyed beauties, who could waltz or dance with such enchanting grace that I was very nearly captivated." In September 1845 the young sailor informed his father that he was engaged to Mary Serena Jesup, the seventeen-year-old daughter of General Thomas Jesup, quartermaster general of the army. [9]

A Kentuckian, General Jesup had been one of the few authentic heroes of the War of 1812, and Blair had once ardently defended his policies in the Seminole Indian War. Mrs. Jesup was the daughter of Major William Croghan, the brother of frontier hero George Croghan, and her mother was a sister of George Rogers Clark and William Clark, who had explored the West with Meriwether Lewis. It was a proper blending of frontier bloodlines, and Blair was delighted. He and the Croghan brothers had been schoolmates and friends in childhood. The wedding on January 14, 1846, enabled Blair to preside over an assemblage so varied as to include Calhoun, Webster, Buchanan, and President Polk, as well as most of Blair's somewhat more intimate political friends.

In 1849 James took a year's leave from the navy and sailed for San Francisco, where with $10,000 from his father he started a small shipping business in partnership with the Aspinwall brothers. He took the timbers for three ships by sea around the Cape of Good Hope and reassembled them in California in large part with his own hands. Meanwhile, he asked his father to build a cottage for Mary on the Silver Spring estate and promised to repay its cost. Blair was delighted to have his daughter-in-law and small granddaughter so near, and promptly complied. Appropriately enough for a sailor's home, Mary's house was called the Moorings. After his leave expired, the navy assigned James to shore duty in San Francisco, which did not interfere with his private activities.

Life in frontier California for James Blair was rough, dangerous, exciting, and highly profitable. By late 1850, however, he was desperately homesick for Mary, and announced that he would resign from the navy. He would return home and settle $50,000 along with the Moorings on Mary and daughter Violet, build her father a townhouse in Washington for which the general could pay rent to Mary, and then return to California to sell out his business. His father and brother Montgomery advised against his resigning, but James was adamant. If war should come, he wrote, he would get command of a ship anyhow. Meanwhile, in the peacetime navy there was no opportunity for a normal family life. A sailor endured "banishment from all a man holds dear for two-thirds of his life in the hope of enjoying the other one-third." The navy granted his leave to come home, but word that Mary and little Violet were en route to California with the Frémonts arrived before he could depart, and Mary persuaded him to keep his commission. She had brought his home and hearth to him.[10]

In May 1851 James had Frank invest $20,000 for him in St. Louis, and in December he urged his father to accept the repayment of his initial $10,000. "If you prefer not to receive it," he wrote, "then hold it in trust for my child if not then for any of your grandchildren that may want the most."

The father was equally magnanimous. The payment was unnecessary: "I am but a trustee for my children . . . If I have the use during my life of enough to supply my wants without calling back what I have given my children, such a call is superfluous. . . . If it should ever . . . be otherwise there is none of my children, to whom I would sooner make it known than to you." Blair did agree, however, that investing the sum for "dear little Violet" was a good idea, and advised James to send the money to Frank for that purpose. Lizzie was much impressed by Jim's offer, but concluded that it was probably Mary's idea since "no Blair would have ever thought of such a thing." [11]

The Blairs were grateful to John and Jessie Frémont for escorting Mary and little Violet to California, but a harbinger for the future relationship of the two families soon occurred. Mary reported from California that the Benton sisters, Jessie and Nina, were treating her like an enemy because James had refused to sign a second $1,500 note for Frémont. Frémont had failed to pay an earlier note, and James, while willing to loan Frémont the money himself, was unwilling to be his security again. James, meanwhile, dutifully followed his father's orders and worked for the reelection of Frémont to the United States Senate, but his original enthusiasm had been greatly diminished. [12]

Francis P. Blair was certain that he and Benton would "be blended together when we have left the stage of life in history," and he was much distressed by the apparent break between James and Frémont. He suspected tale-bearers and was sure that Frémont, though "shy and reserved," was a man "of candor & honor." "I would not have you to bend to Col. Fremont or any man on earth," he wrote James. "If he misconceives you & is too reserved to ask explanations you do right to let him 'wag his way.' . . . But . . . he has served his country & California particularly at much hazard & with great credit throughout the World, & you ought not to allow any unexplained misunderstandings between you and him to work up such a state of feeling in your mind as to make you want to see him 'bite the dust, both in political & in financial fortunes.' " Also, Blair concluded, Frémont's political enemies in California were also his own enemies, and to have them influential in the Senate "would have a very unpropitious bearing upon my '*political & financial fortunes.*' "

In November 1852 James Blair sent his family back to their Moorings at Silver Spring. Mary was expecting another child in February and he was still enmeshed in efforts to sell his business interests. The Aspinwalls had failed in their other business interests in the East and were trying to recoup in part at the expense of James Blair in California. James had also refused various requests to run for the legislature because he was certain he would lose. He considered himself too radical a Democrat for the Whigs. He had also strongly opposed the California Vigilante Committee during "its hanging mania," and he was a free-soil man "thoroughly opposed to the extension of slavery." "My devotion for the true pure and progressive democracy rises almost to a religion," he wrote his father. "Purify, educate, and elevate the masses and thus give permanence & strength to the Union & the hopes of human liberty. This is my utmost inherited education in politics from you." [13]

For two more years James Blair wrote long, loving letters to his wife and parents, complained about his painful rheumatism, and struggled to get clear of his commitments and controversies and satisfy his desperate longing for home. Then on December 15, 1853, he suffered a ruptured aorta and died within a few minutes.

A month later Montgomery Blair sailed for California to settle his brother's estate. The trip by sea was dangerous, and there would be sharp controversies with his brother's former partners. Montgomery, therefore, left a letter to his wife with Elizabeth. It was to be opened only in case of his death, and was not finally returned to its author until 1875. The departing father's instructions for the rearing of his children may have been a clear-cut projection of his own self-image, but they did offer a sound path to responsible citizenship. Since it was more important to "be honest & devout than distinguished," Minna should "endeavor in all ways to fill their minds with the love of God, with benevolence and kindness toward every one." They "should not seek station or position in society . . . except as a means of doing good and therefore, mere self-seeking in the attainment of position should be checked and discountenanced. I would impress them with the political opinions of their father and grandfathers as a part of their religion. The liberty & equality which they have struggled to secure among men being tenets in accordance with the Spirit of the Gospel to do unto others as you wish they should do unto you." [14]

Mary's in-laws wrote her long, tender letters of solace, and the elder Blair begged her to stay on at the Moorings to fill the void left by the loss of James. In California, Montgomery was overwhelmed by examples of James's goodness and generosity. There were countless uncollectable notes ranging from twenty-five cents to thousands of dollars. Fortunately, Montgomery pushed the dispute with Aspinwalls to a successful conclusion, and managed also to help straighten out the confused affairs of John C. Frémont. After many long weeks he finally put his brother's body and possessions aboard a ship and commenced his long journey home. Mary, only twenty-seven at the time of her bereavement, spent the rest of her eighty-seven years at the Moorings.[15]

And finally, there was young Frank, the most troublesome and the most exciting of all the Blairs. After leaving Princeton the errant scholar had followed his brother's example by studying law at Transylvania and emigrating to St. Louis. Then, suffering from ill-health and always looking for adventure, Frank took the Santa Fe Trail westward just in time to be at Bent's Fort in New Mexico when the Mexican War began. General Stephen Kearney, whose bloodless conquest of New Mexico was accomplished through previously arranged bribes to the Mexican generals, appointed him attorney general. Frank's service in this role was brief but vigorous. He helped draw up a legal code for the territory and successfully prosecuted a number of criminals as well as a handful of Mexican leaders who stirred up a final resistance and were therefore convicted of treason. The outdoor life restored his health. He warned his mother not to be shocked by "seeing a great fat rough bear of a fellow squeeze her up in his arms and call her his dear mama." [16]

Lizzie wondered if Frank was staying away to avoid his

announced forthcoming marriage to his cousin Apolline Alexander. She confided to Phil that "Frank ambles after Apo slowly. He would be too slow a nag for me. I would have kicked him many a day since." Upon his return, however, Frank headed straight for Woodford County, Kentucky, where on September 8, 1847, he married Apo. She was the granddaughter of the intrepid war hero and short-lived Kentucky governor George Madison, who had been Francis P. Blair's favorite uncle, and needless to say, she had her father-in-law's full approval and affection. It was a long and happy marriage. The first of the couple's eight children was born in 1848 and the last in 1872, when their mother was in her mid-forties. Apo, however, remained somewhat aloof from the rest of the Blair family, and may have influenced Frank to stay in St. Louis after Montgomery had moved back to Maryland. The elder Blair wrote her the same long, endearing letters he wrote to all of his children and their mates, but somehow long-sought-after and eagerly awaited visits often failed to materialize. Apparently Apo simply did not wish to belong to her in-laws and felt that being managed by one Blair was enough. At one point Lizzie, who rarely had an unkind word for anyone, confessed to her husband a deep sense of guilt because she could not make herself love Apo, and indeed felt uncomfortable in her presence. As time passed, however, Lizzie and Apo found themselves with more and more in common and with increasing bonds of sympathy, while both came to consider Montgomery's wife, Minna, a cold-hearted Yankee who judged other people much too harshly.

Among other virtues, Apo contributed a gallant but often unsuccessful fight against Frank's constant extravagance. In April 1851 Frank complained to his brother-in-law Phil Lee that he was in dire straits, and as the son must have expected, the letter was immediately read and answered by his father. Blair authorized Frank to draw upon him for $1,000 and added a strong admonition:

If, as you say, you *don't charge* & *don't collect;* it is not hard to see how you became straitened. . . . There was never anything so thoroughly ruinous to me as not charging & not collecting. The character once established, & no man thinks he owes you anything and still his conscience will suggest that it may be you think he does, & he will hate you for it. I do hope you will correct all my vices. . . . all

the sins your father visits on your head, I am afraid I shall be accountable for; and of all my infirmities I fear my disastrous propensity to
procrastination, is the most likely to beset & destroy you.[17]

Frank had shortcomings as a financial manager, but he gained
an immediate reputation in St. Louis as an able and aggressive
lawyer and politician who spoke his mind on all questions and
usually threw caution to the winds. The aging Benton dubbed
him "the Young Ajax," and his father hopefully saw in him the
characteristics of another Andrew Jackson, who had been equally
deficient in business matters. By 1850 Frank was a confirmed
Free-Soiler, and was ready to spend the following decade denouncing on every possible occasion both the institution of slavery
and every real or imagined southern threat against the Union.

The Blair family was also entwined with the endless string of
children, brothers, sisters, cousins, aunts, and uncles of Ben Gratz
and his Philadelphia relatives. Eliza Blair's younger sister Maria,
the wife of Ben Gratz, had died in 1841, leaving four of her six
sons alive to mourn with their distraught father. Having found
happiness once in the Gist clan, the fifty-one-year-old Ben Gratz
wisely went to the same source for another mate. In 1843 he
married Anna Boswell Shelby, the widowed thirty-four-year-old
daughter of an elder sister of Eliza Gist Blair and Maria Gist
Gratz. Ben dutifully accepted her young son as his own; adopted
Mary Boswell, a niece of Anna's first husband; and soon fathered
two daughters.

Maria's sons remained the favorite Blair cousins, Ben's sister
and brother in Philadelphia were Aunt Becky and Uncle Joe, and
all Gratzes were always welcome at Silver Spring. "Dear Uncle
Blair," wrote a future Missouri governor and senator, B. Gratz
Brown, in 1852:

> I have a debt of gratitude to acknowledge. . . . from yourself I
> first received favorable impressions in regard to Democratic principles.
> During my retreat from Yale, and in our twilight converse at 'Silver
> Spring,' I first began to cast off the prejudices of early education &
> conventional thought & to enquire for myself into the merits of the
> great questions which had divided parties in the U.S., and the true
> foundations upon which our political institutions rested. It was the first
> strong impulse ever given to my mind, and the first effort disenthralled
> me at once from the shackles that constant education from very early

youth is so apt to build around the intellect. . . . Conviction of the truth—the wisdom—the large bearings—deep sympathies—and majestic prospect of the Democratic Faith took hold upon my thought. . . . a true appreciation of the history of my country.[18]

In 1850 Ben Gratz gave Frank Blair $20,000 to invest for his youngest son, Cary, who soon moved to St. Louis to seek his fortune. Unhappily, Cary Gratz lacked his father's business shrewdness, and in such matters his cousin Frank Blair was no fountain of wisdom. During the following eleven years young Cary managed to lose most of his stake in various enterprises, with Frank usually committed as his security. By 1861 Francis P. Blair was heavily involved in efforts to save both son and nephew from bankruptcy. Frank and Cary became skilled politicians and able soldiers, however, and as might have been expected they remained the favorite sons of their respective fathers.

Chapter 14

The Free-Soiler

ANDREW Jackson had wished for Blair a "triumph over all enemies," and Blair was more than ready to honor this trust. From the day he walked grimly from Polk's office in 1845 until the moment he joyfully toasted the election of Abraham Lincoln in 1860, Francis P. Blair pursued and dreamed of one major triumph: the election of a president who would stand up to the southern leaders who had destroyed the *Globe*. He accepted without question the concept of a southern "Slave Power" determined to rule or ruin the nation. Though a slaveholder himself, he was utterly opposed to any extension of the system, and he believed the southern demands for slavery in the territories to be mere excuses for building a disunion conspiracy.

Though he held no office and published no paper, Blair continued to wield a remarkable amount of political influence. A wide range of close personal friends respected his judgment, and the longtime habit of looking to him for information and counsel remained strong among local Democratic politicians. Also, of course, there was always the possibility that he might return to the editorial wars. Perhaps one secret of his power was the fact that he boldly continued to act like a prime mover in national affairs, and large numbers of people apparently accepted his self-evaluation. Because he acted like a man of influence, others believed he was. Because they considered him powerful, he in fact was.

For several months Blair and Benton supported the Polk administration. Secretary of State James Buchanan drove out to Silver Spring for counsel on how Polk should deal with the British on the Oregon boundary problem. Blair advised a settlement at 49°, and Benton delivered an interminable but meticulously documented three-day Senate speech to defend this arrangement. Blair also supported the administration's Walker tariff in numerous conversations with doubters, and Benton guided the bill through the Senate. Like Benton, Blair deplored the Mexican War until it began, but he supported the resulting acquisitions of western territory. Both men, after all, were thoroughly steeped in the doctrine of America's "manifest destiny" to spread freedom and enlightenment around the Globe, although neither had previously thought of this in military terms. Benton brought the Santa Fe trader James Magoffin to the White House, after which Magoffin arranged the bloodless surrender of New Mexico by bribing the Mexican generals, and Frémont played an effective if controversial role in the conquest of California.[1]

When the Mexican War quickly turned sour in the Northeast and Northwest and both sections blamed it on the slave power, its prolongation threatened the Democratic party. At this point Benton urged Polk to order a two-pronged invasion of Mexico by land from the north and by sea at Vera Cruz, with the armies to have a commander empowered to make peace on the spot. Polk agreed and tried to give the new command to Benton, who spoke Spanish, had numerous Mexican contacts, and had once been an active army colonel. Congress, seeing this as a move to elect Benton president, refused to create the new rank of lieutenant general. Later Polk appointed Benton to the highest existing rank, that of major general. The Congress approved, but refused to authorize the president to appoint a commander-in-chief without regard to seniority, and four professional major generals outranked Benton. Unwilling to go to Mexico without the authority to make peace, Benton refused to be substituted for the four major generals already in the field and declined the appointment.[2]

In California, meanwhile, the dashing Frémont, who had once explored the West after his teen-aged wife had destroyed the official orders canceling the expedition, engaged in stupidity even beyond salvation from a senatorial father-in-law. Having been appointed governor of California by Commodore Robert F. Stockton of the navy, he refused to relinquish the post when ordered to do so by his newly arrived commanding general, Stephen Kearney. Frémont was returned to Washington under arrest, and after a long, bitter court martial in which Benton,

chairman of the Senate Committee on military affairs, served as
his attorney, "the Pathfinder" was sentenced to dismissal from
the service. Unwilling to alienate either the army or Frémont's
father-in-law and friends, President Polk compromised by approving the verdict but remanding the penalty. Insulted by Polk's
approval of the verdict, the angry Frémont resigned from the
service to become a national martyr, and Benton's previously
well-publicized services to the administration came to an abrupt
halt.[3]

Although Polk's diary indicates otherwise, Benton and Blair
now believed that the offer of a military command had been a
hoax and that fighting the president's battles in the Senate had
been the only real assignment Polk had ever had for Benton.
Blair continued to hope that he and the Democrats could make
Benton president, but the chances for a military career to bring
this about in 1848 were gone.[4]

Meanwhile, as the outlines of the vast empire being taken
from Mexico became clearer, the sectional quarrel that Blair and
Benton had feared burst into flame. For the North, David
Wilmot offered a permanent restriction against slavery in any
of the territories. For the South, John C. Calhoun demanded
equal rights for slavery in all territories. Unlike Benton, who
thought both arguments unwise, dangerous, and unnecessary,
Blair supported the Wilmot Proviso, because he believed that
Calhoun and the Slave Power must be stopped immediately.

The war and the resulting sectional conflict, the compromise
on the Oregon boundary, and Polk's veto of a western rivers-and-
harbors-improvement bill left the Democratic party in a shambles.
Blair's editorial successor, Ritchie, tried vainly to satisfy everyone, but the Calhoun faction itself took the lead in getting him
barred from the Senate floor. In August 1846 Polk came to
Silver Spring for a friendly visit, and a few days later Navy
Secretary Bancroft informed Blair that the president was dis-
gusted with Ritchie and would like Blair to resuscitate the *Globe*.
Blair, however, ignored the suggestion and instead defended
Ritchie. John Rives compared Ritchie's efforts to please everyone with the fable of the man and his son trying to humor every
passerby while taking their jackass to market. "They both rode
him at one time, then one rode him, then both walked and led

him, & then they tied his legs together and carried him on a pole. Every person . . . pronounced them fools. . . . . I think it probable that every body will pronounce the same judgment against Mr. Ritchie (when his ass shall be turned out to grass two years hence)." [5]

By June 1847 Blair was certain the Whigs were planning to nominate General Zachary Taylor for president in 1848, and he decided that Taylor's opponent should be a Democratic general. By August he was scratching away on an adulatory sketch of the life and services of his former schoolmate William O. Butler, the least known of America's four major-generals in the Mexican War. In December the Butler eulogy was published in *Graham's Magazine* in Philadelphia, and it was soon reprinted in various newspapers. [6]

Meanwhile, Blair was also urging upon Van Buren the possibility of a third-party candidate for 1848. He thought Polk would run for reelection and could beat Clay, but he also feared that Taylor would get the Whig nomination with the support of Calhoun and the ultra-southerners. The "extraordinary zeal" with which Calhoun had recently greeted Taylor's former son-in-law, Jefferson Davis, made Blair suspect a possible understanding between "the nullifyers & the no party President." Above all, he insisted to Van Buren, the times called for "an independent body of Democrats . . . to sustain every wise & strong measure for the public good without being held responsible for Polk's sins." "All I have troubled you with is literally nothing to me," wrote Blair at the end of his long and intense letter. "I look out of my window & see fifty acres of the most beautiful wheat growing where four years ago poverty grass could not even germinate, and what is all Mexico to a man who would rather see his own sweet region covered in mid winter with the robes of spring & blooming & bearing though summer & autumn, than to tear out the entrails of others to get at mines which, no matter how rich, can never satiate avarice or ambition." [7]

His fertile fields, however, did not interrupt Blair's visits to the Capitol or his concern with the next election. Senator John A. Dix and other Democratic friends disagreed with his public opposition to the administration, but Blair was adamant: "If the other apostles had stood by Judas & countenanced him before the public, I think in the eye of their master, they would not have been altogether blameless." Blair was honest enough, however, to suspect his own motives. "It may be," he wrote Van Buren, "that I am activated by my avenging disposition & miss the true policy. . . . Still, I think, that I propose justice, and sound policy—not wrong & revenge." [8]

The anger of Blair and Van Buren against Polk was magnified further by the death of their dear friend Silas Wright in September 1847. In 1844 Wright had been persuaded to abandon a safe senate seat and run for governor of New York. Elected, he had served vigorously and well, but in 1846 the Democratic faction led by Secretary of War Marcy gave his campaign for reelection only lukewarm support. He was defeated, and the Van Burenites considered this a rank betrayal. It was only a step to blaming Wright's untimely death on his disappointment, although the tragedy was probably caused at least in part by Wright's many years of heavy drinking.

Another Democratic presidential possibility was Montgomery Blair's father-in-law, Justice Levi Woodbury of the Supreme Court, whose New Hampshire background was well diluted with southern sympathies. For Blair and son Frank, principles were more important than family connections. Montgomery, wrote Frank, "is a perfect *Woodburyite* but thank god he has stopped talking to me about him." Van Buren was Frank's choice. Van Buren agreed with the Blairs on Woodbury, but was unwilling to seek the nomination for himself. He had also heard from Martin, Jr., that Blair was ailing, and warned him to be careful: "Honest people are scarce. Particularly in the neighborhood of Washington." [9]

On May 22, 1848, the Democratic party's warring factions finally convened at Baltimore to nominate a president. Blair and other delegates tried to launch a boom first for Van Buren and then for Butler of Kentucky, but Lewis Cass of Michigan had achieved the most neutral status with a letter recommending that territorial inhabitants settle the question of slavery for themselves. The dramatic climax occurred when each of two opposing delegations from New York presented itself as the true Democrats of that state. The Democratic party, as usual, tried to spread its umbrella wide enough for both by voting to seat both delegations and grant half a vote to each delegate. The Van Buren faction, which opposed the extension of slavery and was known as the Barnburners, angrily rejected the offer and withdrew, leaving their opponents, the Hunkers, as the official representatives of the New York Democratic party. Cass was nominated on a platform that ignored the slavery question entirely, and Butler, who was a candidate largely through Blair's efforts, was the choice for vice-president.

Benton was satisfied with Cass as a non-southern candidate, but Blair had wanted a platform and a candidate openly dedicated to free soil. Benton urged Van Buren and other friends not to start another party and thereby allow the other faction to go before the country as the official Democratic party. Blair, on the other hand, virtually demanded that Van Buren head up a new party. The crime against New York, he wrote, should be punished and the wrong redressed. It was "accusing providence to suppose that wise & good men cannot devise the means." [10]

On June 4, in a letter including high regards "especially for my good *friend* Mrs. Blair," Cass invited Blair to accompany his campaign entourage on a tour of the major northeastern cities. Blair promptly declined, but Benton joined several other senators on the trip and received more attention than the candidate himself. In New York, Benton infuriated many of his old friends but caused a sensation before a packed throng when he invoked the name of Silas Wright for the cause of party unity and the hopes of Lewis Cass.

Always the loyal friend, Blair urged forgiveness for Benton because of the latter's political problems in Missouri, and assured Van Buren that Old Bullion was with them in spirit. In fact, however, a vital difference separated the two old friends. Benton considered the southern demands for territorial slavery nonsense and felt that the southern fire-eaters led by the hated Calhoun were using the issue as an excuse for stirring up disunion. Until his death in 1858 he continued to hope that the voices of reason in the South would triumph. Opposing every specific policy that might expand slavery, he nonetheless sought to reassure the North and minimize the sectional friction. Blair, however, took the Southern effort to expand slavery at its face value and was ready to fight the free-soil battle on every front. Agreeing with Benton that a disunion conspiracy existed, Blair saw no hope except through superior northern power and determination, and he was as ready as any abolitionist to stir up northern emotions and antagonism. If Blair and Benton occasionally disagreed on issues, tactics, and candidates, however, they were fully united in their choice of enemies.

On June 6, 1848, an enormous crowd of Barnburners met in New York City, listened to a brilliant attack on slavery and the tyrannical Slave Power by John Van Buren, and announced a convention to be held at Utica on June 22.

On the following day the Whigs met in Philadelphia. Once again, with victory in its grasp, the party abandoned its deserving statesman, Henry Clay, and turned to a military chieftain. Senator William H. Seward, soft-pedaling his own often-expressed antislavery principles, had convinced the slaveholding General Taylor that his best opportunity for greatness lay with the Whigs. Among those working hardest for Taylor's nomination was a young congressman named Abraham Lincoln, who had hopes that a presidential victory would make him the commisioner of the general land office in his home state.

On June 16 Blair suggested that "our Utica friends" should call a general convention in September of all those united against southern domination of the government and against the "extension of slavery as the certain means of perpetuating it." Meanwhile the convention should put forth several names rather than nominate a single candidate.

The Barnburners, however, exceeded Blair's fondest hopes. They nominated Martin Van Buren himself, and six weeks later held a national Free-Soil convention at Buffalo. With all the spirit of a religious revival, the Buffalo convention of Barnburners, antislave Democrats, and "conscience Whigs" who could not accept the slaveholding Taylor listened to blazing speeches and adopted a platform of Free Soil, Free Speech, Free Labor, and Free Men. The delegates then nominated Van Buren, with Charles Francis Adams, son of old John Quincy, for his vice-presidential running mate. Van Buren and Blair may have wondered if Andrew Jackson was observing this alliance from beyond the grave, but neither broached the subject. Blair thought Adams an excellent choice and remembered that "even his father was never wholly identified with the Whig party."

Van Buren's letter of acceptance to the Utica convention delighted Blair further by winning son Montgomery over to the cause. Montgomery, like Benton, had opposed the intrusion of the slave question into the election. "He has an ingenious & honest mind," wrote the happy father, "which although warped by the well plied efforts of interested & industrious ambition, which has worked upon him through his tender affections, is yet able, when the veil is rent, to see & feel the power of truth & honor. It is a great satisfaction to me, that your hand has done this service for him." [11]

In August Blair discovered that his "barn-burning propensity" had "well nigh destroyed" his own "well-earned congressional harvest." Rives was struggling to keep as much government printing as possible despite Blair's public denunciations of President Polk and the Democratic convention that had nominated Cass. Congressional Democrats attacked the *Globe*'s congressional printing contracts and threw out a $21,000 bill for work already completed. Unwilling to "shuffle off the penance" for his "sins" upon his "innocent partner," whose fortunes, after all, underlay his own, Blair finally persuaded Rives to dissolve their partnership officially. [12]

The election campaign coincided with a long and angry debate in Congress over whether or not Oregon could receive territorial government with a law barring slavery. Calhoun insisted that restricting slavery in Oregon would degrade the South and justify disunion. Benton denounced Calhoun, after which Senator Andrew Pickens Butler attacked Benton in language so harsh that only fast action by colleagues kept the two old men apart. Benton announced that he would "cram the lie down his throat." Butler then sent Benton a duel challenge, which Benton, who had already fought his share of duels, ignored. [13] In two all-night sessions the Senate worked out two compromises, but in each case the House tabled the bill while the weary senators were sleeping off the effects of their all-night labors. Finally, on the Sunday morning following the last day of the session, by a scant margin of two votes supplied by the southerners Benton and Houston,

Oregon received a territorial government. In all of this Blair was an excited behind-the-scenes participant, and every event only added to his conviction that the South was determined to rule or ruin and must be stopped by defiance rather than compromise.

In early August 1848, Eliza, now fifty-three, was developing some alarming symptoms "from the alteration process she is undergoing." Her nervous system was "exceedingly deranged," and she was suffering from an irregular pulse, nausea, depression, and terrible dreams. On August 21 the Blairs left for the mountains and mineral springs at Sharon, New York, where a miraculous cure quickly occurred. Soon the elderly lovers were eating enormous meals, sleeping soundly, and walking hand in hand for miles each day over the windy mountain heights. Blair also used the waters to bathe, eat, and drink himself into his best condition in years, but then "sulphured" himself into a distressing cold. At Sharon they were inspired by the news of the Buffalo convention, and went home by way of Lindenwald for another happy visit with Van Buren.[14]

In the November election, Van Buren received 10 percent of the popular vote and ran ahead of Cass in New York. Once again a third party in the state of New York had decided the result of a close national election, and the Whigs for the second time had put their own hero general in the White House. Blair felt that his new party had compelled aspiring politicians throughout the North to take a stand against the extension of slavery, and he predicted that any further weakness on the issue would expand the Free Soil party into "a power which will shake the lofty pedestals of those who gained them by hollow professions."[15]

John C. Calhoun, of course, had other ideas. In January he called the southern members of Congress into a secret caucus, to which Benton and Houston were conspicuously uninvited. Houston attended anyhow and tried to keep the affair within moderate channels. Benton and Blair considered the movement sheer treason. The caucus produced Calhoun's memorable "Southern Address," which consisted primarily of exaggerated complaints of northern aggressions and frightening predictions of eventual race war and Negro supremacy unless slavery could attain equal rights in the territories.

Houston was already under heavy fire in Texas for his vote to admit Oregon with a slavery restriction, and Blair was more than willing to help "the Raven" prepare a defense. The ex-editor wrote a nineteen-page address "To my constituents," in which Houston met Calhoun head-on. The long, eloquent, and often humorous denunciation of Calhoun for threatening the Union over impossible demands in Oregon ended with Jackson's well-known words: "The *federal union*. It must be *preserved*." Surely Texas had not forgotten its debt to Old Hickory! [16]

Even more than Houston, Benton was under the gun because of his forthcoming campaign for election in 1850. The Missouri legislature instructed him to vote like a southerner on all matters related to slavery, and Benton responded with an angry speech of defiance. He would vote his own conscience, appeal to the people for support, and accept the verdict of his constituents. Through the summer and fall of 1849, the "Old Buffalo," as a state paper called him, campaigned by horseback and carriage in every part of Missouri, and his message was always the same: Calhoun and the southern ultras were trying to destroy the sacred Union, the world's great experiment in free government, in the name of territorial rights for slavery that were impossible anyhow because of geography and climate. Calhoun answered in a widely published ten-column letter, and the bitter controversy attracted national attention.

The Blair sons, of course, were thoroughly immersed in Benton's campaign. They wrote public letters, made speeches, and kept their father regularly informed of each battle. In March 1849 a would-be assassin shot at Frank on a dark street in St. Louis. An editor named Pickering was indicted, but was acquitted because of what Blair called "suborning witnesses." By August Montgomery and Frank, misled by the vigor of Benton's style and the enthusiasm of his audiences, were certain Old Bullion was going to win, and their father happily relayed the information to Van Buren: "He plays his part like a great Bear surrounded by a yelping pack of whelps. He slaps one down on this side—another on that—and grips a third with his teeth—then tosses him with his snout." [17]

Missouri, however, was a slave state, and the Whig party had spent too many years hating Benton. The assembly elections in August 1849 were a triumph for the principles of Benton and the Blairs but a personal defeat for the old senator. Sixty-four Whigs, fifty-five Benton Democrats, and only thirty-seven of the Calhoun Democrats were elected. Various attempts to reunite the Democrats were made, but Benton adamantly refused all overtures. He would prefer a Whig in his seat to any bargain with the nullifiers.

The threat of disunion made the Whigs more acceptable to Blair also. In December 1849 he made peace with Henry Clay, who was fresh from his role in Mary Boswell's wedding and an extremely pleasant stay with Blair's friends and in-laws in Philadelphia. "I read with interest the friendly message of Mr. Blair," wrote Clay to John Minor Botts of Virginia, "and reciprocating the spirit of it, I authorize you to say to him, that I willingly consign to oblivion all our past differences." [18]

Chapter 15

Hope and Frustration

WHEN Congress met in December 1849 for the long and angry session of 1850, the old protagonists Clay, Webster, Benton, and Calhoun were back for a final performance. Northerners and southerners immediately accused each other of provocation. Ritchie's Democratic *Union* charged that the administration, working with Senator Seward, "a well-known abolitionist," was plotting to *"foment the anti-slavery excitement of the North to such a pitch as to produce reaction of the South to such an extent as may demonstrate itself in attempts to secede from the Union, in order to give General Taylor and the cabinet an opportunity to run up the Union flag, call its party the Union party, and thus rescue itself from inevitable defeat and prostration."* [1]

Blair, however, believed that the southerners in Congress were trying to pick a needless quarrel with the North, and he was angered by "the tameness of Northern Senators." He wanted "the greed arrogance & ingratitude of the South for the long & unmerited indulgence extended to it" publicly condemned, and he regretted that Silas Wright and "old Johnny Q." Adams were no longer around to assume the task. The southerners' purpose, he wrote, was to whip up a frenzy against a free California and for the Texas claims against New Mexico. If California could be admitted, "Calhoun & his mormons would only have to make the territorial fight with Deseret & its Mormons." And if Calhoun managed to take slaves to Salt Lake, he should be awarded Joe Smith's "chair among the latter day Saints." [2]

As the machinery of government ground to a halt, Henry Clay offered his last dramatic compromise: California should be admitted without federal action on slavery, which meant it would

be free; New Mexico should decide the issue for itself, but only
at the point of statehood; a negotiated settlement between Texas
and New Mexico should be sweetened by the federal assumption
of the Texas debt; the domestic slave trade should be abolished
in the District of Columbia but guaranteed in the other slave
states; Congress should record its sentiments against abolition
in the District of Columbia; and the South should have a stronger
fugitive slave law.

Clay's old Jacksonian enemies immediately rushed to his
side. "Tell Clay for me," Van Buren wrote Blair, "that he added
a crowning grace to his public life . . . more honorable & du-
rable than his election to Presidency could possibly have been." [3]
Blair promptly sent Van Buren's letter to Clay and enclosed one
of his own. Later in the Senate, Clay left his seat to offer Blair
his hand.

The new harmony between Clay, Webster, Douglas, Benton,
and Blair was soon disrupted, however, by a disagreement on tactics. Southerners led by Henry S. Foote of Mississippi concluded
that Clay's compromise was their best bargain if they could amend
its details to their advantage. This, however, required keeping
the various measures combined in a single "omnibus bill." In the
words of South Carolina Senator Andrew Pickens Butler, "California was a large and safe ship, and the other smaller boats in
danger were to be attached to her and she would carry them all
safely into port." [4] With an endless string of amendments the
southerners sought to add most of present-day New Mexico to
Texas and worked for an ever-stronger fugitive slave act. These
would be their price for the admission of a free California.

Because of James Blair and Frémont, Blair and Benton had a
personal interest in the immediate admission of California, and
they had promised friends in New Mexico every effort to keep
the region from being swallowed by the slave state of Texas.
They were also realists and knew that the compromise could
never pass as a single package. Each of Clay's points could command a majority separately, but most of the representatives and
senators who could support one or more did not dare support
them all. Clay, however, was persuaded by Foote and others
to keep the measures together in one bill.

Throughout the long, hot summer the struggle raged. Blair's family went off to the seashore, but he could not leave the battle-field. Once again he sat enthralled as Clay and Benton for the last time went at each other with a brilliance neither had ever excelled. Like Benton, Blair considered Calhoun's last great speech a fitting expression of the treason they had always felt his doctrines to be, and he agreed with Benton's refusal to join the eulogies when Calhoun died. When Foote, who had already been shot in three of his four duels, pointed a pistol at Benton on the Senate floor, Blair considered it just another example of the way slavery had corrupted the conduct and principles of the southern "chivalry."

To their surprise, Blair and Benton found President Taylor their strongest ally against the effort to sacrifice New Mexico. Taylor owned 110 slaves but he did not advocate extending the institution, and his most influential advisor was the antislavery New Yorker William Henry Seward. Also, Taylor had devel-oped strong prejudices against Texas during the Mexican War, and he was ready to defend New Mexico against Texas personally —at the head of the army if necessary. On July 4, however, the president sat for several hours in a broiling sun at the Washington Monument while Henry Foote delivered an interminable ora-tion. Back at the White House he sought comfort from several bowls of cherries and ice-cold milk, and five days later he died.

The new president, Millard Fillmore, was a personal enemy of Seward's and already a supporter of the omnibus bill. Blair concluded that with Fillmore's pressure the omnibus would pass, and he was much disturbed by this prospect of a southern victory.[5] On July 31, however, Benton mailed a letter to Eliza Blair from her husband and added his own postscript. They were "all in the clouds triumphing over Clay, Webster, Cass, Foote, the omnibus, and the devil!" James Pearce of Maryland, an om-nibus-bill supporter, had moved to strike everything related to New Mexico from the bill. He intended to reinsert it in a more acceptable form, but when New Mexico was stricken by a vote of 33–32, angry southerners did the same for Texas by a margin of one vote. In quick succession every item but Utah was elimi-nated from the bill. The bill, wrote Lizzie Lee, had "died of amendments and passed the Senate with no passenger in the Omnibus save the Utah travellers. The Mormons alone got thru' living—the Christians all jumped out." [6]

As Blair and Benton had predicted, the compromise measures passed quickly once they were separated. Clay and Benton had obviously enjoyed their last great encounter, and Blair and Van Buren agreed that both were "truly great men." Soon, however, as expected, Missouri replaced Benton with a Whig senator. Blair with his usual optimism decided they must now "mount Old Bullion & ride him into Battle" for the 1852 presidential campaign. To his great disappointment, however, Benton would not be ridden. He had always kept himself free from presidential ambitions, and to the consternation of his friends, his considerable national following, and his future biographers, he would not abandon this resolve.

In late September 1850 Senators John C. Frémont and Henry S. Foote exchanged angry words and almost fought a duel. Frémont appeared eager to avenge Foote's previous insults to his father-in-law, but after the Benton and Blair women had suffered some anxious moments, the affair was settled peacefully. Soon the Frémonts and Mary Blair with little Violet were preparing for the long sea voyage to California, where James Blair anxiously awaited them. [7]

The departure drew the two families even closer together. Francis P. Blair's sense of propriety, goaded by his love of travel, persuaded him that he should escort his daughter-in-law and granddaughter to New York City. There he again enjoyed numerous lively conversations with local politicians and editors. Poor Mary, already apprehensive about the long and dangerous journey, was upset further by the conduct of her brother, Willie, who had come to see her off, but spent most of his time in certain infamous hotels. All in all it was an exciting trip. In a restaurant Blair hung up his hat and expensive new coat. A lady passed by carrying a very similar hat and coat, and feeling much satisfaction from being in style, Blair looked toward his own for a comparison. His own were gone, but with all the speed of his fifty-nine years he raced into the street and caught the lady and her husband as they were entering a hack. With a show of embarrassment she explained that she had thought they were her husband's. The man, who was already wearing a hat and coat of another color, said "No, my dear," and politely handed Blair the stolen items. Blair returned to his group in triumph, "proud of his attire and prouder of the vigilance that had saved them." [8]

Blair was certain the Whigs would nominate General Winfield Scott for president in 1852, and he now felt a genuine sympathy for Henry Clay. He was delighted at a Jenny Lind concert when Scott, Webster, Crittenden, and Fillmore drew only perfunctory applause, after which the crowd rose and rocked the hall at the appearance of Clay. Later Blair assured the old statesman that Jenny had asked to see him because she had heard the public "proclaim you above all our great men." Clay was obviously pleased that Blair had seen his triumph. [9]

The editor of the *Western Atlas* in New York proposed Blair himself as a candidate. Blair was proud of the honor but ashamed of the "poverty in the Democratic party" indicated by such a suggestion. In a kind and witty note he suggested that the editor look elsewhere, and he sent the editor's letter to Van Buren with a request for its return. He wanted it "as a memorial to my descendants, that though sorely tempted I refused the Presidency." [10]

Above all, Blair wanted a candidate who would defy South Carolina's threat to the Union. "The negro question," he wrote Van Buren, "has no more to do with the Charleston plot as a motive than Calhoun's heart had to do with patriotism." The southern chivalry, he added, had just settled an affair of honor without bloodshed right at his own gate. Two congressmen intending to fight a duel had "puffed off two loads of powder & shook hands and . . . told it that the salt petre had saved their honor & their bacon both." Eliza had met the three carriages carrying the participants and surgeons, who were very polite in giving her the road for fear the smell of powder might frighten her horse. Blair only hoped that South Carolina's honor might be saved in the same way. [11]

Blair's willingness to take Woodbury only "as the old maid does 'a do no better,' " ended abruptly in September 1851, when the judge died. On the same day his daughter, Minna Blair, who had already had one child stillborn, gave birth to a ten-pound boy. Having lost one wife in childbirth, Montgomery Blair carefully kept the news of her father's death a secret for several weeks, until she learned of it by reading about the appointment of his successor to the Supreme Court. The Blairs concluded that Woodbury's life had been much shortened by overeating, and Lizzie promptly filled her next letter to Phillips Lee with dire warnings and pleas for him to curb his appetite.[12]

Blair now settled once again on William O. Butler, and spent the next few months writing long letters on the general's behalf. At this point Lizzie Lee, whose transcriptions for her father were only slightly more legible than his own, concluded that her communications were too significant to risk prying eyes at the post office. She therefore began writing in metaphors and spelling all proper names in a simple reversed-alphabet code. That anyone unscrupulous enough to open her letters would probably be able to decode a cipher that included "Olsm Ezm-Yfiem" for John Van Buren and "the Nztrxrzm" for his father, "the Magician," apparently did not occur to her, and the mysteries thus attempted made writing the letters more exciting.

Planning for the election of 1852 was interspersed with the usual family and personal affairs that made life in the Blair household a constant adventure. In September 1851 Lizzie informed Lee that slave Mary wished to buy her grandchild with her small savings, and asked him to send a deed. The elder Blairs heartily approved of the arrangement because it would give Mary "a motive for soberness & industry." In the following month Ben, a trusted slave under hire to the Blairs who, according to Lizzie, produced the only profit at Silver Spring, badly injured another man's slave in a fight. Ben's master sent word that Lizzie should help him escape the magistrates, and he was allowed to run away with the full connivance and assistance of both his master and his employers. A short while later, Eliza suffered a painful loss when the very elderly slave who had been her childhood nurse died. Joanna, wrote Lizzie, had been "the last association with her childhood's home" left to her mother, and it was "a comfort that she made her comfortable of late years." In December 1851 Eliza and Lizzie were trying on hats from New York when they suddenly smelled smoke. A slave, James, " with his obstinate habit of making big fires," had made one that overheated the stove pipe and set the house on fire. Lizzie gave the alarm and fought the blaze with axe and water until others came to put it out. Her father, meanwhile, was seriously ill with influenza and could not help.[13]

After Blair recovered in January 1852, his first visit was to the dying Henry Clay. Eliza sent the old statesman a batch of her honey-and-whiskey cough remedy, and until Clay's death six months later the Blairs and Mary Boswell Riggs were his most faithful attendants. Six of his children, including the brilliant son killed in the Mexican War, were dead, and he apparently preferred death alone in Washington to the company of his aged wife. Blair also served as an intermediary for Van Buren and for Benton, who sent a promise that Clay would receive full justice and credit in his memoirs entitled *Thirty Years' View.* "Make my grateful acknowledgments to Mr. Clay for his kind assurances," wrote Van Buren, "and say that they are most sincerely and feelingly reciprocated." Blair urged Clay to come to Silver Spring, where Eliza and Lizzie could nurse him full-time. Clay pleaded immediate social obligations but promised to come in the spring. In June he died.[14]

In January 1852 Washington was greatly excited by the presence of the great Hungarian revolutionary Louis Kossuth, who was seeking American help for another attack on the hated Austrians. The ladies, including Lizzie and Eliza, were thrilled by his dynamic presence, and Blair invited him to deliver the major address at the annual Democratic dinner at Jackson Hall commemorating the Battle of New Orleans. With the help of Eliza and Lizzie, Blair composed the toasts for the banquet, but he was forced to compromise and accept compliments to John Tyler in exchange for his own eulogies of Van Buren. Van Buren's brief message to be read to the assemblage never arrived, and Blair was convinced that his southern enemies had stolen it from the post office. Kossuth's words, appearance, and delivery left his listeners singing paeans for days.[15] Like others before and since, however, Kossuth found Americans unwilling to translate their enthusiasm into dangerous or expensive action, and Kossuth County, Iowa, has remained his only permanent American memorial.

Wishing a stronger voice for the candidacy of General Butler, Blair decided that Montgomery should become the editor of a new Washington press, but Van Buren threw cold water immediately: "No inducement . . . should induce you to hazard the independence you have assumed by connecting yourself as proprietor with anything of the sort. You are too honest & too confiding for the business people of the present day." Blair accepted his friend's advice, and in return offered a cure for the ex-president's gout: "burning the spot with *Moxa,* a moss rolled up in small volume covering the space of two pence placed on the spot & set fire to. Have the blister dressed with garlic." [16]

Blair's hope for Butler suddenly collapsed in January 1852, when the general publicly approved a series of pro-slavery-extension resolutions passed by the Kentucky legislature. Blair could only conclude that his old friend and schoolmate had been unfairly pressured and duped. In an angry confrontation he accused John C. Breckinridge and other Kentucky Democrats of out-Heroding Herod, and only the soothing intervention of Preston King kept the quarrel from reaching a dangerous stage. To John Van Buren, Blair confided that his "vocation of President making" was over. "I am willing to follow you free soilers wherever you choose." "Prince John" answered with a friendly but sharp scolding, but Martin Van Buren sent a kind and understanding letter. "I hope you may escape your next fit of the gout," Blair answered gratefully, "& that John may have the visitation in your stead." [17]

By June 1, 1852, when Blair and his fellow delegates met at Baltimore to choose a Democratic nominee, Blair had settled on Houston, but the nomination of a slaveholding heretic was clearly impossible. Cass, Douglas, and Buchanan were the front-runners, but they soon destroyed each other's chances. The New York delegates leaned briefly toward Buchanan, but Blair assured them "that there could not be a worse man chosen." To Blair's relief "Old Buck" faded with the others, and on the forty-eighth ballot the convention turned to Franklin Pierce of New Hampshire. Pierce had taken no position on any of the issues, and Blair, Benton, and Van Buren, like everybody else, thought he was their man.

In early August Benton crushed his opponents in the congressional election in the St. Louis district, and for the rest of the summer and fall he campaigned vigorously for Pierce. Frank Blair, who was elected to the Missouri legislature, did likewise.

In September Frank's public tongue-lashing of a Benton detractor almost caused a duel between himself and a local doctor, but to Blair's relief the latter's friends persuaded him "to take Frank off with his pills & not attempt it with pistols."

Ex-editor Blair, meanwhile, became the propaganda clearinghouse for the Pierce campaign. "I am required here," he wrote Van Buren, "to contribute my mite to assist the Pierce Commee. in providing campaign documents. The feebleness of the organ renders this sort of desultory aid in pamphlets & letters indispensible." His major effort was a long and occasionally unfair attack on the military record of the Whig candidate, General Winfield Scott. Though he compiled the material, Blair did not put his name on it because of his long personal friendship with Scott's daughter. He thought it fair, however, because the Whig presses had "assailed Pierce's private life with the grossest falsehoods." He assured Van Buren that he had only tried "to furnish our distant village friends, something to say, when borne hard upon by adversaries. Pray do not set it down to vindictive temperament—for I assure you it was almost coercion that brought me to it." [18]

In October George Peaslee, Pierce's campaign manager, asked Blair to prepare a letter on possible cabinet appointments. At first Blair insisted only that the cabinet should not include any of the recent candidates for the nomination. By election time, however, he was convinced that Montgomery should be in the cabinet, preferably as attorney general. Asking the advice of Rives and Van Buren, Blair wrote that his elder son was an able and sound lawyer with an unblemished personal character and morals that were "not only pure but religiously pure." He was sure that "the old Jackson party everywhere would be glad to see some amends made in his person for the cavalier treatment I received from Mr. Polk." Rives and Van Buren agreed, but suggested that the idea should come from Benton. [19]

In November Franklin Pierce won by an overwhelming majority, and the Whig party was to all intents and purposes dead as a force in American political life. Several hundred thousand northerners had voted for Pierce without any inkling that he would turn out to be a strongly pro-southern president. Blair's contribution to the result cannot be measured, but his well-known identification with the candidate and his record as a Free Soiler must have limited the doubts of a great many northern voters. Perhaps Pierce's greatest advantage was the national image of his opponent— the huge, pompous, and overly dramatic general known as "Old Fuss and Feathers." Winfield Scott ran a poor campaign and did not emerge as a viable candidate. Americans have never been reluctant to elect generals to the presidency, but they have consistently rejected those who have demonstrated an excessive awareness of their own importance.

The new president-elect was either a genius at deception or so weak and vacillating in conversation that he invariably became in the eyes of his supporters whatever they wished him to be. His national image had been produced by the wishful thinking of individuals and factions who agreed with each other on almost nothing. Free Soilers, professional Democrats, moderates everywhere, and southern fire-eaters alike had high hopes for Franklin Pierce. He was a blank page upon which each group had drawn its own image, and his administration was certain to leave a trail of anger and betrayed expectations. Only once did he command universal sympathy. His only child, an eleven-year-old son, was killed before the parents' eyes in a train wreck shortly before the inauguration, and Mrs. Pierce never fully recovered her sanity. The Pierce White House was a bleak place, and this may have affected both the president's choice of friends and his judgment.

Blair's cabinet choices were John Dix for secretary of state and Peaslee for postmaster general, and he also praised James Guthrie of Kentucky and Joseph Medill of Ohio. As expected, Benton suggested Montgomery Blair for attorney general. Peaslee reported that Pierce had described Blair as "an old friend in whom he had great confidence." A new swarm of letters poured in on Blair from political job-seekers led by his prominence in the campaign to consider him a major power in the administration.[20]

Blair, Benton, and Van Buren, however, were living in a fool's paradise. Pierce and his associates had used them to good advantage, but the president-elect was actually controlled by friends who had no intention of rewarding them or any other Free Soilers. Pierce was probably a weakling rather than a shrewd conniver, but this meant that his decisions would be shaped by those who applied the most direct personal pressure. William Marcy, the able New York Hunker who was anathema to Van Buren, became secretary of state. Jefferson Davis, recently defeated for governor of Mississippi by the moderate Henry S. Foote, was rescued and restored to great personal power in the South by appointment as secretary of war. Caleb Cushing of Massachusetts, who had been a Whig until the end of the Tyler administration and was strongly pro-southern, was the new attorney general. In Missouri Benton's recommendations were ignored completely and every political appointment in the state went to the Old Buffalo's enemies. Pierce did appoint Montgomery Blair solicitor of the federal court of claims, but it was hardly the cabinet post or judgeship for which his father had hoped.[21]

At the end of 1853, Blair's last lingering hopes for Pierce abruptly ended. Stephen A. Douglas, another party leader ignored by Pierce, tried to solve several problems simultaneously with a new bill to organize governments for the territories of Kansas and Nebraska. Douglas needed a territorial act that would open the land for a northern railroad to California, mollify southerners, and reunite the Democratic party behind his own efforts to become president. After long consultations, he finally produced a bill that would allow the territorial settlers themselves to decide on the question of slavery. When others pointed out that the territory was already pledged to freedom by the Missouri Compromise of 1820, Douglas added a final provision repealing the Missouri Compromise.

The suggested repeal of the sacred compromise brought a scream of rage throughout the North. Anti-abolition Free-Soilers as well as abolitionists could now rouse people who had previously given slavery no attention at all. The longstanding prohibition against slavery in the vast area from Missouri and Iowa to the Rockies was to be destroyed, and, in theory at least, southerners with slaves could now seize it for their own. Charles Sumner, Salmon P. Chase, and other radicals issued their famous "Appeal of the Independent Democrats in Congress," and the northern press and pulpit took up the cry against this allegedly wicked and Godless attempt to extend further the national rule of the Slave Power.

As expected, Benton in the House and Houston in the Senate defied their fellow slaveholders and denounced the bill as a measure that would only damage the South while tearing the nation apart. Both insisted that slavery had no chance in the region and that the southern people had no need nor wish for the bill. Blair was equally indignant, and blamed it all on the "railroad mania engendered by the jobbing speculators." He begged Pierce to oppose the measure, but the president instead threw the full power of his office behind it. At last, Blair accepted what had always been clear. Pierce would use Blair's talents in any way possible, but had never intended to accept his advice on anything.

Meanwhile, in April 1853, three American ambassadors abroad—James Buchanan, John Y. Mason of Virginia, and Pierre Soulé of Louisiana—had issued the Ostend Manifesto, threatening to buy Cuba from Spain even if Spain refused to sell, and citing the danger that Cuba might abolish slavery as a valid justification. Blair concluded that the South was "making a prodigious stride to . . . make a Slave empire that will stand alone when they cut the connection & unless I am grievously deceived the North will rally to prevent the fatal advancement." It was a sound prediction, and he would play a major role in its fulfillment.[22]

Chapter 16

The Republican

LATE in May 1845 some railroad companies invited Blair to join an excursion from New York City to St. Anthony's Falls on the Mississippi in present-day Minnesota. His womenfolk objected strenuously because of his ill-health and the presence of cholera in the St. Louis region, but Senator Preston King wanted him to confer with the New York Democrats, and he was eager to see Frank. At 5:00 A.M. on May 28, with Phillips Lee's latest $250 check to Lizzie in his pocket, Blair left for New York with what Lizzie called "the notables and fashionables." He was painfully ill from too many strawberries, but King had agreed to be his personal attendant and nurse. King had promised Eliza to make him eat properly, and Blair had promised her he would not go to St. Louis. Lizzie had promised Lee that Rives would repay the money by July 1.

At Buffalo Blair became desperately ill again, but a day of rest and further nursing by Senator John A. Dix "almost after mother's fashion" brought a quick recovery. A few days later he and Frank arrived almost simultaneously at Rock Island, Illinois, and boarded a steamboat for the ride up to the falls. It was a very scenic journey, but father and son spent most of their time discussing politics. Blair had decided it was time for Frank to run for Congress. On June 15 Eliza received from Chicago her husband's long letter hinting that he might go to St. Louis despite his promises, and on June 18 came a letter from Lee describing his meeting with Frank and his father-in-law in St. Louis, where Lee was on a tour of navy duty. On June 24 Blair finally arrived home, weary and angry because Eliza had not sent a carriage for him on the strength of Lee's letter saying that he would get home that day. Lizzie had never seen him looking so well.[1]

On the journey he had renewed friendships and helped launch a movement destined to put the Barnburner and Free-Soil Democrats in a new antislavery Republican party. In New York, also, he had begun a useful relationship with John Bigelow, associate editor of the *New York Evening Post*. Until well after the Civil War, the *Post* was ready to print anything Blair wished to write. This gave the former editor a new opportunity for widespread influence and perhaps with a greater illusion of power than he actually had. As always in politics, however, the illusion of power creates power over those who accept it. "Keep your poker hot," wrote Bigelow in July 1854; "your letters can not come too often nor too long." [2]

In August 1854 Blair's worst fears were confirmed in St. Louis. The anti-Catholic and anti-immigrant Know Nothing party mustered a large vote against Benton because of his lifelong opposition to bigotry, and his battle against the Kansas–Nebraska Act could not be satisfactorily explained in Missouri. His defeat was "the great triumph of the hour for the administration & its Southern friends," Blair wrote bitterly. Blair now believed that the Kansas–Nebraska agitation would bring the Whigs back to power, and for the first time in his life he approved the success of his longtime political opponents.

Occasionally, however, Blair had to turn from political concerns to more personal affairs. His final settlement with Rives, theoretically at least, guaranteed him $7,500 annually. Lizzie thought this would be quite enough if he could only be persuaded to stop buying and trying to improve more land. In addition to his farm, Blair was also preoccupied during 1855 with research for the memoirs of Martin Van Buren, who was touring Europe with his dying son, Martin, Jr., but finding time between banquets to write an autobiography. Young Martin had been like one of their own children to the Blairs, and his death gave them much sadness. Soon Blair was writing the bereaved father a description of his own melancholy task. With his own hands, Blair had built a flintstone and cement mound in his garden for the remains of his "dear son brought from California." The area was "already planted with holly & laurel, long lived & self propagating evergreen in the first bearing, the deepest scarlet berries in the winter. The latter a fine bloom in the spring." [3]

It was a sad year also for the Bentons and Frémonts. Mrs. Benton died in September 1854, and in February 1855, while Benton was denouncing a land bounty bill at the Capitol, the family home burned to the ground. Gone were the personal effects and mementoes of a lifetime as well as the almost-completed hand-written manuscript of the second volume of Benton's *Thirty Years' View*. President Pierce was his usual overtly affectionate and generous self, and invited the family to live in the White House until a new home could be built. Benton refused, but he did comment that Pierce's errors stemmed from his head rather than his heart. The Blairs of course gave every assistance, and the shared tragedies drew the two families still closer.

Blair compared his son's tomb to that of Ajax as described by Byron, but there was little time to mourn fallen warriors. Soon he had Lizzie almost exhausted from long hours of copying his fierce articles castigating Pierce, the president's southern allies, and his northern "doughface lackeys." After one such effort, Lizzie confided to Phil that she had added "the little touch at Mr. Cushing . . . Father praised it so much that I can't help bragging of it to you alone. Mr. C. deserves some hits from the women as he runs the gauntlet of life." [4]

Events in Kansas were giving Blair much to denounce and were bringing other Northern Democrats to the same doubts about their party. In two fraudulent elections dominated by Missouri voters from across the border, Kansas chose a pro-slavery territorial delegate to Congress and a pro-slavery legislature. The new legislature passed severe penalties for anyone agitating against slavery and authorized a pro-slavery test oath for officeholders. Meanwhile, the New England Emigrant Aid Society and other similar organizations were sending northern settlers and antislavery leaders to Kansas, and southern groups were making similar if much weaker efforts. If the settlers could decide on slavery for themselves, then the right people should fill up the territory. As Douglas himself had expected, the contest was never even. The great bulk of the settlers came on their own from northwestern states, and these immigrants were almost unanimously against both slavery and free blacks. In late

October and early November 1855, a Free-State convention at
Topeka wrote a constitution that prohibited both slavery and the
entry of free blacks, and in January 1856 the Free-Staters elected
a governor and legislature. Kansas now had two governments.
These events were accompanied by sporadic bloodshed, much of
it unrelated to slavery, but enough of the violence was between
pro- and antislavery settlers to make "Bleeding Kansas" a symbol
of the national conflict. President Pierce condemned the Topeka
government as an act of rebellion, and as a result Topeka, Kansas,
still has no Pierce Avenue or Street to go with its other thorough-
fares named after presidents. From late spring until December in
1856, a small-scale civil war raged, although most of the citizenry
probably wished only to be left alone by both governments.

In response to Bleeding Kansas, a coalition of antislavery
Democrats, Whigs, and Free Soilers met at Ripon, Wisconsin, in
February 1855 to recommend the organization of a new antislavery party to be called "Republican." A July meeting at Jackson, Michigan, officially adopted the name. In·Washington,
a Republican Association was organized in June, and Blair was
invited to become its first president. He refused the office, but was
highly sympathetic to the Association. Over the next several
months Silver Spring became a frequent meeting place for Republican converts like Nathaniel Banks, Charles Sumner, Salmon
P. Chase, Preston King, and others.

In September 1855 Blair also found a new candidate, and on
November 17 he shared his discovery with Benton. The ideal
man, "brave and attractive" and "unconnected with past corruptions and misdeeds," was Benton's own son-in-law, John C.
Frémont. Benton was neither flattered nor pleased. Frémont, he
said, had no political experience, and his own sins would be held
against the son-in-law. Blair answered that Benton's influence
would elect Frémont, but Old Bullion angrily disagreed.[5]

However subconscious it may have been, Blair's sudden
enthusiasm for Frémont was not without self-interest. As a national hero allegedly mistreated by President Polk after conquering California and a man untainted by the past errors and sins of
any political party, the Pathfinder was an immensely available
candidate. Also, he and Jessie had always leaned heavily upon
"Father Blair," and owed the Blair family for many services

and kindnesses. They had also named a son after Blair. Frémont, therefore, was not only an excellent practical choice. If elected, he would be likely to follow Blair's counsel in important matters. This admirable trait more than compensated for Blair's knowledge that Frémont was a hopeless financial manager and organizer. Indeed, the confusion that invariably attended his personal affairs was almost a Blair family joke. Blair may have rationalized that Andrew Jackson had never been financially successful either.

Benton, on the other hand, was acutely aware of the deficiencies combined with the courage and energy in Frémont's character, and he desperately feared that the election of a president by an exclusively northern party would provoke a southern secession and a civil war. He would oppose any such candidate, and he did not wish to fight a battle against his own children. Ultimately the Blair and Benton families were completely divided on the issue. The Frémonts made Silver Spring their Washington headquarters and virtually severed communications with Benton. The eldest Benton daughter, Eliza, and her husband, William Carey Jones, agreed with Benton, and this created a further rift. On one occasion, Blair and Montgomery were speaking so angrily of Benton that Lizzie had to find excuses for keeping Eliza Jones, her guest, in another part of the house. Lizzie was thoroughly exasperated with Benton, whom she had loved dearly since his support for Phillips Lee during her courtship. For the next two years she usually referred to him as "Ole Bull." The Frémont children found it very confusing because they still adored Grandpa. They were finally persuaded to blame all the trouble on Jones.

Having found his candidate, Blair agreed to accept the presidency of the Washington Republican Association, but he resigned immediately with a public letter explaining both his inability to serve and the reasons why every northern Democrat should join the Republicans. Dated December 1, 1855, and widely circulated throughout the country, the letter was a masterful appeal to the true followers of Andrew Jackson. Excluding slavery from the territories and rebuking the violation of the compromises, he wrote, were "the most important movements . . . since the Revolution." Every victory by "this element of discord, which has so often threatened the dissolution of the Union, increases the danger. Every surrender of the Free States invites invasion." The "innovating Democrats," he charged, had scorned the voters and had read out of the Democratic party all opponents of the Kansas–Nebraska Act, but the popular response would be "a thunderbolt to those who have violated their rights, spurned their remonstrances, and . . . arrayed brothers from the different sections of the Union to shed each other's blood, in civil war, on the plains of Kansas." [6]

Only a day later, Bigelow asked Blair to send the *Post* a series of articles on possible candidates. Blair wrote a long and eloquent tribute to Frémont but he found no time for the other candidates. Several years later, when Blairs and Frémonts were no longer speaking to each other, Jessie hardly remembered "Father Blair's" contribution to John C. Frémont's nomination, and Nathaniel Banks was generally credited with "discovering" the candidate. Banks, however, spent much time with Blair in 1855, and probably seized upon an idea first suggested by Blair.

The new Republican party coalesced quickly. On January 17, 1856, its leaders called for a preliminary national convention to meet at Pittsburgh on Washington's birthday, February 22. At first Blair refused to make the trip, but Lewis Clephane of the Washington Republican Association got his Quaker friends in Baltimore to nominate Blair as their delegate. Surprised to find a Republican party in Maryland, Blair sent Phillips Lee to Baltimore to confer with his new constituency, and decided that if he could be supported by men of his own Democratic creed in checking the wrongs of Pierce and the South he would go. "The Athenians," he explained to Van Buren, "had a law to compel every citizen to take, in the great contests of the country, one side or the other. If the honest, quiet man, were left to his repose, while the wicked & alert were busy plotting & executing mischievous dangers, things could never go well for the Republic." [7] By the appointed day, only death could have kept him away.

At Pittsburgh, Clephane and various others—including the abolitionist Owen Lovejoy of Illinois and William Dennison and Congressman John Bingham of Ohio—organized the convention, and after a prayer by Lovejoy the commitee unanimously elected Blair to preside over the sessions. The introduction of Blair to the full convention as its permanent president brought a deafening ovation that lasted for several minutes. In the evening session, Blair's address, entitled "the Republicans of Maryland to the Republicans of the Union," was read to the convention. It was his usual fierce denunciation of the southern Democrats and the Pierce administration, and a proposal for a second convention to nominate candidates who would stand against the extension of slavery. Also included, however, was a fervent disavowal of the abolitionist approach to slavery where it already existed. By all contemporary accounts, Blair was the lion of the convention and became the chief force for unity among delegates who ranged in viewpoint from dedicated abolitionism to lukewarm free-soilism untouched by any sympathy for the slaves, and who differed sharply on numerous matters unrelated to slavery. Amid the excitement and emotional oratory he served quietly but effectively on the Committee on Resolutions and Addresses, and accepted a place on the National Executive Committee. If there was incongruity in a lifelong slaveholder presiding over a national antislavery party and receiving the plaudits of abolitionists like Lovejoy, no one appeared to notice it.

Eliza and Lizzie were thrilled by the news from Pittsburgh while fretting constantly about Blair's health. The object of their concern, however, came home snorting fire and eager to begin dictating "A Voice from the Grave of Jackson." On April 26 the *Evening Post* lead editorial urged that no one lay down his paper "without first carefully reading the extraordinary revelations . . . of Mr. Blair. . . . No unprejudiced American can peruse them . . . without feeling that, for the past eight or ten years, the spirit, and some of the very men, against whose disunion projects General Jackson was compelled to level his executive thunders, have been gradually acquiring an absolute ascendance in the federal government, and that at this moment it is under the control of a spirit of slavery propagandism, more desperate and more lawless than Mr Calhoun ever hoped or imagined in his craziest intervals."

In the letter, which appeared also in the *Times*, the *Herald*, and the *Tribune*, and was widely circulated as a pamphlet, Blair charged that Calhoun had agitated the slavery issue to consolidate the South and make himself president. Calhoun and his followers, wrote Blair, had popularized abolitionism by denying petitions against slavery a hearing in Congress, by insisting that abolition literature be censored from the mails, and by linking slavery needlessly with territorial expansion. Using the threat of disunion, insisted Blair, they had ousted Jackson's followers from leadership in the Democratic party, had destroyed the *Globe* against Jackson's wishes, and had compelled all northern candidates for the presidency to kneel at the altar of slavery. The ultimate degradation, wrote Blair, had come when Pierce and the disunionists had made the repeal of the Missouri Compromise the price of loyalty to the party so nobly led by Jefferson and Jackson: "Compare the Kansas act with the Declaration of Independence, and the ordinance of 1787. In the first paper, Mr. Jefferson asserts the rights of humanity—in the other, excludes slavery from all the territories of the Union. The Kansas act would spread it over the continent; and to effect it, establishes a new system of politics and morals for the democratic party, for which it is prescribed as a test. . . . Against this spurious democracy . . . I, as a democrat of the Jefferson, Jackson, and Van Buren school, enter my protest."

Democratic papers throughout the country followed the lead of the *Washington Union* in denouncing and ridiculing Blair as a traitor and as an old, senile, and bitter man. Their anger, however, betrayed their anxiety. Enlisting Andrew Jackson into the Republican party of Charles Francis Adams, Charles Sumner, and Nathaniel Banks was a remarkable feat of grave danger to the Democratic party, and Blair was probably the only living American who could have made the attempt. Many thousands of northern Democrats still felt a strong emotional attachment to the party name and to the party's identification with Jefferson and Jackson. They also remembered Blair, however, as the national spokesman for the living Jackson, and his eloquent claim to be the voice of Jackson from the grave was certain to have an impact. To those Democrats angry and fearful over the possible extension of slavery westward, Blair announced that the true followers of Jefferson and Jackson were those trying to follow Jefferson's lead against the expansion of slavery and Jackson's example in efforts to save the Union. Blair's words were carried far and wide, and they coincided with a steady growth of the Republican party among northern Democrats.

Blair worried more than once about the purity of his own motives, but his belief that the question of slavery expansion was more an excuse than a reason for the southern threats against the Union was entirely genuine. Since he considered slavery an evil and had never felt any need to defend it, the northern attacks against the institution did not bother either his pride or his conscience as a slaveholder. He knew that the nation at large was quite willing to tolerate slavery indefinitely where it already existed, and he could not understand why southerners were unwilling to settle for this acquiescence. To most southerners, however, the immense popularity of *Uncle Tom's Cabin,* the refusal of northerners to obey the fugitive slave laws, and the northern insistence that slavery was an evil to be forbidden in the new territories were highly significant as expressions of moral condemnation against the South. Too many southerners felt threatened by self-doubt and the loss of self-esteem. They were angry at the constant scorn and imprecations of the abolitionists, and feared that a hatred for their unique society was rapidly spreading. They would not settle for a mere condescending tolerance because they were torn by a desperate need for a northern expression of moral approval in the form of equal rights in the territories. Inversely, any denial of such rights was an unacceptable insult. Some of the fire-eaters probably did look with excitement and ambition to the exhilarating prospect of building a new separate nation, and this was always the motive most obvious to Blair. Unaffected by the northern criticism of slavery, he could not understand its psychological impact upon others. Passionately convinced that the American union was mankind's best hope for future progress, he considered those who threatened it to be the worst of villains. The fact that in 1845 the villains had attacked him first surely added to his zest for the battle, but it did not determine his principles.

By early 1856 Blair's thinking was very close to that of his later friend, Abraham Lincoln, although he was probably not yet aware of what Lincoln had been saying in Illinois. Blair was convinced that concessions to the South would only lead to more

unreasonable demands, since disunion and not the demands themselves were the object. The best hope for saving the Union,
therefore, was to establish once and for all and as quickly as
possible the principle that slavery could not be expanded. This,
he believed, would quiet the North, and thereby pull the teeth
of the southern troublemakers, because the southern people would
quickly realize that territorial restrictions were no practical burden. Thus, firm opposition to the slavery expansionists coupled
with constant assurances for protection of slavery where it already existed was Blair's program.

Among the frequent guests at Silver Spring in the 1850s,
Lizzie had two favorites. One was their tall, handsome cousin
from Kentucky, John C. Breckinridge. The other was the equally
impressive looking and erudite senator from Massachusetts,
Charles Sumner. Eliza Blair had nursed the father of Breckinridge on his deathbed, and the young Kentuckian genuinely
loved the Blair family. The Blairs could not persuade him to
vote against the Kansas–Nebraska Act, but differences of principle did not disturb their personal relations.

Sumner had been coming to Silver Spring since 1851, and
was a vital part of the meetings and caucuses attending the birth
of the new party. He was both gifted and dedicated, and his
character and life were free from the sins that plague most mortal
men. His awareness of this, however, made him also utterly humorless and self-righteous. Reportedly, his brief marriage had
ended because his young wife could not stand living with God,
and numerous associates understood her problem. He was an abolitionist and a genuine believer in equal rights for all races, but
his views of right and wrong were highly simplistic, and he was
totally unconcerned with the sensibilities of anyone who disagreed
with him. Still, however, he did not refuse to be served by the
slaves waiting on Blair's table, and apparently never scolded Blair
for owning them. Blair frequently spoke out against abolitionism,
but he found Sumner entirely compatible, as did Benton. Blair
and Sumner, of course, had one common bond that transcended
their differences. They shared the same enemies, even if not
always for the same reasons.

On May 14 Lizzie wrote her husband that next Monday
would be "a big Senatorial day" because "Sumner is to 'draw the

sword & throw away the scabbard,' & attack Butler. . . . This is all the news save there is intense excitement in the city about Kansas matters."

On Monday, May 18, Blair rose at dawn for the horseback ride to the capital. In the evening he returned with the word that Sumner's speech had been "rather rhetorical—but very able." On the following day Blair awoke with a terrible cough, and Eliza in a fit of panic kept him home. At the Capitol Sumner finished his two-day effort with language unequaled for offensiveness in Congress either before or since. The aged Senator Butler of South Carolina, said Sumner,

> overflows with rage at the simple suggestion that Kansas has applied for admission as a free state, and with incoherent phrases, discharges the loose expectoration of his speech, now upon her representatives, and then upon her people. There was no . . . possible deviation from truth which he did not make, with so much of passion, I gladly add, as to save him from the suspicion of intentional aberration.
>
> Were the whole history of South Carolina blotted out of existence . . . civilization might lose—I do not say how little; but surely less than it has already gained by the example of Kansas against oppression. Ah, Sir, I tell the senator that Kansas, welcomed as a free state, will be a ministering angel to the Republic when South Carolina, in the cloak of darkness which she hugs, lies howling.[8]

This attack, coupled with equally insulting language toward Stephen A. Douglas, served no useful purpose. "That damned fool will get himself killed by some other damned fool," predicted Douglas.

Blair had missed the climax of the speech, but reports of it did not make him indignant. Although later historians would point out that the elderly and usually polite Butler had used no offensive language toward Sumner, Blair remembered Butler's insults and duel challenge to Benton in 1848. Blair would not have used similar language toward anyone, but the general sentiments were close to his own opinions of both Butler and South Carolina.

The concept of family honor is usually more obligatory in the South than anywhere else, and Senator Butler had a young nephew in the House of Representatives. After two days of brooding and tossing in his sleep, Representative Preston Brooks of South Carolina, accompanied by Congressmen Keitt and Edmundson, marched to the Senate floor after the session had ended and shattered his cane against the head of Senator Sumner.

Sumner was painfully hurt, but did not lose consciousness. Estimates of the number of blows varied from six according to southerners up to three dozen counted by indignant northerners. The cane was destroyed beyond repair, although the descendants of Brooks still have some of the pieces as proof that it was a hollow stick rather than the club described by northerners. Dr. Boyle, a southerner, reported two scalp wounds of about two inches each. One healed immediately, but the other became infected. This was corroborated by Doctors Miller and Linsley, who reported much improvement in the infected wound after they had opened and drained it. At this point, Sumner's brother and Dr. Perry from Boston took charge, and alarming bulletins about Sumner's condition began appearing regularly.

The medical evidence suggests that Sumner did undergo an extreme crisis from infection, but the wounds apparently healed rapidly once the initial infection subsided. Sumner, however, left the Senate for three and a half years. He spent long periods seeking medical assistance in Europe, where his travels included an extremely active social life and a trip through the Alps by mule because he felt too weak to walk. A Parisian doctor diagnosed the ailment as a sprained spine that caused deep pain with each deep thought or emotion, and he tried the moxa-burning treatment Blair had recommended for Van Buren's gout. At rare intervals Sumner later returned to the Senate, but he became quite ill each time. A genuinely serious infection and the incident itself had probably left psychosomatic after effects.[9]

The extent of Sumner's injury is academic. More important, a personal brawl triggered by unnecessary and inexcusable insults quickly became another national struggle between slavery and freedom. Massachusetts offered to pay Sumner's medical bills, but the senator asked that "whatever Massachusetts can give go to suffering Kansas." Yale and Amherst granted the Harvard-educated statesman honorary degrees. Hundreds of public meetings throughout the North were brought to the point of hysteria by speakers like Henry Ward Beecher, Ralph W. Emerson, Edward Everett, William Cullen Bryant, and others. Bleeding Sumner had joined Bleeding Kansas.

In all of this Blair played an important role. At first he and Benton were concerned primarily with southern charges that Sumner had played the coward by not defending himself. Blair's doctor had ordered him to "avoid all labor," but he and Lizzie went galloping into Washington to get the true facts from Sumner himself. Later they passed President Pierce, also on horseback, and the usually affable Blair looked straight ahead with no sign of recognition. Lizzie bowed slightly, and "from the expression of his face" could see that the president had "observed the incivility." Sumner assured Blair he did not know Brooks, had expected no attack, and "saw & heard nothing" after the first blow. With their quarrel over Frémont temporarily shelved, Blair and Benton cooperated in defending Sumner. Soon Blair was dictating the true version for the *Evening Post*: Brooks had deliberately struck Sumner when he was pinned behind his desk in a defenseless posture, and Sumner had actually lunged at Brooks before losing consciousness. The Yankee reputation for being "a fighting people, when attacked" had been upheld. By the second week of June, Sumner was convalescing at Silver Spring under the watchful care of Eliza, Lizzie, and various house slaves.[10]

On the Sunday following the attack, Lizzie, Minna Blair, and Mary Boswell Riggs sat in church while the Reverend Mr. Pyne announced that the "man who made the Senate a place of bloodshed & violence, had insulted every man who loved his country." Contrasting the prominence of Brooks with the fate of a local young man on trial for killing his sister's seducer, the minister proclaimed that Washington justice was "a lamb to the strong and a lion to the weak." This took considerable courage because Pyne's most powerful parishioners were the family of South Carolina congressman William Aiken. Aiken, who had just given a well-attended party "to glorify Brooks for his Sumner achievement," sat fuming in his pew, while half the women present, not including Lizzie, began sobbing. At the end of the sermon Minna and Mary, with red eyes and swollen faces, passed by Aiken, who extended his hand. " 'Oh Mr Aiken What a noble sermon so full of religion & justice,' " exclaimed Mary.

" 'I think you ought to get a copy of it & read it every day for a week at your house.'—Mr. A. very gruffly replied—'I shall read them a very different sort of a sermon madam." When Lizzie asked the usually timid Mary why she had been so rude, Mary answered that in her excitement she would have said it to Brooks himself if he had been there.[11]

With anger over the Senate violence still echoing throughout the North, the Democrats on June 2 met at Cincinnati to nominate their presidential candidate. For a time Blair considered making an effort for Frémont at that convention. He assumed that his group would be excluded or expelled, and thought a nomination on the spot by the "outsiders" might be very effective. By convention time, however, he had placed all his hopes on a Frémont nomination by the forthcoming Republican gathering at Philadelphia. At Cincinnati, neither the discredited Pierce nor Douglas could overcome the desire of the party for a winner, which meant a candidate uncontaminated by recent events. On the sixteenth ballot, the sixty-five-year-old bachelor James Buchanan of Pennsylvania, who had been absent throughout the Pierce administration as minister to England, was chosen by acclamation. As in the case of Pierce four years earlier, many northern and southern Democrats alike considered him a supporter of their own principles. Blair's kinsman, John C. Breckinridge of Kentucky, was nominated for vice-president.

Buchanan had been anathema to both Blair and Benton for years, but in 1856 Benton decided that sectional harmony was the overriding issue. A Benton delegation from Missouri had tried unsuccessfully to fight its way into the Cincinnati convention with their fists, but Benton had remained on hand to work for the nomination of Buchanan. The thought of becoming the power behind the throne in a Frémont administration apparently did not even cross Benton's mind.

Blair, meanwhile, was angry because Frank had not gone to Cincinnati to cultivate support for Frémont among disaffected Democrats, and poor Lizzie accepted the blame for not having made his wish clear enough to Frank. Blair was also concerned about the cost of attending the Republican convention at Philadelphia, but Rives insisted that there could be no convention without him and offered financial assurances. On June 7, the

Republican and Free Soil leaders of Washington and Maryland brought their wives to a formal dinner at Silver Spring. Such affairs were usually "a bore" to Lizzie and "a horror" to her mother, but this was a productive political caucus amid pleasant circumstances. Blair then stayed ill all week, and Lizzie, terribly worried that there would be "too much mental labor for him there," accompanied him to Philadelphia as nurse and guardian. At the convention, observers commented that he had not looked so well in fifteen years.[12]

For Blair the convention was an exciting and happy event. The thousand delegates were almost entirely northern. Only Delaware, Maryland, Virginia, and Kentucky among the slave states were represented, and their delegations were undermanned. All the free states and the territories of Kansas, Nebraska, and Minnesota had sent a full complement. The excitement was electric, and the moralistic speeches were angry and eloquent. A new movement for free men, free speech, free thought, and free government was being born, and the slaveocrats and stockjobbers were at last to be vanquished. Always the incurable romantic, Blair had found his first chance to strike a blow for humanity since the days of Jackson.

At the convention, the young reporter Murat Halstead found Blair "a little old gentleman, thin, slender, and feeble in appearance, yet moving about with considerable activity. The expression of his face is spoiled by a badly-fitting set of false front teeth. . . . he is given a top-heavy appearance by the fact that his head is too big for his body, and his hat too big for his head. He is treated with distinguished consideration, and the mention of his name is invariably followed by uproarious applause." Halstead later confessed to an error. Blair's teeth were "not *artificial* but *real*. The old fellow's big head glistens with intelligence and he seems to think the result of this convention auspicious." [13]

On the second morning, with some eighty reporters trying to copy his words and with the delegates cheering every sentence, David Wilmot read a brief nine-point platform. After denouncing the alleged atrocities in Kansas, the document upheld the Missouri Compromise, demanded the admission of Kansas as a free state, denied the power of Congress or any territorial government to establish slavery within a territory, excoriated the Ostend

Manifesto, and listed Mormon polygamy and southern slavery as "twin relics of barbarism." Perhaps the most striking plank, however, was as unjustified and useless as the Brooks attack upon Sumner: "It is our fixed purpose to bring the perpetrators of these atrocious outrages, and their accomplices, to a sure and condign punishment hereafter." This could only be interpreted as a promise to arrest and punish severely the president of the United States and the congressional majority that had passed the Kansas –Nebraska Act, although the actions of these gentlemen had been entirely constitutional. It was the most radical statement of the campaign, and it probably cost the Republicans a great many votes.

Frémont was easily nominated on the first ballot. The band played its loudest, while the cheering and shouting both inside and outside the hall was deafening. The delegates then chose William L. Dayton of Ohio for vice-president. Simon Cameron of Pennsylvania was suggested first, but Blair sternly vetoed this choice. Cameron had helped raise the money for the purchase of the *Globe,* and he was connected with various groups seeking railroad grants and other subsidies. The former voice of Andrew Jackson would have no such candidate.

The antislavery Know Nothings supported Frémont, but the remainder of this group nominated former president Millard Fillmore. Thus the American people faced their quadrennial challenge and opportunity with three candidates. James Buchanan had made a career of trying to be all things to all men, and his platform called for the acceptance of popular sovereignty as the solution to the sectional conflict. Whether this meant a decision on slavery by a territorial government or by a constitutional convention at the point of statehood was not explained. Millard Fillmore, with a personal record of opposition to intolerance, was the candidate of a party dedicated to bigotry and prejudice, and was supported in part by men hoping to replace the slavery quarrel with a common enmity toward Catholicism and other imaginary dangers. And finally, John C. Frémont was the unpredictable choice of a party divided on most issues except opposition to extending slavery and united on a platform calling for the "condign punishment" of the existing administration. In most of the slaveholding states no Frémont ballots would even be printed, and the possibility of his election soon triggered a wave of secession threats.

After playing a dominant role in Philadelphia, Blair went on to New York for two weeks with Frémont and the New York Republicans. On June 27 Lizzie reported that despite a bad cold he was seeing throngs of people and was being told daily of the "immense good he is doing by being the medium for bringing into a common action & movement very discordant and opposing elements. This house has people pouring in from all quarters from 6 oclk in the mng until late at night." On July 29 father and daughter started home, much heartened by a rumor that Benton had seen the light and would soon be trying to make amends.[14]

For once Blair had gone to New York without visiting Van Buren, who in firm but friendly language had declined to join the Republicans. He assured Blair, however, that such differences could never weaken his "faith in the purity or integrity of your character." Blair answered in kind: "The most painful feeling I have in this contest is the sense that we are separated in it—and yet I console myself with the thought that we do not differ in principle nor in the measures by which we would establish it." Eliza, who disliked Frémont but preferred anyone to Buchanan, was not always so forgiving. Blair warned that after hearing that Van Buren was again suffering twinges of gout in his toes, she had "declared if she lived to get near you she would tread on those toes." [15]

The next five months were probably the happiest Blair had known since the days of Jackson. News of tremendous Frémont rallies came in daily. Twenty-five thousand cheering supporters met at Massillon, Ohio. Thirty thousand gathered at Kalamazoo, Michigan. At Beloit, Wisconsin, a crowd of similar size cheered a procession six miles long. Lincoln addressed 10,000 people at Princeton, Illinois, and 35,000 at the state fair at Alton. At Indianapolis occurred the largest rally of the campaign. The procession, marked by bands and floats, with one carrying thirty-two girls in white (one for each state) and a thirty-third in black (for Bleeding Kansas), lasted for hours, and orators at five different stands took turns denouncing slavery, the border ruffians, and "Bully Brooks." Songs, flaming orations, and eloquent edi-

torials stirred the emotions of thousands attracted by the Pathfinder's clean romantic image and his high moral stand on slavery.
Jessie, as Benton's daughter and an appealing figure in her own
right, was featured as no other candidate's wife had ever been
before.

The Democrats had a dull candidate, but they lacked no imagination in their assaults on Frémont. Constantly, they repeated
the false charge that he was secretly a Catholic, and cited his
marriage by a Catholic priest as proof. Frémont and Jessie in
fact had eloped and been married by a priest because the Protestant ministers they approached first were unwilling to risk the
well-known temper of her father. The *New York Express* declared that Frémont had been seen crossing himself in the Catholic cathedral in Washington, that he had confessed his Catholicism to a West Point professor, and that he had been heard avowing the doctrine of transubstantiation. In response, a committee
of Protestant clergymen called upon the Frémonts and obtained
adequate proof that he worshipped at Grace Episcopal Church,
that Jessie had become an Episcopalian after being reared a
Presbyterian, and that the children had been baptized as Epis-
copalians. Blair advised Frémont to make no answer to the
charges at all, and Frémont, to his credit, took the stand that
denial would be an admission that the issue was relevant. Numerous local leaders, however, felt that the charge was costing
him a great many votes among the Know Nothings, while the
Catholics were all solidly against him anyhow. Blair wrote numerous letters avowing that as a kinsman of Jessie and a longtime
personal friend of both, he knew them to be Protestants.

In September a crowd of Washington Democrats held a
Buchanan rally on Blair's own land within sight of his house, and
left a tall hickory pole graced by an American flag and an antlered
deer head symbolizing Buchanan's nickname, Old Buck. This
gave Blair the excuse for a letter, "To My Neighbors," which
they could read first in the *New York Evening Post*. A buck,
Blair wrote, was a poor "emblem to be exalted above the flag
of the country, and on the hickory tree," which had "given its
name to one of its greatest heroes." Of all animals the deer was
"the most timid. . . . The great antlers [were] evidence only
of that species of gallantry that . . . gives to a class of gentry

of our species the name of bucks, young or old." The old buck, he continued, was "a sort of old bachelor, like his fellow of the woods, and whose insignia of horns, have . . . been held to characterize his pursuits." Should this ensign "be exalted above that of the country, and chosen to exemplify the virtues of one who aspires to the Chief Magistracy?"

Having taken care of the bachelor candidate, Blair appealed to the non-slaveholding southern whites in language that would soon be amplified in an angry book by a North Carolinian named Hinton Rowan Helper. The effort to bar slavery from the territories, he wrote, was a class struggle to benefit the white masses against the slaveholders and not a sectional conflict. Charleston, South Carolina, was "the headquarters of the oligarchy which originated the design of dissolving the Union, to bring under its subjection the laborer of the white race as well as of the black race." The Republicans, he promised, would give each man a 160-acre homestead, and he would "fight the battle for the rights of the white cultivator of the soil and the white mechanics against all who would pursue him into the new territories" with slavery.[16]

Whatever the national influence of Blair's "neighborly" letter, it delighted John Rives, who charged him with "running down my old Buck, the largest & fattest one in my forest. . . . I fear if you get after him 'with a sharp stick' again, you will make him 'piss his tallow.' " Old Buck, he continued, had gone to the Bubbling Gap Springs the first of the month but it was "to get clear of the *hunters for office,* & not to harden up his horns." Rives thought the letter "the most incendiary article for the South" he had seen. The poor white men there would "exclaim, in the language of the man who had been beaten in a small affray, 'I did not know how much I had been bruised & abused; until I heard my lawyer tell the jury.' " [17]

The strongest force working against the Republicans was the southern threat of disunion. Buchanan did not campaign in the modern sense, but his public letters and the speeches and letters of his supporters emphasized his conservative, safe-and-sound image, in contrast to the allegedly dangerous radicalism of the Republicans. The Republicans in fact were the first entirely sectional party in the nation's history, and the rash language in their platform did accentuate the uneasiness of a great many voters.

The southern press and politicians refused to accept any assurances that Frémont was no threat to slavery where it already existed. In their view his election would end the fugitive slave laws and bring on slave insurrections and a war of slaves against whites. In the words of a Mississippi judge, a Frémont victory "would present, at once, to the people of the South, the question whether they would tamely crouch at the feet of their despoilers, or like their ancient forefathers, openly defy their enemies, and assert their independence. . . . Anything short of immediate, prompt, and unhesitating secession, would be an act of servility that would seal our doom for all time to come." [18]

Still, there were enough northern electoral votes to elect Frémont if he could get them. His major task was to overcome the doubts of a great many northern Democrats, and Blair was the primary agent in this effort. Opposing him, however, was another former spokesman for the Jacksonian Democracy, Thomas Hart Benton. Still hoping for a change in the old man's heart, Frank Blair had engineered the nomination of Benton for governor by the liberal Democrats in St. Louis. Benton accepted and delivered twenty-one speeches at twenty towns in forty days. To the Blairs' chagrin, however, he ignored the governorship and campaigned for James Buchanan. Everywhere he drew large crowds, and his words were echoed in Democratic papers throughout the country. By the end of September Blair was "in an exceedingly ill humor" with his old friend, but he could still report to Van Buren that Jessie had visited her father and that Benton had come out to Silver Spring for dinner. Van Buren's sympathies were all with Benton, and he was happy to learn that personal affections were not succumbing to political differences.

Just before the election, Benton returned to St. Louis for his final speech to the people of Missouri. Frémont, he said, had endured great difficulties and dangers: "I stood by him in every one of them as a father would stand by a child." The election of a sectional candidate, however, would destroy the Union, "the world's last hope for a free government on the earth." The nation's guide, said Benton, should be the late Henry Clay, who "loomed colossally in the Senate . . . declaring that for no earthly purpose, no earthly object could he carry slavery into places where it did not exist before. At the same time he would bare his breast against any infraction, against the rights of the slaveholder wherever it existed. . . . It was a great and proud day for Mr. Clay. . . . I could have wished that I had spoken the same words." The speech was the campaign's most eloquent appeal for the election of Buchanan, and it was as dramatic in print as when spoken.[19]

In August the Blairs enjoyed a triumph in St. Louis. Frank Blair won election to Congress, and Lizzie exulted in the fact that he owed nothing to either Benton or Buchanan. Frank had campaigned as a free-soil Democrat, advocating a free Kansas and supporting Benton for governor and Frémont for president. While Benton ran third for governor, he too carried St. Louis, which augured well for the future of Missouri's unionists.

Blair spent the last few weeks of the campaign in New York at Frémont's headquarters, and was hopeful to the end. Frémont's supporters remained enthusiastic, and ministers throughout the entire North were preaching and praying for his victory. Unfortunately for them, however, neither the state nor the national elections were held on the same specific day, and the results in some states were usually known in others that had not yet voted. In 1856 the Pennsylvania state elections on October 14 went to the Democrats by less than 3,000 voters, and this cast a pall over the Republican effort in other states. In later years Frémont argued that he would have carried Pennsylvania if Blair had permitted the nomination of Cameron for vice-president, and that the resulting bandwagon effect would have brought Indiana or Illinois into the fold. Pennsylvania and either Indiana or Illinois would have changed the result. Buchanan won 174 electoral votes, Frémont 114, and Fillmore 8. With 1,341,264 popular votes, Frémont had carried the North resoundingly, but with no votes at all in the lower South he was 500,000 votes behind Buchanan. Fillmore received 900,000 votes, which meant that with virtually the entire South behind him, Buchanan would still be a minority president. The Republicans would now have four more years to discredit the Democrats and find a candidate who could win a few more votes in two additional northern states and become president.

At dawn after an all-night vigil at campaign headquarters, Blair and the Frémonts went home for breakfast. Noting that

Buchanan had carried Missouri, Jessie remarked, "Colonel Benton, I perceive, has the best of the family argument." Frémont smiled, but Blair could not hold back the tears as he answered, "Tom Benton's stubborn stand cost us many a vote outside Missouri." Young Lily Frémont, who was just old enough to share the disappointment, broke into loud sobbing. Jessie rebuked her and sent her for a walk. Blair blew his nose and said contritely, "That will do for me too, Jessie Ann." [20]

A month later, Blair confessed to Van Buren that he had been "lost since the last month in that sort of trance which confounded the fallen angels when 'hurled headlong from the precipice of heaven.' " He feared that Buchanan would "not be able to withstand the bullying of the Southern Conspirators. If he goes on with the system of submission & concession to the Southern Bravos, the peace of the Union must be lost. Indulgence to slaveholders, who carry everything with the whip is only provocation to their contempt & assumption." Blair's evaluation of Buchanan was not entirely accurate. The new president-elect was so emotionally attached to numerous southern friends that no bullying whatever would be required to make him attempt to solve the crisis by meeting all their wishes.[21]

And the South would take all Buchanan could give. Frémont's large northern majority had rubbed salt into nerves already raw. As one editor put it, "Frémont, the candidate . . . of the free-soilers, abolitionists, and haters of the South generally," had won the North on a platform "which would inflict immeasurable degradation upon the Southern people—would reduce them to the level of serfs—would deprive them of every vestige of manly equality, strip them of respect at home and abroad and render them the laughing stock of the governments of the Old World." [22] A strong, wise, and eloquent president might try to reassure the southerners that Frémont's vote was a reaction to their own aggressiveness and was neither a threat to slavery nor a mass accusation of sinfulness or immorality. A president with less understanding, however, might try to ease the southern sensibilities by policies aimed at giving them concessions that would only stir the North to greater opposition. It was all a vicious circle. The South craved examples of northern respect and goodwill in the form of impossible concessions largely unusable even if granted, but the southern demands for the concessions only magnified the northern anger and resistance that had led to the southern aggressiveness in the first place.

Slaveholder Francis P. Blair, like most northerners, did not fully understand the southern drive towards disunion. He was correct, however, in believing that any policy that encouraged the South to make further demands would thereby lead inevitably to secession and war.

Chapter 17

Cold War: North and South

JAMES Buchanan quickly fulfilled Blair's worst expectations. He was a man of both energy and intelligence, but had powerful emotional ties with the South and was remarkably oblivious to northern public sentiment. In early manhood he had taken a vow of celibate bachelorhood after the sudden death of his fiancée—the couple had been estranged just before the tragedy, and her parents had forbidden him to attend the funeral. During a long political life in Washington he had found congenial companionship primarily among the southern leaders, who were more prone than northerners to leave their wives at home. For years he had roomed with Senator William R. King of Alabama, and on one occasion a contemptuous opponent had referred to them as Buchanan and "his wife." [1] He believed in the agrarian principles of Andrew Jackson at a time when the country's economic needs and advancing technology were making such a philosophy obsolete, and his southern friends appeared to be the only serious defenders of this true faith. Ironically, on economic matters he and Francis P. Blair were usually in firm agreement, but here the affinity stopped.

The one event most likely to bring about a southern secession would be the election of a Republican president in 1860. Knowing this, Buchanan should have given first priority to the healing of the wounds within his party and the development of a policy toward slavery extension that both southern and northern Democrats could at least tolerate. Unfortunately, he felt no repugnance to the idea of giving slavery equal rights in the territories, and he could not believe that the majority of the northern people did either. He had run for president as the unionist opponent of black abolitionist Republican fanatics threatening the Union, and to him the only real disunionists were in the North.

Thus, in his cabinet selections and patronage policies, Buchanan turned to his southern friends and ignored the northwestern Democratic followers of Stephen A. Douglas, without whose support the Democratic party could not possibly win the White House in 1860. The result was a cabinet of four able southerners, two northerners with strong southern leanings, and one senile northwesterner, Lewis Cass. Ultimately, several historians would call the group "the Directory" and imply that the president was their helpless tool, but this is incorrect. Buchanan picked his cabinet members because he shared their attitudes, and the administration's policies resulted from harmonious agreement rather than impositions upon the president by anyone.

In 1857 the Democrats were badly split over the real meaning of popular sovereignty. To the southerners it meant that a territory could decide the question of slavery only at the point of statehood. If a state decided against slavery after a territorial period without restrictions, this was neither a threat nor an insult to the South because it could be attributed to geography, climate, or other impersonal reasons. If, however, a territory, while still a territory, made the same decision without giving slavery at least a legal chance, this would be a moral condemnation of slavery and a denial of the South's equal rights. The distinction may have seemed foolish to those convinced that slavery could not thrive on the western plains, but to angry southerners the symbolic difference was real enough. On the other hand, the northern Democratic aspirants for federal and state offices knew that popular sovereignty would be acceptable to northern voters only if the inhabitants of a territory could bar slavery as soon as they were authorized to elect a state legislature. Three-fourths of the southern whites, after all, were non-slaveholders who probably would not vote to introduce the institution if there were no slaves already in their midst, but they now stood ready to defend

it to the death. Once installed, slavery as a system of racial
control had built-in life preservers even among those who
hated it.

James Buchanan agreed with the southerners, but he believed
that his position would be stronger in the North if the decision
could be made by the Supreme Court. He knew that a case involving the question was already before the Court, and he honestly believed that appeasing the South was the only requirement
for ending the sectional strife.

While Francis P. Blair and Frank, Jr., were struggling to
elect Frémont throughout 1856, Montgomery Blair was serving
as the attorney for a Missouri slave named Dred Scott. In 1834
Dr. John Emerson, a United States Army surgeon, had taken
Scott from Missouri into Illinois and then to Wisconsin Territory. Four years later Emerson brought Scott, who had acquired
a wife and two children, back to Missouri. Soon Emerson died
and left Scott to his widow and daughter, who found the slave
and his family a financial burden. Ultimately Henry Blow, the
son of a former owner, was supporting them, and to escape this responsibility, Blow in April 1846 financed Scott in a suit for freedom on the grounds that residence in a free territory had made
him legally free. A lower court agreed, but the Missouri Supreme
Court judges reversed this decision with an angry ruling that
eight earlier precedents set by their own court were no longer
applicable because in recent times individuals and states had "been
possessed by a dark and fell spirit in relation to slavery, whose
gratification is sought in the pursuit of measures whose inevitable
consequences must be the overthrow and destruction of our
government." [2]

In 1856 the case finally reached the United States Supreme
Court. On the advice of his father, Montgomery Blair agreed to
represent Scott without fee, and an abolitionist group agreed to
pay the extra expenses. By this time, Scott's owner had married
an antislavery Massachusetts congressman, and her brother had
assumed the ownership of their controversial ward. All agreed
that whatever the decision of the Court, Scott would go free.
Grave constitutional questions were involved, however, and people
on both sides wanted the Court to answer them.

Montgomery Blair was never an exciting orator, but he en-

joyed a long and lucrative career because of his knowledge of the
law, painstaking research, and clear-cut logic. On December 15,
1856, with his proud family watching, Montgomery addressed
the Court for three hours on the major questions. In the earlier
trials Mrs. Emerson's attorneys had argued that Scott could not
sue in a federal court because as a Negro he could not be a citizen,
and that in all similar cases earlier, the Supreme Court had accepted the verdict of the state supreme court. Blair, however,
cited precedent after precedent to show that the Court had assumed
jurisdiction in similar cases and that at various times numerous
Indians and free blacks had been citizens. The state of Missouri
required a certificate of citizenship in another state from any free
black wishing to move into Missouri, and the United States
Supreme Court owed a state court verdict no more respect than
the wisdom and validity of the decision deserved. And finally,
Blair confronted the really crucial question. The federal courts,
he said, had long since decided in numerous cases that the Constitution authorized territorial legislatures to pass laws only "as
the agents of Congress, and dependent wholly on the will of
Congress for their force." A long string of precedents clearly
delineated by Blair showed that the power of Congress to prohibit
slavery in the territories had often been exercised and had never
before been questioned.[3]

Blair's more renowned colleague, George Ticknor Curtis,
declaimed brilliantly that Congress had full authority over the
territories in all cases whatsoever. Unlike Blair, however, Curtis
argued that in certain areas the Congress should not use this
power against territorial slavery. His oration won more immediate
plaudits, but the heart of the case was really in Montgomery
Blair's forty-page brief.

In reply, Reverdy Johnson of Maryland and Henry S. Geyer
of Missouri took the opposite view on each of the major questions
and dramatically stressed the rights and needs of the slaveholding
states. Johnson offered numerous degrading remarks about
Negroes in general, and insisted that slavery would exist forever
and must be allowed to expand as the only way to preserve the
constitutional freedom of the nation.

However brilliant or correct the arguments on either side,
the most important fact was the composition of the Court—five

from slaveholding states and four from free states. The majority first decided tentatively to accept the Missouri ruling and avoid the constitutional questions, but Justices Benjamin R. Curtis of Massachusetts and John McLean of Ohio prepared a minority report supporting Scott and the Blair–Curtis constitutional arguments. This led to further angry discussions and a new inclination by the southern judges to produce a majority opinion on the same questions. President-elect Buchanan had already written his old friend, Justice John Catron of Tennessee, to ask if a sweeping opinion was forthcoming, and at this point Catron replied that the southern judges were reluctant to make such an important ruling on a strictly sectional basis. If, however, Justice Robert C. Grier of Pennsylvania, who agreed with the southerners, could be persuaded to join them in a public stance, the six justices would settle the argument over slavery rights in the territories once and for all. Buchanan immediately wrote Grier a strong letter advising him to support the southern judges, and Grier willingly complied.

Knowing what the decision would be, Buchanan in his inaugural address called attention to the impending action of the Court and predicted that the ruling would end the sectional quarrel. Within a few days, Chief Justice Taney read the opinion: Scott could not sue because no Negro could be a citizen; all property including slaves was protected by the federal Constitution in all territories; as a result, neither the federal government nor any territorial government could bar slavery from any territory; and the Missouri Compromise had been unconstitutional from its beginning. In effect, slavery could never again be barred in any territory until that territory should become a state.

For once, Francis P. Blair did not have to help rouse the opposition. For northern politicians, editors, ministers, and other noisemakers in both parties, this was the Slave Power's most brazen effort yet, and the president by his own words was openly allied with it. Thomas Hart Benton quickly produced a 192-page *Legal and Historical Examination of the Dred Scott Case.* Many more thousands of northern Democrats crossed the line to the Republicans, and in Illinois an ex-congressman named Abraham Lincoln gained a new and powerful issue.

Having improperly influenced the Court to render an unnecessary and highly inflammatory decision, Buchanan soon gained an opportunity to undo at least some of the damage. If Kansas could become a free state with a minimum of friction, the arguments of Douglas and others that the Dred Scott decision could not really put slavery in the territories would gain some weight. Buchanan sent Robert J. Walker, who had already confessed to Blair his freesoil leanings, to Kansas as governor. Walker tried to hold down the fraudulent voting and give the Free-State majority an opportunity to win the state, but the pro-slave minority won a temporary victory in part because the Free-Staters permitted it. For several reasons, most of them justified, the Free-Staters boycotted both the election for delegates to a state constitutional convention and the referendum on slavery prescribed by this convention. The result was a pro-slave state constitution ratified by a vote that included only a small fraction of the Kansas population. The Free-Staters, meanwhile, finally won control of the legislature in another election, and held their own referendum on the so-called Lecompton Constitution. This vote rejected the pro-slave constitution overwhelmingly.

Faced by this evidence, the president should have asked Congress to authorize a new convention, but instead Buchanan submitted the Lecompton Constitution to Congress and announced that Kansas was "as much a slave state as Georgia or South Carolina." Stephen A. Douglas, of course, could not accept this view and hope to be reelected senator from Illinois in 1858. Breaking openly and violently with Buchanan, the "Little Giant" led a small faction of northern Democrats to the Republican side of an angry debate that lasted throughout much of the 1857–1858 session of Congress and ended in a defeat for the president and the South.

Throughout these months, Francis P. Blair watched with mingled anger and satisfaction as the Democratic party tore itself apart and the Republicans gained daily. He wrote numerous letters soliciting financial support for the *Republic,* a Washington paper designed to help "democratize" the Republican party without weakening its free-soil principles. He also sent a letter of praise and encouragement and a "large and generous contribution" to Elihu Burritt, the "learned blacksmith" of New Britain, Connecticut. Burritt was trying to promote emancipation with federal compensation in a small paper called *The North and South,* which Blair found both wise and provocative.[4]

Buchanan made a mild overture to the Blair family by offering to let Montgomery keep his job as federal solicitor. Montgomery answered that he had not asked for the place and would do nothing to keep it. Minna, who enjoyed the extra money, found her husband's attitude provoking. In November 1858 the president finally discharged Montgomery and added that he would have done it sooner but for his friendship with the late Judge Woodbury.[5]

In May 1857, Blair coughed up a small trace of blood. This threw Lizzie and Eliza into a panic resolved only by the decision that he needed a long trip. Frank was in New York, and would return to St. Louis via Washington. Blair and Eliza decided to accompany him back to St. Louis if Lee would come home to take care of Lizzie. "He mends so slowly," wrote Lizzie, "& is so feeble—that something prompt must be done." The doctor was "more impressed with the necessity of it than any of us." No one enumerated the therapeutic effects of a slow and rough 800-mile trip before Pullman cars had been invented, but Blair and Eliza departed on May 24. From St. Louis Blair soon wrote Montgomery that "my strength grew, by the action of the cars, which instead of fatiguing me as it did others, called out a latent vigor, that I did not know I possessed. Your mother, too has improved by the travel; though, indeed, there was not much room for it." Three weeks later the pilgrims were back at Silver Spring with the old man's spirits bubbling from the evidence of Republican strength along the route.[6] Any travel lover must admire Blair's success in convincing his family that an expensive trip was the automatic cure for any and all ailments.

Throughout much of 1857 the Blair family was also occupied with another major event. At thirty-eight, Lizzie was finally expecting her own contribution to the family line. Her daily reports to the absent father-to-be were full of happy pride, but following the accepted standards she wore high-waisted dresses and large hoops to keep the secret as long as possible, and cringed with proper modesty when people finally began noticing her condition. In the process of having clothes made for herself and the expected infant, Lizzie was much impressed with Minna's new sewing machine, described by its owner as "more interesting than a Baby—more profitable & less trouble." Blair promised to get one for his daughter, but Eliza put her foot down. No such machine "could come in the house to take bread out of the mouths of her poor neighbors." Lizzie considered this "practically loving one's neighbors rather than oneself." [7]

On August 7 a large and strong baby boy was born to Lizzie and was promptly christened Francis Preston Blair Lee. The family considered naming the baby Frémont, but Martin Van Buren's son Smith had named his daughter Eliza and suggested a future affiance between the children if they would name Lizzie's son after Blair. Blair later wrote Martin Van Buren that "if a descendent of Richd. Henry Lee . . . could blend the name of Van Buren with Blair in the course of that lineage, I think the latter name might be proud of the conjunction—& with this possibility in view, I shall take extraordinary pains with the education of the young aspirant. He is admitted on all hands to be perfect as a babe . . . with a temper as genial & happy as yours & with sympathies alive for music, dancing, laughing—for glee of all sorts, I have no doubt he exceeds you in your best days, although he is only in his seventh month." If the baby's proud father was consulted in the choice of a name, he apparently acquiesced without protest. Lee would have to wait until his second grandson to get his own namesake, and even then the boy would shorten his full name of Phillips Blair Lee to P. Blair Lee.[8]

A year later a baby was abandoned at the front door of the Moorings, the home of Mary Jesup Blair, James Blair's widow. Mary decided to leave the child at the church home until she paid off some pressing debts and then adopt it as her own. Learning that another baby had been left on a doorstep in Washington, Eliza Blair decided that this sinful desertion of helpless children was encouraged by "the immunity given by *hoops* which with the aid of corsetts so completely conceals a woman in that condition." [9]

On December 7, 1857, the Blair family proudly watched Frank take his place in the House of Representatives. Freshmen congressmen rarely began orating immediately, but Frank and his father had already prepared a major address. On January 14 Frank Blair asked the House to appoint a committee to study the expediency of acquiring territory in Central or South America to be colonized voluntarily by free Negroes and those "who may hereafter become free." This was a direct blow at those southerners who had been supporting filibusters and other efforts to gain new territory for slavery. Blair would "put it out of the power of any body of men to plant slavery anywhere in this continent" by settling any vulnerable areas with free blacks. The southern states, he declaimed, should voluntarily free all their slaves under an agreement by the federal government to colonize them in Latin America. They could be protected by the United States Navy, and even though inferior to whites in the northern climate, their associations with the Anglo-Saxon whites had made them superior to the mestizos and Indians of Latin America. Thus, said Frank Blair, they would actually raise the social and political levels of that region and benefit humanity as a result. Eventually, he concluded, slavery would surely be doomed, and both North and South should now support a plan for gradual emancipation that would remove slavery's strongest bulwark, the racial prejudice of the South's non-slaveholding white majority.[10]

Despite its racial assumptions Blair's speech had a definite virtue. It was the first serious suggestion since the days of Washington and Jefferson that slavery was a national problem rather than a sectional crime that the southern people must eliminate by themselves. Colonization would never be a practicable solution, but the idea that North and South should cooperate in mutual efforts was highly constructive. If the North was ever to persuade the non-slaveholding southern whites to accept a peaceful emancipation process, the policy would have to include the dispersal of the freedmen out of the more heavily concentrated slave areas. It would also require a sharing of the responsibility for the education, vocational training, and economic assistance necessary for the peaceful integration of more than 4 million black slaves into a highly prejudiced white society. If the Blairs had not found a viable answer, they had at least identified the major problems. They had also become even more anathema to the southern leadership.

As the battle over the pro-slave Lecompton Constitution for Kansas continued in Congress, Frank Blair on February 2, 1858, spoke again in the accents of his father. Slavery, he charged, had controlled the last three presidents, had dominated the Congress for years, and had now taken over the Supreme Court. Buchanan, he continued, was deliberately trying to fix slavery upon the people of Kansas, but the territories could not be "wrested from the freemen to whom they belong, to be given up to slaveholders and their slaves, in order to strengthen the oligarchy which rests upon this servile institution." Comparing the slaveowners with the greedy Roman nobility of the days of Tiberius Gracchus, Blair harshly attacked slavery as a dead weight upon the whole South. Various southern leaders in earlier times had pointed out the burdens of slavery upon the free whites and the southern society in general, and Blair had the help of his father in remembering and researching their remarks. Amid much laughter he assured the House that although reared a Democrat, he made "no complaint . . . of having been read out of the party. I should as soon think of complaining of being read out of a chain gang." [11]

On March 23, 1858, the Senate voted 33–25 to admit Kansas as a slave state under the Lecompton Constitution, but on April 1 the House voted 120–112 to send the constitution back to Kansas for another popular vote. A face-saving compromise eventually enabled the Kansas electorate to reject it by more than six to one.

The Blairs, however, had no time for celebrating because a new personal loss was at hand. After two years of a secret struggle against cancer of the colon, Thomas Hart Benton was dying. Hiding his condition, he had sent Jessie and her children off to join Frémont in California, and he was now being cared for by his daughters Nina and Sarah, and their husbands, William Carey Jones and Richard Jacob. Dictating to Jones, he was determined to finish the final pages of his sixteen-volume *Abridgement of the Debates of Congress*. Blair and Lizzie visited the old man frequently, and were momentarily even friendly with Jones, who was an ardent Buchanan Democrat. Benton's "patience & tenderness to attendants," wrote Blair, "is amazing & love for his friends increases, as his vitality decreases." On April 4 Secretary of State Cass called, and later he remembered that the dying statesman had only kind words for the Buchanan administration. On April 7 Blair came with Lizzie, who reported that Benton "spoke more distinctly & so kindly to me that the words will long live with me." "Ole Bull" had rewon Lizzie's heart by predicting that her baby son would become a great man. Her father informed Van Buren that their old friend had expressed a strong faith that the "Conspirators of the South . . . were again foiled in their plans of overthrowing the Govt." On April 9, the day before Benton died, President Buchanan himself arrived. Sarah Jacob heard her father whisper to Buchanan that they were friends, even though they had "differed on many points." The president must "look to a higher power" for support and guidance. Later Benton assured his children that he was "comfortable and content," and a few hours afterward he was dead.[12]

As Benton had once said of Calhoun, however, death did not always remove a man from his battles. Two days earlier the *New York Tribune* had already reported the whispered confidence of the "dying patriot" to "an old and intimate Missouri friend" that "among the greatest consolations in dying was the consciousness that the House of Representatives had baffled these treasonable schemers, and put the heels of the people on the neck of the traitors. Few events in our history had given him so much satisfaction as the defeat of Lecompton. He warmly praised the intrepid and the incorruptible Douglas Democrats who had resisted the power and wiles of a corrupt and deluded administration." The friend was actually Francis P. Blair, although Frank had supplied the story and thereby became the "Missouri friend."

William Carey Jones immediately wrote an angry denial that soon became a pamphlet. According to Jones, there had been no such friend and no such conversation. Instead, he insisted, Benton had been a loyal supporter of the president until the moment of his death. Jones was a Buchanan Democrat in sentiment as well as an administration appointee, and his bitterness against the Blairs was probably compounded by jealousy and dislike toward Frémont, who had been the favorite Benton son-in-law until the election of 1856. Old Blair, Jones wrote, had spent his life since 1845 in "vindictive attempts on the integrity of the Democratic party—to which party, nevertheless, he owed all that he had," and "to carry that purpose, he would sacrifice any friendship, betray any confidence, and not hesitate at the ruin of his country." Richard Jacob also added a statement that Benton's final interview with Buchanan had been friendly.[13]

Blair answered with a long public letter that editor Bigelow judged had left Jones "like a shot skunk . . . not worth picking up." Actually Blair had privately reported the same final conversation to Van Buren, and his version was entirely consistent with everything Benton had said and done for several years. On the other hand, the dying statesman had probably been both charitable and friendly with both Buchanan and Jones.[14]

The dispute was more than an empty exercise in semantics and name calling. Benton had always had a tremendous following among northern Democrats, and the tearful thousands in St. Louis who filed as he lay in state would soon be voting for or against Frank Blair in the August election for Congress. Like Andrew Jackson, Old Bullion was a valuable ally in death if his allegiance could be established.

Whatever the influence of Jones or Benton, Frank Blair's public calls for gradual emancipation and his all-out opposition to the Lecompton Constitution made the congressional election in St. Louis a virtual draw. Over 1,800 more ballots were cast than in the April elections, and the votes against Blair included that of Ulysses S. Grant. Blair's opponent, Richard Barret, claimed victory by 426 votes. Blair charged various frauds and claimed a majority of 91 votes. Six months later, after the Committee on Elections had compiled a 1,000-page report on the charges and countercharges, Congress voted 93–91 to seat Blair. It was not exactly a landslide victory, but St. Louis again had an antislavery congressman. During the contest Montgomery Blair received a $6,000 legal fee and generously gave his brother half of it to help him weather the period of unemployment.

In August 1858, while waiting for the results of Frank's election in St. Louis, Blair was stung in the eye by an insect and suffered terribly for months. He could not stand the light at all, and had to depend upon Lizzie for his reading and writing. Among the reading he enjoyed most were the Lincoln–Douglas debates in progress in Illinois. Lizzie reported that Blair seemed to "enjoy our standard bearer—who is an acquaintance—& a 'poor white' from Ky." [15] Blair had probably met Lincoln on one of his trips west, and Frank already knew him well. Blair must have been impressed with Lincoln's wisdom, because the rail splitter's ideas were so close to his own. Lincoln's major thrust against Douglas was the argument that there could be no peace until slavery was legally contained within its present boundaries and the South accepted it as such. Once the North was convinced that slavery could not expand and was on the road to ultimate extinction, argued Lincoln, northern attacks against the South would cease, the South would stop making unrealizable demands, and slavery could run its natural course unmolested by enemies and under pressure only from its own weaknesses. Above all, such a process would prevent disunion and a civil war. And finally, regardless of the consequences, any serious efforts to expand slavery or destroy the Union would have to be resisted, with force if necessary. No two people were closer in basic viewpoint on the national problem of slavery than Abraham Lincoln and Francis P. Blair.

In November 1858 Blair received a letter from Hinton Rowan Helper, a former North Carolinian, who had written a book denouncing slavery as a political and economic curse for the non-slaveholding whites. Helper called upon the slaves to rebel and the poorer whites to revolt until the institution was destroyed, and like Frank Blair, he considered colonization of the slaves in another land to be the ultimate solution. Blair approved of the attack on slavery, but not the violence included in Helper's recommendations. Helper wished Blair to endorse the book and add three or four pages of his own views. Frank Blair later helped raise the money for the distribution of a cheap abridged version, but his father never did become involved with Helper.

In October and November 1858 the Republican party won most of the elections for Congress, governorships, and state legislatures throughout the North, and Blair's health was quickly restored. The most important issue may have been the economic depression that afflicted the country in 1857–1858, but southerners saw the election only as a triumph for the party that considered slavery an evil to be prevented in the new territories. One of the Republican losers was Abraham Lincoln, but the legislative candidates pledged to his senatorial election actually polled more votes than those pledged to Douglas. Lincoln had suddenly become a national figure with a conservative doctrine on slavery that put his followers on the side of righteousness against evil without requiring them to take any risks or make any sacrifices.

In Frank, the older Blair had a powerful voice for the ideas he and his sons shared. The Mercantile Library Association of Boston invited Frank to deliver an address on January 26, 1859, and father and son quickly produced another dramatic version of free-soilism and colonization, with some added inspiration from the late Thomas Hart Benton. Published widely as *The Destiny of the Races of this Continent,* the speech was an eloquent appeal to the morality, self-interest, and nationalism of the Northeast and the Northwest alike. It called upon Blair's listeners to march profitably and safely ahead in the armor of righteousness toward a better world cleansed of slavery, racial conflict, and all painful contrition with regard to the western Indians. The merchants of Boston, declaimed Frank Blair, faced two great challenges: reaching the spices, teas, silks, and gold of the Orient through a railroad that could be built across the heart of America by Yankee ingenuity and industry; and creating a "new empire for their commerce within the tropics of America, requiring for its maintenance the peculiar organization of the colored races." The first objective could be attained only by settling the magnificent plains, valleys, and mountains of the great West and creating rich new states, but standing in the way were the Indians and the pernicious evils of slavery. The Indian menace, predicted Blair, would eventually disappear through natural processes. Overcoming slavery, however, would require great sacrifice and effort.

In both cases, Blair insisted, the Spanish solution of racial amalgamation must be avoided because "hybrid races" were degraded and could not "perpetuate themselves." The Moors and Spaniards had lived together for eight centuries without propagating a common stock, and "the celebrated African explorer, Dr. Livingstone," had reported "that in the old settlement of Angola, where the Portuguese . . . amalgamated generally with the natives, the hybrid race does not survive but a few generations." The same principle, said Blair without mentioning the vast mestizo population of Latin America, applied also to the French and Indian half-breeds and to mulattoes.

Slavery, warned Blair, might engulf the West if not checked. Rome, he said, had been destroyed by slavery. The advance of modern Europe had begun only when slavery was ended. By the admission of the tsar himself, slavery was the reason why millions of Russian serfs had failed to defeat small British and French armies in the Crimea. Turkey was an even more miserable example of slavery's evils. And every comparison between free and slave states showed what a frightful economic and moral weight the institution pressed against the American South.

The Supreme Court, Blair continued, had ruled that the Negro was "a being so alien to our nature as to have no rights which we are bound to respect . . . that he is not included . . . in the great declaration of the rights of humanity . . . that he has no soul." If by this "monstrous doctrine" humanity could be denied the slaves, this degradation would apply "in time to all who are constrained to labor in service of another, no matter of what class, or how compelled." The slaves were human, and to save them from destruction by the whites, a place in Spanish America must be found where emancipated blacks could enjoy free homesteads and civil liberties. This would open up new resources and markets, and the present Caribbean and Gulf countries would soon fall under the benign influence of the new black nation. It would be "our India, but under happier auspices; for instead of being governed by a great company, to drive the people to despair and insurrection. . . . it would have its own Government, which would owe a fealty to ours as Canada does to England." The United States should not only restore freedom "to the race which has so long and faithfully served us and our fathers," but should also "recompense them for their long servitude, by giving them all homes in regions congenial to their natures, and guaranteeing to them a free government of their own." Lizzie reported that the speech was a sensation among "not only the politicians—but the Literati—& State street gentility." Lincoln, Emerson, Massachusetts governor Nathaniel P. Banks, and numerous editors praised it highly.[16]

During the next few months the colonization idea was strongly supported by a large number of Republican political leaders and editors, but neither the Blairs nor anyone else offered a specific program. The Blairs were hoping for a gradual process whereby the southern whites over a period of many years would voluntarily emancipate the slaves by state action and send them to a new satellite nation. They would begin with the blacks already free, and they believed that the border states would abolish slavery quickly as soon as the program proved to be viable. It was an impossible dream. The cotton-state leaders already considered any statement or policy against slavery to be a moral condemnation and a mortal insult, and after John Brown's raid their political control over the frightened and angry nonslaveholding whites would be absolute. Even if this had not been so, the colonizationists never really faced up to an equally difficult obstacle. The Liberian experience had proved that a new black nation in a poverty-stricken land could not prosper and although Central America was not exactly barren, it was already filled with a population afflicted by hunger, disease, exploitation, and dictatorial misgoverment. No Central American government or people would willingly surrender enough of its best land or mining resources to support an influx of 4 million former slaves. Any such areas taken by force would have to be retained by force. The potential cost in blood, treasure, and moral principle could be ignored in dreams and political speeches, but it would not disappear.

Frank Blair's Boston address and his status as the only Free-Soiler elected to Congress by a slave state soon made him a national figure. Invitations to speak came from New York, Cincinnati, St. Paul, and other cities. He would accept, Frank wrote his father, only if the elder Blair would write the speeches: "I think you could handle the subject in a way to make it worthy of a New York audience. You have already raised my reputation so high that you are bound to maintain it." During the summer and fall of 1859, Frank's orations won high acclaim in several northern cities, and in November he went almost into the lion's mouth at Cincinnati, just across the Ohio river from slavery. Among those continuing to praise Frank's efforts and ideas was the recently defeated senatorial candidate and former poor white, Abraham Lincoln.[17]

The Blair hopes for support among the non-slaveholding southern whites were rudely smashed in October 1859 by the raid of John Brown at Harpers Ferry, Virginia. Brown clearly intended to arm slaves with guns from the arsenal, and he brought along several hundred spears, which added to the general spirit of horror. No slaves rose to join him, however, and he was quickly defeated. Most northerners condemned him at first, and the Republican leadership vehemently denied that their party was in any way responsible. "Did anyone ever hear of such atrocious madness & malignity?" wrote Frank Blair.[18] Brown, however, was tried hastily under circumstances considered unfair by most northerners, and before the court he lied about his plans and intentions with eloquence, histrionic talent, and dignity. John A. Andrew of Massachusetts urged Montgomery Blair to defend Brown, but Montgomery instead sent Samuel Chilton of Virginia. Like some others, Montgomery urged Brown's attorneys to offer a plea of insanity, but Brown refused, and Governor Henry Wise of Virginia refused the psychiatric examination that might have proved the case. In the end Brown went to the scaffold with great courage and dignity, and his death stirred the sympathies of many who had condemned his deeds. A sizable portion of the northern intellectual and religious community elevated him to martyrdom and sainthood, and a senatorial investigation further angered the South when various witnesses successfully defied subpoenas and some who appeared refused to testify. The investigating committee, however, did establish the fact that Brown had been financed by a group of wealthy abolitionists, all of whom denied any knowledge of his intentions. The hearings also exonerated the Republican party from any responsibility.

Brown's raid, however, was a godsend for the southern radicals, who could cite it as proof that the hated Yankees really did intend to abolish slavery by violence and race war. It generated and magnified anger and fears that could no longer be overcome by realistic southerners who could see no danger to slavery where it existed, and as a result it was probably the most powerful single event pushing the nation toward a civil war. The southern wing of the Democratic party would henceforth be dominated by radicals who would make demands that the northern Democrats could not accept without losing all hope for election victories in their own states.

At Cooper Institute in New York City on January 25, 1860, Frank Blair repeated his call for colonization, and added a pow-

erful effort to reassure northern voters that a Republican victory
would not really cause a secession. He called for a new Jackson
to convince the slaveholders that they were safe and to destroy
the fireeaters. John Brown, he said, had no Republican support,
and the use of Brown's raid to terrify the southern people was
nothing but play-acting. Evoking cheers and laughter, he rid-
iculed the southern threat of disunion as an attempt to defy providence—as foolish as trying to stop America's rivers and reverse
the flow of the Gulf Stream.[19]

Frank and his father, however, were still misjudging their
opponents. The Republican party would soon elect a president
who met all of the Blair's ideal standards. He would try to reassure the South, but the result would not be what they predicted.
As 1860 dawned, however, Francis P. Blair dreamed only of
righting his own and the nation's wrongs by electing a Republican
president, and he still believed that a moderate free-soil president could hold the Union together.

Chapter 18

Triumph and Vindication

THE late 1850s were singularly happy years for Francis P. Blair. He was sixty-eight in 1859, but despite periodic illnesses he had never felt better. Vacationing in Pennsylvania in August 1858, he wrote Montgomery that "it is a great thing to be relieved at my age from having cares of the heart, the hands, & the thought. Your mother and I take long walks and long rides in the mountains & find something new at every turn."[1] "You ask how long I calculate to live," he wrote Van Buren several months later.

> I am fortunate in being delivered now in my old age from hemorhage of the lungs & cough & dyspepsia & debility that threatened me with death in early life. I then prayed to God that I might reach forty, that I might live to educate my children. The boon, I believe will be doubled & that I shall reach 80 at least & see my grandchildren educated. I had 12 (twelve) of them seated around my table the other day, all of them marked by sense, goodness, and beauty. The 13th (Blair Lee) was then in the mountains & is now returned fat & hearty & best looking of all. When I cast my eye upon this fine group I calculate that I shall live to eternity, in this world as well as the next.

Indeed, comparing his condition at age twenty-five with the present could indicate a hope for "immortality on earth without depending for it on my children." Almost as an afterthought, Blair added: "Your handwriting is a sort of puzzle too, but this is an advantage, as I am flattered by the length of time employed in the perusal. That I have a long letter from you however short or long is always a high gratification." The historian involved with Blair and Van Buren can only sympathize with the cryptographic problems of both men.[2]

A minor vexation in 1859 was Amos Kendall's continuing refusal to surrender Andrew Jackson's most important papers. The controversy was rekindled by James Parton's work on a multi-volume biography of Jackson. Parton wanted Blair to contribute his views on Jackson, but Blair still hoped that George Bancroft would be the one to enshrine Old Hickory properly. Kendall was still ignoring Jackson's written deathbed-orders that the papers be given to Blair. Finally Blair wrote a eulogy to Jackson that Parton duly summarized in his book along with comments indicating his own lack of agreement. Parton's biography generally was a Whiggish and patrician treatment that Blair found wholly unsatisfactory. However, Parton was much impressed with Blair and could not understand how he could feel such adulation for a backwoodsman like Jackson.

Neither the pleasures of grandfatherhood nor his concern for Jackson's reputation could divert Blair's attention from his main objective: the success of the Republican party. "Tomorrow," he wrote Montgomery on December 19, 1859, "I start to New York to meet the Nat. Commee. of party who are to fix place of meeting of the convention. . . . Will you look into my Bank acct. to see whether I have money to bear my expenses?" [3] The committee later selected Chicago for the convention at the suggestion of a Lincoln friend that it would be a neutral city because Illinois had no candidate for the nomination.

The Blairs already liked Abraham Lincoln, but they had not yet thought of him as a presidential possibility. Their choice was the conservative Whig from Missouri, Edward Bates, who had taken a firm stand against the Kansas–Nebraska Act and the Lecompton Constitution, although he had also joined the Know Nothings in 1856. Coming from a slaveholding state, he might be less anathema to the South than most Republicans, and he shared the Blairs' view on colonization. Their agreement on this policy was probably the strongest bond between Bates and the Blairs, because their economic views had always been quite divergent.

The sectional quarrel, of course, divided friends as often as it united former opponents. In March 1860 Elizabeth Blair Lee drove to the home of her longtime friend Varina Howell Davis, wife of Mississipppi senator Jefferson Davis. Approaching the door, she heard her hostess cry out to a servant, "That's the Blairs' carriage. Don't let any of them in but Mrs. Lee." Lizzie had her usual pleasant afternoon because the ladies tactfully avoided politics in her presence. But personal relationships could only stand the strain if buttressed by an affectionate nature and even temperament like Lizzie's. All over Washington the social lines had long since been drawn between North and South, Republicans and Democrats, and Buchanan and Douglas Democrats, with the latter in many ways the bitterest enemies of all.[4]

In February Blair had tried to recruit his old friend John J. Crittenden into the Republican ranks and had even suggested that Crittenden might become their presidential candidate. He sent Crittenden a collection of Frank's speeches and assured him that the Republicans would adopt their recommendations "to defeat, with the least injury to the public interest, the schemes of the party seeking a separation of the States." To all who would listen, Blair continued to urge the nomination of a Republican whom the South would have no legitimate reason to fear.[5]

For the southern radicals, however, pride was as important as fear. On April 23, 1860, some 2,500 Democratic delegates and visitors descended upon Charleston, South Carolina, to nominate a candidate for president. Stephen A. Douglas was the only aspirant with any real hope of winning a substantial popular vote in both North and South, but the southern leaders had not forgiven him for opposing the pro-slave Lecompton Constitution in Kansas or his Freeport Doctrine, which proclaimed that territorial legislatures could bar slavery by refusing to pass positive laws for its protection. The Buchanan-dominated delegates from the northeastern states added their voices to the southern enmity against Douglas, and reason fled the hall. The southern radicals wanted a split party that would elect a Republican president and produce a southern secession.

The climax of the convention came when a majority of the delegates refused to include in the party platform a pledge of federal protection for slavery in the territories. The crux of the dispute was perhaps never more clearly stated than in the dramatic address by William Lowndes Yancey, the "Orator of Secession." The northern Democrats, charged Yancey, had committed the unpardonable sin of accepting the Republican abolitionist heresy that slavery was wrong. They had defended southern slavery on the basis of state laws, but not on the assumption that slavery was right according to the laws of God and nature, and this made the northern Democrats as bad as the Republicans. Only a northern affirmation of the righteousness of slavery in the form of a call for federal protection of slavery in the territories could keep the party united. Yancey's demands were impossible, but his charges were correct. Most northerners, including those in front of him, were willing to tolerate slavery, but they were not ready to admit that it was right according to the laws of either God or nature. Yancey's northern listeners could not support a federal slave code for the territories and hope for election or reelection to offices in their own states. The northern Democrats stood firm, and seven southern delegations withdrew from the convention. Ultimately the southern Democrats nominated Vice-President John C. Breckinridge on a platform demanding federal protection for slavery in the territories, while the northern and some of the border Democrats nominated Douglas with a program accepting the Dred Scott decision but stopping short of the more extreme southern demands.

On May 9, 1860, a group of former Whigs and Know Nothings from both North and South met in Baltimore to form the Constitutional Union party and nominate John Bell of Tennessee and Edward Everett of Massachusetts for president and vice-president. Their brief platform spoke only for sectional peace, although in the immediate past the southern members had often tried to outdo the Democrats in demands for slavery rights. There were significant differences, however, between the Constitutional Union southerners and the southern radicals supporting Breckinridge. Men like Bell, Sam Houston, John J. Crittenden, and William C. Rives did not believe that a failure to achieve their demands or even the election of a Republican president would justify secession.

Despite threats of violence, the Blairs called a Republican state convention in Baltimore. With Montgomery as president the group chose national delegates and passed resolutions calling for emancipation and colonization. In May, after the Democratic party had split at Charleston but before either faction had made its final choice, the Blairs and their fellow Republicans poured into Chicago on a wave of euphoria to choose a candidate. Their opponents were divided, and only some foolish mistake could prevent their victory. The Blairs and their friends were determined to write a platform acceptable to northern voters and choose a candidate who would not give the South a legitimate excuse for secession. Above all, the Blairs considered William H. Seward anathema. Seward's phrases like "the higher law" and "irrepressible conflict" had convinced the southern rank-and-file that he was their most dangerous enemy and had stirred up uneasiness in the North as well. The Blairs still favored Edward Bates, but they would accept almost any equally conservative candidate. "The old gentleman is much looked up to," wrote Montgomery to Minna on May 11. "Everybody seems to regard him as the Nestor of the council & I believe his advice will go far towards settling matters both as to candidates & to platforms."

It was another happy convention for Blair. A special escort conveyed him to and from the office of Chicago's mayor, John Wentworth. He received a great ovation when introduced to the assembled delegates, and he was promptly named to the Committee on Resolutions, which wrote the platform. Whatever his influence, the platform principles on slavery were exactly what he had been advocating except for the omission of a plank on colonization. He proposed this, but gave up quickly rather than upset the existing harmony with a controversy. The final platform promised something to almost everyone except those wishing to take slaves to western territories. A protective tariff, a homestead act, river and harbor improvements, liberal naturalization laws for immigrants, and a railroad to the Pacific would be the people's rewards for electing a Republican president. For the radicals the platform repudiated the Dred Scott decision, damned James Buchanan for the Lecompton Constitution, and described popular sovereignty as a delusion and a fraud. Equally important, it also condemned John Brown's raid as a terrible crime, reaffirmed the right of each state to control its own domestic institutions, and said nothing about the Fugitive Slave Act. The president should ask Congress for legislation to protect the new territories from slavery, but only if he should judge such action necessary.

Only one delegate was conspicuously unhappy with the platform. The white-bearded old abolitionist Joshua Giddings complained passionately because the preamble from the Declaration of Independence had been omitted, and walked off the floor in protest. Immediately, George William Curtis and Frank Blair rose to support Giddings. Jefferson's immortal words were added by acclamation, and amid thunderous cheers the tearful Giddings was escorted back to his seat.

The defeat of Seward was surprisingly easy. While his thirteen-carload New York entourage was parading behind brass bands through the streets, the Lincoln supporters, many of them armed with bogus tickets, grabbed the seats in the convention galleries and shouted leather-lunged approval at every mention of the rail splitter's name. Many delegates also agreed with the letters Blair had been writing for months to the effect that Seward had talked too much and was a risky candidate. Also, the party's leading editor, Horace Greely, had quarreled with Seward and was filling both the air and his *New York Tribune* with warnings that Seward could not win. The other candidates quickly decided to unite on a single opponent. Bates had alienated recent immigrants by supporting the Know Nothings and Fillmore in 1856. Cameron of Pennsylvania and Chase of Ohio also had enemies and handicaps. The logical answer was Abraham Lincoln, who had taken a strong moral stand against slavery and its extension while promising over and over that he would never disturb it where it already existed. The deafening cheers from the galleries and shrewd promises by his managers of cabinet posts to Indiana and Pennsylvania brought a victory at the end of the third ballot. With their usual stubborn loyalty the Blairs supported Bates to the end, but they found Lincoln entirely acceptable.

Once again, Francis P. Blair had a candidate he could support with all his heart, and at long last he had a winner. In the North the Republicans had money, organization, strong emotional issues, and the most marketable candidate since Andrew Jackson. Lincoln had been born in poverty and reared on the frontier, and he was self-educated. He had served in an Indian war, farmed, labored, kept store, and become a successful lawyer and politician strictly through his own talents and hard work. He was a symbol of America's most cherished values, and attempts to picture him as a backwoods barbarian backfired in his favor just as similar efforts had only strengthened the popularity of Andrew Jackson.

Perhaps remembering that the only two Whig presidential victories had been won by candidates who remained virtually silent throughout their campaigns, Lincoln followed the urging of William Cullen Bryant that he "make no speeches, write no letters, . . . enter into no pledges, make no promises, nor even give any of those kind words which men are apt to interpret into promises." He assured various individual southerners that he would protect their constitutional rights, but he made no public statements. Privately, he pointed out that his previous speeches and the party platform were available for all to read, and argued that no more words were necessary.

Lincoln's silence helped the southern radicals conduct a thoroughly distorted campaign against both him and his party. Seward was now speaking everywhere for conciliation, but the New Yorker's earlier extreme phrases were quoted night and day by those seeking to frighten the southern people into secession. Lincoln's own previous statements were also taken out of context, and his position that slavery was a moral evil by far outweighed his assurances that the institution would remain undisturbed in the South. Also, various radical Republicans upstaged their silent candidate and the moderate Republican majority with unnecessarily violent language. The Bell campaign, supposedly for unity and peace, also helped the southern fire-eaters by circulating a pamphlet quoting the more extreme statements of the Republican radicals and arguing that abolition really was the Republican party's primary goal.

In the North the major problem was to convince the voters that Lincoln was a peace candidate as well as the candidate with the proper moral attitude toward slavery. None worked any harder at this task than the Blairs. The summer of 1860 was even hotter than usual, but Francis P. Blair worked night and day on pamphlets, public letters, and speech material for his sons. Early each morning Blair and Eliza took their daily horseback rides with their little grandsons Jesup and Woody on their mules in tow, but the rest of the day Blair usually spent scrawling his interminable communiqués to the political front. In August Blair combined a political visit to Simon Cameron in Pennsylvania with a brief vacation in the Alleghenies, but he was soon back at his desk. "Frank has come with father after speaking 6 times in 36 hours in Pennsylvania," wrote Lizzie in September. After a long sleep, Frank and his father worked all day on two new speeches to be delivered in Philadelphia. Montgomery also made several well-publicized speeches throughout Maryland, which in some areas took considerable courage. The Blairs' message was essentially what it had always been. The Republicans, they argued, were not abolitionists and would not touch slavery where it existed unless at some future date a majority of the southern people should agree to abolition combined with colonization. The only real issues were the extension of slavery and the preservation of the Union against those deliberately stirring up the false notion that the Republicans were a threat to slavery. "No Marylander," said Montgomery Blair at Iddins Store in Montgomery County, "supposes he is deprived of his property in Slaves because he cannot take them into Pennsylvania." [6]

Whatever the Blairs' impact may have been on northern and border-state voters, the voices of moderation were drowned out in the lower South, where the campaign was one long brainwashing exercise in preparation for secession. Politicians and editors warned daily of northern plots, new John Brown invasions, slave uprisings, burning homes, and the future murders of women and children. The horrors that would accompany the election of Lincoln had become the prevailing orthodoxy, and the threat of mob violence hung heavy over anyone with the sense or courage to question it. The southern Democratic candidate, John C. Breckinridge, was not a secessionist, but virtually all of the secessionists were in his party. Douglas, for one, believed a rumor that if Breckinridge could carry the border states the radicals would seize Washington and make it the capital of a new southern Confederacy.

The election results indicated that most Americans were still conservative. Breckinridge carried Maryland by only 700 votes over Bell, and Lincoln himself got 2,300. Bell carried Virginia, Kentucky, and Tennessee, while Douglas carried Missouri. Lincoln also received 17,000 votes in Missouri, where Benton and Frank Blair had kept the southern radicals so busy denying their disunion sentiments that no really powerful secessionist impulse had developed. Lincoln won a resounding electoral majority with less than 40 percent of the popular vote, and he would have been elected even if all the votes of his three opponents had gone to one candidate. Breckinridge won a majority in only seven of the fifteen slaveholding states, and even in those states Bell and Douglas together won 48 percent of the votes. The combined vote of the slave states was 570,000 for Breckinridge and 705,000 for Bell and Douglas.

Equally important, the Republicans failed to carry either house of Congress. They lost nine seats in the House while gaining five in the Senate, but they still held only thirty-one of the sixty-six senate seats until the southerners from the seceding states resigned. If the southerners had remained in the Union, no cabinet member unacceptable to them could have been appointed, but they continued to parrot the fear that Lincoln would fill the South with antislavery officeholders. The Supreme Court, also, was the same court that had delivered the Dred Scott decision.

Lincoln and his party were pledged not to interfere with southern slavery and he lacked the power to touch the institution under any circumstances, but these facts were irrelevant. Because Lincoln had said over and over that slavery was a moral evil, his overwhelming election by the North was the supreme insult. As one editor put it: "Lincoln's triumph is simply the practical manifestation of the popular dogma in the free States that slavery is a crime in the sight of God, to be reprobated by all honest citizens, and to be warred against by the combined moral influence and political power of the Government. The South, in the eyes of the North, is degraded and unworthy, because of the institution of servitude." [7] Shortly before becoming vice-president of the Confederacy, Alexander H. Stephens would assure Lincoln that southerners really did not fear his antislavery opinions any more than they had feared those of Washington and Jefferson. The election, however, had made the antislavery view a national policy, and the South would not permit its beliefs to come "under the ban of public opinion and public condemnation. This . . . is quite enough of itself to arouse a spirit [not only] of general indignation, but of revolt on the part of the proscribed." [8]

Secession, however, offered a solution to an inescapable moral dilemma. By creating an independent, powerful, prosperous, progressive empire based on slavery, the southerners could prove to the world, to the hated Yankees, and to themselves that slavery was not the great evil of which they had been accused. It was both a magnificent challenge and a glorious dream for people whose sensibilities and self-esteem had been under constant attack for three decades, and no realistic assessment of the actual danger to slavery could be allowed to get in its way.

Three-fourths of the southern whites had no direct connection with slavery at all, and therefore suffered very little if at all from either guilt feelings or northern criticism. As the Blairs and others had pointed out, however, the racial prejudices and fears that had made them accept slavery in the first place had been heightened rather than diminished by the slavery debates and conflicts. Since the first blacks had landed as indentured servants in 1619, the slaveholders had had little difficulty in persuading the non-slaveholding whites that the institution was preferable to racial conflict, competition and miscegenation. Constant reminders of the Haitian revolt, numerous domestic slave rebellions both real and imagined, and the recent John Brown raid had long since laid the groundwork for the 1860 presidential campaign and its hysterical rumors and charges of revolts, murders, arson plots, well poisonings, and northern invasions. Racial prejudice and fear came naturally enough to people whose white skins were a social premium and who knew the slaves only through the propaganda of their masters. The same prejudices, after all, existed also throughout the North where free blacks were obviously no threat to anyone. Under certain circumstances, fear and bigotry are natural human instincts that do not have to be taught and can be overcome only by dynamic intellectual and moral efforts. Without racism neither slavery in the beginning nor the Civil War in 1861 would have occurred. The subsequent loss of some 630,000 lives should forever be remembered as the price paid by Americans for allowing racial prejudice to dominate their reasoning and guide their conduct.

Francis P. Blair understood the feelings of the southern non-slaveholding whites, and he still clung to the hope that they could ultimately be separated from their allegiance to the slaveholding aristocracy by colonization for the slaves. Their leaders, however, he could not fathom at all. He saw no threat to slavery, and he could not believe that they really did either. In his eyes they were being driven by unholy ambitions to destroy a nation chosen by the Almighty to exemplify free government everywhere. He was overjoyed that the southerners and their supporters had finally been cast out of the White House, and although he dreaded a civil war he did not shrink from armed conflict if it should be the only alternative to disunion. The president-elect, he wrote Frank, should study Jackson's proclamation against nullification. As for himself:

> I hold that this continent belongs to the American people as a nation, and not only for the time of existing lifeholders, but for all time. The Nullifiers have no right to cut off the communication of the Northern people by direct route by land—nor have the Negro owners of Mississippi and Arkansas the power or the right to arrest the commerce of the river—or subject it to cannon they may plant on what they please to call their soil. It is theirs to plant cotton on, but not to plant force, to arrest the progress of the nation. There is a right of eminent domain in the whole people of the Union, to this country, that rises above that of individuals granted in their parents or that of States growing out of their local sovereignty.
>
> The mad men who have begun the Revolutionary movement in basing it on Slavery . . . necessarily make a war on the Institution for its removal as an element of discord and national danger a consequence. . . . the pretext has not the slightest influence on the mind or rather the motives of the Machinator. Not one of the States breeding commotion ever lost or fear to lose a slave, nor can they spare a slave or Slaveowner—least of all to tap the waters of the Rio Grande in New Mexico to make bread—or to compete with Brigham Young in Utah.[9]

If the expected secession should occur, the influence of Francis P. Blair upon his friend Abraham Lincoln would not be in the direction of peace.

Chapter 19

In the Midst
of a Revolution

TO James Buchanan life must have seemed terribly unfair in December 1860. He had done his best to keep the southern states happy, and in his recent annual message to Congress he had blamed the sectional crisis almost entirely upon the North. Surely the southern radicals could at least wait until Lincoln took office before seceding. His fire-eating friends, however, were in no mood for patience. The southern people were angry, insulted, and fearful because of the recent election campaign, and they must be led out of the Union before Lincoln or anyone else could make concesssions sufficient to allay their emotions. One at a time, beginning with South Carolina on December 20, 1860, and ending with Texas on February 1, 1861, the seven states of the lower South passed ordinances separating themselves from the United States. Only South Carolina and Mississippi followed the Jeffersonian example of 1776 by explaining their reasons in detail, and the delegates were clearly straining for justifications. The northern states, they charged, had refused to return fugitive slaves, had permitted their citizens to comdemn slavery and make efforts to arouse the slaves to revolt, had denied the southern states their constitutional rights in the territories, and had shown their eternal hostility to slavery by electing Abraham Lincoln president. Ironically enough, the reasons cited by the seceding states were far more applicable to the eight slaveholding states that did not secede. Four of the eight would eventually secede after the Battle of Fort Sumter, but they would do so for a different set of reasons.

Buchanan suffered from pangs of deep frustration and sorrow, but apparently felt no anger or condemnation toward the South. He announced that although secession was unconstitutional, the federal government had no constitutional right to coerce a seceded state back into the Union. He called upon the northern states to end the crisis by repealing their personal liberty laws designed to aid escaping slaves, and he pleaded for a constitutional amendment that would protect slavery in the territories until the point of statehood. This solution had been rejected by the northwestern Democrats at Charleston and by the North as a whole in the election of Lincoln, but Buchanan was still strangely oblivious to northern anger at the South's demands.

Moderates in the northern and border states worked desperately to find compromise solutions, while senators and congressmen from the seceding states remained in their seats as long as possible to hamper all such efforts. A Senate committee of thirteen headed by John J. Crittenden, a House committee of thirty chaired by Thomas Corwin of Ohio, and finally an ad hoc peace convention of delegates from twenty-one states headed by John Tyler worked long and hard, but none of them could find mutually acceptable ideas. The lower South would settle for nothing less than a symbolic affirmation that slavery was right and justified by all the highest standards of God and man, and the northern people and their representatives would make no such admission.

The only practical question remaining was whether or not the president-elect would accept the views of his predecessor that military coercion was unconstitutional. James Buchanan hoped violence could be avoided long enough for the seceded states to see that slavery was in no way threatened by Lincoln in the eight slave states that had not seceded. Then, perhaps, the seven malcontents would recognize the error of their ways and voluntarily rejoin the Union. William Henry Seward, already selected to become Lincoln's secretary of state, shared this hope, and was prepared to make any necessary concessions to keep the peace. This approach might save the Union without bloodshed. It might also result in the permanent formation of two separate nations.

Francis P. Blair feared that the secessionists would "make it a point of honor . . . to die altogether rather than live & continue to be rebuked by the prosperity of the free States which in condemning their domestic Institution, seems to condemn that by which only they will consent to live. Like the point of honor in modern chivalry, that which is essentially wrong is the only thing which they hold worth dying for." This may have been Blair's most realistic assessment of southern motivations yet. He and his sons were certain that the Union could be saved only if the president-elect followed the stirring example of Andrew Jackson in 1833. They hoped that the threat of military force would succeed without a massive war, but they were quite prepared for an armed conflict if the alternative meant risking a permanent division of the Union. In early December 1860 Montgomery Blair suggested to Lincoln that a private home might be better than a hotel for his stay in Washington while awaiting the inauguration. Why not stay in Blair's own "very plain old fashioned" house? Jackson had often stayed there, and the Blairs would be delighted for Lincoln "to begin where he left off." Lincoln had not yet decided to be another Jackson, however, and he was too busy finding a balance among the factions of his party to commit himself so obviously to one of them.[1]

Throughout the period between Lincoln's election in November and his inauguration in March, Francis P. Blair found himself once more besieged with visits and letters from office seekers high and low. His major concern, however, was Lincoln's selection of the cabinet officers who would help deal with the rebellion. He would support Lincoln under any circumstances, but he did feel that Montgomery would make an outstanding attorney general. As he wrote Frank, Andrew Jackson had prophesied that Blair's proscription "would be fatal to the Democracy & my restoration a consequence of the putting down of Calhoun's heresies. If Lincoln should make this good in the person of my son, it would endear him to all who love the Old Chief's memory." Also, Montgomery's birth, education, and connections in Kentucky could be important in the effort to keep the border states in the Union.[2]

Above all, Blair did not want either William H. Seward or Simon Cameron in the cabinet. Whether justly or not, Seward's closest friend and alter ego, Thurlow Weed, was noted for a long string of political and financial dealings widely considered less than totally honest, and Seward's radical reputation, however undeserved, would further alienate the southern people and strengthen the forces of secession. Blair had long since forgiven Cameron's role in his own dismissal in 1845 to the point of tramping through the Pennsylvania mountains with him in search of deer and bear, but he remained acutely aware of the Pennsylvanian's reputation for finding the main chance in financial dealings. In short, he did not believe that either could be entirely trusted, although Cameron was playing the role of a close personal friend. Ironically enough, his fear that Seward would be a needless goad to the slaveholders was mixed with objections to Seward's apparent willingness to make concessions to the South. The New Yorker was frantically trying to undo the impact of his own earlier radical statements, and Blair could never understand inconsistency in terms of anything but dishonesty. In letters to Frank that were promptly relayed to Lincoln, Blair argued eloquently against the nominations of Seward and Cameron. Even if his opposition should destroy Montgomery's prospects, he would rather sacrifice Montgomery than have either of them in the cabinet.[3]

On January 14 Blair offered his views on both the crisis and the cabinet directly to Lincoln. "It is said," he wrote, "that men who have the destiny of great nations in their hands never hear the truth: I will try in this instance to make you an exception." Crittenden's compromise plan to extend the Missouri Compromise line to the Pacific would not "reconcile the nullifiers. . . . whose discontents grow out of the constitution itself. . . . They think a Slave Oligarchy the best Government the World ever saw; & they think, & justly, that association with the free Institutions of the North must in the end prove fatal to it. The Union is abhorrent to them . . . & nothing but force will bring them to submission to it again." Lincoln would soon head "the best government ever framed on earth, in the midst of a revolution, deep rooted & wildly extended & pressed onward by the machinations of able & daring men." He would have a "greater responsibility than Washington ever occupied," and the stakes would be "as much greater as our states are greater than the colonies." The

Francis Preston Blair. The voice of Jacksonian Democracy and defender of the Union.

Eliza Gist Blair. Loving Wife and able Partner. Her children called her "The lioness."

Elizabeth Blair Lee (Lizzie). Navy wife and political scribe with a soft heart and indomitable spirit.

Samuel Phillips Lee. Lizzie's beloved, and commander of the Union blockade against his native Virginia.

Postmaster General Montgomery Blair. An unselfish but occasionally vindictive puritan. *Reproduced by courtesy of the
Library of Congress.*

General Frank Blair (seated, center) and staff. Prodigal son and warrior-politician. *Reproduced by courtesy of the Library of Congress.*

Preston and Eliza Blair. The romance never dimmed.

Silver Spring. Where the mighty gathered and where a drunken Confederate orgy helped save Washington.

The Blair-Lee Houses in Washington, D.C., where "Mrs. Number 4" and "Mrs. Number 6" rarely communicated.

Blair's Washington, 1849. Jackson Hall, lower left inset, built by Blair and Rives with their winnings from 1844 election bets. *Reproduced by courtesy of the Library of Congress.*

Brutality in defense of family honor. The caning of Sumner on the Senate floor. *Reproduced by courtesy of the Library of Congress.*

The Republican convention, 1860. The ladies cheered for Lincoln and the Blairs found a winner. *Reproduced by courtesy of the Library of Congress.*

The election of 1860. Left to right: Bell, Douglas, Breckinridge, and the winner. *Reproduced by courtesy of the Library of Congress.*

President Lincoln and his cabinet. Montgomery Blair is third from left. General Scott offers counsel, probably against reinforcing Fort Sumter.

The Emancipation Proclamation. Left to right: Stanton, Chase, Lincoln, Welles, Smith, Seward, Blair, and Bates. *Reproduced by courtesy of the Architect of the Capitol.*

Francis Preston Blair Lee. Favorite grandson and future senator.

North was "as much bound to resist the South Carolina Movement, as that of planting a monarchy in our midst by a European potentate," and this could "only be done by an exhibition of the superior power of the North & the certainty of its application to the uttermost if necessary." Seward, wrote Blair, had offered to "meet prejudice with conciliation, exaction, with concession, which surrenders no principle, & violence with the right hand of peace." To Blair this was Buchanan's program, and it could only increase the threatening dangers. "No constitutional compromise could ever be devised for a new constitution to meet the exactions of the South, & preserve the character of popular Institutions for the Nation." [4]

In the same letter Blair also pointed out that Washington had been assisted by the genius and virtue of men like Adams, Jefferson, Hamilton, Madison, Lee, Henry, Franklin, and others who upheld Washington's reputation for "probity & disinterested love of country." Confidence in Lincoln's "honesty & patriotism" was now the mainstay of the Union, and the president should not weaken it by including Seward and Cameron in his cabinet. Blair listed Charles Francis Adams, John Andrew, Edwin D. Morgan, Preston King, Salmon P. Chase, Sam Houston, John Minor Botts, and some others as eminently preferable, but he admitted that Chase was "liable to the objection of eagerness for the Presidency which would make him obnoxious to rivalry—but his introduction would make him indispensible to counteract the machinations of Seward . . . if there was no deliverance from him."

Lincoln apparently agreed with Blair's views of the crisis, but as president he needed the broadest possible support. He needed the Seward–Weed influence in New York State, where the nation's largest city was marked by strong pro-southern sympathies among commercial giants and common laborers alike. Also, without permission, his followers had promised a cabinet seat to Cameron at the convention. Seward was offered the Department of State, while Cameron could be secretary of war. From the border states he chose Montgomery Blair for postmaster general and Edward Bates for attorney general. Salmon P. Chase, ardently disliked and opposed by Seward, became secretary of the treasury, and as Blair had predicted, soon became both a counter-

weight to Seward and an intriguer for the presidency. Gideon
Welles of Connecticut and Caleb B. Smith of Indiana were appointed secretary of the navy and secretary of the interior, re-
spectively. Blair, Welles, Chase, and Cameron were former
Democrats, and the Seward Whig faction protested angrily that
only three Whigs were included. Lincoln, however, replied that
the score was even because he himself was a former Whig. As
Blair had predicted, the announcement of Cameron's appointment triggered a storm of protest and accusations related to his
past deeds and associations. Lincoln actually wired Cameron a
request that he decline the appointment, but Cameron wanted the
position and ignored the president-elect's wish. Advisors other
than Blair persuaded Lincoln to let the matter stand.

Seward and Weed, who realized Lincoln's need for their
cooperation, tried even harder to prevent the appointment of
Chase, Welles, and Blair than Francis P. Blair had labored to
block the selection of Seward. Only two days before the inauguration Seward wrote Lincoln that he would not accept the Department of State unless his wishes were followed on the other
appointments. Lincoln responded with an ultimatum giving
Seward until 9:00 A.M. the next morning to make up his mind,
and Seward quickly capitulated. At the inaugural ball a *New York
Herald* correspondent asked Lincoln if he had any message for
his editor, James Gordon Bennett. "Yes," answered Lincoln.
"You may tell him that Thurlow Weed has discovered that
Seward was not nominated at Chicago." [5]

The new administration took office on a cold, windy March 1,
1861. While waiting to escort Lincoln to the inauguration, James
Buchanan was signing last-minute bills in the president's room at
the Capitol. Suddenly his postmaster general, Joseph Holt,
rushed in with a surprising and ominous message. After weeks of
sending reassurances that his post was defendable without reinforcements, Major Robert Anderson had just reported from Fort
Sumter, South Carolina, that a successful defense would take at
least 20,000 men. A short while later, Buchanan and Lincoln
rode through heavily guarded streets to the Capitol, where they
could see a huge crane swinging from the dome. The great
bronze statue of Freedom, which had been cast by slaves, was
waiting to be lifted to the top of the building and was still lying

on the ground. After taking the oath, the new president delivered a highly conciliatory inaugural. He repeated that he had neither the lawful right nor the inclination to interfere with slavery where it already existed. He would support the proposed Thirteenth Amendment just passed by Congress, which forbade forever any federal interference with slavery in the states. He would hold, occupy, and possess the federal property, and collect the duties and imposts, but beyond this there would be no "using of force against, or among people anywhere." At the insistence of Seward, any threats to retake federal property already seized by the South was conspicuously absent. "In *your* hands, my dissatisfied fellow countrymen, and not in *mine*," said Lincoln, "is the momentous issue of civil war. The government will not assail *you*. You can have no conflict, without being yourselves the aggressors."

Unfortunately for the peacemakers, however, Fort Sumter was still in federal hands, and the new southern government considered it an unbearable symbol of Yankee authority. James Buchanan had rejected military coercion as a national policy, but he had remained convinced that his constitutional oath included the protection of federal property wherever this was possible. Forts at Pensacola and Key West, Florida, and at Charleston could be reinforced and defended from the sea, and he had turned a deaf ear to southern demands for their surrender. His military commander-in-chief, General Winfield Scott, had offered strangely conflicting advice, and Buchanan had actually showed more determination to hold the forts than had Scott. The seventy-year-old Scott, a massive figure of six feet five inches and almost 300 pounds, had never been endowed with much political judgment. In October 1860 he had written a letter declaring that peripheral states had a right to secede, and that the federal government could use force only against a seceded state that blocked the way to another state that had chosen to remain in the Union. Allowing the nation to form itself into as many as four new confederacies would be preferable to the horrors of a civil war. Along with these peaceful sentiments, however, he recommended reinforcing the southern forts even as he pointed out that only five companies totaling 400 men were available for the assignment. The total army numbered only 16,000, and virtually the entire force was

stationed in the western Indian regions. The president ordered
the powerful warship *Brooklyn* with troops, stores, and provisions to sail to Fort Sumter, but was persuaded by Scott to substitute the unarmed shallow-draft side-wheeler *Star of the West*.
When the shore batteries at Charleston opened fire, the *Star of
the West* beat a hasty retreat. Buchanan was widely criticized
because the *Brooklyn* had not moved in against the Charleston
batteries, but the commander had simply followed the recommendations of General Scott.[6]

Fort Sumter was uniquely qualified either to become the
tinder-box of a civil war or to elicit a symbolic northern statement
that a peaceful secession was possible. Fort Pickens at Pensacola
and Fort Taylor at Key West were easy to defend and remained
in Union hands throughout the war. Fort Sumter, however, was
situated within Charleston Harbor, and any reinforcements would
have to come through a channel highly vulnerable to coastal
batteries. In its existing state the fort was no danger to Charleston
and of no great value to the United States. South Carolina was
eager to pay the federal government for its property and equipment, and had tried vigorously to open negotiations with Buchanan for that purpose. If Buchanan had given up the fort
several weeks before the inauguration, a wave of anger would
have swept through the North, but whether this feeling would
have remained high enough to support a war by Abraham Lincoln
cannot be determined. If Lincoln should abandon the fort or if the
Carolinians should allow a token Union force to remain there
indefinitely, no explosion would occur, the border states would
remain in the Union, and peaceful efforts to win back the others
could continue. The efforts might not succeed, but for the time
being at least a war would be avoided. If South Carolina attacked
the fort, however, it could not be defended without a massive
naval effort by the Union. A southern assault would also immediately swing northern public opinion in favor of an all-out war,
and it was the only issue in sight that appeared to have this
potential. The longer secession remained peaceful, the more time
the northern people could spend getting accustomed to the idea,
and if the South left the channels of trade open, the actual
difference secession would make in the lives of most individual
northerners would be minimal. In retrospect, the Confederate

unwillingness to leave Fort Sumter alone until some future date when passions might be cooler appears to be a foolish decision, but pride and rationality are often strangers. Also, Jefferson Davis was being advised on all hands that a collision at Fort Sumter would bring most if not all of the as-yet unseceded slave states into the Confederacy. If both Maryland and Virginia seceded, Washington, D.C., would find itself in the midst of the Confederacy, and if Kentucky and Missouri also seceded, a victorious war for the Union would be almost impossible.

Having been informed that Fort Sumter must be either re-provisioned or abandoned, and well aware of what had happened to the *Star of the West,* Abraham Lincoln also had to make a decision. His secretary of state, William H. Seward, and the great weight of northeastern business opinion represented by Seward and Weed wanted a peaceful evacuation, and Seward, not yet convinced that Lincoln was his own master, began making promises to various southerners that this would happen. At one point every cabinet member except Montgomery Blair was ready to acquiesce. General Scott assured the president that neither Sumter nor Pickens could be held, even though Buchanan's despatch of the *Brooklyn* to Pickens had made that fort quite invulnerable. Former cabinet members Jeremiah Black, Edwin M. Stanton, and Joseph Holt all wrote James Buchanan that Sumter would be abandoned and that Buchanan's own efforts to find a peaceful solution would be continued. All of this, of course, ran counter to remarks Lincoln had made before his inauguration, but whether his resolve was weakened by the overwhelming pressures to avoid a conflict cannot be determined. At one point, however, his only official advice to hold the fort came from Montgomery Blair, and various associates came to believe that the Blairs were most responsible for Lincoln's final decision.

On March 11 Francis P. Blair went to the White House to speak for those who would fight for Fort Sumter if necessary. The conversation was not recorded, but after returning home Blair was for once astounded by his own temerity at having used such passionate language to a president of the United States. "If I said anything which has left a bad impression on the President," he quickly wrote Montgomery, "you mush contrive some apology for me." He had said "that the surrender of Fort Sumter, was virtually a surrender of the Union unless under irresistible force—that compounding with treason was treason to the Govt. etc. There may be circumstances, with which I am unacquainted, rendering this very improper language & I am sure Genl Scotts patriotism, would not propose, what would warrant it." Knowing that Montgomery would hand the letter to Lincoln, Blair urged a national proclamation that would stress the defenseless condition in which Lincoln had found the government so that the fall of Fort Sumter, if it should happen, would not bring disgrace on the new administration. Lincoln, he wrote, should announce that he would maintain such defenses on the Gulf and eastern seaboard as were in the hands of the government and necessary to protect all states against foreign invasion, but declare that he would not use them against the seceded states. This "would reconcile the border Slave States to their retention & maintenance by the Govt. of the Union, if they mean to remain in the Union. . . . I think there never was an occasion when an eloquent appeal by the President to the people, like that of Genl Jackson in the Crisis of 1832, could be of more use." [7]

Gideon Welles always believed that Blair's warning had been a vital force in Lincoln's decision. To his diary he confided that Blair's "earnestness and indignation aroused [and electrified] the President," and when Blair, "in his zeal, warned the President that the abandonment of Sumter would be justly considered by the people, by the world, by history as treason to the country, he touched a chord that responded to his invocation. The President decided [from that moment] that an attempt should be made to convoy supplies" and reinforce Anderson. (Welles added the bracketed phrases at some later date.) [8]

At this point Lincoln asked his cabinet for written opinions on whether Fort Sumter should be reprovisioned "under present circumstances." Montgomery Blair's quick reply reflected what the Blairs had been saying for months: Ambitious leaders had inflamed the peoples' disappointment over the loss of the last election; the weakness of the previous administration was responsible for the present size of the rebellion, which was now being regarded at home and abroad as a successful revolution; and every hour of acquiescence was strengthening the rebels' claim to recognition as an independent people and forcing the southern unionists to accept the situation. A war between North and South, wrote Blair, could only be avoided by "firmness which gains respect." In 1833, the boldness of Andrew Jackson had prevented bloodshed and inspired respect. In 1860, however, contempt for Buchanan had inspired and expanded the rebellion, but it was not alone Buchanan's weakness: "They for the most part believe *that the Northern men are deficient in the courage necessary to maintain the Government.* . . . No men or people have so many difficulties as those whose firmness is doubted. The evacuation of Fort Sumter . . . will convince the rebels that the administration lacks firmness, & will therefore tend more than any event that has happened, to embolden them, and so far from tending to prevent collision will inspire it unless all the other forts are evacuated and all attempts are given up to maintain the authority of the United States." A continuation of Buchanan's policies would bring a war and "go far to produce a permanent division of the Union." A successful relief of Fort Sumter, however, "would completely demoralize the rebellion. The impotent rage & the outburst of patriotic feeling which would follow this achievement would initiate a reactionary movement throughout the South which would speedily overwhelm the traitors." And finally, the result would not be "materially different to the nation if the attempt fails & its gallant leader & followers are lost. It will in any event vindicate the hardy courage of the north, & the determination of the people & their president to maintain the authority of the Government, & this is all that is wanting, in my judgment, to restore it. You should give no thought for the commander & his comrades in this enterprise. They willingly take the hazard for the sake of the country & the honor which, successful or not, they will receive from you & the lovers of free government in all lands." [9]

On March 29 the Lincolns gave their first state dinner for the cabinet members and their wives and most members of the diplomatic corps. It was a tense and excited gathering, and afterwards the president asked the cabinet to stay for a conference. He had a written recommendation from General Scott that both Fort Sumter and Fort Pickens should be evacuated at once. The army's commanding general had announced that "Our southern friends . . . are clear that the evacuation of both the Forts would instantly soothe and give confidence to the eight remaining slaveholding states and render their cordial adherence to the Union perpetual." [10]

Clearly, Scott was speaking in the accents of Seward, who had been his close friend for many years. The usually self-composed Blair looked straight at Seward and burst into an angry tirade: "Mr. President, you can now see that General Scott, in advising the surrender of Fort Sumter, is playing the part of a politician, not of a general. No one pretends that there is any military necessity for the surrender of Fort Pickens, which he now says it is equally necessary to surrender. He is governed by political considerations in both recommendations." Realizing that he had gone too far, Seward offered another long argument for surrendering Sumter, but agreed that Pickens should be held. [11]

Seward's machinations were probably the result of a bad conscience. His own "higher law" and "irrepressible conflict" doctrines had done much to produce the secession, and he had apparently never expected to be confronted with realities inspired by his careless phrases. Despite his arch-radical reputation in the South he was essentially a conservative and peaceful man. He really did believe that conciliation would keep the border states and lead them to try to get their sister states back into the Union. He and James Buchanan had travelled in opposite directions for twenty years, only to arrive at the same crisis with almost identical policies, the exception being Buchanan's unwillingness to surrender Fort Sumter.

The statesmen of the new Confederacy, however, saw Seward as an unwitting ally. Georgia congressman Martin J. Crawford was certain that Seward's conciliatory approach would "build up and cement our Confederacy and put us beyond the reach of either his aims or of his diplomacy. . . . It is well that he should indulge in dreams which we know are not to be realized." The Confederate secretary of state, Robert Toombs, responded: "It is a matter of no importance to us what motives may induce the adoption of Mr. Seward's policy by his government. We are satisfied that it will rebound to our advantage." Crawford and Toombs may have been right, but neither Jefferson Davis nor Abraham Lincoln would wait to find out. [12]

On April 1, Seward made a last desperate effort with a memorandum to the president. He would evacuate Fort Sumter while holding the other federal property in the South. Then the nation should be reunited by involving it in a foreign war or at least in an energetic resistance to French and English intervention in Mexico or against Spanish interference in San Domingo. Lincoln ignored this flight of fancy, which remained secret for another thirty-three years.

The Blairs, meanwhile, with the approval of Navy Secretary Gideon Welles, had already brought Montgomery's Blair's brother-in-law Gustavus V. Fox into the argument. Earlier, Fox had tried unsuccessfully to persuade President Buchanan to send a convoy of large ships carrying men and light-draft tugs carrying supplies that would run the batteries at night and reach Fort Sumter under cover of darkness. Married to Minna Blair's younger sister, Fox was an experienced naval commander who several years earlier had left the service for a successful business career. On March 12 Fox explained the plan to Lincoln and was then taken to General Scott, who disagreed completely on the grounds that the new batteries on both sides of the harbor entrance made a safe entry impossible. Fox, however, insisted that a naval force propelled by steam could pass any number of guns there because the course was at right angles to the line of fire, and the distance would make accurate shooting impossible in the dark. Seeing that "Mr. Blair was fighting this battle alone," Fox thought it would strengthen his arguments and Blair's position if he made a visit to Fort Sumter. Lincoln agreed, and Fox reached Charleston on March 21. He had traveled the last part of the way with former South Carolina congressman Issac Holmes, who in Fox's presence informed the secessionist leader Lawrence Keitt on "the highest authority for what I say" that Sumter was to be given up. Fox and Major Anderson at the fort agreed that April 15 at noon would be the point beyond which the fort could not be held without new supplies. Fox returned to Washington still convinced that his plan would work, and he furnished Lincoln with a list of examples where ships had passed shore batteries with impunity, "notably the English gunboat squadron which ran the batteries at Kinburn in the Crimean War." [13]

On the afternoon of April 4, Abraham Lincoln ordered Gustavus Fox to reprovision and reinforce Fort Sumter. He would notify Charleston that a relief expedition was coming and promise not to send troops if the southerners would allow the supplies to reach the fort peacefully. At the same time Lincoln gave Seward the responsibility for Fort Pickens. The most important vessel in Fox's plan was the expedition flagship, the *Powhatan,* a powerfully armed steam frigate loaded with munitions needed at the fort and considered by Fox to be strong enough to protect the boats and tugs that were to land the supplies. Unhappily for Fox, however, Seward communicated the entire plan to James E. Harvey, a well-known newspaper correspondent who was also a native Charlestonian. Harvey, whom Seward had already appointed to be United States minister to Portugal, immediately wired a Confederate friend in Charleston: "Positively determined not to withdraw Anderson. Supplies go immediately, supported by naval force under [Commodore Silas] Stringham if their landing be resisted." [14]

On April 5 Gideon Welles ordered Captain Samuel Mercer on the *Powhatan* to sail to a point ten miles east of Charleston Harbor. On the following day, as Mercer was preparing to get underway, Lieutenant David Porter stepped aboard the *Powhatan* with orders signed by Abraham Lincoln with an addendum, "Recommended, Wm. H. Seward." Porter was to go on secret service without communicating with the Navy Department and sail the *Powhatan* not to Sumter but to Pickens, where neither the ship nor its munitions supplies were needed at all.

Mercer immediately wired a complaint to Seward, and late that night Seward and an angry Welles went to the White House for an explanation. Confronted with the conflicting orders, Lincoln insisted that it was all a mistake. He had been signing routine papers and had signed the orders to Porter without reading them. The president curtly ordered Seward to telegraph Porter immediately to return the ship to Mercer for the original mission. Seward complied, but signed the telegram "Seward." Porter had already sailed, and when a messenger boat caught up with the *Powhatan* the intrepid lieutenant simply ignored the order. He had taken the ship with orders signed by Lincoln that superseded those signed by Welles. Orders signed by a mere secretary of state obviously carried no weight against those signed by the president. The flagship and major offensive power of the Sumter expedition thus proceeded to Fort Pickens where it was not needed.[15]

As if Fox did not have difficulties enough, a major storm scattered his ships, and he arrived off Charleston Harbor virtually defenseless just in time to bounce around helplessly on the high seas while the Carolinians shelled the fort. Anderson had assured South Carolina's governor, F. W. Pickens, that he would be starved out by April 15 if he were not reprovisioned, but knowing the expedition was enroute, the southerners did not wait. Beginning at 4:30 A.M. on April 12, they bombarded the eighty-five soldiers and forty-three workmen in the fort for thirty-four hours. The fort caught fire several times and it was badly damaged, but no one was injured. If Fox had had sufficient firepower to engage the batteries successfully, the fort might have been reinforced and kept in northern hands. Running out of food, medicine, and ammunition, Anderson decided that he had upheld the honor of his command, and he surrendered with the stipulation that he be allowed to fire a fifty-gun salute to the American flag. The only reported casualty of the battle was "one horse—Confederate." Unhappily, however, when the fifty-gun salute was being fired during the surrender ceremony, an accidental explosion killed two soldiers and wounded four others.

Fox and the Blairs always believed that if Seward had not sabotaged the expedition by informing Harvey and diverting the *Powhatan*, the fort might have been held and the ensuing war avoided. This, of course, rests upon the doubtful proposition that the *Powhatan* would have been strong enough to make that much difference. The Blairs, however, never did face up to another possibility—that Abraham Lincoln might have preferred to lose the Battle of Fort Sumter because a defeat would be a far greater rallying force in the North than a victory. There is no evidence that the president ever said a harsh word to Seward for openly trying to thwart his chief's announced purposes. Seward suggested that Harvey's diplomatic appointment should be revoked, but when he changed his mind and kept Harvey in the post, Lincoln did not object. "Thinking it over cooly," said Seward, "I thought it wrong to punish a man for his stupid folly, when really he had committed no crime."[16] Apparently a capacity for stupid folly was not a disqualification for the position of minister to Portugal.

To the degree that they had reinforced Lincoln's instinctive willingness to fight a war rather than risk the dismantling of the great worldwide experiment in free government that he and they conceived the United States to be, the Blairs had done their job well. Lincoln might have responded to the attack by sending a naval force to retake Fort Sumter and announcing to the border states the limited nature of this objective. The southerners had tried unsuccessfully to prevent the landing of additional troops and supplies at Fort Pickens, and the event had caused scarcely a ripple. Virginia, North Carolina, Arkansas, and Tennessee might have seceded because of a limited struggle over Fort Sumter, but the absence of any threat to the other Confederate states and a disavowal of any intention to conquer South Carolina might well have kept them in the Union. South Carolina, after all, had never really been popular with the other states, and numerous border-state editors had already been denouncing the deep South for risking a war that would be fought on their soil. Lincoln, however, had decided to strike while the iron was hot. With angry condemnations of the South ringing throughout the North, he called for 75,000 militia to put down the rebellion and then summoned Congress to a special session beginning on July 4. Buchanan had asked the Congress for authority to call the militia, and had probably breathed a sigh of relief when his requests were denied. Lincoln carefully gave himself eleven weeks of freedom from Congress and acted with breathtaking boldness in exercising his authority as commander-in-chief of the armed forces and his responsibility for the security of the nation. His reaction to the events at Fort Sumter rather than the battle itself started the war and brought the immediate secession of Virginia, North Carolina, Arkansas, and Tennessee, through whose territory northern soldiers would have to march en route to the cotton states. Kentucky refused to furnish any troops, while Maryland and Missouri went through crises. All three remained in the Union.

Clearly, Abraham Lincoln and Jefferson Davis had used Fort Sumter for their divergent purposes. Davis had no reason to doubt that his attack on Fort Sumter would start a war, and Lincoln almost eagerly grasped the opportunity Davis had provided. On May 1, with northern soldiers flocking to the colors from every direction, Lincoln consoled the disappointed Gustavus

Fox. The gale had scattered the tugs, he wrote, and "an accident, for which you were in no way responsible, and possibly I, to some extent was," had deprived Fox of the "war vessel with her men, which you deemed of great importance to the enterprize. . . . You and I both anticipated that the cause of the country would be advanced by making the attempt to provision Fort-Sumpter, even if it should fail; and it is no small consolation now to feel that our anticipation is justified by the result." [17] Although the Blairs continued to blame Seward for the failure of the relief expedition, they, like Lincoln, preferred war to any possibility that secession might be permanent.

Three days after the battle, a handsome, gray-bearded soldier rode past the White House and dismounted in front of Montgomery Blair's plain, square old residence to keep an appointment with Montgomery's father. The soldier was a Virginian, but he had freed his own slaves and had written that "there are few in this enlightened age who would not acknowledge that slavery as an institution is a moral and political evil." He had also denounced secession as the destruction of a government "that has given us peace & prosperity at home, power and security abroad, & under which we have acquired a colossal strength unequalled in the history of mankind." Francis P. Blair had been authorized by Abraham Lincoln to offer Robert E. Lee the command of the Union armies, but his guest could not accept. "Mr. Blair," said Lee, "I look upon secession as anarchy. If I owned the four millions of slaves at the South, I would sacrifice them all to the Union; but how can I draw my sword upon Virginia, my native State?" A few days later he joined his fellow southerners and thereby guaranteed that the war would be greatly prolonged and infinitely bloody. [18]

Chapter 20

The Warriors

IN September 1860 Eliza Blair's favorite horse, "the Sluggard," stepped on a hornets' nest and promptly threw sixty-five-year-old Eliza directly over his head. She landed on her face, which was badly cut, but she was not seriously injured. The incident rated only a casual mention in Lizzie's next letter to her husband, because the Blair women were preoccupied with more important matters. They were intensely involved in the election campaign, and deeply concerned that its results might bring a war. In St. Louis, where Phillips Lee and Frank were watching the signs, Lee was still writing with guarded optimism, while Frank was already convinced that a conflict was inevitable.[1]

In early October Lee took command of the sloop of war *Vandalia* in New York with orders to sail to the China Sea. Fortunately the fitting-out took several weeks, which Lizzie and young Blair spent with him in New York. It was a happy if brief period, and Lizzie had difficulty explaining to three-year-old Blair just why his father had to leave. She was quite proud of the little boy when he informed a stranger in a New York park that his "papa" was Captain Phillips Lee who would have to sail his ship "a long way from mama and me."[2]

Lee did not spend all of his time getting ready for sea and enjoying his family. One evening he met with Congressman Francis E. Spinner of New York and senators Preston King of New York, James Doolittle of Wisconsin, and Lyman Trumbull of Illinois. They all believed that the Buchanan administration was deliberately dispersing the fleet and sending its loyal officers as far away as possible. Lee announced that as "a southern man and a Virginian," he "would stand for the Union and its flag to the last." He would delay his departure as long as possible and then make his way slowly to the west coast of Africa, where he would "leisurely cruize" [*sic*] for slavers and not arrive at the Cape of Good Hope until news of Lincoln's inauguration had reached there. If events then indicated that either he or his ship was needed for the aid of the country, he would return home immediately.[3]

Lee followed this plan to the letter. At Cape Town he learned that the states were seceding and that Buchanan had denied the right of the federal government to coerce them back into the Union. Against orders to go and without orders to return, Lee sailed back to New York and reported to Washington. For this unprecedented violation of military custom he was greeted coldly by Gustavus Fox, who had once been a midshipman under Lee's command. Fox informed him that he "did not know how the Secretary would take his return." Welles and Lincoln, however, were looking for all available ships and commanders, and they immediately assigned Lee and the *Vandalia* to the Charleston blockade.

For the next four years Lee performed with heroism and great efficiency. He had spent several years in coastal surveys and was thereby superbly equipped to direct operations requiring ships to sail into dangerously shallow waters. After winning much favorable attention at Charleston he was assigned to the larger sloop of war *Oneida* and ordered to the mouth of the Mississippi. There, under Admiral David Farragut, Lee commanded the advance division when Farragut's ships fought their way past the two forts guarding the approaches to New Orleans. At one point the smaller ships were deliberately attacking the forts to draw the fire away from the bomb vessels, and the *Oneida* was engaged alone against both forts. Admiral David Porter later said that he had never seen "a ship more beautifully fought and managed." Lee, added Porter, "had much more than his share of killed and wounded; and said less about it than those who did not take the bull so closely by the horns." After successfully engaging several Confederate ships and participating in the capture of New Orleans, Lee commanded the advance division below Vicksburg and twice ran the Vicksburg batteries.[4]

On July 16, 1862, Lee was promoted to captain. On September

2, 1862, he was named acting rear admiral, and ordered to the command of the North Atlantic blockading squadron. It was an assignment requiring imagination, technical skills, and administrative talent rather than a flair for heroics, but in terms of winning the war it was the most important command in the navy. Many of the more spectacular naval exploits of the Civil War contributed little to the final result, but the Union blockade damaged the Confederacy severely and helped keep either Britain or France from becoming involved. Lee designed a blockading system by which the heavier ships remained in close while the lighter, faster, and more maneuverable cruisers in successive "girdles" were spread farther out to sea. The blockade captured or destroyed a total of sixty-five blockade running steamers, fifty-four of them during Lee's period of command.[5]

In all of this, however, there was much frustration because his achievements and services gained only minimal recognition, and he received no regular promotion until after the war. His career was hounded by the personal dislike of Assistant Secretary of the Navy Gustavus Fox and his own brother-in-law Montgomery Blair, and this was compounded by Montgomery's strong influence over Secretary of the Navy Gideon Welles. Also, the New Hampshire Woodbury girls who had married Montgomery Blair and Gustavus Fox were no more shy and retiring than the Blair women. Minna Blair was not fond of either Phillips Lee or Lizzie, and her sister probably helped keep Fox from forgetting his own earlier resentments. Many years earlier, when Levi Woodbury was secretary of the treasury, he had transferred the coastal-survey operation from the navy to the treasury department. No one had complained more loudly than Phillips Lee, who considered it a change from professionalism to political patronage. It is barely possible that the Woodbury feud with Lee began at that early date. In any case Francis P. Blair respected Montgomery's attitude even while deploring it, and Montgomery managed to remain on reasonably good terms with his mother and sister even after relations among the women were broken. During the last two years of the war, Lizzie and her parents spent much of the time in the Lee house at 4 Pennsylvania Avenue, which was connected by a common wall to 6 Pennsylvania Avenue, the house Francis P. Blair had given to Montgomery.

By 1864 Lizzie was referring to her sister-in-law as "Mrs. No.6," and she and Eliza, who also adored Lee, were no longer communicating with Minna across the wall. Whenever Lizzie met Fox away from "No. 6," he was invariably complimentary and affectionate in his remarks about Lee. Indeed, she wrote, he was always far more cordial "anywhere else than at that locality. His entente is complete there & he evidently doesn't want to complicate it." [6]

Fox tried to keep Lee from getting the North Atlantic command, but the strong recommendations of other officers and possibly the friendship of Welles and Lincoln for the senior Blair prevailed. Fox and Montgomery Blair may have acquiesced in the knowledge that this assignment would afford minimal opportunities for flamboyant heroism, but if so they forgot a compensating advantage. During the Civil War the navy was still operating under the prize-money system by which the officers and men divided the value of their captured cargoes. As blockade commander, Lee received one-twentieth, which eventually totaled some $150,000 and made him by far the most highly rewarded member of the armed services. This led to increased jealousy at "No. 6" and encouraged false rumors that he had made $300,000. On one occasion Montgomery told Lizzie and his parents that nobody cared about getting Lee promoted because they felt the money was quite enough compensation. [7]

In mid-July 1864 a Confederate army fought its way to the outskirts of Washington and established headquarters in Blair's Silver Spring house. The newspapers were spreading the alarming news that the city was protected only by green troops and was in great peril. Communications had been cut between Washington, Baltimore, and Philadelphia. At Hampton Roads, Virginia, where his blockade operation was functioning smoothly and routinely, Admiral Lee assumed the worst rumors were true. He promptly sent four steamers, including one ironclad, with heavy batteries up the Potomac to Washington and followed in his own flagship. Fortunately, adequate reinforcements had already arrived, and his services were not needed—a fact relayed to him in no uncertain terms by Gideon Welles: "The Department disapproves your leaving your station without orders in an emergency like the present. Return to Hampton Roads without an-

choring your vessel." Before leaving, Lee sent a full and contrite
explanation. From all available information, it had seemed "that
the emergency appeared not to be there, but here at the national
capital." [8] Ironically, Welles later complained that Lee was short
on initiative and boldness, even though their only disagreements
had been over Lee's daring return home from Africa without
orders and his unauthorized expedition to defend Washington
during the brief crisis of July 1864.

For several months in 1864, Welles tried unsuccessfully to
get soldiers from General Henry W. Halleck for a joint army-
navy attack upon Fort Fisher, near Wilmington, North Carolina.
The fort was a haven for blockade runners, and Lee was also
eager for its capture. Finally Welles authorized Lee to take the
fort alone if he could. By sending small boats up the Cape Fear
river almost to the fort, however, Lee discovered that the water
was too shallow for a purely naval attack. Ultimately General
Ulysses S. Grant supplied a force smaller than Lee thought
necessary, and Fox reported that Grant wanted a different naval
commander for the assault. Welles and Fox happily obliged,
and Lee was replaced by Admiral David Porter and transferred
to the command of the Mississippi squadron, where prize money
was scarcer. Welles confided to his diary that Lee was a good
officer but much too cautious. The subsequent assault by Porter
and General Butler on Fort Fisher was an ignominious failure
that ended in wild recriminations on the part of all concerned.
Lizzie considered the quarrel between Butler and Porter "a hot
fight between two gas bags—who may puncture each other." [9]

Lee ordered his wife and father-in-law to make no complaint
over this transfer, but, as usual, Blair had already protested bitterly. Lizzie did not mind at all because the orders included a
leave of absence for her husband between stations, but she predicted that "Mother's resentments will be intense." When Eliza
did hear the news, she first went off by herself for a while. Then
she praised both Lizzie and Lee for their fortitude. Lizzie
laughed and said that "it didn't take fortitude to have him come
home." [10]

In January 1865 a combined naval and army operation identical
to that proposed by Lee finally took Fort Fisher. Lee, meanwhile,
had again put his navigational and tactical skills to good use on

the western rivers. He kept the Confederate armies of Generals Edmund Kirby-Smith and John B. Hood on opposite sides of the Mississippi, and he contributed much to the routing of Hood's army by General George Thomas.

At "No. 4," the family controversy over Lee's fortunes centered on his long periods of service without leave, the navy department's refusal to make his acting rank a permanent promotion, and the refusal of Fox and Welles to ask Congress to give him a resolution of thanks, even though General Thomas had sent Lee a letter of glowing praise. In January and again in June 1865, Francis P. Blair finally asked Charles Sumner for assistance: "It may be that I am held too close to my son, to make it agreeable to some in the Senate, that the latter should receive its thanks. But Capt. Lee is as radical as you are especially on the point of State responsibility, & does not agree with me about my States rights doctrine but you about your doctrine." [11] By 1865 Montgomery Blair was out of the cabinet and the Blairs were anathema to the congressional leadership. After having been proscribed by his in-laws when they had influence, Lee was now handicapped by his relationship with them. He was thanked by each house of Congress separately, but did not get the joint resolution that marked the exploits of some other favored heroes.

While Phillips Lee was loading ammunition and supplies on board the *Vandalia* in November 1861, Frank Blair in St. Louis was preparing for the war he knew to be inevitable. His immediate personal concern was the fact that like his father many years earlier he had signed too many security notes for friends and made too many unsound investments. In particular he was heavily committed as security for his favorite cousin Cary Gratz, as well as for the firm of Howard Gratz and Joseph Shelby, who were also his cousins. Cary and Howard were the sons of Ben and Maria Gratz; Shelby was the son of Anna Maria Boswell Shelby, whom Ben Gratz had married after the death of Maria. Since the second Mrs. Gratz was a neice of the first Mrs. Gratz, the children were cousins as well as stepbrothers. During Frank Blair's youthful sojourns at the home of Ben and Maria Gratz, he had become very fond of the Gratz brothers, Jo Shelby, and a neighboring boy named John Hunt Morgan. In the 1850s Howard and Cary Gratz and Jo Shelby had followed Frank Blair's example by moving to Missouri. The firm of Gratz and Shelby had been badly hurt by the depression of 1857, and the thought of refusing to sign security notes for them or for Cary Gratz would have never occurred to Frank.

Largely through the talents of his agent, Franklin A. Dick, Francis P. Blair had more than $48,000 invested in St. Louis securities and mortgage loans. It was safe insurance against his old age, but his son needed help. Dick reported that Frank owed a total of $56,340 plus $5,000 as security for a friend whose farm and property would probably be an adequate reimbursement. His assets, wrote Dick, totaled $85,000. Dick proposed that Francis P. Blair use his own securities to take up Frank's debts, which Frank would secure to his father with first liens on the property. Frank would also pay interest and assign his rents from the property to Blair. The $15,000 that Frank already owed his father would be included in the securities. Blair dreaded the thought of losing his financial independence, but he did not hesitate to throw his fortune into the breach for his favorite son. Frank felt "great mortification," but he was certain the arrangement would keep his father's capital and income safe. Above all, he would "not be under the apprehension of having everything swept from my children & wife in case anything should happen to me."[12]

And Frank did have more important concerns. Blair had always considered him another Andrew Jackson, and Benton had dubbed him the "Young Ajax." Their appraisal was quite accurate. Whatever his deficiencies in professional and business affairs, Frank was a man of fierce determination, boundless energy, vivid imagination, instinctive courage, and a taste for grand homicide on a massive scale if exercised in a noble cause. In short, he was eminently qualified to be a great soldier, and the Civil War gave him the opportunity. He was also a member of Congress and a politician, however, and this meant that his time and talents could be divided according to Lincoln's needs.

The first priority for Frank Blair was keeping Missouri in the Union. When the secessionist governor, Claiborne Jackson, persuaded the legislature to call a convention, Blair organized the Union forces for the election of delegates. He also converted the Wide-Awake Clubs that had supported Lincoln into Union

Clubs, and began drilling and arming them with money raised from private sources. These groups had a strong German nucleus, but were joined by a great many other Missourians ready to fight for the Union. The election for convention delegates went overwhelmingly unionist, and the convention resolved that the conflict was caused by the "alienated feelings existing between the Northern and Southern sections of the country, rather than the actual injury suffered by either, in the anticipation of future evils, rather than in the pressure of any now actually endured." Missouri would remain in the Union and seek compromises that might induce the erring states to return.

What Missouri might do, however, if the North actually made war upon the South remained unpredictable. Governor Jackson had asked the legislature for authority to call up the militia for Missouri's defense against the North. Frank Blair's Wide-Awakes and Home Guards, meanwhile, were drilling in various secret places. Ultimately he had eleven companies totaling 750 men. Pro-Confederate groups in St. Louis were also organizing and drilling; their headquarters was in a local mansion already decorated with a Confederate flag. An important fulcrum of power in Missouri was the federal arsenal in St. Louis, which covered fifty-six acres and supposedly held some 60,000 stands of arms. If captured by the secessionists, the arsenal might have a pervasive effect upon the large number of citizens who always waver in violent situations. The commander, Major William Bell, was ready to surrender the arsenal to the governor upon request, but Blair persuaded General Scott to remove Bell before this could happen. Bell's successor, Major Peter Hagner, was also suspect in Blair's eyes, and the overall commander of the Department of the West, General William S. Harney of Tennessee and Louisiana, was torn between southern sympathies and a stern sense of duty. Ultimately Blair persuaded Lincoln to replace first Hagner and then Harney with forty-three-year-old Captain Nathaniel Lyon, who was short, red-haired, aggressive, and dedicated to both the Union and the abolitionist cause.

The real crisis occurred after the Battle of Fort Sumter. Governor Jackson refused Lincoln's request for four regiments of infantry and asked Jefferson Davis for seige guns and mortars. He also called a special session of the legislature for May 2, 1861, and ordered the state militia into camps for drilling and discipline. General Daniel M. Frost of the Missouri state militia established Camp Jackson in St. Louis with 750 men and began preparing to seize the arsenal. Soon a large quantity of mortars, artillery, and ammunition arrived from the Confederacy.

On April 17 Frank Blair returned to St. Louis from Washington with orders placing the Home Guards and all other loyal soldiers under Lyon. Blair and Lyon recruited volunteers to fill the four regiments that Jackson had refused to give Lincoln, and actually mustered in more men than had been requested. Lyon became the brigadier general, and Blair was elected colonel of the first regiment.

After several weeks of shadow boxing while both sides waited for more men and supplies that never came, Blair and Lyon suddenly surrounded and captured Camp Jackson with all its men. The 750 prisoners were marched back to the arsenal under guard by the Germans and the regulars. The streets were lined with angry and excited people both unionist and secessionist, and at one point a street fight ended with the Union soldiers firing into the crowd. Twenty-nine people were killed or mortally wounded, and the victims reportedly included a child in its mother's arms. On the following day another six or seven persons were killed. General Harney took back his command of the city from Lyon, and the disorder gradually stopped. St. Louis and the arsenal were henceforth safe for the Union, although the event left a heritage of bitterness. A few days later, Frank Blair narrowly escaped death from a bullet fired through an open window of his home. Seizing a camp of 750 men with an army of 7,000 was easy enough, but recruiting and organizing the Union forces while the Confederate sympathizers remained separated and uncoordinated was a major feat. Frank Blair had persuaded the president and the War Department to change the military leadership and issue the necessary orders, and his foresight, energy, and decisiveness guaranteed that St. Louis would remain in Union hands.[13]

Ultimately Claiborne Jackson and his brother-in-law, General Sterling Price, took some 40,000 Missourians with them into the Confederate army, but another 110,000 fought for the Union. Frank Blair offered commissions to both Cary Gratz and Jo

Shelby. Cary accepted but his stepbrother angrily went off to join the Confederacy.

Nathaniel Lyon was a fighting man of the Blair stripe, but Frank's efforts to get his new friend promoted to major general and made commander of the Department of the West were opposed by both General Scott and Attorney General Bates. An older man of higher rank and less radical reputation must be found. At this point Francis P. Blair and his sons went to Lincoln with a new suggestion. John C. Frémont had a national reputation and was popular with both Congress and the St. Louis Germans. He had always been a man of action. Lincoln accepted the Blairs' evaluation, and Frémont and his indomitable wife, Jessie, suddenly found themselves with another opportunity for greatness. Apparently, no one pointed out that a force of sixty-two men was the largest command Frémont had ever held.

In June Frank Blair returned to Washington for the special session of Congress that was to meet in July. He ran second to Galusha Grow of Pennsylvania in the balloting for speaker, but was immediately named chairman of the Committee on Military Affairs. In this capacity he guided through numerous bills legalizing actions already taken by the president and providing for the creation of a massive volunteer army to fight the war. He also publicly defended Lincoln against charges of responsibility for the Union debacle at the First Battle of Bull Run, and he openly called for the replacement of General Scott. His father was kept busy writing the speeches.

Meanwhile, Governor Jackson, Sterling Price and General Ben McCulloch took control of western Missouri with an army estimated at 30,000 men. To check them, Nathaniel Lyon marched to Springfield with a much smaller force of some 7,000 to 8,000. In St. Louis all was chaos while the army waited for its new commanding general. Frémont delayed three weeks in New York and Washington while trying to procure munitions and supplies. It was a difficult task because most of Lincoln's advisors and officers were concerned primarily with the East. The Blairs and Lincoln became more and more impatient over the new general's delays, and were much relieved when he and Jessie finally reached St. Louis on July 25. There Frémont was immediately accosted by messengers from Lyon begging for reinforcements. Lyon was separated by 120 miles of bad terrain from the nearest railroad, he was running out of supplies, and many of his men were leaving because their enlistments were expiring. He was also facing a much larger force under General McCulloch. The Confederates hoped to destroy Lyon's army, take St. Louis if possible, and then move against Cairo, Illinois, on the Mississippi.

Simultaneously, Frémont began getting calls for help from Cairo. Correctly considering Cairo more important, but mistaken in his belief that the city was in serious danger, he sailed with 4,800 men to Cairo, where he was greeted with enthusiasm. Meanwhile, he sent two regiments to the railroad center at Rolla, and wrote Lyon that he should fall back to Rolla if he could not hang on at Springfield. Lyon, however, feared that the 120-mile retreat across rough country and difficult streams would turn into a rout by the pursuing enemy. On August 10 Captain Cary Gratz and his cousin and stepbrother Captain Jo Shelby faced each other at a place called Wilson's Creek when Lyon with only 5,000 men attacked McCulloch's army of 13,000. Following Lyon's heroic personal example, his men held their own until he was killed. Demoralized in the face of superior numbers, the Union army retreated and straggled back towards St. Louis. Both sides had suffered heavy casualties, but the Confederates had won control of western Missouri. As news of the battle filled the northern press and Lyon's body was taken the long way home to New England, Frémont was widely criticized for not having either sent reinforcements or ordered Lyon to retreat sooner.[14]

At first the Blairs did not share in the condemnation of Frémont, but the Battle of Wilson's Creek left them badly shaken. Even worse than Frank's sadness over the death of Lyon was the whole family's grief when word came that Cary Gratz had also been killed. Poor Ben Gratz deserved their sympathy. His stepson Jo Shelby eventually became a Confederate general, and when Robert E. Lee surrendered, Shelby and his men buried their battle flag in the Rio Grande and crossed into Mexico to join Emperor Maximilian. The other Gratz sons remained unionists, but whatever her politics, Anna Maria's heart probably went with her own first born. Perhaps fortunately, the teen-aged children of her marriage with Ben were both daughters.

Returning from his brief triumph at Cairo, Frémont worked hard to bring order from chaos and get an army ready for battle despite severe shortages of arms, horses, and wagons. In letter after letter to Washington he called for more supplies and equipment that were simply not available. Frémont's difficulties had already been described by Jessie in a plaintive letter to Lizzie Lee on July 27. They had found "an arsenal without arms or ammunition—troops on paper, and a thoroughly prepared united enemy. Thick and unremitting as mosquitoes. The telegraph in the enemy's hands. . . . Western troops on their way to the Potomac—the western waters left to defend themselves as best they might." She had begged Frémont to let her go directly to Lincoln, but he would not risk her health with the trip and insisted that he could not do without her. "It's making bricks without straw out here and mere human power can't draw order out of chaos by force of will only. . . . I believe in the United States. . . . but this is a day for men, not rules, to govern affairs." Jessie added that she was proud of Phillips Lee for returning from Africa without orders and that they were anxiously waiting for Frank Blair. It was the last letter signed "love" that Jessie Benton Frémont would ever write to a Blair.[15]

In early August Frank Blair returned to St. Louis with a personal order to keep the president informed on conditions there. Lincoln had offered to make him a general, but they had agreed that for the time being at least he should keep his seat in Congress. Ohio congressman Clement Vallandigham, who would eventually be convicted of treason, had already tried to get Frank expelled from the house as a military officer constitutionally ineligible to serve in Congress, but others had pointed out that the restriction did not apply to a militia officer.

On August 13 Francis P. Blair wrote a long letter to his favorite, Jessie. He hoped they would begin a correspondence

about the great things which are to make history hereafter and in which we are to be equally interested—you for your husband's exploits and I for my sons, as well as his. I will let you have what your father called "the inside view of things" at Washington and you must make me up "Ceasars [sic] commentaries" of the civil war in Missouri. . . . I want you to have Frank made a militia major general for the State of Missouri. This I presume Govr. [Hamilton]

Gamble can do, and as Major General Frost nipt his military honors
in the bud by turning Traitor and absconding with Claib Jackson, it
would seem but a completion of what was begun by substituting
Gamble for the abdicating Governor to make Frank . . . take the
position deserted by Genl. Frost. . . .

I hope and believe Genl. Fremont will make a glorious campaign
in the great valley. . . . To be the Chief to conduct to such results,
is a superiority vastly more eminent than that at which he arrived
in 1856.[16]

Later biographers of Frémont and Blair have mistakenly
cited the above letter as one written to Frémont himself.[17] It
was not a demand upon an overworked general with no power
to appoint state militia officers anyhow, but a request to a lifelong friend that she ask the new provisional governor to take
what seemed a logical step. On August 18 Frémont did ask Governor Gamble to commission Frank Blair a brigadier general, and
Gamble, who was a friend and ally of Blair's would probably
have done so if he had had the constitutional authority.

Within two weeks after his arrival in St. Louis, Frank Blair
was convinced that the choice of Frémont was a catastrophic error.
The Pathfinder worked with great energy and zeal, but his
efforts were poorly organized, and confusion and bad judgment
dogged his every step. He fortified St. Louis, built a useful new
railway station, and organized an effective riverboat fleet and
service. He selected a formerly cashiered officer named Ulysses
S. Grant to command one of his armies. He also surrounded
himself with a staff of gaudily uniformed Hungarian and Italian
officers, and had so many guards blocking the doors at his headquarters that people with valuable information could not reach
him. When the Confederates continued to expand their control
of the Missouri hinterland, he seemed paralyzed. He refused
to enforce strict discipline, and there were constant complaints
of corruption and inefficiency in the awarding of contracts for
supplies. Officers in Washington could not evaluate the complaints objectively because Frémont ignored the traditional army
methods of bookkeeping and accounting. Numerous favorites
received high-ranking commissions that he had no legal power to
grant. When the local press began criticizing his policies and decisions, he suppressed several newspapers, including the strongly
unionist St. Louis Republican.

Frank Blair recommended to Frémont the services and products of various people and companies, and most of his suggestions were honored. Frémont later claimed that the refusal of a contract recommended by Blair had started their quarrel, but there is no evidence that Blair ever considered the neglect of his business friends a serious grievance.

Always sensitive to any kind of criticism, Frémont resolved to silence his opponents with a masterly political stroke. On August 30 he proclaimed that he would thrust aside the provisional governor and rule the state entirely by himself; Missouri would henceforth be under martial law. Any persons caught with guns in their hands north of the Union lines would be court-martialed and shot; the property of those proven to have been active with the enemy in the field would be confiscated and their slaves would be "hereby declared freemen." [18]

The proclamation made Frémont the overnight idol of the northern abolitionists and was praised highly in many newspapers. The southern response was immediate. General Jeff Thompson announced that for every Confederate put to death in accordance with Frémont's order he would " '*hang, draw* and quarter' a minion of Abraham Lincoln. . . . I intend to exceed General Frémont in his excesses." Lincoln answered quickly also. Shooting people, he wrote Frémont, would lead to a retaliation, "and so, man for man, indefinitely. It is, therefore, my order that you allow no man to be shot under the proclamation without first having my approbation or consent." As for the liberation of slaves, Lincoln feared that this would "alarm our Southern Union friends and turn them against us; perhaps ruin our rather fair prospect for Kentucky. Allow me, therefore, to ask that you will, as of your own motion, modify that paragraph so as to conform to the . . . act of Congress" authorizing the confiscation of "property used for insurrectionary purposes, approved August 6, 1861." [19] This act had authorized the confiscation of slaves actually used for military purposes such as the construction of forts or the digging of trenches.

Lincoln was trying to save Missouri and Kentucky without humiliating his general, but the stubborn Frémont answered that the president would have to change the orders himself. Lincoln immediately complied by giving the press a letter to Frémont ordering the proclamation to be modified to conform to the act of Congress, which should "be published at length with this order." Frémont, however, refused to help publicize Lincoln's letter and actually printed and circulated some 200 copies of his original proclamation without the accompanying modification.

At first Frank Blair assured his brother that Frémont would succeed if given enough men and supplies. Shortly afterward, however, he and General John Schofield, who had been with Lyon at Wilson's Creek, left a conference with Frémont and walked for several minutes in silence. Then Blair asked "Well, what do you think of him?" Schofield later remembered that he had "replied in words rather too strong to repeat in print, to the effect that my opinion as to his wisdom was the same as it always had been." Blair answered: "I have been suspecting that for some time." [20]

On September 1, Frank Blair wrote Montgomery a letter filled with concern and sorrow, but entirely lacking in vindictiveness. Indeed, he even praised Frémont's emancipation proclamation, but he was dismayed by the general's military incompetence. Missouri, he warned, was in grave danger, but men with information could not gain access to Frémont:

> He talks of the vigor he is going to use, but I can see none of it, and I fear it will turn out to be some rash and inconsiderate move—adopted in haste to make head against a formidable force which could not have accumulated except through gross and inexcusable negligence. Oh! for one hour of our dead Lyon—many have been disposed to blame Fremont for not sending reinforcements to Lyon. . . . It is very certain that if he had sent the reinforcements to Lyon that he took to Cairo . . . Lyon would have driven McCullough [sic] from the State. . . . Probably you have information which will satisfy you that Fremont was not to blame. If so the public here should know it also in order that the confidence of the people should not be withheld from the Commanding General. I could not think when I first returned here that any part of the blame could rest with him but my observations since have shaken my faith to the very foundation. . . .
>   . . . you and I are both in some sort responsible for Fremont's . . . being placed in command of this Department and therefore I feel another and an additional motive to speak out openly. . . . My decided opinion is that he should be relieved of his command and a man of ability put in his place. The sooner it is done the better. . . . if the Govt. knows more of his plans than I do—if you are satisfied with

him—then you can view this paper and say that I am an alarmist. . . . I shall be but too happy if anything occurs to restore my confidence in Fremont.[21]

When Montgomery Blair handed his brother's letter to the president, Lincoln was already much disturbed by Frémont's proclamation and his refusal to change it. Still, however, he and Montgomery Blair, by Lincoln's account at least, felt only sadness and concern. On September 9 the president wrote to Major General David Hunter, whose rank precluded an order that he join Frémont as a subordinate, that Frémont needed "to have by his side a man of large experience. Will you not, for me, take that place." Still hoping to save Frémont if he would accept advice and assistance, Lincoln sent Montgomery Blair and Quartermaster General Montgomery Meigs to St. Louis with instructions to investigate, report, advise, and admonish.[22]

At some point along the way west, Meigs and Montgomery Blair passed an angry woman with an English maid coming from the other direction. Jessie Benton Frémont, in the style of her father, was prepared to fight for her own. After sitting up for two days and nights in hot, uncomfortable, and overcrowded trains she reached Washington late on September 10 and drove to a hotel. She was carrying a confidential letter from Frémont, and even though the hour was late she immediately sent a card to the White House asking when she could deliver the letter. The answer came back quickly: "Now at once, A. Lincoln." She had hoped for a bath and some badly needed sleep before the interview, but without hesitation she walked to the White House still in the dusty clothes she had worn since leaving St. Louis. Predictably, she and Abraham Lincoln later remembered the event in different terms. According to Lincoln: "She sought an interview with me at midnight, and tasked me so violently with so many things, that I had to exercise all the awkward tact I have to avoid quarreling with her. She surprised me by asking why their enemy, Montgomery Blair, had been sent to Missouri. She more than intimated that if General Fremont should decide to try conclusions with me, he could set up for himself." [23]

Jessie, however, remembered that the president had not even offered her a seat, and that his hard and repelling voice indicated immediately that his mind was already made up against Frémont "and decidedly against me." When she explained that she had brought the letter to make certain it would be received, Lincoln "answered not to that, but to the subject his own mind was upon, that 'It was a war for a great national idea, the Union, and *that General Frémont should not have dragged the Negro into it— that he never would if he had consulted with Frank Blair. I sent Frank to advise him.*'" Lincoln promised her an answer on the following day.[24]

No answer came, but on the second day Francis P. Blair came to confer with the erstwhile friend who had always called him "Father Blair." Again the memories were selective. Jessie later wrote that Blair "was very angry with me for not letting Montgomery 'manage things.' He talked angrily and freely as was natural to one who had grown up to defer to him, and in his excitement uncovered the intentions of the administration regarding the protection of slavery." He also assured her that Montgomery would talk with Frémont "and bring him to his senses," and he told her quite frankly that Montgomery had gone to St. Louis because of a letter received from Frank. None of the Blairs had ever been reticent or secretive.[25]

Blair later recounted to Montgomery and Lizzie that he had reminded Jessie of everything the Blairs had done to promote Frémont's career and save his property in the courts. "She bridled up at this & put on a very *high look*. I told her she saw she was to play the part of Empress Catherine. Not Catherine but Josephine, she said. I said You are too imperious for her & too ungrateful for me." Montgomery Blair later recorded that Jessie also threatened "that Frémont should hold Frank personally responsible expecting that she could make the old father quail at the thought of losing the Son of whom he is most proud in a duel with a skilled duellist. But the old man told her very gently that the Blairs did not shrink from responsibility."[26]

The furious Jessie fired off another note to Lincoln. She had learned that Montgomery Blair's trip to investigate Frémont had resulted from charges made by Frank Blair and she demanded copies of Frank's letter. Lincoln, whose domestic life had occasionally been hectic, was no novice at handling angry women. "It is not exactly correct . . . to say that I sent Postmaster-General Blair to St. Louis to examine into that department and report,"

he answered. "Postmaster-General Blair did go, with my approbation, to see and converse with Gen. Fremont as a friend. I do
not feel authorized to furnish you with copies of letters in my
possession, without the consent of the writers. No impression has
been made upon my mind against the honor or integrity of General Fremont, and I now enter my protest against being understood as acting in any hostility towards him." [27]

As Jessie made her long trek back to St. Louis, Montgomery
Blair reported to Lincoln from that city, and his natural bias
toward Frank did not make his words untrue. He had had a long
talk with Frémont: "He seems stupefied & almost unconscious,
& is doing absolutely nothing." The feeling, Montgomery reported, was almost unanimous that Frémont was unequal to his
task, and there was a widespread impression that he had not done
his duty by Lyon. Rebel strength was growing daily, and Frémont was simply not defending the state properly. The situation
betrayed "what my father said his proclamation showed, that
his mind is busy with petty aspirations & of course he is prey to
the petty jealousies incident to such a condition. I have telegraphed you to say that I think General Meigs should be immediately put in command here." [28]

Before Jessie left Washington for St. Louis, she wired her
husband a coded warning that Montgomery Blair was no friend,
and whatever impact Montgomery's advice might have had on
Frémont disappeared when she arrived. As soon as Montgomery
left for Washington, Frémont, at her insistence, arrested Frank
Blair for insubordination and confined him to barracks. The whole
affair, of course, immediately burst into print throughout the
country, and nowhere were the sides more bitterly drawn than
in St. Louis itself. The Frémont press charged that Frank Blair
drank too much, which may have been true. Blair's friends spread
a rumor that Frémont was an opium eater, which was undoubtedly false, although Lizzie Lee found it the only credible explanation for such a change in the man she had once so admired.

Still trying to convince Frémont that no personal enmity
was involved, Montgomery Blair sent the general a conciliatory
telegram. "I will send Frank's letter. It is not unfriendly. Release him. This is no time for strife except with the enemies of
the country." On the following day, Montgomery sent Frank's

letter and one of his own, urging that the controversy should "cease for public reasons." [29]

Frémont and Jessie were not mollified, but Montgomery's efforts did offer a face-saving way to undo their error in arresting Frank. On September 24 Frémont's assistant adjutant, Chauncey McKeever, handed Frank Blair a new order; he was being released because of "a telegram from your brother . . . followed by a letter asking for your release for public reasons." He had been arrested for using his "family position . . . to lay private letters, with unsustained accusations, before the President, disturbing the President's confidence in the Commanding General, and seriously impairing the efficiency of this Department." Frémont trusted that Blair would henceforth "avoid so evident a breach of military propriety." [30]

The commanding general had trusted incorrectly. The angry Colonel Blair promptly mailed a copy of his release order and a letter to Lorenzo Thomas, the adjutant general. Blair was furious at the charge that he had used family position "to lay private letters, with unsustained accusations, before the President." He had performed his "simple duty to the Government . . . at the instance of the President himself," and he would not avoid responsibility "by influence or favor of any individual." To defend his "character as an officer and a gentleman" he would prefer formal charges against Frémont, and sustain his accusations in a court-martial, and he would demand a Court of Inquiry to review his own conduct. [31]

Only three days earlier, Frémont had suffered another devastating blow. At the important town of Lexington on the Missouri River, Colonel James A. Mulligan with the Chicago Irish Brigade and some Illinois and Missouri troops had surrendered to a much larger force under Sterling Price. With a loss of only 25 men killed, Price had captured 3,500 men, seven guns, large quantities of munitions, and $100,000 worth of commissary stores. Mulligan had expected help, but more through the failures of generals leading the reinforcements than the direct fault of Frémont, it did not arrive. Frémont had sent Mulligan to Lexington without protection against enemy movements that might cut him off, and according to military custom he had to bear the responsibility for the ineffectiveness of his subordinate generals. For a week the nation had followed developments at Lexington in the press, and the surrender brought another storm of public anger against Frémont.

On September 23 the *St. Louis Evening News* sharply condemned Frémont for the fall of Lexington, and the general promptly closed down the paper for a day and arrested the editor, who was a close friend of Frank Blair's. On September 26 Frank Blair made formal charges against Frémont. Later in the day, assistant adjutant Chauncey McKeever handed Blair still another order: He should "proceed without delay to Jefferson Barracks and report himself 'in arrest.' "

Frank was almost as angry with his brother for sending Frémont the telegram and letter as he was with Frémont himself, and he let their father know it in no uncertain terms. He had told "the Judge" plainly and explicitly that he would not stop the controversy—the "talk about the quarrel being detrimental to the public service" was *"bosh."* Frémont, he wrote, was about to lose Missouri and had disobeyed the president's orders: "I believe firmly that he is such an ass that he is determined to refuse obedience to the order of the President if he should be superceded. You may think this absurd but I have good reason to know that his flatterers have persuaded him that he can do this successfully. . . . As for my controversy you need not give yourself any trouble. I will take care of that myself." [32]

The elder Blair apparently restored the family peace, because Frank soon wrote his brother that while he had been "exceedingly annoyed" by the telegram and letter to Frémont, he knew that Montgomery had acted "with the best interest of the country and my own at heart." Montgomery, meanwhile, asked their father to advise Frank against pressing his charges: "Frémont will be forced out of his command I think by public opinion. That is sufficient revenge if revenge were an object worthy an honorable man's thoughts at such a time of National calamity. I think that Frank is really in danger now of letting his thoughts run too much into such a channel & unless you prevent him from doing so by strong language he may ruin himself." [33]

The Blair–Frémont quarrel never had its day in an official court. Lincoln sought the advice of Generals Hunter, Pope, Meigs, and Curtis, and all agreed with Blair. Congressman Elihu

B. Washburne visited St. Louis at the head of a congressional subcommittee and reported that "such robbery, fraud, extravagance, peculation as have developed in Frémont's department can hardly be conceived of." With his usual sense of fairness, Lincoln sent War Secretary Cameron, who had been leaning to the Frémont side of the argument, to St. Louis with authority to remove the general if he thought it expedient. Cameron found Frémont's new headquarters at Tipton, Missouri, in wild disarray, but he succumbed to the general's plea for one more chance. Cameron agreed to withhold the dismissal order until his return to Washington, during which time Frémont must capture the enemy or give way to some other officer. A few days later Lincoln sent a messenger with orders replacing Frémont with General Hunter and ordering him back to Washington, although the message was not to be delivered if Frémont had either won a battle or was on the verge of fighting one. Frémont had already taken Springfield and was preparing for a battle with McCulloch, who he thought was near. He had also posted sentries to deny access to anyone bringing orders from Washington. The messenger, however, found the general's tent, and the long drama was over. Frémont read the order, slammed it on the table, and demanded: "Sir, how did you get admission into my lines?" If he had ever thought of defying such an order, a Missouri battle camp away from St. Louis was not the place for it. On the following day he did inspire a storm of enthusiasm among his officers and men by announcing that if General Hunter did not arrive first, he would lead them into battle the next day. Fortunately for Frémont, Hunter arrived at 10:00 P.M. Otherwise Frémont might have become a laughing stock, because the enemy was more than sixty miles away.[34]

Some historians and biographers have suggested that the Blair–Frémont quarrel occurred simply because Frémont received more popular attention than Frank Blair. The previous and subsequent careers of both men, however, belie this simplistic explanation. The judgments, ideas, and policies of the Blairs can be debated, but their disdain for self-interest when taking a stand was a lifelong trademark. Frank Blair decided honestly and wisely that Missouri might be lost through Frémont's incompetence, and he reacted accordingly. When he concluded that Frémont might have saved Lyon and Cary Gratz, and when Frémont put the affair on a personal basis, he was also motivated by grief and anger. A Blair biographer's suggestion that Montgomery might have smoothed the rift and saved Frémont but for the intervention of Jessie is nonsense.[35] If Frank Blair had not spearheaded the drive to remove Frémont, the Pathfinder's disobedience of Lincoln's orders, the complaints of other officers, or a genuine military catastrophe would have accomplished the same result. Frémont was later given command of a well-trained army in Virginia with only a few of the handicaps faced in Missouri, and his performance again indicated a total lack of military capacity. Of course, he had the misfortune to be pitted against Stonewall Jackson, but Jackson might not have gained such a brilliant reputation if he had had abler opposition.

Was Lincoln correct in his feeling that Jessie was threatening him with a possible mutiny to be followed by an appeal for popular support? Were Frank Blair's suspicions that this might really happen based upon anything but prejudice? Quite possibly. Frémont might not have considered such an action, but Jessie was a different matter. As an eighteen-year-old bride, she had deliberately destroyed orders from the secretary of war canceling a projected Frémont expedition, and the success of the exploit and her father's influence had saved him from punishment. In California, Frémont had defied the direct orders of his commanding general, and in the emotional climate caused by northern objections to the Mexican War his court-martial conviction had only made him a national martyr. Jessie had written Lizzie Lee that "this is a day for men, not rules, to govern affairs," and she had angrily informed Francis P. Blair that her model was Josephine, who had helped Napoleon overthrow the French Directory. Frémont may have been fortunate that she was not by his side when he received the relief notice. Poor Frémont. His marriage to Jessie Benton brought fame and opportunities he might otherwise have missed, but the opportunities also caused his greatest failures and humiliations. He spent his later years blaming his mistakes on the faults of others, and the generous historian should be willing to hope that he really believed what he wrote.

Unhappily, the quarrel had to go one more round. A congressional Joint Committee on the Conduct of the War plagued

Lincoln throughout with its harassment and support of various
generals on the basis of their political attachments, and the Frémont case immediately received its attention. The committee
was dominated by its rough and aggressive radical chairman,
Senator Benjamin F. Wade of Ohio, and usually began with a
bias toward anyone ready to abolish slavery immediately and
against anyone wishing to proceed with caution. It also tended
to discover that while Republican generals were endowed with
military genius, those with Democratic backgrounds were incompetent, traitorous, or both. After weeks of hearing testimony by
Frémont's friends and foes, the committee exonerated Frémont
without, however, condemning his accusers. Frémont, meanwhile,
had published his own defense along with his correspondence
with Montgomery Blair. Frank Blair ignored his brother's advice and denounced Frémont in Congress. Radical papers were
pressuring Lincoln to give Frémont a new command and complaining he could not get a fair trial. Blair charged that Frémont
could have a formal trial anytime he wished, damned Frémont's
testimony before the committee as an "apology for disaster and
defeat," and angrily defended Lincoln against the charge that
Frémont had been dismissed for trying to abolish slavery.
Schuyler Colfax answered for the radicals with an eloquent and
widely circulated defense of Frémont. Numerous Americans
who had marched for Frémont in 1856 continued to believe that
their hero had been sacrificed on the altar of slavery, and he remained an important political force. A few months later, Montgomery Blair sent Frémont a bill for $5,000 for legal services
rendered over a period of many years. Frémont offered $3,000
which Blair accepted. It was their last communication.

By June 1862 Frank Blair was tired of Congress and was
chafing with anger and impatience over various Union military
defeats. He accepted an appointment as brigadier general and returned to St. Louis to recruit his own army. His efforts were hampered by the newspaper attacks of Frémont partisans, but he soon
enlisted seven regiments and marched off to join General William Tecumseh Sherman in Arkansas. He believed passionately
that the war could best be won by taking control of the Mississippi River and attacking in the deep South where the Confederacy was weakest. The Union had been making halfhearted

attempts to take the almost invulnerable city of Vicksburg, and Frank demanded that his father and brother persuade Lincoln to give it his full attention. Located on a high bluff overlooking the Mississippi, Vicksburg controlled the river traffic much like Gilbraltar commands its strait. Frank argued that the western armies should unite "to untie the knot the rebels have tied at Vicksburg & open this great artery of our life." [36]

In late December 1862 General Blair joined General Grant near Vicksburg. Like most of the regular army officers, Grant had had his troubles with politician-generals and he expected Blair to be an annoyance. He soon found out, however, that this politician would obey orders and fight. On December 28 Blair led 1,800 men across the bayou at Chickasaw Bluffs and engaged the Confederates in their rifle pits. He and his troops fought their way through a net of young cottonwood saplings piled among a thick stand of stumps, and through a deep and miry bayou. They continued up a steep bank in the face of the enemy rifle pits and heavy guns, and carried the first and second tiers of rifle pits. They actually reached the last Confederate entrenchments, but found themselves without support and had to retire. Blair did not complain except to his family, but he always believed that with more support from the other generals the charge might have succeeded. He had lost a third of his men. Two horses had been shot from underneath him, and when his last horse sank in the mud he leaped off and led his men on foot to the rifle pits. Sherman lost a total of 1,929 men in the overall attack. Blair now had the reputation for personal heroism necessary for any successful commander of western troops. In April he was promoted to major general and given command of the Second Division of the Fifteenth Army Corps.[37]

Whether or not the decision was affected by Blair's advice, Vicksburg did eventually fall to a united army under Grant, who fought his way into position to lay the city under seige and simply starved the inhabitants into submission. On May 19, 1863, Blair and his men again fought their way to the enemy's breastworks, but had to retire with a loss of 881 in killed and wounded. When word came that Confederate reinforcements were being sent to Vicksburg, Blair's command provided accurate intelligence of the Confederate forces, cleared out the enemy between the Black and Yazoo rivers, destroyed the Mississippi Central Railroad bridge over the Black River, destroyed stock and forage, and obstructed the roads—all under orders not to get cut off from Vicksburg. When Vicksburg surrendered on July 4, 1863, Blair was there to celebrate with Grant and Sherman.[38]

After a rousing reception in St. Louis, a visit with his family and with President Lincoln in Washington, and several highly controversial political speeches, Frank rejoined the army in October 1863. At Corinth, Mississippi, General Sherman appointed him "second in command to me giving you full power to act over all troops in my corps at whatever part of the Line or Column you may be. . . . all the cavalry I have will be under your command." On October 29, 1863, Blair assumed command of the Fifteenth Army Corps near Chattanooga, Tennessee. Once again he led his men with great success throughout the fighting that finally ended with the Union victory at Chattanooga on November 25. Commenting on Blair's Fifteenth Corps, Sherman asserted that there was "no better body of soldiers in America than it, or who have done more or better service." [39]

On December 11, Blair relinquished his command to John A. Logan and returned once more to Congress. Sherman again took the "opportunity to thank General Blair for the zeal, intelligence, courage, and skill with which he has handled the corps during the eventful period he has commanded it." After another angry congressional session during which Blair continued to serve the purposes of Abraham Lincoln, he was again commissioned a major general, and he assumed command of the Seventeenth Army Corps on May 4, 1864. In June he arrived in Georgia with some 8,000 men, and Sherman was greatly relieved to see "the two good old divisions of the Seventeenth Corps that General Blair had just brought up." In the battle of Atlanta, his corps repulsed a major Confederate charge and lost 1,801 men. At this point Sherman began his devastating march to the sea, with Blair and his men doing their full share of the destruction. On December 16, 1864, he wrote his father that they had "inflicted more damage upon the enemy than could be done by a dozen victories." They had destroyed 400 miles of railroad, burned millions of dollars worth of cotton, "the only thing that enables them to maintain credit abroad & to purchase arms & munitions of war," and "gobbled up enough provisions to have fed Lee's army for six months." At Dayton, a twelve-pound shot passed just over Blair's head and killed a captain and an orderly's horse just behind him. On December 21, Sherman's army captured Savannah and then turned northward. South Carolina received its share of the same treatment given Georgia, and when Lee surrendered to Grant, General Blair was in North Carolina. On April 17 came the last act of the war. General Sherman, accompanied by Generals Howard, Schofield, and Blair, accepted the surrender of General Joseph E. Johnston.[40]

If Frank Blair had felt moved to keep faith with the ghosts of Nathaniel Lyon and Cary Gratz, he could be comfortable in the knowledge that he had done so. He had also kept faith with his family. From Smyrna Camp Ground near Marietta, Georgia, he wrote his father an apology for being too busy to thank him often enough for the kindness of letters:

> It recalls to me the recollection of all that I owe to my dear parents whose love and goodness has followed me all my days. I trust I shall never do anything unworthy of your exalted character & that you may never have any occasion to be ashamed of me.
>
> When the war is over it will be time enough to talk over my plans for the future. . . . but I have had enough of politics & I do not think that anything will again induce me to enter upon that career.[41]

Chapter 21

To Win a War

BY all accounts, Montgomery Blair was a superb postmaster general.[1] Equipped with a puritanical sense of duty, an innovative mind, and enormous energy, he was intolerant of the waste and inefficiency for which the Post Office Department had long been known.

Politicians have often joked that the eager partisans demanding post office jobs after every election are numerous enough to have prevented all past defeats if they had really done half the work they claim. Following his appointment, Montgomery Blair was almost overwhelmed with office seekers. His interviews with the hopeful occasionally lasted until 2:00 A.M. and were then renewed at 8:00 A.M. the following morning. One request, incidentally, came from an ancient friend turned enemy. If changes should be made, wrote former postmaster general Amos Kendall, "please spare my brother, George M. Kendall who is now in the dead letter office." George was seventy-three, needed the job, and was too old for other duties. Also, Kendall's son-in-law was in the department and had no other income. Both were Democrats, but they were for the Union and would support "any party which will save the Union 'peaceably' if they can." Presumably, they kept their jobs. At breakfast one morning, Eliza berated Montgomery severely for ignoring her recommendation that he give a job to the widow of an old Kentucky friend. The postmaster general replied meekly that he had been unaware of the request, but his angry mother insisted that she had asked more than once. Lizzie concluded that "brother will not invite another such attack by neglecting her wishes."[2]

Blair did not formally suspend the federal postal service in the seceded states until May 31,1861, because "the mails alone afforded the means of diffusing any correct information among the people of the South and disabusing their minds of the prevalent errors which the conspirators had availed themselves of." With the coming of all-out war, however, he closed the accounts of the secession postmasters and declared them to be defaulters and embezzlers.

To prevent disloyal employees from handling mail vital to the Union war effort Blair decreed that all postal employees must take an oath of loyalty or resign their places, and inspectors were assigned to hunt out disloyal postmasters in the loyal states. He also suspended the postal privileges of twelve disloyal newspapers. In his view, freedom of the press did not include government services for papers aiming "blows at the existence of the government." The department, he said, could not suppress treasonable publications, but it had no obligation to circulate them.

Sensitive to the needs of the 2 million men who served in the Union forces, Blair created a system whereby every regiment had its own postmaster who received and distributed the mail, sold stamps and money orders, and forwarded letters. He also allowed the servicemen to send letters unstamped; the postage was to be collected from the recipients. Several high-placed leaders argued that officers should have free stamps, but Blair refused to make this discrimination. His efforts, however, did not prevent occasional angry complaints from his brother the general that the soldiers were not getting their mail on time.

Mail carriers were exempted from military service, and humorists like Artemus Ward regaled the public with stories like that of the sixteen mailmen riding into the same small town each carrying one letter. In fact, however, waste was held to a minimum. Blair discontinued unnecessary post offices, eliminated the fraudulent reuse of stamps by adopting a new indelible ink for cancellations, and installed cancelling machines to replace inefficient hand labor. He also withdrew the franking privilege from postmasters, personally reviewed contracts to make certain they went to the lowest bidders, and substantially reduced the extortionate rates usually demanded by railroad contractors. He put the postmasters on fixed salaries rather than commissions, and Congress on his recommendation divided the mail into three separate classes with uniform rates of postage for letters. By 1863 Blair had reduced the deficit of $5,656,705 to a deficit of only $120,000. When he resigned in 1864, the department was on its way to an 1865 surplus of $161,000.

The financial savings, moreover, were accompanied by greatly expanded services. Since 1825 the mail had been delivered only in large cities, with the recipients paying the carrier two cents per letter and one-half cent per newspaper. Blair persuaded Congress to establish free delivery for all city mail. Soldiers and sailors constantly on the move needed safe means for sending and receiving money. In 1862 Blair pointed out the widespread theft of money from mails and argued for a money order system, which Congress authorized in May 1864. Meanwhile, by higher fees, mandatory return receipts, and strict accountability, Blair greatly strengthened the registration system. In 1862 he established the modern system whereby mail is sorted in railroad cars on the move.

And finally, Montgomery Blair was the prime mover in the establishment of a uniform system for the international exchange of mail. On May 11, 1863, in response to his overtures, the representatives of fifteen nations and areas that sent 95 percent of the world's correspondence met in Paris and adopted thirty-one recommendations. The actual achievement of the Universal Postal Union took several more years, but the movement began with Montgomery Blair. John A. Kasson of Iowa was Blair's top aide in the Department, and represented the United States at Paris. Blair gave Kasson full public credit for his achievements, including the Postal Union idea, and Kasson considered Blair the greatest of all postmaster generals.

As usual Montgomery often turned to his father for advice and assistance. Seeking to reduce the railroad rates for carrying mail, Francis P. Blair composed a brief to persuade Congress that the Post Office Department had a right of eminent domain to force the railroads to carry the mail for a reasonable price. He also advised Montgomery to suggest federal subsidies for the building of new railroads willing to carry troops and mail in return. This would "have great effect, & favorable, on existing railroads. Congress might employ it in legislation, to put them very much at your service." The combination of arguments and threats apparently worked, because Montgomery was able to get the rates reduced.[3]

Managing the postal department was only part of Montgomery Blair's job, because throughout most of his presidency, Abraham Lincoln leaned heavily upon the Blairs. He recognized their intense loyalty, agreed with most of their viewpoints, and found them personally congenial. He and Francis P. Blair shared a taste for humorous stories. Lincoln's close friend and occasional bodyguard, Ward Lamon, wrote later that "between Francis P. Blair and Mr. Lincoln there existed from the first to last a confidential relationship as close as that maintained by Mr. Lincoln with any other man. To Mr. Blair he habitually revealed himself upon delicate and grave subjects more freely than to any other. When he had conceived an important but difficult plan, he was almost certain, before giving it practical form, to try it by the touchstone of Mr. Blair's fertile and acute mind." [4] Montgomery Blair's children played with the Lincoln children on the White House lawn, and the president occasionlly joined them. Young Woodbury Blair would later remember vividly the president's long arms and legs and coattails flying in all directions as he ran around the bases in a game of townball.

The Blairs had strong ties of past friendship with Mrs. Lincoln's pro-southern family in Kentucky, and various Boswells and Shelbys from their own tribe were also fighting for the South. They could share poor Mary Todd Lincoln's anguish when two of her brothers and the husband of her favorite sister died in battle for the Confederacy. Lizzie, in particular, was Mary's age, and she was always welcome at the White House as a warm-hearted and sympathetic friend. By July 1861 Lizzie was furious because the Washington ladies were giving Mrs. Lincoln "a cold shoulder," and she tried to make up for this at every opportunity. When gossips reported that Lincoln's affections for Mary were less than fervent, Lizzie scoffed. She knew that Mary had her husband's deepest love because this was "a matter upon which one woman cannot deceive another." When eleven-year-old Willie, the brightest of the Lincoln children, died in 1862, Lizzie was almost the first to offer comfort.[5] Lizzie did not record her feelings when five-year-old Joe Davis was killed by a fall from the high porch of the Confederate presidential mansion in Richmond, but she would probably have also gone to the side of her old friend Varina Davis if the circumstances had permitted. Men's wars are hard on women.

If the happiest days of Francis P. Blair had been spent in the service of Andrew Jackson, his experiences with Abraham Lincoln were almost equally satisfying. Lincoln, of course, differed in character from Jackson. He could submerge his own feelings, accept insults without rancor, and even compromise his convictions temporarily for the achievement of a long-range goal. He was the leader of a coalition party and he was the president of a nation profoundly divided on several major issues. To keep his party and his people united he had to avoid the appearance of strong partisanship except in the case of those few issues upon which most unionist Americans were in harmony. His disagreements with the radicals were probably not as sharp as they chose to believe, but he needed defenders against their attacks and spokesmen for the moderate policies that probably still reflected the sentiments of most Americans in 1862. And if his defenders were aggressive enough and prominent enough to draw the radical fire away from the president to themselves, so much the better. In short, the president needed lightning rods, and the Blairs were ideally suited by temperament, instinctive loyalty, and convictions to play the role.

Because Montgomery Blair was a West Point graduate with military experience and had unvarnished direct communications from the front through Frank, Lincoln often trusted his judgment ahead of that of the military secretaries. Navy Secretary Welles considered Montgomery the wisest of men and often asked his advice. Secretary of War Cameron knew nothing about military operations, and as the senior Blair had predicted, he soon became hopelessly enmeshed in financial dealings in which his innocence could be defended only on the grounds of incompetence. Cameron's replacement, Edwin M. Stanton, was an able lawyer and a competent if harsh administrator. He was also a strange personality. He had once exhumed the body of a dead sweetheart to make certain the report of her death was true, and he later kept the little casket containing the body of his dead child in his bedroom for several months. He was usually quarrelsome and rude with almost everyone, including Lincoln. He had gone from sympathy for the South before service in the Buchanan administration to a radical antislavery and antisouthern position after his appointment by Lincoln, and the Blairs could only interpret this as selfish hypocrisy. He and Montgomery Blair were thoroughly incompatible in almost every matter, whether personal or political.[6]

The Blairs had always been friendly with Secretary of the Treasury Salmon P. Chase, but as time passed they often disagreed with him on principle and sharply condemned his disloyalty to Lincoln. After Fort Sumter, Seward and the Blairs rarely disagreed on anything, but they could never forget his role in diverting the *Powhatan,* and they always suspected him of using others for nefarious purposes inconsistent with his announced viewpoints. For the entire Blair family, Seward was an emotional fixation whose words and conduct could never be believed even when they coincided with the Blairs' own policies.

The independence and strong influence of Montgomery Blair were particularly evident in November 1861, when the ambitious and quarrelsome Captain Charles Wilkes on the U.S.S. *San Jacinto* stopped the British steamer *Trent* and removed two Confederate agents, James M. Mason and John Slidell. Wilkes proudly announced his feat to a northern public already starved for a victory and became a national hero overnight. On the morning the news broke, Secretary of War Cameron led a large crowd in "three cheers for Captain Wilkes!" Even Gideon Welles congratulated Wilkes, whom he detested and would later dismiss from an important command. The British press and people, however, were furious, and popular clamor for war was rising in Britain.

Montgomery Blair's other cabinet colleagues, including Seward, were as jubilant as Welles and Cameron, but Blair insisted that Wilkes had violated international law and that Mason and Slidell would have to be handed over to British custody. Lincoln listened and considered carefully. Seward also reviewed the facts, and perhaps influenced in part by Senator Charles Sumner, he later agreed that a capitulation must be made. At the final cabinet meeting before the decision was taken, only Blair and Seward argued for the release of the agents, and Lincoln wisely ignored public opinion and followed their advice.[7] It was one of the last decisions upon which Lincoln's cabinet disagreed without rancor.

The sharpest controversy within both the Lincoln administration and the wartime Congress was over the issue that had already split the nation. What should be done about slavery, and when should the action, if any, be taken? The war had begun with no public demand for abolition, and there was a real possibility that a quick northern victory could end the conflict with no action on slavery at all. The longtime abolitionists like Sumner, Thaddeus Stevens, Benjamin F. Wade, George Julian, Owen Lovejoy, and others were a relatively small but very loud faction in Congress. From the war's beginning they demanded immediate emancipation and lacking the congressional strength for a constitutional amendment, they concentrated their pressures on Lincoln. Frémont's proclamation had affected them like a divine revelation, which totally obscured both his military deficiencies and the military necessity for holding the border states. Lincoln, however, had a habit of putting first things first. A northern statement of emancipation would be meaningless if the South won its independence on the field of battle, and the loss of Kentucky, Missouri, or Maryland because of a premature action might tip the balance. Lincoln intended to destroy slavery, but not by jeopardizing the Union victory without which emancipation would be impossible.

The Frémonts openly blamed their problems on the president's alleged softness toward slavery, and the radicals who had been thrilled by the Pathfinder's emancipation order accepted this indictment of Lincoln. Publicly and privately they expressed their contempt for the president in the most insulting language. Since Frank Blair had been the most direct agent involved in Frémont's downfall, he and his father and brother were also cast as conservatives with regard to slavery. Actually, of course, the Blairs had never doubted that the war would end slavery and they were entirely ready for abolition at the proper moment. They still feared that emancipation without colonization would bring tragic results, but they had no qualms about taking the first step.[8]

On November 21, 1861, Montgomery Blair urged Lincoln to recommend that Union men be compensated for slaves lost by the war, with the money to be raised by confiscating the estates of traitors. This should be done, he wrote, "in view of the not improbable necessity of emancipation by martial law in the Gulph States." Union General Benjamin F. Butler had already set a precedent by defining escaped slaves as contraband and keeping those who entered his lines. The Blairs agreed fully, and were soon arguing the matter with doubting friends.

Throughout most of 1861–1862 Abraham Lincoln was under constant pressure from both the abolitionists and those who wished slavery to remain untouched, and he had every reason to believe that the northern public was not yet ready to support emancipation for moral and philanthropic reasons alone. Various historians believe that he might not have reached an emancipation policy in 1862 without the constant pressure of the radicals in Congress, and this may be true. He must have also been influenced, however, by those who thought as he did and who supported his every step toward emancipation while doing battle with those who were trying to push him into dangerously premature action.

Lincoln the consummate politician carefully avoided any appearance of a public break with the radicals. Francis P. Blair and his sons, however, had always believed that democracy functioned ideally when voters were presented clear-cut polarized issues and candidates. The Blairs agreed with the radicals that the war must end slavery, and many radicals, including Chase, Wade, Greeley, and Stevens, supported colonization, but the Blair temperament always preferred conflict to compromise. The clan's patriarch had never forgotten Andrew Jackson's advice: "Temporize not. It is always injurious." For ideological reasons, the radicals were supporting Frémont and other incompetent generals, and were hounding much abler generals who were not abolitionists. They were attacking the president personally and viciously for his unwillingness to abolish slavery under circumstances that might endanger the war effort and allow the South to destroy the Union and thereby preserve slavery. The radicals, therefore, were the enemy, and must be opposed openly in speeches and public letters. Also, personal loyalty had always been a Blair trademark, and the family bitterly resented the personal nature of the radical attacks upon Lincoln. Through the Blairs Abraham Lincoln's position on controversial matters could be eloquently and widely stated without the president himself getting involved in the quarrels at all.

Frank Blair in particular could trumpet defiance on the floors of Congress, and no one ever enjoyed such a role more or had better credentials for the assignment. Whatever his views on race, he had taken and would continue to take greater personal risks for the Union and against slavery than anyone else in the Congress. He had been shot at in the streets of St. Louis and had been narrowly missed by a bullet fired through his living room window. He was also preparing to lead troops into the face of death at Vicksburg, Chattanooga, Atlanta, and other places. If the radicals wished to be his enemies also, he would not deny them the pleasure.

Significantly, however, the Blairs continued to enjoy close personal relations with the radical governors William E. Dennison of Ohio and John Andrew of Massachusetts. Also, their friendship with Charles Sumner endured many disagreements all the way through Reconstruction until they and Sumner were again on the same side in 1872.

Abraham Lincoln had been reared in an extremely racist environment in southern Indiana and Illinois, and he understood the Blair argument that any effective emancipation would have to be made palatable to northern voters. Never looking beyond the horizon of possibility, Lincoln led, pushed, and followed northern public opinion step by step toward the death of slavery, while making every concession he thought necessary for keeping the border states loyal. Although Simon Cameron's fiscal incompetence and military ignorance were the ostensible reasons for his transfer from the War Department to the American embassy in Russia, the move was triggered by Cameron's public recommendation that the slaves be armed and encouraged to make war upon their former masters. When General Hunter followed Frémont's example and decreed emancipation for the slaves in Georgia, Florida, and South Carolina, Lincoln revoked the order, although he did not censure Hunter. Such decisions and their timing must be the president's alone. Meanwhile, however, he sternly enforced the existing laws against the foreign slave trade, and refused to commute the death sentence of a young captain convicted of this crime. He supported the Confiscation Act of August 1861, which provided for the emancipation of slaves employed in military service or labor against the United States. He brushed aside another ancient taboo by recognizing and exchanging envoys with Haiti and Liberia. Both nations sent impressive representatives whose social polish, multilingual talents, and intellectual capacities rather stunned official Washington.

Agreeing with the Blairs that a compensated emancipation in the border states would weaken their ties with the Confederacy, Lincoln made various generous offers. On July 16, 1861, a House committee that included Frank Blair reported a plan for giving each border state $300 per slave, but the border-state delegations in Congress were deaf to the suggestion. Despite the efforts of the Blairs and others in Maryland, Kentucky, and Missouri, the legislatures of those states also refused to accept reality.

On April 11, 1862, Congress abolished slavery in the District of Columbia and appropriated a million dollars to pay the loyal masters $300 per slave. Nine of the District's 979 slaveholders, incidentally, were themselves black. Perhaps the freedman whom Blair and Rives had helped to buy his family got back their price.

The public's acceptance of emancipation in the District led to the next step—abolition without compensation in all territories of the United States. In July 1862 the Congress with Lincoln's approval passed a second Confiscation Act that declared free all slaves of all persons who committed treason or supported the rebellion. It was the Frémont proposal on a grand scale, but this time the public reaction was mild. Abolition could be made acceptable if presented as a step necessary for winning the war. The Union's military defeats and the rising casualty lists were tilting northern sentiments rapidly toward destruction of the institution that had caused the war and was a bulwark of the southern military effort.

In all of these matters the Blairs supported Lincoln where he needed it most—among the doubters and opponents. "You seem dissatisfied over abolition," wrote Francis P. Blair to a Maryland friend on April 9, 1862. "All practical men are now sensible that slavery so affects the people whether it ought to do so or not as to make it a terrible institution to our race. They see that it imbues a brother's hand in a brother's blood, and invites foreign despots to plant monarchies on our continent. With this result before us, the only enquiry should be how to get rid of an institution which produces such miseries." [9]

Meanwhile, the Blairs and Lincoln were still trying to launch a colonization program. In 1855 Ambrose W. Thompson had founded the Chiriquí Improvement Company to develop several hundred thousand acres of coal and farm lands in Panama near the Costa Rican border. Thompson had been in touch with the Blairs for a long time, and on April 10, 1861, only hours before the attack on Fort Sumter, Lincoln conferred with a representative of the company on the feasibility of establishing a Negro colony in Panama. In August 1861 Thompson offered to deliver coal in Chiriquí to the Navy Department for half the current price if a colony of blacks could be sent there to do the mining. A commission examined the project, and on November 16,1861, Francis P. Blair sent Lincoln a long brief that included the commission's report, the conclusions of a congressional committee, the confirmation by Colombia of the company's land grant, and a supporting legal opinion by Attorney General Bates. Blair added that only the United States government could accomplish the real objectives: "*The acquisition of safe & well fortified Harbors on each side of the Isthmus—a good & sufficient Railway transportation between them—a command of the coal fields to afford adequate supply for our Navy—a million of acres of land for the Colonization of American Freedmen in Homesteads & freeholds.*" For several pages Blair argued for the creation of an American India in Central America, where "our freedmen of African blood, from their superior intelligence & strength & skill in the cotton culture," would "absorb the influence England seeks to derive from the colonies planted by her from the West Indies in Central America." The minister to Honduras, E. O. Crosby, was ready to negotiate with that country, and the minister to Venezuela, Henry T. Blow, was ready to examine the area still more closely. Blair even drafted an order for Lincoln's signature detaching a ship to take Blow to Panama. The president, however, delayed while Navy Secretary Welles and Interior Secretary Caleb B. Smith studied the matter. In his annual message to Congress on December 3, 1861, Lincoln again strongly recommended colonization as part of the solution to the slavery problem.[10]

By July 13, 1862, Lincoln had reached the great decision. On that day he told Seward and Welles, and on July 22 he gave his cabinet the news that he was planning an emancipation. They could discuss it, but the decision was not debatable. Only two cabinet members approved wholeheartedly. Stanton emphasized the military value of the South's slave labor system that freed the whites for fighting. Bates simply agreed with Lincoln. Montgomery Blair favored the proposed proclamation, which called for an all-out colonization effort, but preferred to have the announcement made after the fall elections, because he feared the step would hurt the Republican candidates for Congress and governorships. The radical Chase was unenthusiastic, perhaps because he had hoped to use the issue to win the party's presidential nomination away from Lincoln in 1864, and he objected to the compensation for loyal slaveholders, which the initial proposal included. William H. Seward had long since abandoned the "higher law" and "irrepressible conflict." He feared that emancipation would further reduce the supply of cotton going to Europe and increase the ire of the British and French governments against the United States. It was a strange miscalculation, because the favorable impact of emancipation upon the British and French peoples would prove far more important than any objections by their leaders. Seward did accept the policy, however, although he quite sensibly urged a delay until the winning of a military victory significant enough to give the policy some practical meaning.

Montgomery Blair asked permission to file his objection, but on the following day he changed his mind. The policy should be unanimous. He did, however, urge Lincoln to propose emancipation as a "necessity to prevent foreign intervention." Otherwise it might put the next Congress in the hands of the war's opponents. If, however, the measure could be used to make an issue "between the Govts. of Europe & the people there . . . our people would hail [it] as judicious." Also, since the effect of freeing those slaves in the Confederacy would be to free all the slaves, why not proclaim them all free so the European nations could not charge that the government was sustaining slavery in the border states and might restore it further south when the war ended. And finally, Blair would make the proclamation effective immediately rather than announce a future date of January 1, 1863, for its enactment. Obviously, Blair's preference for an immediate and total emancipation was in line with the views of his most extreme radical enemies.[11]

Lincoln, however, preferred to keep the entire affair a secret for sixty-two more days. On August 22, in a famous letter to Horace Greeley, Lincoln sorely disappointed both the blacks and the radicals, but he did much to put the coming proclamation on an acceptable basis for the general public. "If," he wrote, "I could save the Union without freeing any slave I would do it; and if I could save it by freeing all the slaves I would do it; and if I could save it by freeing some and leaving others I would do that. What I do about slavery, and the colored race, I do because I believe it helps to save the Union." This letter has often been cited as evidence that Lincoln had no real concern for emancipation except as an instrument for victory. It was written, however, five weeks after he had privately announced his plans for emancipation, and can therefore also be interpreted as an eloquent argument designed to win the support of northerners still anti-black by custom and often desperately afraid of the economic and social competition a horde of newly freed immigrants might become. In the long run, emancipation would succeed only if a majority of the American people would support it. If the Blairs were estimating the racial prejudices of their fellow white Americans correctly, Lincoln needed to justify emancipation as a necessary step for winning the war and saving the Union, and his letter to Greeley did just that.

On September 22, 1862, Lincoln issued his preliminary Emancipation Proclamation. It began with a promise to ask the next session of Congress to vote compensation for slaveholders in all slave states willing to abolish slavery at their own speed, and a pledge to efforts to colonize "persons of African descent, with their consent." Meanwhile, on January 1, 1863, all slaves within any state or designated part of any state whose people were in rebellion would be forever free. In theory the southerners could keep their slaves by surrendering before January 1. Just as Fort Sumter had put the responsibility for the war upon the South, the preliminary proclamation put the responsibility for abolition in the same place. The final proclamation on December 30, 1862, described the action "as a proper and necessary war measure for suppressing . . . rebellion," and included no moralistic pronouncements of any kind. It also specifically exempted most of the Confederate areas actually under northern control, and did not affect the border states at all. Historians critical of the Proclamation's limited scope have usually forgotten that slavery was still protected by the United States Constitution in all states under Union control. The president could announce his future policy against slavery in the rebellious states, but only a constitutional amendment could actually abolish the institution.

The Proclamation inspired much noisy opposition, including a fierce condemnation of Lincoln by the Illinois legislature. Just as the Blairs had feared, the November elections went heavily Democratic. No straw polls existed to provide arguments over why people voted as they did, but the Democrats made their opposition to emancipation a major issue.

In his annual message to Congress in December 1862, Lincoln again strongly advocated colonization and suggested that the actual emancipation be accomplished gradually until completion in 1900. Meanwhile, negotiations with the Chiriquí Company were continuing. On September 12, 1862, Thompson and Interior Secretary Smith actually signed a contract providing for coal purchases and a colony to be led by radical Senator Samuel Pomeroy of Kansas. The plan, however, had already been caught in a fatal crossfire. On August 14, 1862, the president had met with a deputation of distinguished free blacks and had eloquently presented every argument he knew as to why they should be happy to move to same other area where they would not be oppressed by the white majority in either North or South. He stressed the discrimination practiced in the North as well as the bitterness the war would leave in the South. He urged them not to allow their own comfortable situations to divert their attention from the tragic status of their less fortunate brothers, but all to no avail. America's free black leaders would neither emigrate nor urge others to do so, and formal refusals from various groups and meetings began to appear immediately. Even if the black leaders had been willing to sponsor a colonization movement, the governments of Honduras, Nicaragua, and Costa Rica denounced the plan as soon as they understood it, and hinted that they would oppose it with force if necessary.[12]

For the next two years the Blairs defended emancipation before often-hostile audiences and continued to hope for a successful colonization. On May 20, 1863, Montgomery Blair assured a large audience in Cleveland and all who read his speech in pamphlet form that "the mission of the Afric-American race" would "not be concluded in the region which has been his house of bondage. Its destined glory as a redeemed, a free and civilized race is to be consummated in the American tropics. They will there infuse vigor, unity, and enterprise, with aspirations to emulate the progressive geniuses of the country of their birth." [13] The Blairs could support abolition vigorously, but they could not accept the radical idea that military leadership should be selected on the basis of attitudes toward slavery, and they would soon be in opposition to the radicals' proposals for the future reconstruction of the South. Thus, they found themselves under constant fire within the Republican party they had helped to found—without winning any forgiveness or friends in the Democratic party they had deserted.

The Blairs' conflict with the radicals was exemplified by their support for General George McClellan and their opposition to radical favorites like Frémont. In 1861, "the Little Napoleon," as McClellan was dubbed, was only thirty-four years old and appeared at first glance to have all the qualities of a great commander. He was a charismatic leader and a talented organizer who easily won enthusiastic affection and support from his troops. If he had been assigned to organizing and training soldiers for other men to command in battle, his reputation would have been secure. Unlike the great gambler, Robert E. Lee, however, he was cautious to the point of paralysis when faced by an actual battle. He had won his original fame with some brilliant organization in western Virginia and the victorious Battle of Rich Mountain, although historians would later credit the battlefield leadership to his subordinate, General William S. Rosecrans. On July 22, 1861, he assumed command of the Army of the Potomac, and on November 1 he became commander in chief of the army. From July 1861 until March 7, 1862, he organized and trained, but made no move to fight anyone despite sharp denunciations by the radical Joint Committee on the Conduct of the War and periodic entreaties and finally orders by President Lincoln.

McClellan was flamboyant and arrogant. On one occasion he went to bed even though he knew President Lincoln was waiting downstairs for an interview. Commenting to his wife on the administration, McClellan wrote: "But it is terrible to stand by &

see the cowardice of the Predt, the vileness of Seward, & rascality of Cameron—Welles is an old woman—Bates an old fool. The only man of courage & sense in the cabinet is Blair, & I do not altogether fancy him!" [14] The general's overt conceit and bravado, however, apparently masked a deep personal insecurity and self-doubt in the face of genuine crises. Also, perhaps, as historian Bruce Catton has observed, McClellan simply had no taste for massive homicide.

McClellan was a Democrat and he was opposed, however mildly, to the abolition of slavery. He had returned several escaped slaves to their loyal owners in conformity with existing laws, and the radicals from the beginning suspected that he was a traitor deliberately trying to sabotage the war effort. During each of McClellan's periods of command, the radicals were constantly badgering Lincoln to discharge him. Ironically, if McClellan had been a Lee or a Grant, the war might have ended quickly with slavery still intact. The general's delays may have inadvertently promoted the aims of both the radicals and the president with regard to slavery.

The radical enmity toward McClellan was enough to make him attractive to the Blairs, but their support also had a more substantial basis. Francis P. Blair agreed with the general's policy of trying to win with the least bloodshed. "If you can reach . . . Richmond by a slower process than storming redoubts and batteries in earthworks," wrote Blair to McClellan, "the country will applaud the achievement which brings success to its arms with greatest parsimony of the blood of its children." Frank Blair also urged McClellan to remain on the defensive in front of Washington while allowing others to disperse the Confederate army with an all-out effort on the Mississippi. Montgomery Blair, the West Point graduate, apparently offered McClellan no military advice, but his father and brother kept arguing that the Confederacy should be attacked first where it was weakest (in the West and deep South) and left alone for the moment where it was strongest (between Washington and Richmond). By this time the older Blairs had suffered much from the deaths of Cary Gratz and several other young cousins and friends, and they knew how reckless Frank was. Why fight unnecessary battles anywhere? At one point the elder Blair suggested that McClellan make Frank his chief of staff, but no insecure general aware of John C. Frémont's fate wanted the assistance of Frank Blair. Blair's further recommendation that McClellan publicly support emancipation was much more sensible.[15]

Under heavy pressure from the radicals, northern public opinion, and the president, McClellan finally moved on March 7, 1862. He reached the Yorktown, Virginia, area by sea in early April with more than 100,000 soldiers, almost twice the number he would encounter at any time during the forthcoming battles. He also expected support from the army of General Irvin McDowell, but Lincoln suddenly discovered that only 20,000 men had been left to defend Washington. Some of McDowell's men were assigned to Frémont's Mountain Department, while the remainder returned to Washington. During the next few weeks, General Stonewall Jackson fought his way past the armies of Generals Frémont and Banks to get between them and the capital. Then, having terrorized Washington to the point where no additional troops could possibly be sent to McClellan, Jackson led his 15,000 men past, over and through the combined 35,000 men under Frémont and McDowell in time to rejoin Lee for the battle to save Richmond. McClellan, meanwhile, had estimated his enemy's strength at twice its actual numbers, had waited when he should have moved, and had besieged when he should have attacked. Still, however, Richmond was almost within his grasp when Lee and Jackson confronted him directly with an army only half the size of his own. McClellan then retreated when he should have advanced, and fought a desperate and bloody seven-day battle. McClellan was at least a master technician in the art of retreating, and for once the Confederate casualties outnumbered those of the North.

For the rest of his life McClellan blamed the defeat on Lincoln and Stanton for not sending the reinforcements from McDowell. He was still at Harrison's Landing on the James River, within easy striking distance of Richmond, when Lincoln and Stanton ordered him back to Washington. Another Virginia command had been created for the radical favorite General John Pope, and a sizable portion of McClellan's army was to join Pope. McClellan chose this inopportune moment to write Lincoln a strong recommendation that military operations should not be allowed to interfere with slavery. On July 7–8, the president and Francis P. Blair journeyed to Harrison's Landing to confer with the general and inspect the troops. Presumably, the "old gentleman" helped set McClellan straight on the subject of slavery.

General Pope, whom Montgomery Blair considered "a braggart and a liar," greeted his new troops with an inspiring introduction: "I have come to you from the West, where we have always seen the backs of our enemies." By August 27, 1862, nearly half of the Confederate army was between Pope and Washington, and on August 29–30 Lee and Jackson with 48,500 men routed Pope's army of 75,000 in the Second Battle of Bull Run. Pope suffered 16,054 casualties, while the Confederates lost only 9,197. Pope blamed General Fitzjohn Porter for failing to execute an order that Porter insisted was physically impossible, and Porter was later dismissed from the army. Montgomery Blair later made the exoneration of Porter a major project until the general was finally cleared in 1879.[16]

Of vital immediate concern, however, were the chaos and confusion created by the battle. Pope charged that McClellan had not sent adequate reinforcements, and the congressional radicals insisted that Pope had failed only because of McClellan's treason. On August 30 Stanton and Chase drew up a petition against McClellan for approval by the cabinet. All signed but Blair, the conveniently absent Seward, and Welles, who concurred with the sentiments but objected to the method. Blair insisted that although McClellan had obvious faults he alone could reorganize and restore the morale of the soldiers. Supported only by Blair, Lincoln on September 2 infuriated the radicals by restoring McClellan to full command of the army in northern Virginia. "No order to that effect has been issued from the War Department," snapped the angry Stanton.

"The order is mine, and I will be responsible for it to the country," replied Lincoln. Montgomery Blair remembered later that Stanton and Chase had "actually declared that they would prefer the loss of the capital to the restoration of McClellan to command." [17]

McClellan responded brilliantly. Within two weeks he had Pope's demoralized troops reorganized and in pursuit of Lee's troops, who had invaded Maryland with the ultimate goal of capturing the great railway center at Harrisburg, Pennsylvania. Lee had hoped that large numbers of Marylanders might rise to his support, but he was grievously disappointed. On September 13 two Union soldiers at Frederick, Maryland, picked up a piece of paper wrapped around some cigars. It was Lee's detailed plan for the invasion. If Lee had exaggerated his numbers in the plan and left it deliberately in McClellan's path he might have again demoralized McClellan, but the document was genuine, and McClellan for once knew the actual strength of the enemy. On September 17, near Sharpsburg on Antietam Creek in Maryland, McClellan and 75,000 men faced Lee and Jackson with 40,000. After two days of fierce and bloody battle, Lee abandoned the area and escaped even though McClellan had some 36,000 men who had not yet done any fighting. McClellan's casualties were 12,469 as compared to Lee's 13,724. By indecision, however, McClellan had lost another excellent chance to win the war, even though he had stopped Lee's invasion.

The victory enabled Lincoln to announce his preliminary Emancipation Proclamation, and on October 6 he ordered McClellan to advance again. McClellan, however, stood still while the Confederate cavalry hero J. E. B. Stuart rode all the way around the northern army. On October 25 Lincoln wired his reluctant warrior: "I have just read your despatch about sore tongued and fatiegued [sic] horses. Will you pardon me for asking what the horses of your army have done since the battle of Antietam that fatigue anything?" Ten days later, despite last-minute pleas by Montgomery and Francis P. Blair, Lincoln replaced McClellan with General Ambrose Burnside. McClellan had "the slows," and the president was tired of trying "to bore with an auger too dull to take hold." [18]

Anxiously looking ahead to the 1864 election, Francis P. Blair had urged Lincoln to give McClellan one more chance and a direct warning that "absolute & prompt obedience was the tenure by which alone he held his command." Then, said Blair, if McClellan, under this pressure, could win a victory, the peace Democrats in Congress would turn against him. This in turn would compel the general and the war-supporting Democrats to support Lincoln for reelection. Even after McClellan had been relieved, Blair continued to argue that if McClellan became a martyr, the peace Democrats would unite behind him, while the radicals would seek to win the presidency with Chase.[19]

The Blairs also argued that despite his faults McClellan was superior to any available radical generals, and Lincoln's next two commanders quickly proved their point. Ambrose Burnside did not have "the slows," but he was also quite unencumbered with military judgment. At Fredericksburg, Virginia, Burnside suffered a terrible defeat that included several charges up a slope against entrenched artillery and sharpshooters. A newsman reported that "it can hardly be in human nature for men to show more valor, or generals to manifest less judgment." The one-day casualty score was 9,000 Federals and 1,500 Confederates. Watching the carnage, Robert E. Lee observed that "it was well war is so terrible, or we would grow too fond of it." [20]

Lincoln then gave Burnside's command to Joseph Hooker, another radical favorite. Montgomery Blair accurately described Hooker as "too great a friend of John Barleycorn," and he and his father again urged the restoration of McClellan. Lincoln had strong advice for Hooker: "I have heard in such a way as to believe it, of your recently saying that both the Army and the Government needed a Dictator. . . . Only those generals who gain successes, can set up dictators. What I now ask of you is military success, and I will risk the dictatorship." [21]

Praying that "God have mercy on General Lee, for I will have none," Hooker started for Richmond with 134,000 men and reached Chancellorsville on May 1, 1863. Lee and Jackson faced him with only 60,000 soldiers, but for daring gamblers and skilled tacticians they were enough. Before the debacle ended, the North had suffered 17,287 casualties, and the shattered Union army was again straggling back toward Washington. To his credit, Hooker later fought well under Grant at Lookout Mountain. As Francis P. Blair had said, Hooker was "brave enough to fight when led but not to lead . . . too much for a weak head." [22]

At this point, Lincoln stopped trying to please the radicals. His next commanding general was George Gordon Meade, a tough and competent soldier. The Blairs liked Meade, in part because he had been born in Spain and therefore could not be corrupted by dreams of the presidency. The radicals, however, as usual were angry. Having exonerated both Burnside and

Hooker, the Joint Committee on the Conduct of the War turned its verbal guns on Meade, who had remained clear of the slavery controversy. Meade, however, with the aid of Confederate mistakes, won the greatest and bloodiest battle of the war at Gettysburg on July 1–4, 1863. Meade allowed his exhausted soldiers to rest while Lee's even wearier troops escaped, but unlike McClellan at Antietam, he had not ended the battle with a vast force still unused and fresh. Still, however, he had permitted the shattered Confederate army to cross the Potomac, and the radicals continued to suspect sinister plots.

On March 9, 1864, Abraham Lincoln gave Ulysses S. Grant the new superior rank of lieutenant general and the full responsibility for ending the war. The president had finally reached the same conclusion that Frank Blair had been writing home for months: Grant was the best general in the army. The Blairs were delighted, while the radicals were again displeased. Grant apparently shared the typical anti-black attitudes of his native southern Illinois, and he had once ordered all Jews to leave the Western Department on twenty-four hour's notice. Lincoln had quickly rescinded the order. Grant was a competent if unspectacular strategist, and like Robert E. Lee he was willing to shed blood. Like his predecessors he would often suffer losses far exceeding those of the South, but in contrast he did not retreat. In one month Grant lost 50,000 men and stopped only to bring up new men from his ample reserves. After the battle of Fort Fisher, Grant infuriated the radicals by dismissing the ridiculous General Benjamin F. Butler, long a radical hero for his contraband policy toward escaping slaves. Waving the casualty lists, the Joint Committee demanded Grant's removal, but Lincoln stood firm, always supported by the Blairs.

In all of this the Blairs were villains in radical eyes, and the fact that the Blair judgments of the radical generals almost invariably proved correct only increased the animosity. The radical efforts against slavery were noble enough, but ideological purity was a disastrous standard for selecting military leadership. The ineptitude of Frémont, McDowell, Pope, Burnside, Hooker, and Butler prolonged the war and cost thousands of lives. Unwilling to admit this, the radicals could only cast about for scapegoats to explain their own misjudgments.

Chapter 22

To Serve a President

ON March 6, 1862, a great antislavery meeting was held at Cooper Institute in New York, and among those who sent letters to be read was Montgomery Blair. While Blair echoed the antislavery sentiments of the other speeches and letters, he sharply attacked the radical idea that the southern states had been destroyed as political entities, and he made another impassioned plea for colonization as the only alternative to either radical amalgamation or the destruction of the black race. It was the only sour note of the meeting, and the longtime abolitionist Gerrit Smith quickly published a letter taking issue with Blair's view that the races could not live together peacefully on an equal basis.[1]

In December 1862 Montgomery again exemplified the Blair habit of choosing principle over personal feeling by defending his old enemy, William H. Seward. Various radicals, encouraged by Chase and perhaps Stanton, decided that Seward was the influence holding Lincoln back from an all-out emancipation policy. A committee of nine radical senators demanded Seward's dismissal, an end to the president's "all parties" policy, and more frequent cabinet meetings, which presumably meant more influence for Chase. After a five-hour session at the White House, however, Lincoln asked for a show of hands, and only four of the nine senators still thought Seward should be replaced. In the discussion, Montgomery Blair argued persuasively that the committee was proposing an unconstitutional plural executive. The president alone, insisted Blair, "was accountable for his administration, might ask opinions or not of either and as many as he pleased, of all or none, of his cabinet." While he had often disagreed with

Seward, Blair added, he believed it would be a serious mistake if Seward should be forced out of office by meddlesome senators.[2]

After Gettysburg and Vicksburg, the arguments over how to end slavery and reabsorb the southern states into the Union became still more divisive within the political parties as well as between them. A wide range of opinions and convictions had to be adapted to the American habit of making national decisions through the conflict of two, or sometimes three, significant political parties. Most northerners were neither radicals nor copperheads—neither anxious to make all blacks free and equal nor willing to stop the war short of total victory. The wartime sacrifices, sufferings, and hatreds were on the radical side of the argument, however, and the future rights of the Confederate states were hardly a priority concern for the average northerner.

In both Missouri and Maryland a strange polarity had developed between conservatives unwilling to accept even a compensated emancipation and radicals on the side of immediate full emancipation and racial equality. Among the Missouri radical leaders was Benjamin Gratz Brown, who had carried the democratic ideals taught him by "Uncle Blair" to conclusions far beyond those of his cousin Frank. Several other Missouri radicals, however, had been proslavery when Frank Blair was risking his life to found a Republican party in Missouri, but for personal advantage they had later followed the popular drift in St. Louis to a radical position Blair would not accept. The large German population still considered Frémont a hero, and even southern sympathizers could support the radicals as a means of striking back at Frank Blair. In short, the labels were clear-cut, but the divisions behind them were not.

The chief radical in Maryland was Representative Henry Winter Davis, who had changed from conservative to radical almost overnight after the Blairs had emerged as the leaders of conservatism. By the fall of 1863, Maryland conservatives and radicals were locked in a fierce primary contest between Davis and Thomas Swann. Speaking at Rockville, Maryland, on October 3, 1863, Montgomery Blair as usual sharpened the issues when political expediency would have dictated an attempt to blur them. "The Abolition party," he charged, was prolonging the war by trying to impose "*amalgamation, equality,* and *fratern-*

ity" upon "the free white labor of our land." The traitors who had misled the southern people should be punished, but the mass of the southerners should again have control of their own destinies through their state governments. The president, insisted Blair, would continue to follow the program exemplified in the restoration of governments in Missouri, Kentucky, Maryland, and West Virginia, and all true patriots would stand by him. Whether or not the Rockville speech was a trial balloon for Lincoln, it apparently had his approval. It was published far and wide, and the reactions to it gave the president a useful survey of the political and popular sentiment on the issues it covered.[3]

Well aware of the mixed reactions to Montgomery Blair's Rockville speech, Lincoln on December 8, 1863, issued an amnesty proclamation. He offered a full pardon to all rebels—except a few selected top leaders—who would take an oath of loyalty to the Constitution and swear to support the Emancipation Proclamation and all other congressional acts related to slavery. Also, when, in any seceded state, a number of citizens equal to one-tenth of that state's voters in the election of 1860 should take the prescribed oath and establish a democratic government, it would be recognized as the true government of the state and be given full federal protection.

In turn, the postmaster general, on January 22, 1864, addressed the Maryland legislature with an ardent plea for Republicans and war Democrats alike to support the president. Both parties, said Blair, agreed that the Union must be saved and that slavery must go, and should work together for these common objectives: "We are all Republicans—all Democrats." [4] This speech was also circulated nationally, and for once even the radical press did not attack Blair's conciliatory language.

In 1864, America faced a crucial wartime presidential election. Just as the senior Blair had feared, the radicals hoped to elect Chase, while the peacemakers were turning to General McClellan. Chase yearned for the nomination, but was unwilling to give up his cabinet seat and make an open effort. Apparently at least in part to get a stalking-horse for threatening the regular party into nominating Chase, a handful of extremists met in Cleveland on May 31, 1864, and nominated General Frémont. The general had no chance to win, but he could still endanger the regular party candidate in a close election. Frémont announced that he would support any other candidate with "fidelity to our cardinal principles," but if Lincoln should be renominated there would be "no other alternative but to organize against him every element of conscientious opposition with a view to prevent the misfortune of his reelection." [5]

At this point Frank Blair again exploded on the political scene. In 1862, while campaigning with Sherman, he had been reelected to Congress over a radical candidate, Samuel Knox, by a mere 153 votes. The radicals had turned to Knox after B. Gratz Brown had refused to oppose his cousin Frank. Both sides claimed fraud, and Knox formally contested the result with a charge that fourteen or fifteen hundred paroled prisoners "were marched to the polls sober, but returned drunk loudly hurrahing for Frank Blair," and that thousands of nonresidents had "voted *early and often,* to save this amphibious, hybrid, hermaphrodite faction from disgraceful defeat." [6]

On June 3, 1863, a lately converted radical congressman from Missouri charged that General Frank Blair had ordered $8,651 worth of whiskey, ale, wines, cigars, and smoking tobacco at government expense and had sold most of the items for an immense profit. While the general was away on the battlefield, the accusation was circulated widely in radical newspapers and speeches.

In October 1863, a few days after his Rockville speech, Montgomery Blair asked Lincoln whether Frank should remain with the army or take his seat in Congress. Frank preferred the army, but would follow the president's wishes. Montgomery and Lincoln, and probably the elder Blair, must have discussed the matter, and they understood each other completely. The result was a letter from Lincoln to Montgomery Blair suggesting that Frank should come to Washington, surrender his commission to the president, caucus with his friends, and help organize a House that would support the administration. If elected speaker, he should serve. If not, he could retake his commission and return to the army. Above all, Frank should not allow the provocations of "insincere time servers to drive him from the house of his own building." Frank, wrote Lincoln, was "young yet," with "abundant talents—quite enough to occupy all his time without devoting any to temper," and was "rising in military skill and usefulness," as proven by his appointment to a corps command "by one so competent to judge as General Sherman." There Frank could "serve both his country and himself more profitably than he could as a member of Congress." [7]

Military events, however, kept Frank from following these directions exactly. When Congress was being organized in December 1863, he was fighting the bloody battles of Chattanooga and Knoxville. He then decided to remain with the army even though Secretary Stanton transferred his corps to General John Logan, but the complaints of his friends in St. Louis and his anger over the charges of personal dishonesty changed his mind. Also, even though they had marched 500 miles and suffered heavy battle losses in Tennessee, his troops had been ignored in Stanton's official reports.

On the morning of January 9, 1864, Lizzie was awakened by Frank's arrival and the excited voices of her parents. The general went next door for breakfast with his brother and then took up residence with his sister and parents. For the next three and a half months Lizzie served as Frank's secretary and scribe, while their father performed his usual chores of research and writing. Having just returned from the sights and sounds of real battlefields, Frank was feeling even more aggressive than usual, and despite his feigned indifference he was deeply hurt by the charges of corruption. He also suffered terribly from headaches, which in the light of his subsequent medical history were probably caused by high blood pressure, and this did not improve his temper. He was trying to cut down on smoking, but thirty cigars a day for years had already taken a toll. At one point his headaches abated when word came that Apo was en route to Washington, but they quickly returned when she delayed her departure for several more weeks.[8]

General Blair soon renewed his personal relations with the president. On January 16 he and Lizzie spent a long evening with the Lincolns and Lizzie reported that "we got very intimate." On the following day she presented some ladies at the White House and hoped that Mary Lincoln would not notice that she was again wearing her only black gown.

Lincoln and Frank Blair shared a common problem—Treasury Secretary Salmon P. Chase. In his quest for the presidency, Chase was using the immense patronage of his office in St. Louis and other areas to build up the radical party. Two years earlier, when Chase had begun issuing individual trade permits to merchants conducting exchanges between the warring sides, Frank had protested the wisdom of exchanging food badly needed by the South for cotton of far less importance to the North. The awarding of the permits soon caused angry complaints of political favoritism. Many Democratic newspapers were soon charging corruption in the Treasury Department's local operations in New York and other places as well as in St. Louis. A number of Frank Blair's conservative-turned-radical enemies in St. Louis were profiting from Treasury Department patronage, and he concluded, naturally enough, that this was their motivation.[9]

Chase, of course, considered himself a thoroughly high-minded patriot and humanitarian, but he was nonetheless involved in a serious conflict of interest. Laudatory newspaper editorials and magazine articles, as well as several campaign-type biographies, were promoting his presidential candidacy, and financing most of this was the great banker Jay Cooke. Chase had given Cooke a monopoly for the sale of the nation's war bonds, as well as the privilege of transferring government money, which could be loaned at interest when not actually being spent. Cooke had 2,500 war-bond salesmen electioneering for Chase, and his enormous advertising contracts were a powerful lever over a great many newspaper editors. Cooke personally financed a sketch of Chase for the *American Exchange and Review*. Thurlow Weed in the *Albany Evening Journal* accused Chase of "converting the Treasury Department into a political machine," and Chase responded with an angry letter to Seward. The Chase organization, headed by the corrupt and greedy Samuel Pomeroy of Kansas, distributed 100,000 copies of a pamphlet called *The Next Presidential Election* at government expense under the frank of Senator John Sherman. The six-page document excoriated Lincoln and argued that his reelection would be both absurd and dangerous. Two weeks later Pomeroy distributed a secret but quickly publicized "circular" that repeated the attacks on Lincoln and added a eulogy of Chase as the only man who could avert catastrophe.[10]

Chase also had powerful financial backing from his son-in-law

William Sprague, whom his ambitious daughter Kate had married to get the wealth she hoped would make her father president. Sprague, who had inherited his fortune, was more irresponsible and foolish than greedy, and his interest in Chase was personal rather than financial. Nevertheless, the Sprague firm was heavily involved in the cotton trade being regulated by the Treasury Department.[11]

Chase protested his innocence, and for the fourth time offered to resign. Lincoln refused, but Chase noted that "there was no response in his letter to the sentiments of respect and esteem which mine contained." On March 5, 1864, Chase formally withdrew his name from consideration for the presidential nomination, but neither the Blairs nor the rest of Lincoln's cabinet took this seriously. During the same period, the president and Frank Blair had long and friendly conversations.

Abraham Lincoln probably had mixed emotions. He was reluctant to sharpen further the divisions between the radicals and conservatives in his party, but he must have recognized that Chase might become a dangerous rival if left unchallenged. Also, even though he was more impervious to insults than most presidents have been, he could not have ignored entirely the personal attacks attributed to Chase and the secretary's supporters. Although Lincoln did not ask Frank Blair to enter the lists against Chase, he also did nothing to restrain his Missouri tiger, and he must have enjoyed the results.

In the House, Blair began with a resolution for the appointment of a special committee to investigate the granting of trade permits, but Speaker Schuyler Colfax blocked the effort. On February 27, after the "Pomeroy Circular," the general delivered a long and angry speech called "The Jacobins of Missouri." He not only described the chameleon-like habits of his Missouri enemies, but also went after Chase for undermining and betraying the president. His words probably reflected both his own hurt feelings and the vocabulary of his father: No "man having the instincts of a gentleman should remain in the cabinet after the disclosure of such an intrigue against the one to whom he owes his position. I suppose the President is well content that he should stay; for every hour that he remains sinks him into the contempt of every honorable mind." [12]

In response, Missouri radical J. W. McClurg repeated the

corruption charges against Blair. Blair answered with a demand for an official investigation. As for McClurg, said Blair, he had "taken the place of the forger and falsifier, and I pronounce him an infamous liar and scoundrel (Great Sensation.)" A month later, on April 23, 1864, an impartial committee reported that "one Michael Powers, representing himself to be an agent of the Treasury Department," had offered to procure not more than $175 worth of liquor, tobacco, and cigars for General Blair and his staff. After Blair and others had signed the order, Powers, by his own admission, had inserted additional figures to change the order completely for his own profit. General Blair was entirely innocent.

Anticipating this verdict, Blair and his father and sister had already drafted his response, and the proud family was in the gallery when he delivered his swan song in the House of Representatives. He began by apologizing for his attack on McClurg: "I found it impossible to restrain myself, and used language for which I am willing to apologize to the House, but for which I shall never apologize to him." The real culprit, however, was the secretary of the treasury. The forgery had been "perpetrated by a person in the employ of the Treasury Department, uttered and put into circulation by a special agent of the Treasury Department, and printed in a paper pensioned by the Secretary of the Treasury."

"You are out of order!" shouted Speaker Colfax.

"Go ahead!" answered Blair's supporters.

"These dogs have been set on me by their master," Frank roared above the confusion, "and since I have whipped them back into their kennels I mean to hold their master for this outrage and not the curs who have been set upon me." The false accusation had been circulated in newspapers pensioned by the Treasury Department, and he "was simply endeavoring to show the motives which caused me to oppose Mr. Chase and which opposition caused him to retort upon me by an assault upon my character and reputation by the forgeries committed and disseminated by his understrappers." Again Colfax called Blair to order, and again Blair's friends shouted for him to continue. Sprague's cotton permits would make millions, Blair charged, and the bond bankers had already earned $1,750,000 in only nine months. No wonder there were "a great many newspapers in favor of Chase for President and very few people." Chase's withdrawal, said Blair, was not to be taken seriously. The secretary was working "under the ground" and "in the dark" in Frémont's name, and "that poor creature" was "unconscious of being made a cat's paw to accomplish the objects of his intriguing rival." The plan was "to hold a convention of Jacobins and red Republican Germans at Cleveland" to threaten the regular party with an independent Frémont candidacy if it should renominate Lincoln. If the delegates instructed to vote for Lincoln could "be bought with greenbacks or frightened by the Jacobin hobgoblin, it is expected that Chase, who has so magnanimously declined to be a candidate will then be taken up as a compromise candidate. . . . It combines the tactics, the intrigues, the corruption and the frauds of Calhoun and Biddle combined." To a loud mingling of cheers and jeers, Frank walked off the floor.[13]

A few hours later a "troop" of congressmen, mostly Democrats and western men, came to the Lee house to make speeches and present Frank with "a superb sword sash & spurs," engraved with the words "from his friends for his gallant support of the Union." After the party disbanded, Frank crossed the street to the White House where he received his commission back and talked with Lincoln until the small hours. Lizzie awakened him early the next morning because he was leaving to join Sherman. Over breakfast he recounted that Lincoln had told Sumner that "his set" had begun the war on the Blairs, beginning with Frank's arrest by Frémont, and had added: "The B's are brave people & never whine—but are ready to fight their enemies and very generally whip them." [14]

Ohio congressman Albert G. Riddle reached Chase at the railway station where the secretary had just heard of Frank Blair's speech while boarding a train for Baltimore. Riddle remembered later that Chase almost shook the train with his trembling and fury. Most observers expected Chase to resign, but friends quickly persuaded him to wait while they drafted a disavowal of Blair's speech for Lincoln to sign. Riddle and another radical colleague took the paper to Lincoln, who received them politely but not cordially. They argued that Chase's resignation would cost Lincoln the presidential election and urged him to mollify the secretary.

Lincoln reminded them of Frank's work in building an antislavery party in Missouri and stressed the injustice of his "being kicked out of the house which he himself built." He conceded only that he had been annoyed by Frank's first speech against Chase and had known nothing of the second. He did not sign anything.[15] Chase told friends that he would resign unless Lincoln disavowed Blair's speech in writing. Lincoln wrote nothing, but Chase did not resign. If the president was really annoyed by either of Frank's speeches he did not say so to any of the Blairs. Clearly, Frank Blair had served Lincoln's purposes well, since the wide circulation of the speech broke the image of purity Chase's backers were trying to project.

A few weeks later, after a dispute with Lincoln over a patronage appointment, Chase again resigned, expecting thereby to have his way as usual. This time, however, Lincoln accepted the resignation and added: "You and I have reached a point of mutual embarrassment in our official relations which it seems can not be overcome, or longer sustained, consistently with the public service."

In Congress, the angry radicals demanded an explanation from Lincoln: How could Blair constitutionally serve as both a general and congressman? The president responded with a full report of his written agreement with Frank, and the radicals were again angered by this alleged servility to the Blairs. The Committee on Elections finally reached a 5–4 decision that Samuel Knox and not Frank Blair had been elected to Congress in 1862, and the House accepted this verdict by a small margin. From a battlefield in Georgia, General Blair had already written his brother that he did not "care a snap of my fingers whether they succeed or not in turning me out of Congress and the army both. . . . I could enjoy a little quiet retirement; especially as it is now apparent that the rebellion will soon be put down and Old Abe re-elected." He did not add that despite his father's loans, his property was slowly being lost through circumstances and inattention, and that his military and political services would leave him again bankrupt.[16]

Frank Blair's widely publicized speech ended the presidential hopes of Salmon P. Chase for 1864, but in the same month the radicals got another boost at the expense of those counseling forbearance toward the South. At Fort Pillow, near Memphis,

Tennessee, the uneducated but enormously talented and aggressive Confederate general Nathan B. Forrest stormed an undermanned garrison that was already in the process of surrendering. Over half the 600 men present, including 262 Negro soldiers, were killed, wounded in escape, or buried alive after all resistance had stopped. It was a brutal massacre, carried out only because so many of the soldiers were black, and however prejudiced the average northerner himself might be, he could still feel nothing but anger toward the South. Various editors demanded retaliation against Confederate prisoners, and Lincoln asked his cabinet for advice. Seward suggested the rigorous confinement of an equal number of prisoners as hostages until the Confederate government should disavow the atrocities and give a pledge that they would not be repeated. Chase agreed, but wished the hostages to be of the highest rank. Stanton would have the president demand that the Richmond government hand over Forrest and his aides for punishment, and if the demand were refused, take such measures against the hostages as existing circumstances made necessary. Welles agreed with Stanton. Montgomery Blair, however, insisted that retaliation against anyone but the actual offenders would not be civilized warfare. He would "pursue the actual offenders alone . . . order the most energetic measures for their capture, and the most summary punishment when captured." No further action was taken.[17]

With Fort Pillow still in northern minds, the Republicans and war Democrats met in a Constitutional Union convention at Baltimore to nominate a candidate for president. The radicals were not in the majority, but they were influential beyond their numbers. Lincoln had already pulled their teeth, however, by proposing a Thirteeth Amendment to abolish slavery everywhere throughout the nation. Despite anti-Lincoln speeches by Henry Winter Davis and others, they knew that the renomination of the president was their only alternative. They were still angry, however, at those who had torpedoed the chances of Salmon P. Chase.

Convention delegates then as now were often chosen by state conventions composed of delegates selected by poorly attended local conventions and caucuses. Thus convention delegates often were, and are, those with either intense convictions about the

issues or strong personal interests. Equally often, they are selected by only a handful of people, and may not reflect the sentiments of the bulk of their constituents. Also, delegates are sometimes exhausted, drunk, or both by the second or third day of
the sessions. Committees make important recommendations and
only in rare instances are the recommendations rejected. In June
1864 the radicals were strong in the committees, and they had
the Fort Pillow massacre on their side.

The major conflict occurred when two delegations arrived
from Missouri. The radical, or anti-Blair, faction had already
indicated its ideological purity by pledging its support to the
nomination of General Grant, whose only vote for president to
date had been cast for James Buchanan, and who had once voted
for a pro-southern Democrat for Congress against the radical Republican Frank Blair. The conservative, or Blair, faction was en-
thusiastically for Lincoln. Frank Blair himself was fighting in
Georgia and had nothing to do with the selection of the delegates.
The Blairs' close friend, Governor Dennison, was the convention's
permanent chairman, but the radical-dominated Committee on
Credentials moved to seat Missouri's "Radical Union Delegation." Amid great shouting and applause, the convention voted
440 to 4 to comply. Historians have cited this as a warning to
Lincoln against the Blairs, but the president actually contributed
to the decision. Anxious to avoid giving the radicals any valid
excuse for switching to Frémont, he had asked the delegation from
his own home state of Illinois to support the Missouri radicals,
and the other delegations recognized the Illinois vote as an expression of Lincoln's wishes. Also, he had probably done this
with the acquiescence if not the agreement of the Blairs, who
were entirely ready to sacrifice their personal interests for his
reelection. The first ballot was unanimous for Lincoln except
for the Missouri votes for Grant, which were quickly changed
to make the vote unanimous.

The platform pledged the delegates to lay aside all political
differences and work together for victory; to offer no terms of
peace except unconditional surrender; to work for the abolition
amendment; and to uphold the national faith pledged for the redemption of the national debt. It also praised Lincoln's Emancipation Proclamation and his decision to use Negro troops, and

it warned that any violation of the laws of war against such soldiers would be avenged. At the insistence of the Missouri delegation another plank announced that "harmony should prevail
in the national councils, and we regard as worthy of public confidence and official trust those only who cordially indorse the
principles proclaimed in these resolutions and which should
characterize the administration of the government." There was
considerable disagreement as to whether this proposition was
aimed at Blair, Seward, Bates, Welles, or all of them, with Blair
generally considered the most likely prospect. In fact, however,
the resolution did not really apply to any of them, because they
were all in favor of the rest of the platform. The radical proposition to confiscate rebel property was conspicuously missing,
and the convention nominated for vice-president the Tennessee
unionist and former slaveholding Democrat Andrew Johnson.
The Blairs were pleased with the choice.[18]

Some three weeks later, Lincoln pocket-vetoed the Wade–
Davis Bill, which had repudiated his amnesty proclamation.
Sponsored by Ben Wade and Henry Winter Davis, this bill decreed that a majority rather than Lincoln's 10 percent of the
white voters in a seceded state must take the oath of allegiance
and create a new state government acceptable to Congress as well
as the president. As expected, the radicals were again angry,
and several actually circulated a secret call for another convention to replace Lincoln. The movement, however, was stillborn
for lack of another viable candidate, although Frémont was still
in the race.

In early July 1864, as rebel troops approached Silver Spring,
Francis P. Blair sent Eliza, Lizzie, and Blair Lee to the seashore
at Cape May, while he and Montgomery and his grandchildren,
Preston and Woody, went deer hunting in Pennsylvania. Shortly
afterward, Blair entrained for New York in the same railway car
with his daughters-in-law Minna and Mary and their children,
Admiral Porter and his family, Charles Sumner, and Salmon P.
Chase. He and Chase had a pleasant, good-natured chat. At Phila-
delphia Blair learned from the Gratz family that Eliza had been
ill, and he promptly changed course for Cape May. Eliza and
Lizzie, meanwhile had been terribly upset by reports that Silver
Spring had been destroyed and that Blair might be in danger. His

sudden and unexpected arrival at Cape May cured Eliza immediately. Having delivered the good news that Silver Spring was
safe and the bad news that Montgomery's house had been burned,
he continued to New York. There he visited the city's leading
editors and argued for the necessity of Lincoln's reelection. Then,
in a two-hour interview, he urged General McClellan to shun the
upcoming Democratic convention in Chicago. Lincoln was certain to win, Blair argued, and McClellan should not allow himself to be used as a divisive force. Instead, he should ask for
reinstatement to a major command, which Blair thought would
be granted. McClellan was polite and friendly, but would make
no promises. A few weeks later he accepted the Democratic nomination but repudiated the peace plank in the platform. Blair
later wrote that he had gone to McClellan without Lincoln's
knowledge because he feared that a campaign with McClellan
running on a peace platform would hurt the war effort. Many
years afterward, Lincoln's friend Ward Lamon wrote that Lincoln had sent Blair to McClellan, but since Lamon had the date
of the visit incorrect by three months, his memory of the incident
itself was probably faulty. General Alfred Pleasanton also remembered in later years that Blair had told him that he had
gone to McClellan for Lincoln. Montgomery Blair wrote later
that McClellan would have received the Virginia command later
given to Philip Sheridan if he had declined the nomination and
supported Lincoln. And finally, McClellan's biographer became
convinced that Lincoln and Grant had decided against giving
McClellan this command only because of his presidential candidacy. Whatever the origins of Blair's effort, it was worth making.[19]

John C. Frémont's radical stance may have been sincere, but
his supporters, claiming to speak for their leader, tried to get
him nominated by the Democrats with an agreement to seek a
negotiated peace. Rebuffed in this effort, his former aide Justus
McKinstry, who had been particularly anathema to Frank Blair,
offered Frémont's support for the Democratic nominee in exchange for the Pathfinder's restoration to the command in St.
Louis.[20] Whether or not Frémont had actually authorized these
overtures, he was a candidate without hope and he needed a face-
saving exit. He was not, however, without bargaining power.

The microscopic vote for James G. Birney in 1844, after all, had cost Henry Clay the presidency. Who could know what the Frémont impact might be in the more closely divided states? The military situation in the summer of 1864, when the rebels were threatening Washington and horrendous casualties were being suffered by Grant's army, also worked against the president. At one point Thurlow Weed told Lincoln that he could not possibly be reelected, and Lincoln himself had serious doubts. Also, on August 5, Greeley and other editors published the Wade–Davis Manifesto, an abusive statement denouncing Lincoln for refusing either to sign or officially veto the radicals' Reconstruction bill.

In short, by late September 1864 Lincoln needed to propitiate his radical opponents and eliminate the Frémont candidacy. Frémont and Blair biographers later described a northern electorate seething with hatred for Montgomery Blair, but no real evidence justifies this conclusion. Certainly John C. Frémont had not forgiven Blair, and other radicals hated him not only for his principles and self-righteousness but also as a surrogate for the Lincoln they could not harm. Henry Wilson warned Lincoln that the retention of Blair would cost him thousands of votes, but this did not make it true. Despite the hatreds and fears created by the war, most northerners and border-state citizens were apparently still moderates on the subject of Reconstruction. Henry Winter Davis lost his next bid for reelection.

Still, however, only a few votes might decide the presidency. After the Republican convention, Montgomery Blair offered his resignation but Lincoln refused it, and throughout the summer the president continued to resist the radical pressures against Blair. After the rebels burned Montgomery's house, valued at $20,000, there was much talk that he should be reimbursed either by the government or by a private subscription. Montgomery, however, flatly rejected the idea on the grounds that he was no different from any other citizen. When General Benjamin F. Butler retaliated by burning the Virginia home of the Confederate secretary of war, James Seddon, Montgomery objected strongly. He appreciated Butler's concern, but found the act indefensible. Shortly afterward, Lizzie walked home from church with General Grant and relayed Montgomery's feelings.

Grant agreed to issue a general order against any such future occurrence. Toward Secretary Stanton and General Halleck, however, Blair was less forbearing. When a friend offered sympathy, he answered that "nothing better could be expected" with "poltroons and cowards" in the War Department. Halleck and Stanton soon heard the story and angrily insisted that Lincoln dismiss Blair. The president, however, did not "consider what may have been said hastily in a moment of vexation at so severe a loss . . . sufficient for so grave a step. Besides this, truth is generally the best vindication against slander." [21]

In August, a few weeks later, Francis P. Blair met Lincoln at the Soldiers' Home for a talk about the election. The president was gloomy, and Blair assured him that Montgomery would gladly resign if this would help. Lincoln replied that he "did not think it good policy to sacrifice a true friend to a false one or an avowed enemy." Blair repeated the offer, and assured Lincoln that he could sacrifice Montgomery Blair with a clear conscience.[27]

In late September the radical senator Zach Chandler of Michigan appointed himself to serve as a harmonizing agent. He first went to Ohio to see Wade, who agreed to support Lincoln more vigorously if the president would give more recognition to the radical element and dismiss Blair. Wade also specified that he would follow any course approved by Henry Winter Davis. Chandler next went to the White House, where Lincoln reluctantly agreed that Blair would resign if the result would unify the party. The next stop for Chandler was Baltimore, where Davis was also willing to accept the replacement of Blair as an adequate olive branch. And finally, from Baltimore Chandler continued to New York for negotiations with the friends of John C. Frémont. Chandler offered Frémont another high military command and the dismissal of Blair. Frémont formally refused to ask for either of these concessions, but he knew that Blair would be dismissed. His friends and advisors clearly considered it part of a bargain. On September 22, 1864, Frémont formally withdrew from the race.[23]

On the following morning Montgomery Blair found a not entirely unexpected note from the president: "You have generously said to me more than once that, whenever your resignation could be a relief to me, it was at my disposal. The time has come.

You very well know that this proceeds from no dissatisfaction of mine with you personally or officially. Your uniform kindness has been unsurpassed by that of any friend, and . . . in the three years and a half during which you have administered the general postoffice I remember no single complaint against you in connection therewith." However strongly he may have felt that Lincoln's reelection superseded his own interests, Montgomery Blair, like anyone else, did not find his dismissal pleasant. He explained to the astounded Welles that it was undoubtedly a peace offering to Frémont and his friends. "In parting with Blair," Welles wrote regretfully, "the President parts with a true friend, and he leaves no advisor so able, bold, sagacious. Honest, truthful, and sincere, he has been wise, discriminating, and correct." [24]

The new postmaster general was the Blairs' close friend, former governor of Ohio William Dennison. According to Lizzie, Dennison was selected on the recommendation of her father. The elder Blair wrote Frank a long explanation of Montgomery's resignation, and Lizzie sent Phillips Lee a copy of this letter. The family's unanimous feeling that Montgomery had done the right thing for the all-important cause was unmarred by the slightest rancor toward Lincoln.[25]

In New York on September 27, twenty thousand people crowded into Cooper Institute to hear and cheer the ex–postmaster general. He had resigned, Montgomery announced, on the recommendation of his father, who looked only "to the grandeur of this nation and the happiness of this great people," and who "would not permit a son of his to stand in the way of the glorious and patriotic President who leads us on to success and to the final triumph that is in store for us." The victory, he declaimed, depended entirely upon the reelection of Lincoln because the Democratic party platform advocated a peace acceptable to the slaveholding South. It was a great performance by Blair only four days after his dismissal, and he repeated the speech in various western states. Many of his Missouri friends, in particular, were furious at Lincoln, and many strong personal letters were required to keep them in line. Frank Blair, meanwhile, electioneered daily among his troops for the president, and the soldiers' vote was an important part of the total.[26]

On November 8 the people spoke and Lincoln was reelected with 53.6 percent of the popular vote. The electoral margin of 212 to 21 was overwhelming, but a change of only 202,000 votes out of the 4 million cast could have given McClellan a popular victory. Lincoln's efforts to blur the differences within his party, his balancing of the scale by eliminating both Chase and Blair from his cabinet, and the withdrawal of Frémont were all important to his reelection.

On October 12, 1864, the death of Chief Justice Roger B. Taney gave Lincoln a chance to repay the Blairs. After the election, Francis P. Blair, Gideon Welles, and others made eloquent and logical pleas for the appointment of Montgomery Blair, with the elder Blair ending his letter on a customary note: "You will not infer that I set up any claim. You have done enough for the Blairs to entitle you to their gratitude & of their posterity." Abraham Lincoln, however, was looking ahead to four years of struggle with Congress over Reconstruction, and he did not wish a senatorial conflict over the confirmation of a chief justice. The moderates would not oppose a radical of legal and judicial ability, but the radicals would certainly oppose Montgomery Blair. The seat was important to the radicals. Before the election, when it appeared that Lincoln might lose, Ben Wade remarked: "No man ever prayed as I did that Taney might outlive James Buchanan's term, and now I am afraid I have overdone it." Several radicals favored Stanton. Seward, Weed, and the New York editor James Gordon Bennett supported Montgomery Blair as the best hope to prevent the nomination of Chase. [27] Lincoln consulted, listened, and received promises from various friends of Chase that he would be satisfied with the judgeship and stop craving the presidency. Then Lincoln ignored the advice of his own most loyal supporters and appointed Chase. It was shrewd politics and a wise choice. Being human, Lincoln also probably enjoyed showing the self-righteous Chase just how forgiving a man of principle could be.

As usual, the Blairs complained briefly to each other, but they quickly renewed their expressions of friendship and loyalty to Lincoln. Only Frank showed any anger—less at the rejection of Montgomery than at the selection of Chase.

Montgomery Blair's efforts for Lincoln had not gone entirely unnoticed. On November 23, 1864, a meeting of the Maryland Unconditional Union party formally offered thanks for his "long, consistant [*sic*], bold & fearless advocacy of free-soil principles & for his able & efficient efforts in favor of emancipation & the adoption of the new [Maryland] Constitution, & for the wise & prudent manner in which he has sustained & strengthened the cause of the Union in our state. . . [and] his earnest & ardent endeavors to secure the renomination & reelection of President Lincoln . . . necessary for the speedy suppression of the Rebellion & restoration of the Union." [28]

Chapter 23

The Home Front

ON Francis P. Blair's seventy-first birthday, his four-year-old grandson Blair Lee awakened him with a kiss. After breakfast, amid great peals of laughter, the old man and the little boy lathered their faces and shaved together, with Blair Lee using a toy whalebone razor. Then the grandfather galloped off six miles to the city to get the latest news and send a letter urging General McClellan not to allow his critics to stampede him into any rash actions. Lizzie wrote her daily report to Captain Lee, while their son played happily in the nearby woods. Soon a captain from Massachusetts would give him a St. Bernard dog that would become an inseparable companion. It was not entirely a typical day. More often, Blair would send his letters to the city with a teen-aged slave named Vincent, who would bring back the Blair mail and other communications from Montgomery and various friends on the return trip. Occasionally Lizzie would do Vincent's work in the pantry to free him for his pony-express duty.

When Blair did not go to the city, he and Eliza would take a morning ride. After Frank sent home "the General," the horse he had ridden through the Vicksburg campaign, Eliza had her safest mount in years. Blair Lee learned to ride alone just in time to take over "Jenny Lind," a gentle little mule owned first by the children of James and Mary Blair. Mary's children had moved up to somewhat faster ponies. It was an exciting day for Lizzie when Blair at the age of seven first rode Jenny Lind all the way to the city and back. After Montgomery finished his mansion at Falkland, only a short distance away, his children, too, were ofter on pony or mule or underfoot at Silver Spring. Then in 1863 and 1864, first some and then all of Frank's children joined the group. Eliza in particular enjoyed having them all, and the children loved playing in the fields and woods. The favorite, however, was always Blair Lee, who spent long hours working with Eliza in the garden and never tired of his grandfather's stories of the horses, dogs, and hunting of his Kentucky youth. The child particularly liked the old man's tales, some true and many probably imagined, about "Old Bonney," the favorite dog of his childhood. Frank's son Preston (Francis Preston III) was a year older than Blair Lee, but they were well-matched in size. For a time Lizzie worried about Blair's new teeth, because Preston was "a very cross fighting boy & Blair, tho good tempered once in a fight sticks to it." Later she reported that the boys were doing well and that her parents had decided "their namesakes were the smartest of their grandchildren." Frank's eldest son, Andrew, entered the Naval Academy at Annapolis in 1864, and avoiding the academic example of his father he made Apo very happy by becoming a model student. His furloughs were usually spent at Silver Spring.

Montgomery's wife, Minna, spent much time in Philadelphia and New Hampshire with their brood, and the Confederate threat occasionally sent everyone scurrying from the Silver Spring area into Washington or to points further north. The children, however, always pleaded for a quick return. In summer the mothers shared their children's aversion to Washington because they associated various diseases with the perpetual odors from the Potomac and from the sewage-filled canal that ran through part of the city. The family's greatest loss from illness, however, occurred in Philadelphia, where Montgomery's eight-year-old daughter, Maria, died in September 1862. Minna had taken the children there because of General Lee's Maryland invasion.[1]

Betty Blair, Montgomery's daughter who had been adopted by her grandparents after the death of her mother, also remained a part of the household until her marriage to Captain C. M. Comstock in 1865. Betty received every advantage of education, music lessons, and travel among Blair friends in various northern states. At the time of Betty's marriage, banker Elisha Riggs and his wife, Mary Boswell, who had once momentarily broken the heart of James Blair, were sitting out the Civil War in Europe. Mary bought a trousseau for Betty in Paris, and Grandfather Blair soon received a request for $400 in gold plus $160 for the customshouse duty, the seamstress's bill, and a hairdresser. It was a large sum for Blair, but apparently no one even suggested that the more affluent Montgomery might shoulder some of this responsibility for his daughter. The grandparents had adopted Betty when she was an infant, and they would play the role of parents till the end. Betty was duly grateful: "I have to say a thank you my father—and hollow sounding is the word —when I dwell on your love and kindness during the whole of my life—May God reward you for the life long goodness you have shown your adopted, & devoted daughter." [2]

Phillips Lee usually sent $200 a month home to pay for Lizzie's expenses, while her father had a fairly stable annual income of roughly $3,000, which was adequate but not excessive. His investments in Frank's property and debts in St. Louis slowly evaporated during and after the war, but he did manage to use wisely the Washington-area assets under his own management and care. John Rives had served him well.

In 1860 Lizzie was already helping manage Washington's orphan asylum, and she continued this effort for the next forty years. Occasionally she had the unpleasant duty of taking children away from parents known to be abusing them cruelly. More often, however, there were great satisfactions. She gave the name Secessia to the infant daughter of a Confederate soldier who had been killed and a Washington girl who had died, and resolved to give the little girl special care. She took Neddy, a thirteen-year-old deaf mute, into her own home, where he did odd jobs until he became old enough to get a job at the Capitol. When Neddy suffered a broken leg from a kick by a donkey, she paid the $50 bill of a doctor who had jeopardized the boy's life by incompetence, and then employed still another physician who helped him to a full recovery. For a gifted boy of fifteen she got the promise of a chance to become a naval engineer as soon as he was old enough to take the proper examination.

Daily life for Francis P. Blair, of course, consisted mainly of the war and politics. Hour after hour he scrawled letters of advice to Frank, Montgomery, and Phillips Lee; recommendations to Lincoln for commissions and promotions for people like Adelbert Ames, Abner Doubleday, John Schofield, and Apo's brother Andrew Alexander; letters seeking information from and giving the latest Washington news to northern and border politicians like John Andrew, William Dennison, and John J. Crittenden; longer, more formal letters designed for publication; and drafts of speeches for Frank and Montgomery. When trying to promote the interests of his son-in-law, Blair conferred with Gideon Welles. On matters concerning the army or Frank's military career, he bypassed Edwin M. Stanton and went directly to Lincoln. At one point in mid-1863, however, he refused to request a leave for a friend of his granddaughter Betty on the grounds that he had danced attendance on the president often enough. Lizzie concluded that this refusal was meant for Apo's ears also.

Silver Spring was surrounded by numerous Confederate partisans, and a certain amount of uneasiness was always present. The Union army at one time pastured 300 beef cattle and a number of horses on the Blair premises, and both Union and Confederate soldiers were frequently in the area. Blair had little sympathy for neighbors who went south to fight for the Confederacy, but when their families became destitute they could always depend upon him for assistance. Union soldiers marching by could always expect a drink of cold water and a refreshing rinse from his fountain, and often some food when their sheer numbers did not make this impossible.

When Lee invaded Maryland after the Union debacle at the Second Battle of Bull Run, the Blairs fled to the city temporarily, but quickly returned to cheer on the soldiers marching toward Sharpsburg and Antietam. Blair reported that "at least 50,000 of the discomfitted army of Pope and other new levies slaked their thirst & washed the dust from their persons" at his "fountain on their march to encounter the hosts of Secession. The troops & trains have been pouring along by me for the last three days & still continue uninterruptedly. The Presidt. told me that one hundred thousand had marched by different roads on the first day." Blair was convinced that the rebels were planning to stake everything on a blow at the capital, while "counting on the demoralization of our troops, defeated & disheartened by the incapacity & cowardice of our wretched Genls. Pope & McDowell." He was so confident that McClellan would beat them, however, that he resolved to "keep open house, as now at Silver Spring, until I see what I never expect to see, the Rebel Flag on the heights beyond me. If we are victors the electric flash that announces the fact will strike off the fetters of every Slave on this continent. It is success in the decisive battle that is to do this, not proclamations." [3]

After Lincoln issued his preliminary Emancipation Proclamation, the master-slave relationship at Silver Spring ended gradually in an atmosphere of mutual trust and understanding. "We were 'solitary & alone' at our quiet fireplace," Blair wrote John Andrew in May 1861, "our children all in the city; our security being well cared for, by that outcast race, who have no rights which a 'white man is bound to respect—' nevertheless I felt safety in trusting them with all the rights & power, guns & powder, I possessed." In April 1862, when Congress abolished slavery in the District of Columbia, many nearby Maryland and Virginia slaveholders sold their unhappy minions farther South. Others, however, offered their slaves the emancipation that had long been forbidden by state laws. Francis P. Blair announced that his servants had always known that they could go when they wished.[4]

Confronted with a direct and immediate choice, all but one of the Blair servants elected to remain "on their own terms." Young Vincent, whose taste for total freedom may have been stimulated by his frequent gallops with the Blair mail, declared that he would "go *into the world* to better his condition." Blair was somewhat taken aback by this loss of a protégé, but Lizzie persuaded him that Alick could be "a better house servant than Vincent & not doing great things either." Middle-aged Henry announced that he was "content" and "not used to knocking about among common folks. Was used to quality all his days & wants to spend the rest of them with them." Nanny said that she knew when she was well off, but she was delighted that her children would be free. Little Blair Lee's nurse, Becky, also remained for the time being, even though most of her sisters, nieces, and nephews were liberated by a neighboring family who had always been emancipationists. Becky's former owner freed Becky's sister

Harriet and her children, but took away a niece, which grieved Becky deeply. Absorbing the opinions of her white family, Becky was a full-fledged colonizationist. She had accompanied Lizzie and Blair Lee on several trips north, and she was apparently quite devoted to the little boy. He loved her deeply in return, while the relationship between nurse and mother involved an intricate conflict between natural affection and restraints imposed by artificial proprieties and circumstances. Becky chose to remain with Lizzie and Blair, but seemed to resent her own weakness that made her willing to do so. Lizzie found her occasional periods of surly and quarrelsome behavior quite incomprehensible.[5]

In late June 1863, the sound of the cannon and a colonel's warning that a battle might occur in their fields sent the household again riding into the city. Blair and Eliza moved in with Montgomery, whose family was in New England, and Lizzie, Blair Lee, and all the servants occupied the Lee house. Lizzie reported that the rebels had appeared "at the crossroad led by the Noland (who Father got out of prison not long since)— they took 100 horses—then instead of coming toward us" they went to the Quaker neighborhood. It was neither the first nor the last time that bread cast upon waters redounded to Blair's advantage. Even though the Confederates were in full force at Rockville, only a few miles away, the Blairs returned to Silver Spring on July 1 and were there to celebrate when the great victories at Vicksburg and Gettysburg were announced. On July 7 the army sent a twelve-man guard to protect Silver Spring from any guerrillas, but none appeared. On July 13 Lizzie went to church where the Confederates had camped only two weeks earlier. She felt a great sense of deliverance, but she could see "in the faces of the secesh [secessionists]" around her that they still had hopes. On July 21 she wrote Phil that a neighbor had been to Gettysburg to see Robert Brown, a wounded southern friend who was "lying on a quilt with 600 other Confederates with none of the comforts of life." She and Montgomery interceded to get Brown transferred home where he could get better care.

Understandably, not all the servants shared the Blairs' preference for the countryside over Washington's distractions. In September 1863 Becky announced that she would not spend another long, dull winter in the country. Lizzie interpreted this as an attempt to browbeat her into moving to the city. The crisis was averted by taking Becky and Little Blair to Philadelphia for several weeks with the Gratz family. There Becky took her young charge along on visits to her Negro friends. One of the families stuffed him with cake, and Blair reported that they had "Uncle Judge's picture and Grandpa's picture" on their walls, and he found Uncle Frank's picture in two other parlors. By Christmas Eve they were back at Silver Spring, where Eliza presumably satisfied Becky by decreeing that they would all move to the city on January 1 and stay until spring. Frank was coming for his last session in Congress, and he would obviously need a mother's care. "The Old Lady" announced that all of her grandchildren would dine with her on New Year's Day, and everyone else, including her husband and daughter, would be excluded unless Phil should come home.

On their tobacco farm near Upper Marlborough, Maryland, Phillips Lee's brother John and sister-in-law Nelly found the demise of slavery a more painful process. On December 30, 1863, Nelly wrote Phil a long letter of thanks for the money he had sent them. She also added a description of the slaves' Christmas parties and a plaintive lament: "Oh Phill why couldn't this state of things be allowed to stand? Mr. Lee says there is a great difference in their manner of working & in their time of getting at their work. We think they remain with us because they know the good time is coming & they know they will be made free without any trouble to them." Three months later, Lizzie and John Lee were standing on a Washington street when a young black dressed in a braided overcoat walked by. Lee angrily complained: "That is one of William Hill's negroes & he turned to let me see his finery & impudence. We are about cleaned out now." According to Lizzie, Nelly was a southern sympathizer until the Confederacy ignored the French army in Mexico, but then decided that she would even "fight cousin Robert rather than consent to 'French' & 'Catholic' dictation on this continent." [6]

A few weeks later, Lizzie and Blair Lee accompanied Gustavus Fox down the Potomac for a visit with her husband at Hampton Roads. She also got permission for Marian Sander, the wife of a lieutenant in Lee's Command, to go with her, and

Lee arranged for the younger couple to spend a day together. On the return trip the ship got stuck in the mud for ten hours, and the passengers had to be rescued by an army steamer with 300 soldiers on board. Gideon Welles teased Lizzie for wrecking his ordnance boat. A few weeks later Lieutenant Sander was killed, and his wife never forgot that Lizzie had made possible their final meeting.

Shortly after Lizzie's trip to Hampton Roads, Uncle Benjamin Gratz arrived from Kentucky. Time had apparently eased Ben's pain over the death of Cary Gratz, and Lizzie thought he looked better than at any time since his second marriage. He greatly enlivened the Blair household with keen jabs at his old friend and brother-in-law; Eliza usually joined in the fun at her husband's expense. One evening Blair and Gratz went to the White House to see Mary Lincoln, who was eager to hear about her Kentucky family, and they arrived in time to watch the White House stables burn to the ground. The Lincoln horses and the children's ponies perished, and guards had to restrain the president to keep him from rushing into the stable to save them. Lincoln was particularly grieved by the loss of the pony that had belonged to his dead son, Willie. Gratz was infuriated by the indifference of the soldiers and the incompetence of the Washington Fire Department.

Washington social and entertainment events were at a minimum in the spring of 1864, but the Blairs did go to a theater to hear Fanny Kemble—the English actress and author of a recent book against slavery—do readings from Shakespeare's *Henry V*. Fanny had been married to South Carolina planter Pierce Butler for fourteen years, but had finally left her husband and lost her children in a bitter court battle because she could no longer endure the life of a slaveowner. The Blairs had sympathized with her, but Lizzie found the performance a failure. The play, she wrote, was "written to brag of the British over the French," and was out of place in the Washington of 1864. There was very little applause, although "Sumner seemed to understand it." [7]

During their sojourns in the city, Lizzie and her mother also spent considerable time visiting the wounded. In May 1864

Eliza brought a young Captain Smedburg to the Lee house, where he could recover more comfortably from the badly botched amputation of a leg on the battlefield. The move probably saved his life, because he ultimately recovered only after suffering a dangerous infection for several weeks.

Francis P. Blair spent much of the spring of 1864 campaigning among his Montgomery County neighbors for a seat in the forthcoming Maryland constitutional convention. Henry Winter Davis predicted correctly that he would be beaten by a secessionist, but Blair at least made a valiant effort to persuade his fellow Marylanders to accept the emancipation with compensation. As usual, he found a bright side to his defeat for the only elected office he had ever sought: As a delegate he would have been held responsible for getting the slaveholders paid for their slaves and he would have suffered through a miserable summer away from home in Annapolis. The convention abolished slavery without compensation.[8]

In July 1864, while the Blair men and two grandchildren were hunting in Pennsylvania, and the women and other children were at Cape May, the troops of Generals Jubal Early and John C. Breckinridge took over the Blair homes at Silver Spring and Falkland. They had already destroyed twenty-four miles of railroad track and numerous mills, workshops, and factories, and had burned the home of Maryland governor Augustus Bradford. The Confederate forces numbered 20,000 men, but as usual the telegraph lines and the press were reporting 75,000 to 100,000. At nearby Point Lookout were 17,000 rebel prisoners, and Early was hoping to free and rearm them.

General Lew Wallace, who would later write *Ben Hur*, led a Union force from Baltimore and was routed by superior numbers at Monocacy, but he caused a vital break in Early's timetable. Another delay apparently resulted when the southern officers at Silver Spring got into Blair's well-stocked wine cellar and staged a wild party in which they scattered the women's clothes and various papers and other valuables around the house. Early and Breckinridge rode up and ended the festivities with a blaze of anger over both the wasted time and the vandalism. At one point Early could have attacked when the city had only

20,000 defenders, most of them raw recruits and recent convalescents, and Gustavus Fox had a steamer in the Potomac ready to take the president to safety.

Early did not attack soon enough, however, and while Admiral Lee was steaming uninvited to the rescue, other reinforcements from Grant were already streaming into the city. At Fort Stevens, on the city's outskirts, Lincoln stood on the ramparts and watched the battle. A sergeant only five feet away was wounded, and an officer only three feet away fell dead from a sharpshooter's bullet. The Union losses were 380 killed and 319 wounded, but the next day Early and his men were gone. The opportunity to pursue them was lost by confusion among Halleck, Stanton, and the president, and Grant finally gave the order after Early had escaped. "Put Halleck in command of 20,000 men," said Ben Wade, "and he would not scare three sitting geese from their nests." Montgomery Blair's anger was not caused entirely by the loss of his house.[9]

Although Montgomery's house had been burned, perhaps from carelessness rather than vindictiveness, the losses at Silver Spring were remarkably low. The crops, valued at $6,000, were untouched, perhaps in part because one old man told the Confederates that the neighbors who had welcomed them had been often fed by Blair and would need his help later. The mules, horses, ponies, cows, and hogs were scattered, but most of them wandered back. Someone reported that Blair Lee's big dog had been shot, but after the little boy suffered a few days of intense grief he had the equal joy of seeing his pet come walking into the yard. Although considerable furniture had been destroyed and numerous papers taken or scattered, the house was relatively undamaged. Just below a picture of General John A. Dix was a note:

A Confederate officer, for himself & all his comrades, regrets exceedingly that damage & pilfering was committed in this house, before it was known that it was within our lines, or that private property was imperilled. Especially we regret that Ladies property has been disturbed, but restitution has been made, & punishment meted out as far as possible. We wage no ignoble warfare for plunder or revenge, but for all that men hold dearest, & scorn to retaliate in kind the unnumbered outrages committed in our homes by federal Satraps—of which the burning of Govr. Pilcher's, Col Anderson's & hundreds of other private houses, are but light matters in comparison with the darker crimes that remain untold.

On the photograph of the Blairs' southern friend Annie Mason was written: "A Confederate soldier has remained here until after eleven—to prevent pillage because of his love of Mrs. Wheaton (Emma Mason) who had found in this home good & true friends." Equally fortunate, General Breckinridge was second in command, and he had not forgotten either the Blair hospitality or Eliza's aid and comfort to his dying father. One observer reported that Breckinridge had "preserved Silver Spring and made more fuss over it than if it had belonged to Jefferson Davis." [10]

Young Ned Byrnes, another of Lizzie's orphan protégés, had taken Blair's rifle and joined the troops at Fort Stevens, and some older men reported that he had shot some five or six rebel sharpshooters. Lizzie was proud of Ned, but she was disturbed that the killing had made him a hero in the eyes of little Blair Lee. A month later she reported that Ned was "still a hero and the most valuable person on the place." Ned later spent many years as director of the National Botanical Gardens.

In the loose way that the Blair family finances were always managed, Francis P. Blair only a few weeks earlier had sold Phil and Lizzie a lot next to their Washington home for $1,000, but had refused to take the money unless he should need it at some future date. Now that much of his furniture and other household equipment was damaged or destroyed, he agreed to accept the money. Additional help also came from an unexpected source. Simon Cameron, whose cabinet appointment Blair had worked so hard to prevent, sent him two thoroughbred cows and a compliment: "You are too good a man to suffer while the land is flowing with the good things in life." Cameron still had a long and lucrative political career ahead of him, and he never missed a chance to mend a fence. Gideon Welles rode out to view the damage and was properly sympathetic, but his host's concern was directed largely to convincing the secretary that Admiral

Lee's unauthorized dash up the Potomac had been justified and should not be penalized.[11]

A few months later, Lizzie added further to the family's comfort by going to Philadelphia to spend $850 on a new carriage. It provided great pleasure to everyone but the family patriarch. Eliza sent the old carriage to be sold at auction, but her husband learned of this foul deed in time to effect a last-minute rescue. He could not bear to be parted from old things, and besides it would be needed on muddy days. Henry and Eliza insisted that it was too worn out to be safe on such days, but Blair would not be denied. He grumpily accused the family of being spoiled by luxury, and rode in the new vehicle only when absolutely necessary.

Blair's nostalgia and grief during the war years were stirred by personal losses more serious than an old carriage. In July 1862, Martin Van Buren died. He had disagreed with Blair on most political matters since 1856, but their friendship had never dimmed. Shortly before his death he wrote the Blairs a request for their picture. A year later the old people were even more stricken by word that John J. Crittenden was dead in Frankfort, Kentucky. Like Ben Gratz, Crittenden had suffered the task of preserving a divided family, with a son serving as a major general on each opposing side, and he had done much to help keep Kentucky in the Union. Despite their many years of strong political differences, Blair and Eliza had loved Crittenden like a brother almost since childhood, and the happiest memories of their youth were associated with him.

Most painful of all, however, was a crushing bereavement close at hand. On February 13, 1864, Lizzie and her father went to see John Rives, who was ill with "inflammatory rheumatism." The sight of the old giant lying prostrate and unable to move anything but his hands made his visitors fight back their tears. "He tried to joke," wrote Lizzie, "& his lame efforts were just as sad as his utter helplessness." On April 9 Blair postponed a visit to Rives because of a heavy storm. At three the next morning Blair's old partner was dead. "We have had a sad loss in the death of Mr. Rives, the best friend my father ever had— & I believe anybody ever had," wrote Lizzie to Phil. "You have so long shared my feelings for this noble man that I know how truly you will mourn with me now." En route to the funeral, the Blairs were joined at the city limits by "what seemed to be a thousand men on foot—⅔ of those at the house were of the laboring class." Many "plain but well-dressed women" grieved openly, and Lizzie had never seen so many men weeping. Lizzie found at least some comfort in her belief that "after my father he liked me best of our family—said I was like my father in everything but intellect of which luckily I had not as much as he luckily as I was a woman." [12]

After Early's raid, Olivia, the wife of the Blairs' faithful servant Henry, announced that she would not return to the country, and Lizzie feared that Henry would follow her even though he wished to remain at Silver Spring. Although there had been no emancipation yet in Maryland, there was no question about the right of Olivia and Henry to do as they pleased. Probably as a replacement for Olivia, Lizzie acquired the services of Mary Ann, an "Old Maid," whom Eliza considered the best servant she had ever seen. Lizzie did not like Mary Ann's manners, but found them "easy to bear in the light of her cleanliness and honesty." Apparently agreeing with Lizzie, Becky blamed Mary Ann's impudence on her previous experience working for Quakers, who never "make any servants know their places." Becky, too, however, soon decided to cut the tie. She and Lizzie behaved with cold formality toward each other, but Blair Lee was heartbroken despite his mother's admonition that he was now old enough to care for himself. A few weeks later he insisted that part of his birthday cake—shared, incidentally, with the black children who were his closest friends on the place—must be sent to Becky. Lizzie, meanwhile, learned that Becky had got married, and decided that this was the reason for her bad temper at the end of their relationship. "Becky is a good woman," she wrote, "and I have missed her." In November 1864, Francis P. Blair put all of his servants on regular wages. [13]

Chapter 24

Peace

LATE in 1864, Francis P. Blair began developing a new project. His New York visit in July had included a congenial talk with editor Horace Greeley, who believed that the South would accept peace with emancipation if direct overtures were made to Richmond. Blair was certain, however, that the Confederates would never stop fighting until their hopes for the defeat of Lincoln were crushed at the polls. Lincoln's reelection met Blair's condition, and on December 1, 1864, the New York editor wrote a persuasive letter asking Blair "to mediate and moderate and bring about a good understanding among all our true men. . . . *You* have Mr. Lincoln's ear, as *I* have not, and can exert influence on every side where it is needed. Do urge and inspire him to make peace among our friends any how, and with our foes so soon as may be." [1]

Two weeks later Greeley continued: "You are an older, and doubtless an abler, publicist than I am. You have long been the counselor and trusted advisor of men high in authority. . . . Please, then, consider these suggestions." The government, wrote Greeley, should offer to receive envoys from the Confederacy. North Carolina had made a peace demonstration in the Confederate Congress, and its legislature had made a peace overture. Why had the government not responded? If willing to buy the slaves of Maryland and Missouri, why not buy those of North Carolina. "I believe *you*, if at Raleigh with large powers, could pull North Carolina out of the rebellion in a month." [2]

On December 20, Blair answered. He had devised a plan to deliver the country from "*the cause of the war, the war itself, and the men* & the *means* essential to carrying it on against us." He

363

would "hint it to Mr. Lincoln on Thursday. So far at least as to test his confidence in me without which my project must be still-born. Meanwhile you will keep my suggestion as Secret as illicit embryos ought to be & generally are." [3]

Blair's idea was not too different from that of Seward for preventing the war in 1861. A French army had helped overthrow the Mexican republican government of President Benito Juárez and had installed the Austrian archduke Maximilian as the emperor of Mexico. This was a clear-cut violation of the Monroe Doctrine, but the civil war had kept the Lincoln administration from protesting very strenuously. With his usual romanticism, Blair convinced himself that Jefferson Davis might be persuaded to make peace with the North on Lincoln's terms and perhaps win instant forgiveness for the South by helping a reunited nation stand firm against the common French enemy. At the very least it would offer the South a face-saving way to end the war. Blair did not explain his plan to Lincoln, but asked merely for permission to go to Richmond and confer with Davis. Trusting Blair's judgment and believing that the effort at worst could do no harm, Lincoln answered: "Come to me after Savannah." On December 22, General Sherman announced the surrender of Savannah as a national Christmas gift. On December 28, Lincoln gave Blair a simple card: "Allow the bearer, F. P. Blair, Sr. to pass our lines, go South, and return."

With the Lee house full of people for Christmas and with Eliza shopping for her annual New Year's Day feast with her grandchildren, Blair prepared for his journey. He decided to take along the servant Henry, who had not followed Olivia after all, as an attendant, and Lizzie and Eliza packed up the cold leftovers from Christmas dinner for him to eat en route. He was seventy-three years old, and he had been suffering terribly from a toothache and general weakness, but as always the prospect of an exciting journey ended the pain, restored his appetite, and inspired new stamina. His departure on the *Baltimore* was delayed for a day when the ship ran aground in a Chesapeake Bay fog, but he finally reached Grant's headquarters at City Point on December 30, and sent two letters to Jefferson Davis. The first asked permission to come South to look for papers taken from

Blair's house during Early's invasion. The other explained his true purpose: "to submit to your consideration ideas which . . . may not only repair all the ruin the war has brought upon the nation, but contribute to promote the welfare of other nations that have suffered from it." [4]

The Confederate secretary of war, James Seddon, answered that no papers had been taken from Blair's house by the authority of any Confederate officer, but he would grant the request to make clear his repugnance to any kind of plundering. Since Blair was a public enemy, his visit must be by passport and under strictest parole, and his activities must be limited to the purpose stressed in his first letter to President Davis. After several delays, General Grant finally got Blair properly transported to Richmond. He was taken through the lines by Captain Deacon from Boston, who handed him over to Captain Davis of South Carolina. The Boston captain took a bottle from his bag and offered to drink to the health of Captain Davis. They drank together "with mutual good will" and shook hands. Blair hoped this was a good omen.

On January 12 Blair faced Jefferson Davis with a long written proposal and asked that Davis be totally frank if he thought the ideas to be the unrealizable dreams of an old man. Every drop of his blood and that of all his children, said Blair, flowed from a southern source, and although he loved his whole country, his "native instincts enforced by habit" still attached him to the South. Davis replied that he was under great obligation to the Blair family for personal kindnesses, "& that even when dying, they would be remembered in his prayers." With rapport thus established, Blair read his treatise. Regardless of future military events, he said, slavery, "the cause of all our woes," was doomed as "the sin offering required to absolve us and put an end to the terrible retribution" it had brought. If this expiation were made, he continued, nothing but military force could keep the nation divided. A continuation of the needless war, however, would threaten democracy and freedom within both the North and the South, and it could weaken both sections to the point where they might be prey to the machinations of European despots. How much better to make peace on the basis of Lincoln's amnesty proc-

lamation and rejoin the Union now under circumstances that
might prevent any vengeful treatment of the South. Louis
Napoleon's puppet emperor and army in Mexico were a threat
to the entire continent. Davis should offer to make peace on terms
that would abandon slavery and send the Confederate armies to
serve the national interest in Mexico: "If in delivering Mexico he
should model its states in form and principle to adapt them to
our union and add a new southern Constellation to its benignant
sky . . . it would restore the equipoise between the Northern
and Southern States, if indeed such Sectional distinctions could
be recognized, after the peculiar Institution which created them
had ceased to exist." Blair was certain that the southerners and
the Mexicans under Juárez could expel the French invaders, but
if they could not, the northern armies, including the troops of
General Frank Blair, would be ready to help.[5]

Davis must have been astounded by Blair's imagination, but
he was eager to talk peace. He offered to appoint persons to meet
in conference, and he agreed that uniting "the arms of our countrymen from the North & the South" against a common enemy
would restore better feelings.

Before leaving Richmond, Blair rode through the streets, and
he was convinced that the people and their leaders were suffering
severe economic hardships and desperately wanted peace. In the
North, meanwhile, Greeley and the *New York Tribune* led a
parade of newspapers publicizing Blair's mission as a genuine
hope for peace, while some others suggested that he had gone
only to help his southern friends. Various southern papers, however, denounced him as a murderer and damned Davis for receiving him. On January 16 he reached home weary but happy. Mrs.
Jefferson Davis had greeted him like a long-lost father and he
had fared sumptuously, wrote Lizzie, but everyone was relieved
and happy that he was "back in his own bed with mother beside
him." [6]

Lincoln carefully read Blair's report, and scrawled on his
"Suggestions to Jefferson Davis" the words: "This paper first
seen by me on this 16th day of January 1865 . . . I having had
no intimation as to what Mr. Blair would say or do while beyond
our military lines." The president was very interested, however,
in Blair's report of low morale in Richmond and the enclosed

written offer of Davis to send or receive commissioners "to enter
into conference, with a view to secure peace to the two countries."
On January 18 he authorized Blair to tell "Mr. Davis" that he
would "receive any agent whom he, or any other influential person now resisting the national authority, may informally send to
me, with the view of securing peace to the people of our one
common country."

Back to Richmond by steamer and carriage went Blair with
the president's offer. Again he emphasized the pressure on
Lincoln from "extreme men in Congress and elsewhere, who
wished to drive him into harsher measures than he was inclined
to adopt." The inference was clear. If Davis wished to avoid a
punitive radical Reconstruction he should make peace as soon as
possible. Blair's effort was over. On January 27 he arrived back
in Washington half-frozen after a 250-mile nonstop trip.

The seed quickly sprouted. On January 29 the Confederate
vice-president, Alexander H. Stephens, and two fellow peace
commissioners arrived at the Union Army lines and asked safe
conduct to Washington. This news was telegraphed to Washington, and Lincoln sent Major Thomas Eckert with written directions to receive the commissioners if they would agree in writing
to talk on the basis of Lincoln's note to Blair on January 18—
peace for "our one common country." Before the president's en-
voy arrived, the commissioners applied to Grant for permission
to proceed to Washington and confer with Lincoln. Apprised of
this, Lincoln sent Secretary of State Seward to meet them at
Fortress Monroe with three undebatable conditions for peace:
restoration of the national authority throughout the states; the
abolition of slavery; and continuation of the fighting until the
disbanding of all rebel forces.

Major Eckert arrived before Seward, however, and presented
Lincoln's requirement that the commissioners accept the phrase
"one common country." Since their own instructions read "between the two countries," they could not accept. The hopes for
peace had apparently ended, but General Grant wired Stanton his
belief that the commissioners were sincerely interested in making
peace. He was sorry that Lincoln could not interview them personally. The president responded by embarking immediately for
Fortress Monroe, accompanied only by a White House valet

carrying his traveling bag. On February 3 Lincoln, Seward, Eckert, and the commissioners met on a ship in Hampton Roads for four hours of friendly but fruitless discussions. Stephens echoed Blair's suggestion that they take on the French in Mexico together, but Lincoln insisted that the question of the Union must be settled before any other plans could be made. He pointed out that many northerners still favored a $400 million appropriation to recompense the South for its slaves, but he admitted that many of the questions related to peace and reconstruction would have to be settled by Congress and the courts. He stated pointedly that the rebel states would be far better off to return at once, because the time might come when they would no longer be considered as erring people to be invited back to citizenship, but as enemies to be exterminated or ruined. If he were a Georgian, said Lincoln to Stephens, he would urge the state to recall its troops, elect congressmen and senators, and ratify the new Thirteenth Amendment against slavery *"prospectively*, so as to take effect—say in five years." It was the best offer the South would ever get, but the conference was stillborn because of the southerners' refusal to admit that they were still part of the United States.[7]

If the Hampton Roads effort had ended the war and thereby saved several thousand lives, Francis P. Blair would have been a national hero. As it was, the southerners threw away an opportunity for bargaining that would be entirely missing after Lee had surrendered his army. In retrospect the suggestion of a war against the French was foolish, but Blair's exploit did bring the warring leaders together under circumstances that might have led to peace if the southerners had been more realistic.

As the war slowly moved to its inevitable end through the winter and spring of 1865, the Blairs remained in the city. The head of the clan kept urging Gideon Welles to promote his son-in-law to regular admiral, while Eliza had a serious talk with her nephew, the radical Missouri senator B. Gratz Brown. Brown introduced an amendment to include Phillips Lee in a Senate resolution of thanks to the war's heroes, but a radical-dominated House committee objected because of Lee's connection with the Blairs. In February everyone celebrated when Blair Lee's former nurse, Becky, rejoined the household and as a paid cook showed none of her former tensions. Lizzie, meanwhile, renewed her friendship with Mary Lincoln, who was always "kind and confidential." The president offered Montgomery a choice of the ministerships to either Spain or Austria, but the judge was too busy with his lucrative law practice and his antiradical politics. In early April, Minna produced her sixth child. Montgomery wished to name the baby Cary, but Minna had other ideas. After a considerable argument, which Lizzie was sure her brother would lose, the infant became Montgomery, Jr.

On March 4, the Blairs thrilled at Abraham Lincoln's inaugural address: "With malice toward none; with charity for all; with firmness in the right, as God gives us to see the right, let us strive on to finish the work we are in; to bind up the nation's wounds, to care for him who shall have borne the battle, and for his widow, and his orphan—to do all which may achieve and cherish a just, and a lasting peace, among ourselves, and with all nations." It was a pledge for them as well as for the president.

Before the inauguration, Andrew Johnson was sworn in as vice-president. He had been seriously ill, and apparently drank some whiskey as a medicine just before the ceremony. The result was an unscheduled and incoherent address that clearly revealed a state of intoxication and brought a wave of harsh public criticism. Johnson's mental agony and the lingering effects of his illness left him desperately needing help, which the Blairs quickly provided. They put him to bed under a doctor's care in the Lee house and nursed him for several weeks. At the same time, Senator Preston King of New York also joined Lizzie's household. Three weeks later Lizzie reported that Becky's cooking had restored Johnson's appetite, and that the vice-president and her father were having great fun teasing King and Betty for eating so much. Johnson, she wrote, "was at first the most mortified sick *hurt* man" she had ever seen, and she was delighted by his recovery. Soon the house was overflowing with southern refugees and prisoners applying to take the oath of allegiance and asking help from Johnson. Meanwhile, the Blairs had every opportunity to impress Johnson with their view that reconstruction should not be vindictive.[8]

On April 9, 1865, General Robert E. Lee surrendered at Appomattox Courthouse. Throughout the North the cannon boomed, bands played, bonfires roared, and a joyful people

shouted and sang until they were hoarse. The long travail of
death and suffering had ended, slavery was dead, and the Union
was secure. It was the strange fate of Lizzie Blair Lee, however,
that two of the three happiest events of her life should be marred
by complications. The birth of her son had occurred under ideal
circumstances, but her courtship and marriage had been clouded
throughout by her family's objections. Her blissful relief at the
deliverance of her husband, brother, and a host of other relatives
and friends from the terrible war was mixed with a sudden fear
for her own life. One morning in early April, when she woke to
begin her usual busy day of managing the overgrown household
and caring for Andrew Johnson, she discovered a large, heavy
lump in one of her breasts. Her doctor and her mother feared
cancer, and insisted upon immediate surgery.

Lizzie pleaded desperately for a delay until Phil could return
home, but he was busy finishing up the war on the western rivers.
She wrote him, and he replied with firm orders to obey the doctor. Eliza, forever the frontier woman, concealed her own anxiety
and scolded her daughter sharply for worrying Phil about her
"lump of lead" until the issue had been settled. The germ theory
had not yet been developed, and the operation would be performed on a kitchen table at home with unsterilized instruments.
The anesthetic would be a chloroform-soaked cloth in the hands
of whoever might be handy—in this case her seventy-year-old
mother. With reason Lizzie was sick with fear that she might
never see Phil again. After breakfast on April 14, she found that
her mother had prepared the chloroform and other equipment
and that the doctor was on his way. He arrived, however, with an
announcement that another emergency would require a postponement until the next morning. After he departed, Lizzie became
violently ill and spent several miserable hours regretting her long
separations from Phil, but at the end of the day she discovered
what seemed to be a miracle. The lump that had been hard and
heavy in the morning had disappeared. Late that night she sat
alone, describing the day's traumatic events and her newly found
hope in a letter to Phil, when she was suddenly interrupted. A
few minutes later she continued: "Oh horror upon us again—I
was surprised just now by the ringing of the door bell—everyone
sleeping but me. I went to the door. Majr. Robertson . . . an-

nounced the assassination of our President & the attempt upon Mr. Seward." She could write no more. The following evening she finished the letter: "This dark & dreary day for us all has a silver lining to the clouds which overshadow all—for you & for me." The doctor had decided that the change in her condition meant that the lump was a bruise rather than a cancer.[9]

There was no time to celebrate her deliverance, however. She and her father went immediately to the White House, and soon Lizzie was spending most of her time with the bereaved widow. Mary Lincoln had told her doctor that Lizzie "had attracted her sympathies and confidence more than almost any one in the city." On April 20 she was with Mary for twenty-four hours. She went home for a brief sleep, but was summoned to return as soon as Mary awakened. Mrs. Gideon Welles and Lizzie were the only persons Mary wanted. After twelve days Francis P. Blair decided that his weary daughter should go to Silver Spring for a rest. She did not go, however, although she did spend less time on duty because of her own doctor's orders. Her lump had returned, although it was nowhere near its former size. On April 30, Lizzie was with Mary from 1:00 P.M. until past midnight. She had found Mary in a terrible state of hysteria, but had managed to calm her down. After a month, Mary was finally able to travel homeward. She sent Francis P. Blair a rustic chair that a soldier had given the president and she insisted upon giving Lizzie a beautiful dress. She added she would never again wear anything but black. Her husband had loved her in gay colors, but he would never see her again. At the railway station on May 22, Lizzie and Mrs. Welles bade the unhappy widow a tearful farewell. Except for Gideon Welles and another gentleman, they were the only well-wishers present.[10]

The shock, confusion, anger, and grief permeating Washington and the nation after the first assassination of an American president have been chronicled many times. After the installation of Johnson as president, Chief Justice Chase took Francis P. Blair by the hand: "Mr. Blair I hope that from this day there will cease all anger and bitterness between us." Blair answered in kind. For many people, however, the unity generated by a common catastrophe did not last very long. Secretary Stanton and the War Department were already attacking General Sherman for the unauthorized generous terms he had granted the southerners who had surrendered to him in North Carolina, and the Blairs were soon in full cry after Stanton for this injustice to their favorite general. The reconstruction argument had been delayed only temporarily by the bullet of John Wilkes Booth.[11]

First, however, the victory had to be celebrated despite the national tragedy. On May 10 General Frank Blair surprised his family by appearing with six horses, a mass of luggage, and a servant. A cow he had acquired in Rome, Georgia, was coming with his troops. He had been ordered to march his army north, but had left before getting the orders. He also brought Betty a pony and gave his mother two of the riding horses for her carriage. Frank wanted a dinner party for his fellow generals, and soon Lizzie and his mother were making the preparations. On May 23 tens of thousands of happy people lined the Washington streets from the Capitol to the White House to see the Grand Armies of the Republic in their final parade. The White House flag was at full staff for the first time since April 14, the bands played, and the children sang patriotic songs. The cavalry pranced and the infantry marched. As each major unit passed the reviewing stand, its commanding general shook hands with the president and his cabinet. In front of the greatest throng Washington had ever seen, General Sherman ignored the outstretched hand of War Secretary Stanton.

The Blair dinner was a huge success. Twenty generals and numerous politicians, including Governor John Andrew and John Van Buren were present, with General Sherman the lion of the evening. Grant had declined at the last moment. Because of the politicians invited by Frank, there was no room at the table for the ladies. Apo, Betty, Evy Alexander (Apo's sister-in-law, Eveline), and even Eliza were much put out by this, but Lizzie, who did most of the work, was happy to retire early.[12]

On June 1, when most of the family was away at Silver Spring, Lizzie had her operation at the Lee house without forewarning either of her parents. Becky and a friend from the orphan asylum assisted the surgeon, while Evy Alexander administered the chloroform. The lump was removed, and she healed quickly. The doctor predicted that the angry scar would eventually shrink to two inches. On June 13 she attended the ground-breaking ceremonies for the new orphanage building designed for twenty children. She was sore and weak for the rest of the summer, but she was strong enough to become very angry at her brother and Gustavus Fox for keeping Admiral Lee busy in the west for several more weeks.[13]

Francis P. Blair also staged his own private celebration for his Silver Spring neighbors. He argued for a picnic with free use of the house, but Eliza was the commanding officer on matters related to her home. The guests could roam freely among the trees and flowers, and they could dance in the barn or in the woods at Mary's place, but her house has been abused enough. A huge crowd attended, and the genial host must have watched the noisy games, prodigious eating, and general merriment with much satisfaction. Slavery was dead, and the Union had been preserved. His sons and son-in-law had survived the war and earned national fame by genuine achievement. All of his own past wrongs had been righted. He was now ready to forgive the South and try to make its restoration and reconstruction both easy and painless.

Chapter 25

The Quality of Mercy

F RANCIS Preston Blair left Richmond in January 1865 with
a list of tasks to be performed immediately. He had promised
Jefferson Davis that he would plead for the lives of two Confederate officers being held as spies. Davis argued that they were
prisoners of war and urged him to prevent Lincoln from "doing
what he shuddered to think of—taking the lives of innocent men."
Confederate senator Humphrey Marshall had asked Blair to try
to save the town of Warrenton, Virginia, from further ruin. A
third problem was truly bizarre. A Mrs. Burnett was being held
in the North away from her children in Kentucky because she
was supposedly the wife of Henry C. Burnett, a well-known Confederate leader, when in fact she was no relation of his at all.
Burnett himself had made a plea for correction of the mistake.
Meanwhile, a Mrs. Schaaf, who had been Frank's hostess in
Savannah, wished to remain there, and Frank had insisted that
his father arrange it. Also, several other ladies wished to come
North. "General Grant told me," wrote Blair, "he had issued an
order to allow all the women to come to the North, but it seems
this order has been suspended. Grant issued it upon the Roman
policy—concluding if we got the women of the enemy in our
hands the men would sue for peace. For my part, I think that
cruelty to women can never answer a good purpose." And finally,
Blair had promised a Mrs. Stanard, "a good union woman after
the war began but having no means of living out of Virginia and
was compelled to go with the State," to ask the president for permission to "send her a pair of shoes—a box of tea—half dozen
shirts for her son & some coarse cotton to cover the nakedness of
her Negro House Servants—some raisins & dried currants." [1]

Blair's preoccupation with the problems of individual southerners was not a recent development. Since 1861 he and Montgomery, and occasionally Frank, had interceded over and over for southerners and northerners alike who had come to grief because of the war. If, as some historians have suggested, Lincoln kept the vengeful and ill-tempered Stanton around to offset his own excessively generous nature toward individuals asking for mercy, the Blairs were the self-appointed antidote to Stanton. Northern soldiers and families who felt mistreated, southerners with relatives in northern prisons, and northerners and southerners alike complaining of unjust property losses all found open ears at Silver Spring and at the Blair–Lee houses on Pennsylvania Avenue.

From Burlington, Iowa, in January 1862, Augustus Caesar Dodge pleaded to Eliza Blair the case of his lifelong friend George W. Jones, "now a prisoner at Fort Lafayette." He was sure that as a wife and mother Eliza would appreciate the plight of Mrs. Jones. In the same month Montgomery Blair complained angrily to Stanton about the treatment of a Dr. Peterson of the Missouri Volunteers, who had been removed because he was a "homeopathic physician." To Montgomery, the "holy zeal" of Peterson's opponents was stimulated by their worldly interests and they were comparable to "priests burning Protestants. . . . If the 6th Missouri Regiment find Dr. Peterson a curing Dr. & prefer to keep him I should be sorry that you would allow the faculty to crucify him." In July 1862 General A. P. Crittenden, son of the elder Blair's old friend the senator, asked Blair to get him a leave to be used in assisting his mother. John Rives's son Wright, meanwhile, after a professional lifetime in the army was denied service because of varicose veins, and he asked the Blairs to get him a place in the inspector general's office without letting his father hear about it. Rives eventually became a secretary to President Grant. Dr. A. Krumsick had a more serious problem. He had been captured by the Texas Rangers and imprisoned at Little Rock for two months. Released because of illness, he had gone home on twenty days' leave before being ordered to rejoin his regiment. He had left home in time, but the ship ran aground and made him a few days late. He finally resumed his duties only to be dismissed from the army for having been AWOL. Several officers enclosed a letter praising his brave, efficient battlefield service, and the Blairs immediately presented the case to Lincoln. More than once in cabinet meetings, Montgomery Blair angrily condemned the practice of dismissing officers without trial, and this was almost the only principle upon which he and Gideon Welles disagreed.[2]

In August 1864 Attorney Charles Gwinn pleaded to the Blairs that his client, William H. Rodgers, who had been sentenced to death as a spy by a military commission in Baltimore, was innocent. Rodgers, wrote Gwinn, had carried letters from Confederate areas, but they were personal letters containing no important information, and Montgomery Blair was the young man's last hope. Twenty-four hours before the scheduled execution, Lincoln commuted the death sentences of Rodgers and three others to confinement at hard labor during the war.[3]

Less dramatic was the request of General Alfred Pleasanton and his wife that the elder Blair get their underage son dismissed from the army. The boy had enlisted without their knowledge or consent. Blair did get young Pleasanton dismissed, for which his parents were very grateful. The Blairs failed, however, to get a certain Cadet Todd of Kentucky restored after his dismissal from West Point. The commandant appreciated their concern, but after three reviews decided that he could not comply with their request without gross favoritism. Another West Point case that continued long after the war pitted the Blairs furiously against Stanton. Cadet Samuel Black was dismissed for pouring Hartshorn liniment down the nose of a sleeping new cadet. His father, however, was a colonel who had been killed in the war. Secretary Stanton ordered the court-martial dissolved, but the presiding officer refused and kept the trial in session until Black was dismissed. As a result the academy superintendent and the commandant of cadets were removed from the academy, and the judge advocate of the court was dismissed from the army. Cadet Black, meanwhile, was placed in coventry by his classmates, and he soon resigned to receive an infantry commission that enabled him to outrank those who had chased him off. For months the Blairs worked to get justice for the officers involved.[4]

Letters of entreaty about one problem or another arrived almost daily. Ben Gratz reported that in St. Louis the wife of Dr.

Moses Gratz was terribly distressed because her husband had been arrested and sent South. Moses, insisted Gratz, had been careful in conversation and had had no southern associations. Many Union people in St. Louis would testify for him; so why couldn't Lincoln pardon him? Almost as an afterthought Gratz added that his own factory had been burnt after being taken by the United States quartermaster and filled with hay and corn for the use of the Union army. The army had set the loss at $5,200, but nobody seemed to have the money for a reimbursement. Could Blair look into it? Lizzie Whiting Critcher wrote that her eldest son had been killed and her husband captured. She was lonely and wretched, and could Blair possibly get her husband paroled or exchanged? If not, could he get her a pass to visit her parents? Equally sad for Blair was the fate of Alice Marie Waring. By April 1864 she and her husband had lost everything and wished only to take the oath of loyalty to the Union and return to Maryland. Their son had died for the Confederacy, and Mrs. Waring, who had cancer, wanted to die at home. In response to Francis P. Blair's plea for mercy, Lincoln allowed them to return and ordered that their daughter also be allowed to live in Maryland "if she behaves herself from this time forward." A few months later Lincoln also restored the Warings' property.[5]

W. V. Bovic, later state's attorney for Maryland, was a frequent go-between. In March 1864 he asked the Blairs to help F. L. Kidwell, "arrested for selling citizens' clothing to alleged deserters." Kidwell, a Rockville merchant, had sold the clothes with no knowledge that the purchasers were deserters. Bovic also begged the elder Blair to seek the release of a Colonel Leonard, who had spent several months in prison because a young Confederate soldier on parole awaiting exchange had been found in his home. The boy was a relation of Leonard's wife, and Leonard was entirely innocent of wrongdoing. Bovic added that "your son, the Postmaster General, has been unceasing in his efforts to alleviate the hardships thrown upon our people by the war, and will be gratefully remembered by them." Another Bovic concern was a "poor, deranged, harmless man" who had been jailed because Early's invading rebels had made him cut down telegraph poles. Also, the son of their mutual friend, B. W. Carter, was dying at

Camp Chase, Ohio. The parents would try to persuade him to take the oath of allegiance, and would Blair please help get him released.[6]

In February 1865 Massachusetts governor John Andrew sent a letter from the Quaker minister Mrs. Elizabeth Comstock asking Francis P. Blair to seek pardons for several people previously imprisoned in Maryland for aiding slaves to escape. "Our noble governor," wrote Mrs. Comstock, "tells me thou art a whole-souled, kind-hearted man, & that thou hast some power or influence with the rulers of Maryland, & that an appeal to suffering humanity will not be made to thee in vain." The fifteen prisoners were "guilty only of following the Golden Rule," and one was an intelligent black man sentenced to ten years for helping his wife to escape. The governor had already pardoned two of them, and Mrs. Comstock hoped that since slavery was now dead in Maryland, Blair could persuade him to show mercy to the others. Soon afterward the governor pardoned all but one of the offenders, and the remaining prisoner was released during the following year.[7]

Mary F. Jackson of Connecticut wrote Blair that her only brother was in prison at Camp Chase. Would Blair please ask Lincoln to parole him and let him rejoin his mother in Philadelphia. He was only a Confederate private, and would not violate his parole: "A sister with tears pleads for an only brother, that you will forget justice and remember mercy . . . prayers of the fond widowed mother and the devoted sister will ascend to the throne of grace, that the choicest blessings both temporal & spiritual that heaven can bestow, may be yours." Pleading for a relative, Apo Blair's sister-in-law Mary Alexander assured Blair that "I would not dare trouble you with my complaints if I did not know how good and kind you are to every body that needs help." [8]

One severe direct confrontation between the Blairs and Stanton involved the case of Frank and Aaron Wooley, two Kentucky boys in their early teens who were attending a Maryland boarding school when the Civil War began. The students were required to take an oath of allegiance to the Union, but the Wooleys, apparently influenced by an older boy, refused. The older recalcitrant was released immediately, but the Wooleys were sent to Fort Delaware prison, where they remained for five months. Both almost died from dysentery, and one lost an ear. Appeals by their distraught mother to Stanton, Lincoln, and Judge Advocate Joseph Holt failed until the Blairs became involved. Then Montgomery secured their release under the promise that they would not return home. The Wooley family was convinced that Holt was directly responsible. According to the boys' older brother, Robert Wooley, Holt had come to Lexington thirty years earlier "dressed in red linsey, without a dollar in his pocket or a correct English sentence in his head." Robert Wickliffe, the grandfather of the young prisoners, had taken Holt into his home and office for many years, where he "acquired as much polish and knowledge as his vulgar person and obscure brain would receive." Holt had left the residence with fulsome expressions of gratitude, and after accumulating a fortune through miserliness had returned to marry Wickliffe's niece. Holt, insisted Robert Wooley, had eloquently taught him that Calhoun was America's only real political philosopher, "that South Carolina was the true school of political faith, that the States were sovereign and the Federal Government subordinate and dissoluble." In short, wrote Wooley, Holt had been responsible for his own decision to fight for the Confederacy. When, however, the family had begged him to help the imprisoned children, Holt had replied that he would not help them if he could and that "if they had what they deserved they would be hanged." According to Robert Wooley, Holt had "the passions of a teaser and the capacity of a eunuch. . . . a lady in Washington . . . can declare that the day after the death of his wife, a death hastened by cruel neglect, and while her body lay still unburied, he begged favors of that lady, which, if she had granted, he had not the means to enjoy." Clearly the Wickliffe children and the interloper in the family bosom had not appreciated each other. Whatever the prejudice in Robert Wooley's view of Holt, the judge advocate general had in fact supported southern extremism until his appointment to the cabinet of James Buchanan in 1860, and the Blairs could never abide those whose principles appeared to change with the winds of fortune.[9]

Another old friend of the Blairs, Liczenko Brown Ewell, also brought them into conflict with Stanton. Her sons had fought for the Confederacy, and she had taken for a second husband the

doughty Confederate general Richard C. Ewell. Even though
he had to be strapped to his horse after the earlier loss of a leg
in battle, Ewell performed heroically until the end of the war.
In March 1865 Blair persuaded Lincoln to grant Mrs. Ewell
the benefit of his amnesty proclamation. Having taken the oath
of allegiance to the Union in St. Louis, she returned home to
Nashville, Tennessee. Only a week after Lincoln's assassination,
however, Stanton ordered General George Thomas at Nashville
to arrest her and return her to St. Louis. Thomas answered that
she was conducting herself as a loyal citizen, and asked if she
could return to St. Louis without military surveillance. The angry
Stanton replied that Thomas should execute the order "without
regard to her representations and without delay." General Ewell,
meanwhile, had been captured, but was soon released. After several
months the Blairs were finally able to get the Ewells pardoned
and have their Tennessee property restored to them. At one point
the elder Blair took Liczenko to see President Johnson, who
berated her for deserting her family and country to "run after
a bad-tempered cripple." Having been thoroughly briefed by
Blair, she restrained her anger over these insults and maintained
a penitent attitude. The chance to emulate the forgiving spirit
of Christ was always an irresistible temptation for Johnson.[10]

Most prominent among those helped by the Blair family
were Varina Howell Davis and her husband, the erstwhile president of the Confederacy. Mrs. Davis was a longtime personal
friend of the Blairs and Lees despite their political differences.
In May and June 1865 she composed a bitter thirty-eight-page
letter to Montgomery. She described her family's exciting efforts
to escape arrest and Davis's capture by Union troops. She complained that they "were treated with less consideration than I
have seen my Knightly Husband show to the beggars who came
to our door for alms." She had heard that Davis was being kept
manacled and was being fed nothing but army rations. She was
desperate for news of him and pleaded for Blair to get permission for her to be with him. Montgomery and his father did their
best, but Johnson's personal relations with Davis had been unfriendly, and he felt little sympathy for the Confederate ex-
president. Francis P. Blair agreed with Johnson that Davis
should have a civil trial, but pointed out that Johnson's "tender-

ness to his wife . . . will touch the finer chords in the hearts of Southerners to reconcile them to the course taken to him and will give you a strong hold on the high traits in their character." For the next two years the Blairs, along with such disparate types as Horace Greeley and Thaddeus Stevens, worked successfully for better treatment and the ultimate release of Davis, but Johnson resisted at every step. The Blairs, however, were able to help Jefferson Howell, Varina's twenty-year-old brother, much sooner. Hearing that the young soldier was destitute and willing to take the oath, Montgomery Blair secured his release from prison and loaned him $50 for the journey home.[11]

The list of beneficiaries could be continued almost indefinitely. Andrew Johnson's reconstruction plan allowed proscribed southern leaders to be pardoned by the president if they assumed a penitent attitude. The Blairs immediately became a transmission belt for dozens of pardon requests each week. Among those helped were the former radical southern editor James D. B. Debow and former Supreme Court justice Peter Daniel. "In . . . the President's House on Wednesday last," wrote N. W. Payne, "no opportunity was afforded me of expressing my grateful acknowledgements, for your kindness in procuring my pardon and restoration." William Preston Johnston, son of the Confederate general Albert Sidney Johnston and aide to Jefferson Davis, expressed his deep gratitude to Blair for his release from "the suffering of solitary confinement at Fort Delaware." Johnston would later serve as president of both Louisiana State University and Tulane.[12]

All of this reflected the wartime enmities between the Blairs and the radicals as well as the Blairs' natural sympathies for their southern relatives and friends once the victory had been won. As Frank Blair asked in a speech probably written by his father,

> What civilized nation on earth would hesitate an instant . . . to incorporate with themselves the brave and heroic people of the South, whose fortitude and endurance in a mistaken cause, challenges the admiration of the world? Would France or England, or any other civilized power, hesitate to give to such men the full and equal rights accorded to all other citizens? Would not those nations be most happy to claim as their own, such men as Lee and Johnson, and a

host of others, and to confer upon these living heroes the reward which genius and courage have always commanded? Would they fail to honor and cherish as a part of their own glory, the memory of that illustrious throng of the dead led by Stonewall Jackson?[13]

Such forgiving sentiments were noble enough, and might have become widespread very quickly but for one major barrier—the problem of creating a new social and political system for a South in which almost 4 million former slaves were now free. Like most victors after most wars, the northern people appeared willing to forgive and forget. Most northerners accepted the doctrine of white supremacy and were not prepared to demand a color-blind equality either in the South or in their own states. The wartime memories, however, were still fresh enough to support immediate objections to white southern violence and economic persecution of relatively helpless former slaves. A terrible price had been paid for the end of slavery, and most northerners were determined to have full value for their sacrifices. Any southern action that even slightly resembled a move back toward slavery would be resisted.

An air of submissiveness and a reasonable acceptance of moderate northern efforts to protect the blacks from physical harm and legal injustice would probably have saved the South from any serious postwar domination at all. This kind of wisdom as an aftermath to their bitter defeat would have required an ultra-superior character on the part of the South quite out of step with the entire history of the human race.

Ironically, with all of their sympathies for the defeated Southerners, the Blairs remained strangely immune to concern for the agonizing problems of the newly freed slaves. They were always ready to defend or help their own servants, or any other blacks they happened to know personally, but the black population in the mass remained an abstraction to be considered only in broad general terms. Every proposed restriction on southern whites affected their own individual relatives and friends, but outside their own small circle of slaves the blacks were an impersonal quantity to whom they could feel no ties of kinship or friendship. The Blairs knew the racial fears and resentments of the white South, and they had always argued that if the blacks could not be transplanted elsewhere, the ultimate result would be either their extinction like the Indians or mass interbreeding to form an inferior mulatto caste. When Francis P. Blair finally recognized that neither of these utterly contradictory fears would materialize, he concluded with considerable realism that the ruling white classes would either use black votes to suppress the interests of the poorer whites or would play upon the racial antipathies of the poorer whites to achieve the same result. He and his sons hoped to see the postwar South dominated by the formerly non-slaveholding small farmers, and they saw every effort to promote racial equality as a threat to this goal.

Also, as Jefferson and Jackson Democrats the Blairs genuinely feared the expansion of federal power that national protection for black civil rights would bring. They still saw the ghost of Nicholas Biddle lurking behind the new financial and industrial leaders created by the war, and they were certain that enhanced federal power would eventually be used for their nefarious purposes. Except for Charles Sumner, whom they liked and respected, they thoroughly distrusted the motives of the radicals. In their eyes, the wartime radical opposition to Lincoln had threatened the Union victory itself, and the lines of combat between themselves and this group had already been irreversibly drawn. They saw the reconstruction struggle as a renewal of their earlier battle to preserve a purer, simpler America uncontaminated by the control of financial or industrial monopolies, and they considered the former slaves to be merely a pawn in this contest. In a sense, the blacks had become allies of the enemies they had been fighting for decades.

In the context of the long-overdue drive for racial equality in the late twentieth century, the Blairs' stand on reconstruction appears utterly inconsistent with the democratic principles of natural rights they had spent their lives preaching and trying to practice. For them, however, the civil rights issue was often obscured by other vital questions. The evidence upon which they acted, after all, would mislead several generations of historians into grossly exaggerating the reconstruction hardships imposed upon the white South and thoroughly misrepresenting the role of American business leadership in the reconstruction process. More recent scholars have reexamined and rebalanced the evidence to produce a different story.[14] In 1865, however, no one really knew what the reconstruction process would bring. The Blairs, fearing the worst for both the white South and the nation, acted accordingly. And, even though often wrong by modern democratic standards, they performed their usual political service by refusing to obfuscate the issues and trying to give the voting public a clear view of the alternatives.

Chapter 26

Reconstruction

AS Abraham Lincoln lay dead on the sad, gray morning of April 15, 1865, a handful of grim-faced men gathered to watch Andrew Johnson place his hand on the Bible and swear to uphold the Constitution of the United States. All of them were badly shaken, and one was also burning with anger. Among those present were Francis P. and Montgomery Blair—and Edwin M. Stanton, who had not invited them, did not appreciate their presence.

A few hours later, the abolitionist congressman George Julian attended a radical caucus where "hostility towards Lincoln's policy of conciliation and contempt for his weakness were undisguised." Julian reported a "universal feeling among radical men here . . . that his death is a god-send." Johnson, after all, had made numerous statements of angry enmity toward his former colleagues. On the following day, the Committee on the Conduct of the War met with Johnson and came away happy. The new president had avowed that "robbery is a crime; murder is a crime; *treason* is a crime, and *crime* must be punished. The law provides for it and the courts are open. Treason must be made infamous and traitors impoverished." [1]

Numerous meetings between president and radical leaders followed. Benjamin F. Wade advised Johnson that ten or twelve, or perhaps thirteen—"a baker's dozen"—of the worst rebels should be exiled or hanged. Johnson replied that more men should be executed, but Wade warned that this might cause a backlash in northern public opinion. At Johnson's request, General Benjamin F. Butler drew up a plan for the punishment of Confederate leaders. Soon Charles Sumner and other radicals had convinced themselves that the president would support an effort to give the liberated slaves the vote.

In any contest for the mind and heart of Andrew Johnson, however, the Blairs and other conservative advisors had every possible advantage. The president was emotionally identified by early life and later political experiences with the smaller farmers and craftsmen who of all people in the South feared black equality the most. Like the Blairs, he worshipped at the shrine of Andrew Jackson, whose reverence for the Union had been equaled only by his conviction that the federal government was bound by the Constitution to leave most political, economic, and social decisions in the hands of state and local governments. The war had already accomplished great triumphs for the economic philosophy of Hamilton, Clay, and Webster, but Andrew Johnson still hoped that the new world of national banks, federal currency, high tariffs, and business subsidies could again be banished. When the Blairs pointed out that black suffrage would mean a permanent victory for all of these old enemies and evils, they were speaking to one already converted. The Constitution of the founding fathers had left all questions of suffrage, as well as the control and punishment of violent crimes, to state and local governments, and Johnson would preserve this sacred document with his life if necessary. He might have reached the same conclusions without the Blairs, but their daily verbal and written advice coupled with his gratitude for their compassionate aid after his inauguration must have reinforced his convictions. Also, when Johnson began to relent toward the former Confederates, both Francis P. and Montgomery Blair were constantly bringing letters from politicians throughout the hinterland assuring them that Johnson's policies of mercy and forgiveness had universal support.

Predictably, Francis P. Blair sent Johnson several long letters offering the wisdom of one "associated with the leading men who have shaped the course of the liberal party during the last half century." In Blair's view the president faced three challenges: saving the white race from several dire possibilities that could result from the imposition of black equality; preserving the constitutional rights of the states as originally defined by the founding fathers; and preventing the potentates of Europe, beginning with France in Mexico, from planting a "monarchy in the midst of our continent to hold the key to the Isthmus."

On the subject of race, Blair differed little from most of his contemporaries, and he and his sons usually cited Thomas Jefferson as the source of their inspiration. The man who had written that "all men are created equal" had also considered blacks inferior, and this helped relieve the Blairs from any feelings of inconsistency. Blair was quite confused. He imagined various tragic possibilities, but had difficulty deciding which was most likely to happen. A new San Domingo might occur, in which the whites would destroy the blacks just as they had exterminated the Indians whenever the two races came into contact. More likely, however, a mass interbreeding or amalgamation might create a new mulatto laboring class that would be forever kept in a state of inferiority by its color and would thereby deny laborers everywhere their chance for equality with the professional and managerial classes. At best, if suffrage became universal, the blacks would turn to the former master class for support and guidance at the polls, and this would keep the aristocracy in control over the southern white yeomanry he and Johnson wished to see triumph. Or the former masters might play upon the exacerbated racial fears and antipathies of the poorer whites to keep themselves in power. And yet, with the blacks voting and the whites disfranchised, the result would probably be the strengthening of northern radical republicans seeking power only for the benefit of their nefarious economic schemes. To Blair the best chance for avoiding any or all of these possible calamities was to allow the southern whites themselves to make the decisions, and in 1865–1866, before the Fourteenth and Fifteenth amendments, he could argue quite correctly that this was the true constitutional position.[2]

Whether or not Blair consciously thought in such terms, he and his sons had already been cast in the role of racial conservatives by the political events of the war. By unhorsing the radical hero, Frémont; by supporting Lincoln's gradual approach to emancipation; and by defending Lincoln's softer approach to reconstruction, they had developed a strong mutual enmity with most of the radicals. For many reasons unconnected with racial attitudes, the radicals were their enemies, and political weapons

must be found to continue the struggle. Jeffersonian and Jacksonian economic principles were dead issues in 1865, but the invincible racial prejudices of most Americans both north and south
were still very potent. And finally, like Johnson, the Blairs had
always been bound to the South by strong ties of kinship and
friendship, and they enjoyed dispensing mercy and basking in
the restored affection of the former Confederates. When they
and Andrew Johnson cited the forgiving spirit of Christ as their
example, they were entirely sincere. The Blairs, being human,
enjoyed reading in a letter to Montgomery from John F. Lee that
"people here who used to denounce you on every fit occasion, as a
base abolitionist, and a d——d rascal generally, now speak of you,
earnestly, as a 'great man'—I added and 'a good'—and that too
was emphatically accepted." [3]

Francis P. Blair and Andrew Johnson feared with reason that
equal rights for the blacks would require a vast increase in federal
power that would inevitably give unfair advantages to certain segments of American finance, commerce, and industry. Ironically
enough, however, the northern economic groups that could be expected to profit most from the continuation and expansion of the
wartime banking, currency, debt, and tariff policies were generally
conservative on the subject of reconstruction. As various recent
historians have shown,[4] they were often divided on the specific
economic policies at stake, and they were rarely zealots in the
cause of racial equality. Their antebellum business relationships
with the southern planters had been both pleasant and profitable,
and they were anxious to see their erstwhile Confederate enemies
restored to full and harmonious productivity as soon as possible.
Some may have even dreamed of collecting part of the estimated
$320 million in southern debts wiped out by the war. As a senator,
William Henry Seward had spoken most often for New York and
northeastern business and banking interests. As secretary of state
he was no more radical on the subject of reconstruction than the
Blairs, and he remained totally loyal to Andrew Johnson throughout. Perhaps some of America's business leaders in 1865 felt a
deeply buried instinctive suspicion that a federal government
strong enough to be an effective engine of paternalism might
someday become an agent of regulation and control in the hands

of their opponents. If any politicians or businessmen consciously looked this far into the future, however, they remained silent.

Whatever the influences, Johnson soon delighted the Blairs with his reconstruction policies. He appointed provisional state governors empowered to hold elections to choose constitutional conventions. These in turn could write new constitutions, after which new elections would select new state governments and members for Congress. When a new state government had repudiated secession, accepted the Thirteenth Amendment abolishing slavery, and disavowed the Confederate war debts, that state could rejoin the Union. With certain exceptions, anyone taking an oath of allegiance could participate in the process. Individuals who had joined the Confederacy after serving the Union in a capacity requiring an oath of office were proscribed, as were persons worth $20,000 or more. Those restricted, however, could be restored to full citizenship by special dispensation from the president. A brief expression of humility in a letter or interview was usually enough to secure the presidential pardon, and the Blairs were active agents in winning forgiveness for a variety of former Confederates. Under these provisions, every state but Texas was functioning by December 1865, and when Congress convened for the 1865–1866 session, the representatives and senators from ten former Confederate states were lined up to take the oath of office.

Many northern moderates as well as radicals were upset by the ease of this process, because the South appeared to have regained the upper hand it had enjoyed before secession. No southern state had granted the vote to any freedmen. Every southern state had enacted "black codes" to control the freedmen, and although these varied in their degree of restriction and discrimination, all clearly made the former slaves second-class citizens if citizens at all. In Mississippi no black could own or rent land. In South Carolina no black could be anything but a farm laborer without paying heavy licensing fees. All of the former Confederate states had severe vagrancy laws under which unemployed blacks could be put to work to pay off exorbitant fines. Blacks could not testify in court against whites or sit on juries, and punishments were consistently unequal and occasionally ludicrous. South Carolina prescribed the death penalty for any black male having sexual relations with a white woman "while impersonating her husband." Freedmen's Bureau officers managed to negate much of this legislation, but the impact on the North was not lessened by their efforts.

Furthermore, the South was showing no signs of repentance. South Carolina refused to invalidate its Confederate state debt, and the Mississippi legislature refused to ratify the Thirteenth Amendment. Numerous well-known Confederate leaders, some pardoned by Johnson and some not yet whitewashed by anyone, were quickly elected to state and federal office. Mississippi chose as governor the unpardoned General Benjamin C. Humphreys over a Johnson-supported rival, after which Johnson pardoned Humphreys to keep the situation legal. Many northerners felt that Alexander H. Stephens, the vice-president of the Confederacy, should be in prison with his colleague Jefferson Davis. Instead, Stephens was back in Washington as a newly elected senator from Georgia.

Perhaps most important was the widespread and senseless violence against the freedmen. Even northerners concerned only with keeping blacks from moving into their own areas could become upset over the constant reports of whippings, beatings, mutilations, and murders filling the northern press. An important primary witness was Major General Carl Schurz, who had been sent as an observer to the South by President Johnson. Schurz reported both in the press and to the Congress that planters were keeping their former slaves on plantations by brute force, that armed bands of whites were patrolling the countryside to drive wandering freedmen back to former homes, and that dead and mutilated bodies were being found on and near the highways. Schurz added that he had personally examined some of the victims. Various historians would later condemn Schurz for using an official position to earn money selling reports to newspapers, but no one ever seriously denied the truth of his statements. Until recently, historians have usually dealt with the problem of reconstruction-era violence in terms of whether the numbers were exaggerated, whether the southern people as a whole should be held responsible, and whether the radicals unfairly used the issue as an excuse rather than a valid reason for their reconstruction policies. Not until the civil rights movement of the mid-twentieth century would the history-writing profession treat the physical suffering and deaths of a great many innocent black Americans as a vital historical fact in itself rather than as merely a phenomenon important only in its relationship to more significant matters. Small wonder that Francis P. Blair and Andrew Johnson, among a great many others, would see the violence in the same light.

In December 1865 the American Congress was not dominated by radicals. It included a great many moderates, however, who would support radical policies if they were the only alternatives to southern actions that made the sacrifices of the war seem wasted. When Thaddeus Stevens and others insisted that the newly elected southern congressmen and senators should not be seated until the Congress rather than the president should judge their states qualified for restoration, they had little trouble getting the necessary support from their Republican colleagues. A Joint Committee of fifteen was established to investigate and recommend. For many years historians incorrectly described this committee as radical. The radical members were in fact a distinct minority, and the moderates and conservatives like Lyman Trumbull of Illinois, William Pitt Fessenden of Maine, James Grimes of Iowa, John Bingham of New York, and Reverdy Johnson of Maryland were much better known than radicals like Thaddeus Stevens, George Boutwell, and Jacob Howard.

In December and January, Trumbull and his colleagues worked out two measures designed to correct the black codes and reassure the northern public that the South really could not restore slavery. The first measure would renew the Freedmen's Bureau indefinitely beyond its scheduled expiration one year after the war. The Bureau had done a necessary and effective job in caring for refugees both black and white, and its continuation was clearly needed. The new act, however, provided that all cases of racial discrimination against ordinary civil rights should be tried by military courts, who could impose fines or imprisonment or both. This jurisdiction, however, was to expire in each state upon its restoration to statehood.

Trumbull's other effort was a civil rights bill designed to confer citizenship upon "all persons born in the United States and not subject to any foreign power, excluding Indians not taxed." All such citizens would have an equal right "to make and enforce contracts; to sue, be parties, and give evidence; to inherit, purchase, lease, sell, hold, and convey real and personal property; and to full and equal protection of all laws and proceedings for the security of person and property as is enjoyed by white citizens," and should be "subject to like punishment, pains, and penalties, and to none other, any law, statute, ordinance, regulation, or custom to the contrary notwithstanding." All offenses under the act were to be tried by United States district courts.

Neither bill gave the freedmen the vote or the right to hold office, and neither suggested any change in the new southern governments beyond the obvious reversal of the black codes. To the Blairs and other Johnson advisors, however, they were unconstitutional efforts to impose racial equality upon the South.

The Blairs had expected an attack upon Johnson's policies, and had already launched their defense. As early as June 7, 1865, Generals Grant, Logan, and Frank Blair had endorsed Johnson's policies before a huge crowd at Cooper Institute in New York, and Frank had eloquently proclaimed that Johnson's program was identical to that of Lincoln. Then Frank had repeated the speech in St. Louis before an enthusiastic crowd gathered in welcome. On July 12, 1865, Montgomery Blair denounced both Seward and Stanton in a speech at Hagerstown, Maryland. His main thrust was a sharp attack upon American spinelessness in the face of the French threat in Mexico, but he also pictured the two secretaries as radical sympathizers who should be eliminated from the administration. On August 26, Montgomery added Thaddeus Stevens to his list. In a widely published speech entitled "The Rebellion—Where the Guilt Lies," Montgomery attacked the Buchanan administration, including Stanton, for not protecting southern unionists and reinforcing Fort Sumter, and denounced Seward's efforts to surrender Fort Sumter. He then described Stevens as a vindictive Marat working for a revolution with Stanton, "who wants a guillotine." The southern masses, argued Montgomery, had not been hostile to the United States and should not be disfranchised. In October, November, and December 1865, Montgomery Blair returned to New York State for speeches at Cooper Institute, Rochester, Auburn, and Brooklyn.[5]

In January 1865, meanwhile, a Missouri convention had written a new state constitution that denied the vote to anyone who had engaged in "armed hostility to the United States . . . or to the Government of this State," or had ever given "aid, comfort, countenance, or support to persons engaged in any such hostility." A test oath denying such activity was required of all voters; and clergymen, lawyers, and teachers could not follow their profession without taking the oath. An eminent unionist, Samuel T. Glover, was fined $500 for practicing law without taking the oath, and a Catholic priest, Father Cummings, went to jail rather than pay a $50 fine for not taking the oath before preaching. Some thirty-six ministers were arrested for the same offense. On November 7, 1865, Frank Blair tried to vote and refused to take the oath on the ground that he had opposed the Missouri government when it was headed by the Confederate sympathizer Claiborne Jackson. His vote was refused, and he immediately sued the election judges for $10,000. The case ultimately reached the Supreme Court, where Chief Justice Chase and the Court ruled that the state could control its elections and that Claiborne Jackson had not been the legitimate authority when Frank had opposed him.

Thus, even though Trumbull's bills were essentially a moderate effort to avoid a split between Congress and the president, the Blairs saw them as just another tactic in a battle that had begun long before the death of Lincoln. The Freedmen's Bureau Bill passed first, and Johnson promptly vetoed it. The opinion that the Blairs had written the veto was widespread, although Seward and General Sherman, among others, had also recommended it. Johnson denounced the bill as unnecessary, expensive, and unconstitutional. Civilian judges, he insisted, would interpret the law according to fixed rules of law and evidence, while bureau officers might well be ignorant of the "principles that underlie the just administration of the law." The Constitution had never contemplated a "system for the support of indigent persons in the United States," and any legislation not based upon expecting the freedmen to look after themselves would have "a tendency injurious alike to their character and their prospects." It would "keep the mind of the freedmen in a state of uncertain expectation and restlessness," and it would be "a source of constant and vague apprehension" for the whites. And finally, any laws concerning the southern states passed without their representatives in Congress "to explain their condition, reply to accusations, and assist by their local knowledge" were unconstitutional. Whereas each member of Congress represented a district or state, said Johnson, the president was elected to serve everyone; thus it was his duty to represent the southern states. After another angry debate, the vote to override the veto carried in the House, but failed by a small margin in the Senate.

Trumbull and others still hoped the president might heal the breach by signing the civil rights bill, which passed a month later. By then, however, the president and his advisors were even more deeply entrenched in their role of embattled defenders of the Constitution. The radicals contributed to this by spreading vicious rumors charging Johnson with complicity in the murder of Lincoln, with running a harem in the White House, and with habitual drunkenness. Thaddeus Stevens suggested that Charles I of England had lost his head for fewer usurpations of power than Johnson had committed.

The personal attacks upon Johnson further strengthened the Blairs' conviction that the radicals were hypocrites, and defending presidents under fire had given Francis P. Blair's long life most of its brightest moments. In a long letter stressing every racial fear the South had ever had, he urged Johnson to veto the Civil Rights Act. Surely, he wrote, southern state and local governments should not be denied the right to discriminate between the races in their applications of the laws.[6]

On March 27, 1866, Andrew Johnson vetoed the Civil Rights Act because it would make whites and blacks equal by imposing federal laws where it had "frequently been thought expedient to discriminate between the two races"; the enforcement of such a law would require a permanent military force; and it would be an "assumption of power by the General Government which must sap and destroy our federative system of limited powers and break down the barriers which preserve the rights of the States."

The House overrode the veto easily. The Senate did so by

a margin of one vote. In July, a new version of the Freedmen's Bureau Bill that limited the extension to two years was also passed over the presidential veto. Ultimately, in 1883, the United States Supreme Court would declare the Civil Rights Act unconstitutional.

Ironically enough, the federal assumption of responsibility for southern reconstruction might have stopped in early 1866 if Johnson had signed the Freedmen's Bureau and Civil Rights bills. In the congressional election year of 1866, even the radicals were afraid to go before the northern public with an open demand for black suffrage. In 1865 three northern states—Connecticut, Wisconsin, and Minnesota—held popular referenda in which amendments extending the vote equally to both races were soundly defeated. During the summer and fall of 1865 five northern-state republican conventions passed resolutions for equal suffrage. Five, including those in New Jersey, New York, Pennsylvania, Ohio, and Wisconsin, refused to do so. Northern consciences demanded at least some efforts to protect the freedmen, but the Freedmen's Bureau and Civil Rights acts might well have filled this need in the northern mind if Johnson had not vetoed them and thereby guaranteed a continuation of the struggle between himself and the radicals. Until the vetoes, most moderate members of Congress were on his side, but his unwillingness to bend at all drove them into the radical camp.[7]

Meanwhile, the Congress, aware that the Civil Rights Act lacked constitutional authority, developed and passed a new Fourteenth Amendment. Some historians would argue later that the amendment was cleverly designed as a shield for big business. The amendment proscribed any abridgement of a citizen's rights by a state, and in the 1880s and 1890s skilled lawyers would argue that corporations were citizens protected by the amendment from state regulation. Actually, a statement by Senator Roscoe Conkling while arguing a case in 1882 has been the only evidence that the framers of the amendment had this purpose in mind, but two generations of antibusiness historians accepted it without question. Perhaps significantly, the Blairs strongly opposed the amendment, but showed no suspicion that it had any purposes other than those stated by the Joint Committee that developed it. They and other opponents mustered every available argu-

ment against it, and it could not have been promoted in Conkling's terms without their knowledge.

While developing the amendment, the Joint Committee
took 800 pages of testimony, most of it related to southern white
threats and violence against former slaves and white unionists.
Whippings, maimings, and murders by the score were described
and documented. Because most of the witnesses were Union army
officers and southern unionists who felt threatened, the committee
has often been accused of trying to build a case for the amendment
rather than seeking the truth. According to this argument, the
undenied and undeniable stories painted a false picture of the
southern situation because they were exceptions to the racial harmony prevalent in most areas. The view that no freedmen should
have been given federal protection because the lives of only a
minority were being threatened would achieve a strange popularity among both northern and southern historians.

Ultimately the Congress produced an amendment with a
meaningless provision on voting and a promise of legal protection that most radicals considered quite inadequate. Almost a
century later, the Fourteenth Amendment, liberally interpreted
by the Supreme Court, would become the constitutional basis
for a second and far more effective reconstruction, but in 1866
it was still a chance for the southern states to avoid any further
northern controls. It decreed that all persons born or naturalized
in the United States were citizens of the United States and that
no state could make or enforce any law to abridge their "privileges or immunities," or "deprive any person of life, liberty, or
property, without due process of law; nor deny to any person
within its jurisdiction the equal protection of the laws." The
enforcement of this provision would depend upon the judgment
of the courts in defining possible infractions, and its limitation
to actions committed by state governments left most radicals
bitterly disappointed. Under another section, if the right to vote
were denied to male citizens of twenty-one years "except for par-
ticipation in rebellion or other crime," the basis of congressional
representation would be reduced proportionately. The enforcement of this provision would be impossible, and it has never
served any purpose. The third section declared that no person
could hold any federal or state office who, "having previously

taken an oath to support the Constitution of the United States shall have engaged in an insurrection against the same." However, by a two-thirds vote of each house, Congress could remove this disability. In effect, this simply repeated a stricture first imposed by Johnson, and it affected only a handful of people, but the power to forgive and forget would now be exercised by the Congress rather than the president.

The Fourteenth Amendment was a cheap enough price to be paid for immediate restoration, and Tennessee, after some questionable tactics by Johnson's enemy, Parson William Brownlow, promptly ratified it and was readmitted. The Blairs, however, along with most of Johnson's other embattled advisors, felt that it should be opposed. The conflict had gone too far for any new surrender of the sacred principles of states' rights. Following the president's advice, the other ten southern states rejected the amendment. Numerous radicals viewed the measure with equal distaste. Charles Sumner spoke for two full days against it. The famous black abolitionist Frederick Douglass denounced it as an insult to his race. The noted reformer Wendell Phillips announced that a Republican defeat in the fall elections would be preferable if the party had no platform beyond the Fourteenth Amendment.[8]

In 1866 the fall elections for Congress would settle the issue. If enough Johnson supporters to sustain his vetoes could be elected, the presidential reconstruction would prevail. By the summer of 1866, however, this was already unlikely. The Republican party was committed to at least a minimal protection for the freedmen, and opponents would have to run as Democrats before a northern electorate that still associated their party with the rebellious South. Later, economic determinists in the historical profession would argue that Andrew Johnson might have changed the outcome if he had stressed issues like tariffs, railroad subsidies, the congressional salary increase, and currency and banking policies.[9] In fact, however, the two parties were not clearly divided on these issues. Radicals and conservatives on reconstruction were split among themselves on the economic questions, and Johnson's own views on such matters were in sharp conflict with those of some of his most loyal supporters on reconstruction. The voting public in 1866 was not presented with

clear-cut alternatives on economic policies because the party divisions did not make such choices possible. The only polarized
issue commanding universal attention in 1866 was that of reconstruction, and although many northern voters had mixed emotions about black rights and black equality, a majority of them
were not yet ready to abandon the party of Lincoln to support
the party of secession.

The Blair–Johnson argument that southern whites could be
trusted to give protection and reasonable justice to the former
slaves could not stand up under the events of 1866. In addition
to the almost daily sporadic violence, two genuinely frightful
massacres occured in Memphis and New Orleans. Between April
30 and May 2 a Memphis mob killed 46 and wounded more
than 80 blacks while burning black homes, schools, and churches
at will. On July 30 a New Orleans mob aided by the police
killed 34 and wounded more than 200 in breaking up a convention assembled to work for black suffrage. Conservative insistence that these were the exceptions to a situation of general harmony could not be swallowed by northern voters.

In some states, most particularly New York, bitter antipathies
divided Republicans who supported Johnson and Democrats who
wanted to get the president back into their party and profit from
his patronage policies. The New York Republicans led by Seward's friend Thurlow Weed were loyal to Johnson, but the
Blairs remembered Seward's long record as a free-soil extremist
and his role in the Fort Sumter crisis. They could never believe
that Seward was not secretly in league with Stanton and the radicals, and they did everything possible to ally Johnson with the
New York Democrats at the expense of his influence with the
Republicans. If they could have accepted what was obvious to
Johnson—that Seward was entirely loyal and in full agreement
with his reconstruction policies—their influence might have been
even greater. Instead, however, they continued to argue that
Seward and Stanton were bound together by "hooks of *Steal*."[10]

The Blairs argued further for a coalition between well-known
war Democrats and moderate Republicans other than Seward.
In mid-1865 Francis P. Blair began urging Johnson to replace
Seward and Stanton with Governors John Andrew of Massachusetts and Oliver Morton of Indiana. Later he urged that

General Grant replace Stanton, although he also suggested that Frank could fill this spot with equal distinction. Actually, Andrew and Morton, though friendly to Blair, did not agree fully with his reconstruction views. Indeed, both had been anxious to have Johnson sign the Freedmen's Bureau and Civil Rights bills.[11]

With their usual optimism, the Blairs believed that Johnson's needed coalition could be achieved through a well-publicized national convention, and they took the lead in organizing and planning one to meet at Philadelphia on August 14. The sponsors of the movement included Senators James Doolittle, Edgar Cowan, and Reverdy Johnson, who was a member of the reconstruction committee, as well as Democrats John Van Buren, Henry Watterson, Dean Richmond, and General John Dix. The elder Blair was consulted at every step and helped prepare the call, while Montgomery served as chairman of the committee on organization. Doolittle took his final draft of the call to Silver Spring for Blair's approval.

The call for the National Union Convention at Philadelphia invited those delegates "who in a spirit of patriotism and love of Union" could "rise above personal and sectional considerations." Among those who felt qualified by this condition were two famous "copperheads," or peace Democrats: Fernando Wood, who had tried to lead New York City out of the Union, and Clement Vallandigham, who had been convicted of treason in Ohio. The Philadelphia gathering was a beautiful affair for those eager to forgive secession, forget the war, and ignore the Memphis and New Orleans massacres and other problems of the southern blacks. In a huge wigwam built for the purpose, the cheers rang out as the bands played northern and Confederate music, and prominent northerners and southerners marched down the aisle arm in arm. The new postmaster general, Alexander Randall of Wisconsin, called the meeting to order; General Dix was the temporary chairman; and Senator Doolittle of Wisconsin was the permanent president. Congressman and *New York Times* owner Henry J. Raymond of New York, who was still the national chairman of the Republican party, read an "Address to the People of the United States." Eloquent speeches called for reunion and a new spirit of nationalism. The unanimous Declaration of Principles, which Montgomery Blair helped write, urged the election of congressmen who would readmit the South; denied all right of secession; reaffirmed the constitutional right of the states to determine their own voting regulations; insisted that the Constitution could not be amended without all states voting in Congress; declared the Confederate debt invalid and the Union debt valid; urged federal aid for Union soldiers and their families; and proclaimed the rights of the freedmen to the same protection of persons and property as that given to whites. Except for the limited black suffrage and restrictions on certain Confederates in the Fourteenth Amendment, the declaration was not significantly different from the radical program.

Much of the press treated the convention favorably, but radical papers attacked it with both ferocity and talent. Particularly effective were the humorous but biting public letters of David R. Locke, writing as Petroleum R. Nasby, and the brilliant cartoons of Thomas Nast. The major theme of both was the picture of Yankees and Confederates loving each other in Philadelphia while blacks were being slaughtered in Memphis and New Orleans. Nast drew Andrew Johnson as Iago trying to persuade the blacks he was their friend; as a snake charmer blowing on a flute labeled "Constitution" while a huge copperhead wrapped itself around a freedman; as King Andrew enthroned with crown and scepter while Seward directed the beheading of various radicals; and as Nero holding the Constitution while rebel gladiators destroyed blacks huddled around an American flag.

Still, however, the affair worried the radicals into staging their own convention of southern loyalists, also in Philadelphia. Hundreds of northern Republicans attended as observers and honorary delegates, and played a major role in its decisions. Frederick Douglass, however, was treated very coldly, and the grand march to National Hall was delayed until religious editor Theodore Tilton volunteered to walk with him. A motion to seat him on the platform was ignored, and he was admitted as a delegate only after a struggle. A caucus of northern governors ruled that black suffrage must be kept out of the campaign, and ultimately most of the northern delegates forced an adjournment to avoid the issue. The advocates, mostly southern, regrouped and in a dramatic scene dominated by Tilton, Douglass, and the beautiful actress-playwright Anna Dickinson passed a black suffrage resolution, but most of the party's national leaders were still afraid to go to the electorate with the issue.[12]

The Blairs threw themselves into the campaign with their usual energy and hopes. Frank had been trying to get out of debt by leasing a cotton plantation in Louisiana, and he had a huge crop planted. By the summer of 1866, however, he was again ready to leave his fortunes in the hands of an agent and resume the more exciting life of a politician with a cause. He made more than thirty speeches in Missouri, returned to the plantation until after the Philadelphia convention, and then rejoined the battle. On one occasion he continued a speech after one of his opponents in the audience had been stabbed to death in a fight. In August C. M. Derringer sent Francis P. Blair two pistols because of a rumor that "General Frank" had lost one of his. He would not have Frank "go without derringers; or let others know he has none. He is so much exposed, that they shd. know he is well armed with them—for they will then be like *you* with the 'Rifle,' *afraid to come in contact with him.*"[13]

In September, the National Union party of Maryland nominated Montgomery Blair for Congress, but he refused and begged his friends to support Frederick Stone, the Democratic nominee. Blair was too busy campaigning in other states, and he knew Stone was the conservative viewpoint's best hope.[14]

At Silver Spring, the family patriarch scratched away at letters and speech materials for his sons. He was once again a member of the party of Thomas Jefferson and Andrew Jackson, and the restored allegiance was a powerful tonic. In August he wrote for Montgomery to William Cullen Bryant at the *New York Evening Post* a long letter eloquently defending Alexander H. Stephens and Robert E. Lee. "It is hard," he wrote, "for a noble mind to tear itself from home, kindred, friends, & native soil & go into opposite ranks to crush them all. This was the case of Stephens as well as Lee. It was the case of all elevated souls in the South." At some point Blair also wrote a speech that never got delivered. It described the indignities heaped upon women in Africa, Asia, and Europe, and challenged the radicals to prove their true devotion to equality by advocating female suffrage.[15]

Montgomery and Frank spoke in several states while the

family waited anxiously for news of President Johnson's disastrous swing around the circle. In New York, incidentally, many of the city's most important bankers and businessmen promoted a huge banquet for Johnson and helped finance his tour. Bennett's *Herald* headlined the radical convention at Philadelphia with epithets like "Renegade Southerners on the Rampage," "Blacks and Whites, Free Lovers, Spiritualists, Fourierites, Women's Rights Men, Negro Equality and Miscegenationists in Convention," and "The South to be a San Domingo." At Indianapolis a riot kept Johnson from speaking. At Cairo, Illinois, the Democrats broke up a radical meeting. At Connersville, Indiana, a radical fired four shots into the crowd and badly wounded one man. Only military force prevented another riot in New Orleans. The campaign ended with two days of steady fighting and rioting in Philadelphia, with each side blaming the other and claiming total innocence.

When the votes were counted, the Republicans had won more than enough seats to override Johnson's future vetoes. The citizenry had not spoken for black suffrage, since neither party had espoused it. When forced to choose, however, between advocates of the limited Fourteenth Amendment and those who appeared ready to restore an apparently unrepentant South with no safeguards against what had happened in Memphis and New Orleans, a majority of the voters still remembered at least part of what the Civil War had involved. The Democratic candidates for Congress would have done better to concentrate on local issues and forego the assistance of the national party and its opposition to reconstruction.

For a brief time after the election, Andrew Johnson enjoyed a wave of sympathy, even from some of his enemies, and it was still not too late for the southern states to check the radicals by approving the Fourteenth Amendment. The national leadership of the Democratic party, including the Blairs, however, continued to give the South bad advice on how to escape any further reconstruction. In Congress, the session of 1866–1867 began with the rejection of a harsh military reconstruction bill by Thaddeus Stevens. Then came many long weeks of acrid debate, during which any one of several moderate solutions might have passed except for the opposition of Democrats unwilling to accept any further reconstruction at all. The Democratic party clearly expected to regain its power through a southern strategy not unlike that espoused a century later by Republicans hoping to profit from the civil rights movement of the 1960s.

The radicals continued to gain, however, from the administration's lenience toward southern whites guilty of senseless violence. Six South Carolinians had killed three Union soldiers on guard duty. A military trial found four guilty and sentenced two to hang and two to life imprisonment. After legal appeals and much publicity, the two death sentences were commuted to life imprisonment on the Dry Tortugas. Johnson, however, had the prisoners sent to Fort Delaware, where a civilian judge issued a writ of habeas corpus and released them on the grounds that the civil courts of South Carolina had been open at the time of their trial. They went home to a grand celebration and welcome. In November 1866 Dr. James L. Watson of Virginia, by his own admission, pursued and killed a local black citizen of good reputation who had done fifty cents' worth of damage to the doctor's carriage by passing it on a narrow road. Watson pleaded that the act of passing had been an insult to his wife and daughter, who were on their way to church. After a local court acquitted him, a military court found him guilty under the Civil Rights Act, but President Johnson promptly ordered the court dissolved and the prisoner released. The federal commander at Little Rock reported that "we can arrest under the present laws of Congress, but we cannot hold anyone in the face of the writ of habeas corpus. . . . I had some half dozen murderers in confinement . . . but they sue out writs of habeas corpus and before I am aware of it are released by one of the *Union* judges of the present State government." [16]

Legally, of course, the administration was correct. In *ex parte Milligan* in 1865, the Supreme Court had ruled that civilians could not be tried by military courts in areas where civil courts were functioning. Essentially, also, Johnson and the Blairs were defending a sound constitutional principle. Justice and justifiable mercy have traditionally come more often from civilian judges and juries than from military courts. Unfortunately, however, in 1867 the sacred principle was not providing either justice or mercy for southern blacks. For a great many northern whites the immediate goal of minimal protection for the former slaves was more important than the constitutionality of the means for accomplishing it.

During the final week of the congressional session of 1866–1867, a rising anger over southern intransigence against the Fourteenth Amendment enabled the radicals to pass a much more comprehensive Reconstruction Act than anyone had expected earlier. The law abolished the existing southern governments and divided the region into five military districts, each under a Union general and military forces. With all males voting except those barred by wartime activity, each state was to choose a new constitutional convention, vote on the convention's product, and elect new state governments. When the new governments had accepted the Fourteenth Amendment and made black suffrage official, they could be readmitted to the Union.

Francis P. Blair pointed out that a formal veto would be overridden and urged Johnson to apply a pocket-veto by doing nothing. Meanwhile, pleaded Blair, the president must go to the country with a clean sweep of his cabinet "as a concession to the discontents." [17] Johnson ignored the advice on both counts. He issued an angry veto message, which the Congress promptly nullified by more than the required two-thirds majority.

Johnson was at least grateful to the point of tossing the Blair family an inedible bone. He nominated Frank to be ambassador to Austria, and the Senate quickly rejected the appointment. Frank sent a letter of thanks and assured Johnson that he was not disturbed by the Senate's action. In December 1866 the president had already commissioned Frank to inspect various sections of the Pacific railroads being constructed with government subsidies. Although Frank was burdened with heavy debts, and the ethics of the Gilded Age and the Great Barbecue were already in vogue, he would not be tempted. John D. Perry, president of the Union Pacific Railroad, asked him for assistance in getting the government subsidy of $16,000 per mile for extending the road to Wyandotte, Kansas, and offered to pay for the service. Frank answered that it would be "improper & impossible" for him "to act as an agent or attorney for the R. Roads or receive any compensation from them other than that provided by law."

For the benefit of his creditors, however, Frank did accept $10,000 from his ever-generous older brother.[18]

For the next few months, as the new reconstruction process unfolded in the South, the Blairs continued to speak and write against it, amid growing evidence that the Democratic strategy of opposition to racial equality had much potential. In the fall the Democrats made a strong comeback in the state elections, and Ohio, Minnesota, Michigan, and Kansas rejected state constitutional amendments for black suffrage. In December 1867 Boston elected its first Democratic mayor since the days of Andrew Jackson.

In the summer of 1867 Montgomery made an unsuccessful attempt to get elected United States senator by the legislature of Maryland, which had bucked the national trend by voting Democratic in 1866. Too many Democrats, however, remembered his Republican apostasy, and he was hampered further by a silly quarrel with the Methodist bishop Matthew Simpson. During Montgomery's term in Lincoln's cabinet the bishop had accused him of anti-Methodism in his appointments. Montgomery had denied any religious prejudice and added that two of his aunts and several of his servants were Methodists. The bishop had publicly interpreted this as a statement that Methodists were "good enough for the kitchen, but not for high office." In 1867 the old bishop, by now a prominent radical, probably damaged Montgomery's aspirations with a grossly exaggerated version of the exchange.[19]

None of the Blairs' horrendous predictions about reconstruction came to pass. The military commanders in the South registered a total of 703,000 black and 627,000 white voters, but the white minority was due to a failure to register rather than direct proscription. No more than 150,000 whites throughout the entire South were disfranchised in the elections for convention delegates, the referenda on the constitutions, and the simultaneous choice of officials for the new governments, and most of these disabilities were soon removed by the new legislatures. Mississippi's voters rejected their new constitution, and Alabama accomplished the same result by keeping the total vote below a majority of those registered. By the spring of 1868 seven reconstructed states were back under civilian government. Mississippi and Alabama were mending their ways, but Virginia and Texas had not completed the process in time to be acted upon by Congress during the spring session. The new southern constitutions included many of the democratic reforms the Blairs had always advocated, and the blacks in the new governments usually took the lead in removing further disabilities from the former Confederates. Only South Carolina had a black legislative majority, and local southern whites, derisively but usually unfairly called "scalawags," predominated in most of the other states. Ex-northerners, designated as "carpetbaggers," won places of top leadership in several states, but the statistics indicate that they received white as well as black votes.

Nevertheless, the psychological impact of blacks voting and holding office was terribly painful for most southern whites. Still smarting from their military defeat, they could not easily abandon the fears and prejudices that had justified the war they had caused. Radical reconstruction, however brief, was the pouring of salt into gaping emotional wounds, and its actual course and the generally responsible behavior of the freedmen were quite irrelevant to southern white feelings. The ex-Confederates would continue to predict dire results, and they would later remember, usually incorrectly, that terrible blows against their well-being had been struck. In response to the threat of black equality, the Ku Klux Klan and other terrorist organizations sprang to life in 1867 and played an important role in the elections of 1868. The Blairs, however, saw only the problems of their southern relatives and personal friends, and ignored the fact that virtually all of the violence was being committed by whites against blacks.

Chapter 27

The Candidate

THE Blair views on reconstruction were not shared unanimously within the family bosom. Apo, who felt humiliated by Frank's family debts and who probably wished only that he would spend more time earning money and less time trying to save the South, defended the radical policies. Phillips Lee, who probably resented the apostolic self-assurance of his brothers-in-law, and who had no political ambitions, agreed with her openly. Lizzie remained discreetly silent. At least one breakfast discussion ended with Eliza giving her daughter-in-law a stern lecture. Still, however, the old people tried to keep Apo and her children with them whenever possible, and they continued to adore Phil.[1]

Despite his distinguished performance in the navy's most important wartime command, Lee was passed over for promotion to commodore, a prerequisite for advancement to admiral. Secretary of the Navy Welles insisted that Lee's $150,000 in prize money from the North Atlantic blockade was enough compensation, and Francis P. Blair believed, and probably correctly, that the animus of Welles toward Lee stemmed from the influence of Gustavus Fox and Montgomery Blair. Montgomery Blair probably added Lee's heresy on reconstruction to his brother-in-law's alleged earlier sins. In April 1866 Welles ordered Captain Lee to take command of the Mare Island Navy Yard in San Francisco.

Francis P. and Eliza Blair were furious. In two long letters to Johnson replete with citations of praise for Lee by his fellow officers, Blair argued that Lee should be promoted and given duty closer to home. Welles had argued that this would look like nepotism to other officers, but Blair insisted that this was pure hypocrisy because Welles had put both of his own sons in public office and had employed his brother to buy ships for the navy at a percentage that had earned a fortune. Also, in the last Connecticut election, wrote Blair, Welles had given his son leave to return to Connecticut and vote against Johnson supporters, and had not bothered to go home and cast his own vote. The Blairs, he added, had never been guilty of such disloyalty.[2]

Blair then begged the secretary as a personal favor not to send Lee into exile in California. Losing Lizzie and young Blair would be such a severe blow, he said, that he and Eliza would have to move to California also, and this would be difficult for people their age. Welles was adamant. He apparently felt that Lee should be willing to go without his wife and child and that the threat to take them with him was a low trick.

Montgomery Blair, who always believed that he acted only from principle and never from personal rancor, was probably stung when his father wrote him a plea to "bury this feud before you bury your parents." A few days later, Welles recorded that "Judge Montgomery Blair, who for nine years, he tells me, has not spoken to Lee, and who would, I have no doubt, feel relieved were Lee in California, earnestly requested for his father's sake that the orders might be revoked." Welles complained further that he had called on the president and found "sixty or eighty children from the orphan asylum with the matron and others," and "was implored for the children's sake, to revoke the orders, that Mrs. Lee could remain." Whether under pressure from Johnson or from his usual willingness to oblige Montgomery Blair, Welles relented. In August Lee was promoted to commodore and assigned to Hartford, Connecticut.[3]

Perhaps even stronger than Blair's concern for justice to Lee was his ambition to see Frank in the White House. Historians John and Lawanda Cox have argued with logic that part of Andrew Johnson's adamant support for the white South stemmed from his hopes for reelection through a North–South coalition. Francis P. Blair's sympathy for southern relatives and friends and his belief in states' rights and white supremacy were genuine enough, but he too may have had subconscious political motivations. Frank's wartime struggles with the radical Republicans precluded any presidential nomination from that direction. This left only the Democratic party rejuvenated by the return of its southern white voters and unthreatened by a horde of new black voters grateful to the Republicans for their emancipation. Blair's long record of affectionate relations with individual blacks indicates at least a possibility that some of his rhetorical appeals to racial prejudice may have been a political tactic as much as a statement of conviction. No Democratic candidate had ever been elected president without carrying the South. From 1800 to 1860, a majority of the southern electors had been on the winning side in every election year except 1824 and 1848, and the margin was 44 to 43 in 1848. Frank was only forty-seven in 1868, and he could wait for the right moment, but rebuilding the Democratic party on a solid southern base was a necessary first step.

By the middle of 1867, Francis P. Blair had decided that Andrew Johnson deserved the "same words appropriately assessed to Charles II—He never *said* a foolish thing, nor did a wise one." The family rather sorrowfully gave up on Johnson and turned to the challenge of electing a Democratic president in 1868. On the basis of his record and actual beliefs, Grant was the logical choice, but the general and his managers would not allow principle or lack of it to dictate his choice of a party. Francis P. Blair believed fervently but briefly that Grant was the new hope, but Frank had no such illusions. If Grant did not accept a radical nomination, wrote Frank, it would "be because he can't get it," and Grant would be a bad candidate even if elected because he had "committed himself to the reconstruction plan of Congress & aided to put it in operation." Frank wanted *"a President who will not permit it to be executed,* who will take the ground that it is void & inoperative because unconstitutional." Frank preferred General Winfield Scott Hancock to anyone but himself. "I cannot forget you saying to me," he wrote Montgomery, "that the Blairs had worked long enough for other people." [4]

In August 1867 Gideon Welles urged Johnson to replace Stanton with Frank Blair as secretary of war. Stanton, said Welles, was a coward and would "fly out of one door as Frank entered at the other." The president laughed and agreed, but in the end he accepted Montgomery Blair's advice that he replace

Stanton with General Grant. Grant accepted an interim appointment, but in January 1868, when the Senate refused to accept Johnson's reasons for dismissing Stanton, Grant resigned and turned the office back to Stanton.[5]

Until January, however, Grant's ultimate allegiance remained in doubt. In October 1867 Montgomery spoke for the Democratic ticket in New York and called upon Grant to take sides openly. Francis P. Blair congratulated his son, and added some revealing comments. They would support Grant, he wrote, unless he abandoned their policies, in which case they would oppose him "to be consistent with our own principles & *his*." As for the New York elections, "an overwhelming over throw of the Radicals there" might "make the Seymours all over the country too presuming." He would be "satisfied with 20,000 or 30,000 majority." A few days later the New York Democrats swept the state by 48,000 votes, and ex-Governor Horatio Seymour suddenly became a presidential possibility.[5]

On May 27, 1868, Frank made a nationally publicized address at the unveiling of an impressive statue of Thomas Hart Benton in St. Louis. His father sent a speech tying Benton to the conservative side of the politics of 1868, and then followed it with a letter adding that Benton had been consistently philanthropic toward blacks. He had freed his own slaves and always showed much solicitude for their welfare. At the ceremony, both Frémonts were present, and for once Frank was tactful and relatively nonpartisan. He stressed Benton's devotion to the Union and minimized the politics of 1868. This, however, won him no forgiveness from Jessie.[6]

In May 1868 the Republicans met in Chicago and nominated General Grant for president. Grant had never voted Republican nor espoused the party's reconstruction policies, but both he and the party saw victory in their combination. They could worry about principles and policies later. The platform regretted the murder of Lincoln, endorsed radical reconstruction, damned Johnson and the Democrats, advocated payment of the national debt in gold, promised pensions to veterans and widows, invited immigration, endorsed the Declaration of Independence, and offered only vague and contradictory statements on black suffrage and the tariff.

In early July, the Democrats convened in the new Tammany Hall in New York City. Although for at least sixty years Francis P. Blair's well-being had invariably been enhanced by political controversy, Frank would not allow the old gentleman to risk his health by attending. Montgomery, however, was on hand a week early to push his brother's candidacy. As a military hero and as a politician who had opposed slavery when Grant was voting for James Buchanan, Frank was obviously a strong dark-horse possibility. On July 3 the New York Metropolitan Club held a great meeting at which Montgomery was one of two main speakers. On July 4 the millionaire banker August Belmont, chairman of the national committee, opened the convention with a call for the Democrats to defeat the radical tyrants who had trampled the Constitution underfoot. Applauding vigorously were various conspicuous long-haired southerners in Confederate-gray suits and slouch hats. General Wade Hampton, who had commanded Lee's cavalry; Robert Barnwell Rhett, the "Father of Secession"; General Nathan B. Forrest, commander at the Fort Pillow massacre and founder of the Ku Klux Klan; General James Chestnut, who had drafted South Carolina's secession ordinance; and Clement Vallandigham, who had been convicted of treason in Ohio, were among those present to do the party no good among northern voters. The unanimous platform called for immediate restoration of the South, amnesty for all political offenders, the plan of Ohio congressman George Pendleton for paying the national debt in depreciated greenbacks, economy in government, and an end to the tyrannical radical governments in the South. It also commended Andrew Johnson and Chief Justice Salmon P. Chase, who had emerged as a surprise defender of states' rights on the Supreme Court and was one again angling for a presidential nomination.[7]

Most of the candidates hoped to blur the emotional issue of reconstruction, but Frank Blair would permit no such hypocrisy. In his view America needed another Andrew Jackson, and he would assume the role. In a public letter to Missouri lawyer James Broadhead, Frank warned that before the next election reconstruction policy would be complete, the states would all be readmitted, black suffrage would be established, carpetbaggers would be installed in both houses of Congress, and the Republicans would be supreme in the South. The new president must therefore declare the Reconstruction Acts "null and void, compel the army to undo its usurpations at the South, disperse the carpetbag state governments, allow the white people to reorganize their own governments and elect Senators and Representatives." It was "idle to talk of bonds, greenbacks, gold, the public faith and the public credit. . . . with a Congress in both branches controlled by the carpetbaggers and their allies. . . . We must restore the Constitution before we can restore the finances, and to do this we must have a President who will execute the will of the people by trampling into the dust the usurpations of Congress known as the Reconstruction acts." [8]

The Democratic convention chose its candidate amid a swarm of Republican press attacks upon Frank Blair, and the letter probably weakened his chances for the nomination. On the first ballot Pendleton received 105 votes, Andrew Johnson 65, and others, including Chase, ranged from 34 down to half a vote for Blair. On the nineteenth ballot Blair had 13½ votes and Chase was making a strong bid. The Blairs and most southerners, however, were implacably against Chase, and on the twenty-second ballot New York suddenly went for its ex-governor Horatio Seymour, a hard-money man who opposed the Pendleton plan. Others quickly fell into line, and Seymour, who had also been a peace Democrat during the early part of the war, was nominated. Frank Blair was quickly nominated for vice-president, in part to offset Seymour's weak war record. [9]

The Democratic chances might have been improved if reconstruction had been deemphasized, but Blair's nomination made this impossible. While Grant was denounced for excessive drinking and smoking, Blair was pictured as a dangerous revolutionary, and Seymour as a copperhead. The Republicans debated and publicized Blair's Broadhead letter at every opportunity—and so did he. Thomas V. Nast did his usual job in *Harper's Weekly*, picturing Blair in the regalia of the Ku Klux Klan planning the assassination of General Grant. Before wildly enthusiastic crowds in numerous states, Blair insisted he was no radical. He wanted only to forget the recent strife, grant the vote to whites, discontinue the black governments, and unite the country in fellowship and prosperity. He also rejected his own party's position on the Pendleton currency plan.[10]

In a widely published pamphlet, the Republicans described Seymour as "A Peace Man in War, a War Man in Peace." He had been nominated, charged the Republicans, by a convention including 110 delegates who had seen rebel service, and his platform had been dictated by men whose hands were still red with the blood of murdered Union soldiers. "Grant and Peace or Blair and Revolution" was the issue. Reminding the voters that General Forrest had been honored at the Democratic convention, the Republicans distributed 100,000 copies of the Fort Pillow report on atrocities against the black soldiers.

All efforts to muffle Frank Blair failed. When asked if he would submit to the Supreme Court, he answered that the Mulligan, Bowles, and Cummings cases had already made the radical program unconstitutional. After Grant had won Ohio, Indiana, Nebraska, and Pennsylvania in October, there were rumors of a plan to replace Seymour with Chase. Blair wrote that he opposed it, but would do anything to defeat the Republicans. Chase blamed the early defeats on Blair, and Manton Marble's *New York World* rebuked Frank by pointing out that his remedy was no longer needed because the black governments were already failing. Marble insisted that no Democratic administration would destroy the existing laws. On October 17 Frank offered to withdraw, and he asked his father and Samuel J. Tilden, the New York party chairman, to make the decision. The elder Blair did not object, but above all did not want Chase. He believed it was a plot of Chase and Seward to replace Seymour with Chase. On October 19 a national committee meeting at Tammany Hall resolved to keep the candidates but decided to send Seymour out to campaign on the other issues. The *World* formally asked Frank to withdraw, but, unconvinced that he was actually hurting the ticket, Frank refused.[11]

American election results can rarely be explained with assurance, but in 1868 the electorate was apparently not overly disturbed by the threat of the Democratic vice-presidential candidate to override the constitutional prerogatives of Congress. The hero Grant, representing the party of Lincoln, should have demolished

the peace Democrat Seymour, but such was not the case. Seymour
and Blair received 47.3 percent of the popular vote, with Mississippi, Texas, and Virginia not participating at all, and with various
abnormal conditions reducing the white votes in several other
southern states. The Democrats carried Delaware, Kentucky,
Maryland, New York, New Jersey, Georgia, Louisiana, and
Oregon, and the states being reconstructed showed some unusual
results. Seymour and Blair carried Georgia by almost 2 to 1, and
Louisiana by 2½ to 1. Grant swept Tennessee by more than
2 to 1, with only 39 percent of the eligible electorate voting, but
he also carried North Carolina by 12,000 votes even though 91
percent of the electorate voted. The vote was very close in Alabama, Arkansas, California, Connecticut, Indiana, and Pennsylvania. On the border, the Democrats carried Kentucky by more
than 3 to 1 and Maryland by 2 to 1, while losing Missouri by
21,000 votes (13.7 percent of the total). The often-repeated
statement that Grant won only because of the black votes is incorrect. If every reconstructed state and the three that were still
disqualified had gone for Seymour, Grant would still have been
elected by 173 to 147 electoral votes. Nationally Seymour and
Blair probably won a popular majority among whites, although
the population statistics indicate that Grant must have also received a considerable number of white votes in the South. Perhaps most significantly, even though Seymour's platform condemned reconstruction and Blair advocated the forcible overthrow of the legally expressed will of Congress, 46.2 percent of
the voters outside the South preferred them to the Union hero
who had won the Civil War. Northern and southern whites were
already well on the road to reunion at the future expense of
American blacks.[12]

A few months later some 150 Union officers gathered at the
Stetson Hotel in Long Branch, New Jersey, to form an association and enjoy a great banquet before a large roomful of observers. Present were Admirals Farragut and Bailey and Generals
Sherman, Sheridan, Banks, and others. By accident, probably
calculated, Frank Blair was staying at the hotel and was hastily
given a belated invitation. After more than an hour of happy
eating, the guests and participants popped the champagne corks
and began the toasts. Amid wild cheering, Farragut, Bailey, and

Sheridan in turn expounded on the heroic exploits of the Union soldiers and sailors. Observers later remembered that Frank Blair was sitting with his feet on a chair puffing furiously on a cigar. He was the fourth speaker, but his oration and toast were never finished. "I will speak," he said, "of the people who were once our enemies, and I know that when I speak of them before soldiers I speak before those who will heartily respond. Those against whom we contended, whom we aspersed as Rebels, and whom we triumphed over as well. They were a great and generous people, they were worthy of the steel of our best. We have heard here tonight only of Farragut and Sheridan; but I tell you in the future we will yet hear of General Lee and Stonewall Jackson." At this point a roar of angry shouts ended the speech. Farragut urged that Blair be allowed to continue, but someone else quoted organization bylaws forbidding political speeches. On this ground Frank was called to order and sat down. Echoes of the affair resounded for days. Most editors felt that such sentiments were an insult to the assembled Union officers. Frank, however, had the last word with a public letter. He had meant no insult. "It was a compliment to our army to speak well of those over whom our army had triumphed as 'foemen worthy of our steel.'" His "intention and meaning could only have been perverted by men who had been taught by such heroes as Butler to relish a different kind of *steal*." [13]

Chapter 28

The Last Hurrah

IN 1869 the North was not yet quite ready for eulogies to southern generals before gatherings of Union soldiers, but the wartime hatreds and fears were ebbing. In 1870 the Democrats gained fifty-one seats in the House and six in the Senate, and a great many Republicans were thoroughly disillusioned by the corrupt regime of Ulysses S. Grant. The Fourteenth and Fifteenth amendments needed the coerced approvals of the southern states to become part of the Constitution in 1869 and 1870, and the Fifteenth which outlawed "race, color, or previous condition of servitude" as barriers to voting, affected more northern states than southern. The Fifteenth Amendment climaxed years of effort by the radicals, and it was followed by a general relaxation of attention to the freedmen's problems. Millions of northerners and many of the radical leaders could now feel that they had done their part. Everything now should depend upon the blacks themselves. In 1869 Virginia was "redeemed" by the election of a conservative government, and Alabama and North Carolina followed suit in 1870. Georgia had elected enough conservatives in 1868 to oust its elected black legislators by decree. Congress had responded by putting Georgia again under military rule until it restored the legislators and ratified the Fifteenth Amendment, but the conservatives obviously controlled the state. Actual northern interference in southern politics after the first two state elections under military rule was much less than most people believed. A total of only 20,000 northern soldiers had been spread thinly over the entire South, and the soldiers themselves were more likely to sympathize with the whites they had come to police than with the blacks they had come to protect. Seven thousand of the total were concentrated in Louisiana and Texas, but this did not keep Louisiana from voting overwhelmingly for Seymour and Blair in 1868, and if Texas had qualified for readmission in time, it might have voted similarly. At any rate, military rule as such ended in the South in 1870, although a scattering of troops remained until 1876. With only a few exceptions, President Grant showed little zeal for use of the troops to protect the freedmen. In September 1875 some fifty blacks were slaughtered by whites in riots at Yazoo City and Clinton, Mississippi, but Grant refused the governor's plea for federal troops.

All of this augured well for the political future of Frank Blair, and his indomitable parents continued to enjoy a happy life marked by great expectations. In September 1868 Eliza's horse, "the Prince," threw his seventy-three-year-old rider over his head. She was badly bruised between the shoulders and on the back of her head but no bones were broken, and she was soon back in the saddle. Nevertheless, she later decided that the Prince was gentle enough for young Blair Lee, and took "Blacksmith," a more fractious horse, for her own mount. According to Lizzie, her mother was afraid of Blacksmith, "but must have the exercise for her health." In May 1869, Frank took his son Andrew to Colorado because of a bad cough and bleeding lungs, and Apo and the younger children descended upon Silver Spring. A few months later, Minna reported from her nearby Falkland estate that she dreaded nothing more than the sight of Apo's boys and Blair Lee, with little Henry, "a darkie we call Sherman's banners," entering her domains. Apo in turn had long since forbidden her son Jim to associate with Minna's son Woodbury. Minna was dismayed by the elder Blairs' extravagance—thirty persons, "all who are fed by Mr. B.," were living at Silver Spring. "Some cook for themselves but all comes from him. Every night but one last week they had 19 or 20 to tea; they are run down with company. Mrs. B. says she is too old to worry or have cake etc made, but has plenty of milk & cream, broiled dried venison & apple sauce or Lawton blackberries." There was "no end to the ponies horses & mules. I let Wood's *stay there to eat* & send for it to use. . . . The other morning at 7 o'clock Mr. and Mrs. B—on horseback with Blair Lee on a mule were passing by after their ride. Gist hailed them said he wanted to go over & breakfast with them. Mr. B. put him on the mule before Blair Lee—Victoria ran by their side & off they went. About 10 o'clock he came home on Pres's pony being led by Jimmy. . . . At the 4th of July dinner every one had what they wanted made for dessert. . . . Mrs. Blair really seems to enjoy giving her grandchildren all the pleasure she can; so does the old gentleman—Everything is given up for them." [1]

The tower of strength in running the Blair household continued to be the former slave Becky, who at one point got her wages raised to $15 per month by threatening to quit. Lizzie was terrified by the prospect of losing Becky, but she resisted briefly because she had been housing Becky's niece free of charge for more than a year. [2] In March 1869 the family all grieved deeply over the death of William, another former slave who had been with them most of his life.

The Grants and the Blair women continued to be personal friends despite the political estrangement. Shortly after the inauguration Betty Blair and her husband, C. M. Comstock, dined at the White House, and a week later Lizzie herself was invited to Mrs. Grant's reception. Although Grant dismissed Frank as railroad commissioner, he appointed Comstock to the same position and took great pleasure in breaking the news to Betty personally. Blair Lee at first refused to join young Jesse Grant's club that met every Saturday morning in the White House guardhouse, but he relented when his mother pointed out "that there was some falsehood in avoiding persons just because their parents held high position, particularly if they had always been friendly." Blair went off to his first meeting, but soon returned to get five cents to pay his fine for having missed the previous week. On at least two occasions, Mrs. Grant sent Lizzie and Eliza beautiful bouquets. [3]

With his family influences, both friendly and otherwise, no longer a factor, Commodore Phillips Lee was promoted to admiral in 1870 and assigned to the command of the North Atlantic fleet. This, however, required him to live on a flagship off Key West, Florida, and soon Lizzie was again keeping her husband and future historians informed on the daily lives of her family.

The America of President Grant was rapidly becoming a land of financial and corporate giants fostered and nurtured by the new powers of the federal government created by the Civil War. The farmer-dominated nation that had inspired Thomas Jefferson and bred Andrew Jackson and Francis P. Blair was gone forever, but the old ex-editor kept fighting. In August 1869 he scratched out a long pamphlet entitled *Letter of Francis P. Blair to the Workingmen* for presentation to the third annual convention of the National Labor Union. The Union was the first attempt in American labor history to mobilize all classes of workers, including women and blacks, skilled and unskilled, into one organization, and Blair heartily approved. The ancient editor of the *Globe* relived a host of memories as he again denounced Congress for transferring power to private corporations and banks, and thereby creating "a worse monopoly than the old United States Bank." The new national banking system allowed banks to print money supported by federal bonds, and to Blair this was just the old bank of Nicholas Biddle in a more virulent and dangerous form. Obviously the times required a new version of "the Irish stripling soldier, who was knighted by a British officer at Camden by the cut of his sword on the head for refusing to clean his boots . . . the instrument of Providence in breaking down the coalition of great men to convert our republican form of government into the British system." He did not add his continuing personal hope that Frank might yet assume such a role.[4]

A few months later, Blair entered the lists again, this time in support of a bill for the education of Indian orphans whose parents had been killed in battle by the United States army. The villain of his twenty-one-page letter to the *New York World* was General Philip Sheridan, whose destruction of the Shenandoah valley during the war and brief term as a reconstruction commanding general had earned him a place just behind Sherman among those most hated by the South. Sheridan had argued that the best way to get the Indians in a mood for peace would be to strike a heavy blow during the snow season when they would be helpless. Under Sheridan's orders Custer had massacred a large camp of peaceful Cheyennes only a year earlier. Citing Sheridan's needless killing of Indian women and children and the wanton destruction of their means of livelihood, Blair compared it to the general's demolition of barns, stock, homes, and food during the

Civil War in an area that Blair insisted was largely unionist in sentiment. Sheridan, wrote Blair, had burned and ravaged a beautiful land without reason and this made his needless killing of some 1,500 Indians easy to understand. Blair unquestionably believed what he wrote, but it was a treatise certain to keep southern voters reminded that the Blairs were on their side against the likes of Sheridan.[5]

In the spring of 1869 Frank toured the South and received a hero's welcome everywhere. This pleasant experience was followed by a stroke of good fortune that enabled him to settle his debts. He had lost most of his property already, but still owed about $30,000. The financial house to which he owed the money, however, went bankrupt, and Frank's lawyer bought the debt for $1,300 from creditors who had taken over the house. His father, of course, never recovered any of his St. Louis investments that had gone into the debt in the beginning. A short while later, Betty Blair Comstock angered the family by remarking in St. Louis that the elder Blair was in poor circumstances because of the sacrifices he had made for Frank. The statement quickly spread, and Frank himself wrote Betty a rather gentle letter reminding her of all the generosity she, too, had received at the hands of his parents and suggesting that his political enemies could use such statements against him.[6]

In Missouri, by 1870, Grant's appointments and policies had completely alienated former radical stalwarts like B. Gratz Brown and Carl Schurz, and suddenly Frank Blair found himself reunited with his former enemies. The question of black suffrage had theoretically been settled by the Fifteenth Amendment, and now most Missourians were ready to restore the privilege to all the whites. In August 1870, at the Missouri Republican state convention, the Committee on Resolutions, with Schurz as chairman, recommended restoring the franchise to all white males. The convention as a whole, however, adopted an opposing minority report. At this point, Brown, Schurz, and William M. Grosvenor, editor of the St. Louis Democrat (the Republican newspaper), led 250 delegates out of the convention to form a Liberal Republican party. Under Frank Blair's influence and leadership, the Missouri Democrats decided to support them. As a result, Blair was elected to the state legislature and Brown became governor. Constitutional amendments abolishing both the voting restrictions and the test oath were soon passed by large majorities.

By the end of the year, Republican Senator Charles Drake, author of Missouri's postwar constitution, feared the loss of his Senate seat and asked Grant for an appointment as chief justice of the United States Court of Claims. Frank promptly wrote Montgomery to get every Democrat to vote for Drake's confirmation: "I should never think of supporting him for a judicial appointment (as he is no more fit for a judge than h—ll is for a powder house) except that by such appointment he will be got out of the Senate and in all probability make room for me." In January Frank was elected to the United States Senate to fill Drake's unexpired term. The Democratic *Missouri Republican* announced a great dinner in Blair's honor, marked by "Eloquent Speeches and Joyous Enthusiasm," and several months later the Jefferson City *People's Weekly Tribune* quoted with obvious satisfaction from an earlier Alabama editorial: "Gen. Blair has never flunked and never lied. He fought us for conscience sake, with as faultless a courage as great Caesar's, and as considerate a courtesy as peerless Bayard's. At the close of the war he turned his back on the party of cowardly hate and malignant proscription, and seemingly sacrificed himself in what appeared a hopeless effort to protect the conquered South." Now, however, he had risen again in Missouri to give "liberty and law to the people of Missouri, who were but two years ago the voiceless and powerless subjects of irresponsible despotism." [7]

Frank's return to Washington was a joyous occasion for the family. He and Apo arrived one evening while Lizzie was at the White House, where Grant spoke highly of Phillips Lee. Frank's new $7,500 salary had restored Apo's spirits, and Lizzie had never seen her looking so well and happy. Lizzie reported that her mother's laugh was "as joyous and light hearted as that of the young girls," and that "Father steps along with an expression of delight in every movement." The children, meanwhile, were ecstatic at the prospect of an indefinite stay at Silver Spring. The only discordant note in the family was the refusal of Betty Blair Comstock to come for a visit because Frank was there.

Another happy development was the success of Frank's son Andrew, who had returned from Colorado in perfect health and was about to begin a long and lucrative career as a metallurgist in the steel business. Andrew was also engaged to Anna Biddle, the daughter of Philadelphia banker Thomas Biddle, who was a distant cousin of the late Nicholas Biddle. Frank was afraid that the Biddle money might make his son a trifler and an idler, but Apo was willing to take the risk. Lizzie concluded that since there were five children in the Biddle family, Anna and Andrew might not inherit enough to do any serious damage. When the Biddles came for a visit, Lizzie discovered that she had known Thomas Biddle during her schooldays as a teen-ager in Philadelphia. They recognized each other immediately, although the once-slender Biddle now weighed 220 pounds.[8]

The new senator's father resumed his earlier role of research assistant and speech writer, and Lizzie again served as secretary and scribe for both of them. An immediate issue was the final gasp of radical reconstruction—an attempt to enforce the Fourteenth and Fifteenth amendments by federal law against the depredations of the Ku Klux Klan and similar organizations. Traditional chroniclers of the period have argued that this was merely a political response to the conservative victories being won in most of the southern states, but a final effort to give teeth to the amendments was a natural and justifiable policy for those who had enacted them in the first place.

An act already passed in May 1870 had outlawed force, bribery, and threats against voters, and had forbidden anyone to intimidate voters by depriving them of jobs or occupations. It also banned "disguised groups from going upon the public highways or upon the premises of another" with intent to interfere with constitutional liberties. Frank Blair arrived in the Senate just in time to oppose the two additional acts that followed. The first authorized federal supervisors to enforce the proper registration and voting procedures and certify election returns in cities where voting irregularities were considered likely. The second was more far-reaching. Called the "Ku Klux Act," it forbade anyone to conspire to overthrow or destroy by force the government of the United States or to conspire to prevent persons from holding office, serving on juries, enjoying equal protection of the laws, or voting. Federal courts would have original jurisdiction in all suffrage cases, and the president was authorized to call out the army and navy and suspend the rights of habeas corpus if necessary to enforce its provisions. These laws were desperately needed, but as the Supreme Court would later rule, they were largely unconstitutional unless they could be justified by principles other than the Fourteenth and Fifteenth amendments. The amendments prohibit discrimination by states, but say nothing about individuals or private groups.

Frank Blair served on the Senate committee investigating the southern disorders that had generated the movement for the new legislation. The usual undenied stories of white violence and threats were again spread on the record, and a majority of the committee wrote and approved the bills. For the minority, however, Frank Blair, aided by his father and sister, wrote a strong dissent on the usual grounds of unconstitutionality, destruction of states' rights, and lack of necessity. In his view the southern whites were the ones being persecuted, and the violence would stop as soon as they were restored to their rightful positions of power. During the debates Lizzie staged a dinner party for fifteen, including twelve senators who supported Blair's position. Among those standing beside Blair against the Ku Klux Act were his Missouri colleague Carl Schurz, whose report on white atrocities against the freedmen had launched the radical movement, and Lyman Trumbull, who had introduced the original Civil Rights Act. The bill passed the House by a thin margin, made possible, according to Frank Blair, because Congressmen Samuel Randall and William Holdman were too drunk to say no. A few days later the Senate also passed the bill, but the former bitterness was conspicuously lacking from the debate. Frank made a long speech, and according to Lizzie at least, "bore interruptions and questioning with imperturbable good humor." There were apparently no objections when Frank arranged for his proud father to sit on the Senate floor during the debates. Father and son were delighted by a critical speech made by Schurz, although Frank was sorry that Mrs. Grant was present to hear the denunciations of her husband. On February 22, 1872, Lizzie and Eliza walked the mile to the bottom of Capitol Hill, but rode the streetcar to the top before walking up the Capitol steps. They sat as honored guests in the diplomatic gallery while Trumbull in a long speech warned that the Ku Klux Act would mean the end of state government. The longtime Blair–Trumbull friendship had been further restored when Phillips Lee wrote the Navy Department a letter defending the character of Trumbull's son, a young naval lieutenant facing a court-martial on a charge of drunkenness. The lieutenant was sentenced to dismissal, but Grant, who had had a few such bouts himself, commuted the penalty to suspension of rank and pay for eighteen months.[9]

Another event that helped divide the radicals and increase the developing harmony among former enemies was President Grant's ill-fated attempt to annex the Dominican Republic. Commercial speculators had convinced the president's secretary, Orville Babcock, that this project would be immensely profitable for themselves and would provide the United States an invaluable acquisition. A treaty of annexation was negotiated, but largely through the efforts of Charles Sumner it was defeated by the Senate in June 1870. Grant responded by dismissing Sumner's friend, John L. Motley, from his post as minister to Britain, and trying to revive the treaty. In December 1870 Sumner delivered an eloquent diatribe entitled "Naboth's Vineyard," in which he condemned Grant, the annexation idea, and the Dominican president in language not heard on the Senate floor since Sumner's attack on Butler in 1856. Sumner had once compared Andrew Johnson to Caligula's horse, but he now found Johnson preferable to Grant. In turn, Grant appointed a distinguished commission, including Ben Wade, to investigate conditions in the island, and the result was another recommendation for annexation. Sumner, meanwhile, was deposed from his chairmanship of the Committee on Foreign Relations, with the acquiescence of several of his radical colleagues.

The Blairs agreed with Sumner, and soon the family patriarch had his daughter reading so much on San Domingo that it began to haunt her dreams. San Domingo had never known a stable government, and the population was no more than 13 percent white. The region's bloody race war with the French in the 1790s had been cited for decades by Southerners as the inevitable result of emancipation. After trying unsuccessfully for years to get America's existing black population removed to a more hospitable environment, and after seeing the United States torn apart for ten years by civil war and reconstruction, Blair, naturally enough, saw this effort to add another million black citizens as sheer insanity. Within a remarkably short time, Blair produced a sixty-nine-page indictment of the annexation for use by Frank or anyone else needing help on the issue. He traced the area's long and tragic history and showed that Spain, France, and Britain in turn had been unable to exploit or improve it. To help the imaginary interests of a group of greedy speculators, Blair charged, Grant was trying to get the United States committed to dangerous responsibilities that could never be profitable. Frank incorporated most of his father's arguments in a long Senate speech, and the family breathed a sigh of relief as the project slowly died on the vine.[10] Grant apparently forgave the Blairs for their opposition, but for years he would ride out of his way to pass Sumner's house and shake his fist at it.

All in all, 1871 and the first few months of 1872 were a happy time for the Blairs. Guests came and went constantly both in Washington and Silver Spring. The old people and their grandchildren rode back and forth between the houses and to various local events. Blair took the boys to a frolic on Pennsylvania Avenue that included races, and they returned certain that "Grandma's horse could have beaten anything on the track." Mary Blair's children at the Moorings were also growing into handsome young adults, although servant Becky complained about their mother's failure to teach them better manners. Violet, who was quite beautiful, improved considerably and gave her grandmother much attention after Lizzie gave her a severe scolding. Apo's newly improved spirits sagged when she found herself pregnant again in her mid-forties. Andrew, her eldest, was already twenty-three, while her youngest, Caroline, was less than a year old and not even walking yet. Her son Cary was only three years old, and the prospect of two babes in arms gave her no joy.[11]

Between copying speeches and letters and franking out 20,000 of Frank's orations to the public (she learned to imitate his signature) Lizzie entertained guests, enjoyed visiting Julia Grant at the White House, managed the orphanage, followed the Senate debates, fretted over her parents and the children, and continued to write long, informative letters to her husband. She worried about fourteen-year-old Blair's passion for novels, and forbade him to read except on Saturdays and Sundays, when he also had other amusements to occupy his spare time. Blair and Apo's son George gave Lizzie a bad day when they persuaded her to let them go fishing for the first time in a boat on the Potomac. She worried herself sick despite her "trust in her heavenly father," and vowed that she could not possibly put herself and her heavenly father through such an experience every day. She was delighted by Frank's comment that young Blair was "a miracle. With his father, mother, & grandparents to pet & spoil him and to be free of selfishness astonishes me all the time." Frank, of course, had never been happier, although he was still troubled by headaches and cramps in his feet—alleviated somewhat when the doctor reduced his wine consumption and limited him to two cigars a day.[12]

Montgomery, meanwhile, was amassing a considerable fortune, and worrying chiefly about the escapades of his son Woodbury. Like his uncle Frank thirty years earlier, Woody was dismissed from a preparatory school and was temporarily saved at Harvard only by his father's personal intervention with old friends on the staff.[13]

When Congress met in January 1872, reconstruction as an issue had been moved to the back row behind corruption, civil service reform, and the monetary system. Sumner's bill to prohibit discrimination in inns, places of amusement, juries, schools, churches, and cemeteries had died in committee in 1870 and 1871. In early 1872, the senator tried to add the provisions as an amendment to a general amnesty bill. With Frank Blair in a leading role, the Senate approved it after striking out schools, churches, cemeteries, and juries, and then overwhelmingly voted for amnesty. The House, however, rejected the emasculated amendment, and only the amnesty became law. Henceforth, all but about 700 of the most prominent Confederate leaders could vote and hold office as they had always done. The voting restrictions were already minimal in most of the southern states, and Alabama, Arkansas, Mississippi, and Texas would soon join North Carolina, Tennessee, Georgia, and Virginia as "redeemed" states under conservative control. The only question remaining was whether the southern whites would now take the vote away from the freedmen or allow them to pursue their best interests as individuals and as a group through the traditional American process of free elections. The new southern constitutions had greatly increased the number of whites who could vote, and thousands of these were already voting for the so-called carpetbagger-scalawag governments. A combination of black and white voters would enable the radicals to win one more election in Florida, Louisiana, and South Carolina, but this could not be blamed upon any restriction on white voters. In October 1871 events in nine South Carolina counties, later described by pro-southern historian William A. Dunning as "shocking conditions of barbarity in the attitude of low class whites towards the freedmen," led Grant to apply the Ku Klux Act. Federal troops arrested hundreds of suspects, but most were discharged before trial and only a handful of the most flagrant violators were convicted. The law was applied rarely if ever in most areas and extensively only in a few. Between 1870 and 1896 some 7,372 caces were tried. In 1871 the government won 41 percent of its cases. The figure rose to 49 percent in 1872, although the number of arrests declined, and after 1874 no more than 10 percent of the cases in any year led to convictions. The act was repealed in 1896, but most of its provisions had already been nullified by the Supreme Court in 1876. Since the law was never applied except in extreme circumstances, the southern whites had obviously already regained the upper hand by the early 1870s.

As early as 1870 many northern presses were calling for an end to radical reconstruction because it was paralyzing southern business and discouraging northern investment in the area. America's financial and business leaders, who had never really supported radical reconstruction at all, were anxious for it to stop, and, looking for the winning side, they were also taking control of the Republican party. The spirit that had destroyed slavery and tried to achieve political equality for the blacks was rapidly losing its political base.[14]

By 1872 Charles Sumner, the most dedicated radical of them all, was smarting from his rejection by fellow radicals on both civil rights and San Domingo. He, too, was ready to leave the Republican party and join with Schurz, Trumbull, Greeley, and other Republicans who had made peace with the Blairs and other Democrats on the basis of a common enmity toward Ulysses S.

Grant. During the subsequent presidential campaign, Sumner chided Senator James G. Blaine for "waving the bloody shirt," and Blaine accused Sumner of treason to their party. It was strange, wrote Blaine, to see Sumner allied with the party of Preston Brooks. "What has Preston Brooks to do with the Presidential election?" Sumner answered. "I will not unite with you in dragging him from his grave where he sleeps, to aggravate the passions of a political conflict, and arrest the longing for accord."[15]

The Blairs, meanwhile, had decided that the successful formula used in Missouri might very well work nationally. Frank still had presidential ambitions, but he was only fifty-one years old, and in 1872 the prospect of persuading Democrats to support a Liberal Republican seemed more likely than any hope of inducing northern Republicans to vote for a Democrat. The Democrats were gaining with every election, but they were still very much the minority party in Congress. A Liberal Republican supported by the Democrats would have a better chance against Grant than any Democrat. Also, Frank Blair was finally ready to accept the fact that reconstruction was a dead issue for most northern voters in both parties. His turn would come later when a new party alignment had been established.

In January 1872 a state convention of the Missouri Liberal Republicans issued a call for a national convention to meet in Cincinnati to nominate a presidential candidate. Their indictments against Grant included his acceptance of expensive presents from corrupt and incompetent appointees, his publicly friendly relations with various financiers in bad repute with liberals for their stockmarket manipulations, and certain high-level scandals either brewing or already exposed.

On May 1 the national convention called by the Missourians met in Cincinnati. The Blairs were in close touch with their cousin B. Gratz Brown, Schurz, Trumbull, and others in the movement. According to Lizzie, the family chronicler, all of them, including Frank, were strongly for Trumbull, but the senior Blair feared that the two candidates from Illinois, Trumbull and Judge David Davis, would split their delegation and "use each other up."[16] Additional hopefuls included Charles Francis Adams, who had earned a distinguished reputation as Lincoln's wartime minister to Britain; Brown, who was the Blairs' second choice; Governor Jacob D. Cox of Ohio; Governor John M. Palmer of Illnois, who felt his state needed a third contestant; editor Horace Greeley; and the eternally desperate Salmon P. Chase. The convention's permanent chairman was Carl Schurz, whose German birth made him ineligible for a nomination.

The Liberal Republican leaders were still imbued with the moral enthusiasm that had elected and sustained Abraham Lincoln, and for them the Grant scandals had replaced slavery, disunion, and the southern denial of black civil rights as the great threat to America. Their platform would reform the civil service, bring back political morality, restore states' rights and traditional constitutional principles, and eliminate the southern question from politics. The platform gave full approval to the Thirteenth, Fourteenth, and Fifteenth amendments while arguing that only the states should be allowed to enforce them.

The movement might have had a chance with a dynamic and popular candidate, but dedicated idealists are often guilty of abysmal political judgment. Charles Francis Adams would probably have been the strongest candidate, but he had expressed indifference in a public letter, and had made no serious effort to organize a following. Brown had earned a large radical and black following, and would have been an attractive candidate. He was in the running for several ballots, but his efforts had been restricted earlier by the Blairs' insistence that he defer to Trumbull. As Francis P. Blair had predicted, the Davis–Trumbull rivalry ruined the chances of both Illinois candidates. Brown and Frank Blair traveled to the convention together, and a Cincinnati newspaper announced that they had come to nominate a ticket of Greeley and Brown.

On the first ballot Adams received 203 votes, Greeley 147, Trumbull 110, Brown 95, and Davis 92. Schurz was for Adams, but could do little in his position of chairman. After five ballots had left none with a majority, Governor B. Gratz Brown took the floor and called for the nomination of Greeley, who in his opinion would have the best chance against Grant. On the sixth ballot, the editor received the necessary majority.

By any standard of practical politics, it was a preposterous selection, although Greeley had a long record of honest idealism. Apparently some felt that Greeley's helping to post bail for

Jefferson Davis and his many denunciations of radical reconstruction would carry the South, while his consistent support for
measures designed to help the West would bring votes from that
quarter. Many southerners, however, had not forgotten his earlier
years of opposition to slavery, and Westerners looking for a
candidate in their own image would not take seriously a man so
long stereotyped as an effeminate, ultra-radical, unstable, and
unpredictable reformer, whose sins allegedly included both an
addiction to socialism and the advocacy of temperance. Some
historians have blamed Frank Blair for the nomination, and explained his position in terms of a belief that Greeley would out-
poll Adams in the South and West. Lizzie Lee, however, reported to her husband that Frank had not really wanted Greeley
and that he was being unfairly blamed. For many the decision
brought an immediate cloud of despair. Schurz reportedly sat
down at the piano of his local host and sorrowfully played
Chopin's "Funeral March." [17]

Whether or not the nomination embarrassed Frank, he and
his family now had the job of helping to sell the candidate and
platform to the Democrats. Francis P. Blair was ready to go to
New York and use his influence for Greeley among the New
York Democrats, but Montgomery talked him out of it. Frank,
however, thought this a brilliant idea, but the moment had
passed. "Brother," wrote Lizzie, "has no prompt political in-
stinct." Then Frank was invited to speak in New York at the
Democratic meeting ratifying the Greeley nomination, but his
father counseled that only the local leadership should be involved. The swallowing of Greeley, who had spent a lifetime
denouncing the Democratic party with rhetoric worthy of Sumner, was not easy for the Democrats, but the Blairs did their best
to sweeten the dose in numerous letters and speeches. On July 9
the Democratic national convention met in Baltimore and accepted both Greeley and his platform. Both parties were now
officially committed to black suffrage, and "to oppose any reopen-
ing of the questions settled by the 13th, 14th, and 15th amendments." [18]

It was to be Francis P. Blair's last active campaign, and it
must have given him much personal satisfaction. The issues of
honest government, civil service reform, and opposition to finan-

cial and business monopolies and dishonest practices, as well as the abstract defense of states' rights and the call for a final restoration of the Union, were items of faith he had defended all his life. And, whatever Greeley's political deficiencies, he was a pure and honest man. Also, Frank's political influence and future prospects had never seemed brighter. Actual events in the South and their widespread acceptance in the North indicated that the Blair position on reconstruction had triumphed. For a time, the Blairs even thought that the corruption of the Grant administration would be punished by a victory for Greeley. The moment of euphoria, however, was ended all too quickly by events within the family.

As might have been expected, Frank Blair threw himself headlong into the presidential campaign, and as usual his finances were in sad disarray. Several of his children were enrolled in expensive schools, and Apo was in St. Louis expecting their latest offspring. In June he sold his buggy and horses because he needed the money, and staying in Washington made them unnecessary. More important, he was rapidly losing the use of his right hand, and was finding movement of any kind increasingly painful and difficult. In June Apo produced another boy, and Frank left his worried parents to join her in Missouri and campaign throughout the state. A few weeks later, while Eliza was out "galloping around with Blair, George, and the other boys," the happy word came that Frank's hand had improved daily since he quit smoking. Then in July he reported that the doctors had prescribed a seaside vacation for Apo, and soon he took her and the three youngest children to East Hampton on Long Island. On July 20, 1872, Preston and Eliza Blair enjoyed their sixtieth wedding anniversary. Blair wanted a family affair, but Eliza was in no mood to celebrate. By the end of October, Frank was completely paralyzed on one side from a stroke, and the family was preparing to bring him to Silver Spring.[19]

In August the worry about Frank was interrupted by another family tragedy. Betty Blair Comstock, Montgomery's daughter who had been the older Blairs' adopted child since birth, had become estranged from Frank by her indiscreet conversations about his finances. She had first refused an invitation to come home because of Frank's presence, but as the time for the birth of her first child approached, she expressed a plaintive wish to return and to stay again in her old room. Francis P. Blair wrote her a firm answer, approved by his wife and daughter, that the time was inconvenient and that under no circumstances could she take back her former room from Frank's children. A few weeks later, her husband reported that she had died in childbirth. The entire family was distraught with grief compounded by remorse, as all thoughts of the recent adult dissension gave way to memories of the child they had all known and loved.[20]

The only bright spot for Lizzie and her parents during the summer of 1872 was the reassignment of Admiral Lee to the Washington area. Unable to go to Norfolk to meet him, Lizzie sent young Blair in her place. Soon father and son were enjoying a rare period of companionship while visiting the Blair, Gist, and Gratz relatives in Kentucky.

Frank Blair responded to the new enemy, illness, in his usual fashion. He taught himself to write with his left hand, and scrawled out letters even more illegible than formerly, announcing that he was still a candidate for reelection in December 1872. His Missouri following, however, could not be kept in line in the face of his obvious physical disability. He was replaced, but the new Missouri governor later appointed him to a $4,000 job as state superintendent of insurance. He could live on the salary, and the work was undemanding. He spent most of 1873 at Clifton Springs, New York, where the hot mineral water supposedly had curative powers.[21]

In October and November 1872, the ticket of Horace Greeley and B. Gratz Brown received far fewer votes from two parties accepting reconstruction than Seymour and Blair had received in 1868 from one party in violent opposition to it. The big problem, of course, was Greeley himself, who lost his mind and died shortly after the results were announced. The Blairs, however, took little notice beyond expressing satisfaction that no fraud had been reported. Their only concern by then was Frank. "I am heart hungry for tidings from your father," wrote Eliza in a firm hand to her grandson Preston in April 1873. "By this time he can tell whether the treatment agrees with him."[22]

At some point in 1873, a reporter interviewed Frank at

Clifton Springs. The general's right arm and leg were almost useless, but his mind was strong. He was still opposed to a high tariff. He was intensely favorable toward the efforts of the Grangers and other western radical agrarian groups, and reviewed their activities state by state. Parting with him, the reporter concluded, was "like taking a final look at some noble wreck stranded on a rocky shore. . . . the strained and shattered hulk still retains some vestige of its once goodly proportions and although it rests in apparent quiet, with a calm sea about it, yet the first gale that dashes the waves against its weather-beaten sides will break it asunder and leave not a plank to mark the spot where it lay." [23]

Chapter 29

Twilight

IN 1873–1874 Montgomery Blair found visiting with his parents a painful experience. He was incapable of deception, and speaking about Frank without betraying his despair was impossible. The easiest way to avoid increasing their heartbreak was to keep them involved with the children, and he was always grateful for their presence. He reported to Minna that his mother looked "calm but painfully sad. There is a look out of her eyes which I have never noticed before. She has to control herself & she has the look of resolve in her face as well as sorrow that is very painful." [1]

In late 1872 Francis P. Blair had followed the example of Andrew Jackson by asking for baptism after spending a lifetime without it. He had always believed privately in Christianity, and he. may have felt a more formal connection might improve the efficacy of his prayers for Frank. An Episcopal bishop came out from Washington for a private evening ceremony, and Eliza prepared a feast of ducks, oysters, and ice-cream for the great occasion. [2]

In 1874 Montgomery diverted his parents for a time by trying to gain the Democratic nomination for Congress. In the end, however, the nominating convention preferred a lesser known and noncontroversial candidate. Montgomery's belief that his status as a former Union Republican ruined his chances was probably only partially correct. Spoils-hungry Democratic and Republican local politicians differed little in the 1870s, and neither group wanted uncompromising moralists like Montgomery Blair looking over its shoulder. Marylanders, like most Americans, were tired of the years of struggle and strife, and

Montgomery Blair was still a glaring symbol of what they were trying to forget. Ironically, the harmony he had fought so hard to accomplish was now a political disadvantage.

Frank, meanwhile, returned to St. Louis in late 1873 to accept the job of insurance superintendent. In December he reported that the family had survived Christmas very well, with "the little ones making the usual amount of noise." His left hand was almost entirely well and his right side was improving steadily. A few days later, Frank suffered another stroke and had to be returned to Clifton Springs.[3]

Poor Apo, struggling with the problems and childhood diseases of children aged six, three, and one, while trying to nurse her disabled husband, was almost irrational from worry. Her plight would have been sad if they had been affluent, but the desperate need for assistance from the family was an added torment. In May 1873 her son Preston, who had just enrolled at West Point, asked Lizzie for a loan. Lizzie offered to give rather than loan him the hundred dollars requested, and to pay him for good grades on the same basis as her son Blair. She insisted, however, that he must get his mother's permission first. She was afraid to become involved in a deception that Apo might discover. Apo finally agreed to accept money from Frank's parents, but indignantly returned $50 sent by Lizzie. She would not be a "pensioner of Mr. Lee." Lizzie answered with a sensitive explanation that she and Phil were being reimbursed from *"Mr. Blair's Estate,"* and assured Apo that no deceit or unkindness had been intended. Montgomery and Lee continued to send $200 monthly to Frank at Clifton, but keeping him comfortable without offending Apo was a delicate task.[4]

For a time, Frank again improved. In May, Secretary of War William Belknap got Preston a leave to visit his father, and Frank wrote that he had never before enjoyed a spring so much. Through the summer his left-handed letters to Montgomery remained full of political interest and hope for the future. He gave his family much comfort by formally expressing his faith in Christianity. His parents traveled to see him at Clifton in the private railroad car of Simon Cameron, who had always remained friendly despite their strong political and public differences. By the end of September, however, Frank had lost all powers of speech, and Apo decided to take him home to St. Louis. There his life slowly ebbed away. On July 9, 1875, while alone, he was knocked unconscious by a fall when trying to walk to another room, and he died a few hours later.

St. Louis was draped in mourning, and the ships in the river flew their flags at half-mast. Public eulogies came from friend and foe alike. General Sherman had infuriated Montgomery Blair by calling Frank a "political general" in his memoirs, but had already explained that he meant only that Frank was not a West Point professional. Now Sherman announced that Frank had been "a noble, generous, honest man. . . . brave, frank, and sincere, and unselfish," one of the "most courageous soldiers this country has produced." Many had opposed Frank's ideas and policies, but everyone agreed that his prompt actions in Missouri had saved that state—and perhaps others as a result—for the Union, and no one had ever questioned his courage. "Take him all in all," editorialized the *New York Evening Mail*, "we think Frank Blair was the bravest man we ever knew. Let us honor his memory." The less friendly *New York Times* pronounced his career "an example of how the most brilliant achievements may be blurred by weakness and inconsistency, and how, at the same time, the honorable record of earlier years may outlive and palliate the waywardness of its close." In 1886 a large bronze statue of Frank was unveiled in a St. Louis park, and shortly afterward the Missouri legislature chose Frank and Benton as the state's two great men to be honored by statues in the United States Capitol.[5]

Until the illness and death of Frank, his parents had remained strong and alert. In 1874 a reporter saw them cantering into Washington from Silver Spring. Before Blair could dismount, Eliza sprang from her horse like a young girl and walked firmly up the steps to the Lee house. The long months of alternating hope and despair, however, were an unbearable strain when coupled with advancing age. In 1876 Blair agreed with Montgomery that Samuel J. Tilden was the Democratic party's best hope to end the corruption and big-business domination of the Grant Republicans, but not even a new political campaign could restore the spark. Slowly and quietly he slipped away in spite of the desperate efforts of Eliza and Lizzie to hold him in place. On October 19, 1876, he died. At his request, six of his grandsons served as pallbearers for the funeral held in Rock Creek Cemetery.[6]

Perhaps more than any other contemporary, Blair had become the symbol of an earlier time, and newspapers throughout the country took due note of this in nostalgic eulogies. A clergyman friend wrote the family that Blair "served to link us to a past age, as brilliant as it was pure; and no living man more fully understood the grandeur of that age or beautifully illustrated it." On a page filled with diatribes against Tilden, the *New York Times* ran a two-column story sketching the origins and influence of the *Globe,* and describing Blair's role in the bank struggle, the founding of the Republican party, and the preservation of the Union. "Mr. Blair," wrote the editor, was "slashing and fierce on occasion, and his whole political training had been aggressive and belligerent." In person, however, he was "slender and unimposing; in demeanor, retiring and quiet; in character amiable, affectionate, and grateful. The man and the editor were as dissimilar as possible." The *Philadelphia Gazette* pronounced an epitaph that would have satisfied Blair completely: "Mr. Blair enjoyed many warm friendships, and almost universal public respect." [7]

Eliza had remained strong until her husband's death, but she wilted rapidly, almost as though she had decided to follow him as soon as possible. She would go only when ready, however, and she would play the role of lioness to the end. In January 1877, not long after her six-year-old daughter had died, Apo wrote Montgomery for some books she believed the senior Blair had given to Frank, and apparently expressed some reservations as to the value of the causes for which Frank had sacrificed himself. "My husband," answered Eliza, "left everything at Silver Spring to me during my life. I intend to keep every article, book, and paper there just as he left them to me as long as I live—When I am gone . . . his wishes will be faithfully carried out. But I think he would have chosen someone else as the Trustee for his Grandchildren than you, if he had read the sneer in your letter to Montgomery upon his and Frank's noble political principles and career, by far the best heritage and example they could have left their descendants—Read this to your children, from their devoted Grandmother." For the next few months she remained alert in mind while slowly becoming physically weaker. Surrounded by her children and many grandchildren, she died peacefully on July 5, 1877.[8]

With Eliza's death, the Blair estate had to be divided according to the last of several wills Blair had prepared with much satisfaction. In each version Eliza was to have everything until her death (except for the Pennsylvania Avenue house, which Montgomery would retain), but the prescriptions for dividing everything else after her demise changed with circumstances. In 1864 Blair decreed that in exchange for the house, Montgomery should give his half of the "land bought from the Carrolls" to Elizabeth Blair Lee and pay Elizabeth and Frank $5,000 each. Frank was also to receive the Silver Spring estate. Violet Blair and her children should have the balance of the Carroll purchase, and all property not previously mentioned should go to Frank. Over the next few years, the extra assets assigned to Frank dwindled while Blair's land holdings expanded. In 1870, therefore, he prepared a new document that also commended his "soul to God my creator believing through the merits of Jesus Christ to inherit eternal life." Everything should go to Montgomery, who should act as trustee for its further disposition. Montgomery and Elizabeth should receive land adjacent to Silver Spring proper, while the estate itself should be held by Montgomery in trust for Frank's family as their family residence. If Frank should choose otherwise, Montgomery should pay him any income from the property with one exception: If any creditor's proceedings existed against Frank, the money should go entirely to Apo and the children. The Lee inheritance should include his and Eliza's graves.

A few months later Blair added still another codicil: "My son Gen F. P. Blair surprised me last summer at Silver Spring with the request that in my disposition of the place by will I should give it to his sister—He said she was so identified with the home of her parents . . . that he could not bear to separate her from it. . . . nothing has contributed to my wife's happiness and mine so much as the constant proofs of love of our children which have always attended us and the endearing mutual attachment for each other that unites them. This has been the great blessing of my family history, and renders even the close of life now in near prospect, to the parents, happy." Silver Spring, therefore, should go to Phil and Lizzie, on condition that within six months after Eliza's death they should pay $20,000 to Frank and his family. In turn, Frank and his family should have the land previously assigned to the Lees. Responsible for seeing that all his debts were paid and that all of these arrangements were accomplished would be Montgomery, to whom Blair expressed much well-deserved praise and gratitude for being such a dutiful son. In May 1872, even before Frank's illness, Blair added a final precaution. The $20,000 to be paid by the Lees should go to Montgomery as trustee for Apo and her children, and remain "free and clear of all control and liability for the debts of said Frank Blair junior." [9]

Montgomery Blair lived six more years after the death of his mother. He unselfishly assumed responsibility for various family debts in order that his father's wishes concerning Frank and Lizzie could be fulfilled. Woodbury ultimately survived his various escapades to finish law school and assume much of his father's practice, which left Montgomery time to write long letters and articles defending and praising Lincoln, and work tirelessly if unsuccessfully to reform the Democratic party into its old Jacksonian image. He was a major figure in the struggle over the disputed presidential election of 1876, and went to Louisiana to monitor the recount in that state. When Rutherford B. Hayes was finally given the presidency, in part through a bargain to remove all remaining troops from the South, Montgomery still considered the result a fraud. He persuaded the Maryland legislature to order the state's attorney general to institute a suit for a further decision by the Supreme Court, but the effort failed. He tried unsuccessfully to get Tilden renominated in 1880. In 1882 Montgomery was finally nominated for Congress by the Democrats, but lost to the Republican candidate in a district becoming more and more business-oriented. On July 27, 1883, he died, and received widespread plaudits for his services to his family, community, state, church, and country.

Phillips Lee retired from the navy in 1873, and he and Lizzie enjoyed twenty-four years of normal domestic life. He ran the Silver Spring farm with the precision of a flag officer, and made it for the first time a profitable venture. According to family legend, for many years he and a favorite black servant drove several miles together to the polls each Election Day to cast opposing ballots. The eighty-five-year-old admiral died in 1897, but Lizzie continued to enjoy her son and grandchildren until 1906. She had managed the Washington Orphan Asylum for fifty-seven years before being forced to retire because of blindness in 1898.

Francis P. Blair had hoped for political immortality through his descendants, and through Lizzie's progeny he appeared to have his best chance. After a distinguished career as a progressive state legislator, her son, Blair, was the first United States senator to be elected by the people of Maryland after the Seventeenth Amendment removed the selection process from the state legislatures. Her grandson, E. Brooke Lee, was for many years a powerful state leader in Maryland, and his children have continued the tradition. His daughter is a highly respected leader in county government, and his grandson is a prominent member of the Maryland legislature. In 1976–1978 his son, Francis Preston Blair II, served as acting governor of Maryland.

Notes

UNLESS otherwise indicated, all letters to and from Francis P. Blair and Elizabeth Blair Lee, except to Martin Van Buren, are in the Blair–Lee Papers at the Princeton University Library, and all letters to Martin Van Buren are in the Van Buren Papers, Library of Congress. I have used the following abbreviations throughout:

Basler: Roy P. Basler (ed.), *The Collected Works of Abraham Lincoln* (1955)

Bassett: John S. Bassett (ed.), *Correspondence of Andrew Jackson* (1926)

BLC: Blair Papers, Library of Congress

BRLC: Blair–Rives Collection, Library of Congress

CG: Congressional Globe

Globe: Washington Globe

KHS: Kentucky Historical Society, Frankfort, Kentucky

LC: Library of Congress

LMSS: Abraham Lincoln Papers, Library of Congress

NYHS: New York Historical Society

NYPL: New York Public Library

P: Blair–Lee Papers, Princeton University Library

PaHS: Historical Society of Pennsylvania, Philadelphia, Pennsylvania

VBMSS: Martin Van Buren Papers, Library of Congress

Chapter 1. The Beginning

1. This generalization is based upon many of Blair's later stories to his children and grandchildren.
2. William B. Preston, *The Preston Genealogy* (1900), 153; George Baber, "Blairs of Kentucky," *Register of the Kentucky Historical Society*, XIV

(1916), 47; William E. Smith, *The Francis Preston Blair Family in Politics* (1933), I, 1–18; F. P. Blair's father, James Blair, to Blair, tracing genealogy, Jan. 4, 1831.

3. *Franklin County Tax Books* (1796–1820), microfilm, KHS; *Franklin County Circuit Court Records* (1798–1819), Franklin County Courthouse.

4. *A Review of the Criminal Law of the Commonwealth of Kentucky*, 2 vols. (1804–1806).

5. Robert Peter, *Transylvania University* (1896), 90; Ewing O. Cossaboom, *A Brief Sketch of Transylvania University's Law Department* (1939), 2–6.

6. Blair to Harry I. Todd, Oct. 12, 1865, attributing his survival to Todd's grandfather, KHS.

7. Jean M. and Maxwell J. Dorsey, *Christopher Gist of Maryland and Some of His Descendants, 1679–1957* (1958), 33–34. I have used this book extensively for family dates and names.

8. Ibid., 38, 41–42.

9. *Deed Books*, E, F, G, H, I, K, for various Blair transactions 1812–1826. Originals in Franklin County Courthouse; microfilm, Kentucky State Archives.

10. L. F. Johnson, *The History of Franklin County, Kentucky* (1912), 71; *Franklin County Tax Books*.

Chapter 2. Struggle

1. Statistical data from Thomas D. Clark, *A History of Kentucky* (1937), 198–218, and Arndt M. Stickles, *The Critical Court Struggle in Kentucky, 1819–1829* (1929). See also George Robertson, *Scrapbook on Law and Politics, Men, and Times* (1855).

2. Copy of Blair's release from these debts in Benjamin F. Gratz to Blair, May 26, 1832; *Globe*, June 6, 1832.

3. *Franklin County Circuit Court Records*. Finding and adding all of these figures left some room for error, but I believe they are essentially correct.

4. Ibid.; *Deed Books*, I, 245, and K, 323; Blair to Crittenden, undated, John J. Crittenden MSS, LC.

5. *Franklin County Tax Books*.

6. Blair to Crittenden, Jan. 19, 1826, Crittenden MSS.

7. Conveyance signed by Judith C. Scott and Benjamin F. Gratz (as trustee), Dec. 21, 1827, P.

8. Jan. 6, 1821, Crittenden MSS.

9. Crittenden to Blair, Jan. 7, 1831.

10. Rabbi David Philipson (ed.), *Letters of Rebecca Gratz* (1929), 43–46; Eliza to Blair, undated except by association.

11. Reports from the bank in Kentucky *House Journal* (1822), 57–61, 111–112; *Senate Journal* (1823–24), 71–74; (1824–25), 41–42; (1825–26), 42–45; (1826–27), 42–45; (1827–28), 42–46; (1828–29), 45–47, 61–62; (1829–30), 64–65.

12. This story is well told in the previously cited books by Stickles, Clark, and Robertson; the latter was a conservative participant.
13. March 3, 1824.
14. June 16, 1824. Also each weekly edition March–June.
15. *House Journal* (1824–25), 388–436.
16. Cited by Stickles, 65–66.
17. Feb. 11, 1825, Henry Clay MSS, LC.
18. *House Journal* (1825), 174–203; Stickles, 67–69; *Argus*, Feb. 9, 1825.
19. Stickles, 81–83; quotation, 82–83.
20. Aug. 30, 1825, Clay MSS.
21. *Argus*, Feb. 22, March 22, 29, April 19, May 3, 24, 31, June 23, July 12, 1826; quotation, March 29; Stickles, 88–89.
22. Stickles, 91; *House Journal* (1825), 282–293; Robertson, 95–96.
23. Feb.21, 1826.
24. Nov. 28, 1825, Clay MSS.
25. Blair to Clay, Jan. 30, 1826, Clay MSS.
26. Ibid., Jan. 4, 1826, Clay MSS.

Chapter 3. Old Hickory

1. Nov. 14, 1827, Clay MSS.
2. Dec. 6, 1826.
3. April 16, 24, 30, May 30, June 6, 1827.
4. *Argus*, Sept. 19, 1827.
5. Ibid., Sept. 26, 1827, and following; Crittenden to Kendall and Kendall Crittenden, Oct. 2, 1827, P.
6. Clay to Blair, Jan. 9, 1825; Blair to Clay, March 7, 1825, Dec. 31, 1827, Clay MSS.
7. Blair to Clay, Jan. 22, Feb. 1, 1828, Clay MSS. Crittenden to Clay, March 4, 1828, Crittenden MSS.
8. *Argus*, March 5, 1829.
9. March 7, Nov. 22, 1829. Kendall believed that Peggy was entirely innocent, but much too "forward in her manners."
10. From January through June 1829 Kendall wrote Blair at least twice weekly.
11. Jan. 9, 1829.
12. Jan. 9, March 10, April 21, 1829.
13. *Argus*, March 18, 25, July 8, Oct. 28, 1829.
14. Ibid., Oct. 28, 1829.
15. Jan. 28, 1830.
16. Kendall was writing Blair about the possibility of a new paper as early as Feb. 3, 1829. See also letters of Jan. 28, March 1, 18, April 20, 25, 1830.
17. Oct. 2, 30, 1830.
18. Voluminous correspondence on these matters among Blair, Gratz, Philip

Swigert (Blair's agent), Dennis Hickman, Lewis Sanders, Crittenden, and others, P and BLC.

19. Oct. 29, 1830.
20. Diary of the journey in Blair's handwriting, P.

Chapter 4. The Editor

1. James Parton, *Life of Andrew Jackson* (1861), III,, 337–338.
2. Kearney to Blair, Nov. 9, 1831, BLC; *Globe*, Feb. 5, 1835. For influence in N. Y. legislature, see A. C. Flagg to Blair, Jan. 11, 1832, PaHS. Many other such letters show its importance.
3. Records published in answer to critics, *Globe*, March 4, April 4, Dec. 26, 1843; E. H. Kincaid to Blair, Sept. 21, 1832.
4. Blair to Kendall, Dec. 24, 1842, VBMSS; copy of Kendall Proposal, P.
5. Kendall to Jackson, Dec. 3, 1831, P.
6. Clipping from *Chicago Daily Democrat*, Dec. 21, 1855, P.
7. April 23, 27, 1831.
8. The lottery and other ads ran for years. Feb. 19, 1841, March 8, 1836, for quotations; Oct. 19, 1836, for the serenaders.
9. April 4, 1837, Nov. 7, 1833, Dec. 17, 1840, Dec. 12, 1843, Nov. 2, 1832, Jan. 19, 29, 1831.
10. *Globe*, Nov. 15, 1842.
11. June 10, 1831, Crittenden MSS.
12. July 9, 1831.
13. Nov. 22, 1831.
14. Dec. 7, 1830.
15. Quote from *Globe*, June 21, 1831.
16. *Globe Extra*, May 10, 1832.
17. Jan. 26, May 4, July 20, 1831.
18. Jan. 19, Feb. 15, Dec. 1, 1831.
19. April 27, 1831; see also Blair to John R. Barker on same subject, Oct. 1, 1832, PaHS.
20. *Globe*, March 24, 1831.
21. Feb. 5, 1831.
22. Aug. 5, 1831.
23. July 30, 1832; also Jan. 8, 1831, editorial praising Ireland's efforts to attain independence.
24. Feb. 2, 1831.
25. Dec. 11, 1830, Jan. 12, 15, 22, 29, Feb. 5, 9, 16, 1831, Oct. 1, Nov. 3, 1832.
26. Feb. 12, 26, June 11, 1831.
27. Feb. 19, 23, March 2, 12, 30, April 2, 13, 16, 1831.
28. *Globe*, April 20, June 13, 24, 27, 1831; cf. Jackson to John Coffee, April 24, 1831, Bassett, IV, 268–269.
29. *Globe*, March 24, 1832.

Chapter 5. Victory

1. Printed article, BLC.
2. Ralph C. H.- Catterall, *The Second Bank of the United States* (1903), 29–30, 32–50, 68–113, 132–137, 145–163. This classic is strongly pro-Bank, but clearly shows the institution's weaknesses. Likewise, Bray Hammond, *Banks and Politics in America from the Revolution to the Civil War* (1957), and Thomas P. Govan, *Nicholas Biddle* (1959), present scholarly, thoroughly documented studies that, in my opinion, do not fully justify their pro-Bank and pro-Biddle conclusions.
3. Marvin Meyers, *The Jacksonian Persuasion* (1957).
4. All references to Benton are from Elbert B. Smith, *Magnificent Missourian: The Life of Thomas Hart Benton* (1958).
5. Ibid., 121–122.
6. July 12, Aug. 5, 1832. Such sentiments were daily *Globe* fare for the next several months.
7. Aug. 30, Sept. 5, 7, 11, 15, 1832.
8. *Prelude to Civil War: The Nullification Controversy in South Carolina, 1816–1826* (1966).
9. Feb. 1, 1832.
10. June 13, Aug. 30, 1832.

Chapter 6. Days of Triumph

1. Printed article, BLC.
2. Edward Alcock to Blair, Aug. 6, 1832, Barry to Blair, Oct. 6, 1832, Staunton letter, undated, B. B. Johnson to Blair, June 20, 1832, Bledsoe to Blair, Nov. 30, 1832, S. Daviess to Blair, Dec. 6, 1832, W. H. Davis to Blair, Sept. 8, 1832, John Nagler to Blair, introducing McCord, May 13, 1833—these and dozens of similar missives in P.
3. *Globe*, Nov. 26, 1832.
4. Dec. 22, 1832.
5. March 2, 27, June 10, 1833.
6. March 5, 1833.
7. March 20, 1833.
8. Martin Gordon to William B. Lewis, March 25, 1833, P; Blair's answer quoting Jackson, April 11, 1833, addressee indecipherable, NYHS. Jackson had been fined $1,000 for defying a writ of *habeas corpus* and arresting a judge after the Battle of New Orleans in 1815.
9. Parton, III, 501–504; Lewis to Blair, Aug. 12, 1833.
10. Kendall to Blair, Aug. 11, 26, 1833.
11. *Globe*, July 31, 1833; C. K. Gardiner to Blair, Aug 1, 1833.
12. Aug. 2, 1833.
13. Moore to Blair, Sept. 22, 1833.
14. Aug. 17, 1833.
15. Cited by Arthur Schlesinger, Jr., *The Age of Jackson* (1946), 102.

16. *Globe*, Oct. 16, 1833; May 15, 27, 1834.
17. Ibid., April 30, 1834.
18. Blair to Van Buren, Oct. 10, 1859.
19. Pleasants to Blair, March 15, 19, 27, 1834, Blair to Pleasants, March 17, 1834.
20. Blair to Jackson, Aug. 18, 1834, Bassett, V, 283–284.
21. July 1, 1834.

Chapter 7. *Golden Years*

1. Jan. 21, 1832.
2. Several letters from Blair to Maria Gratz in Philipson, *Rebecca Gratz*, 290–300.
3. Blair to Van Buren, Oct. 8, 1836, VBMSS; description in Post Office Dept. pamphlet by Rita L. Monroney, *Montgomery Blair, Postmaster General* (1963), 44.
4. Gratz to Blair, May 31, 1831, BLC.
5. Jan. 8, 1831.
6. Aug. 7, 1831, Feb. 12, 1834.
7. Montgomery to Blair, May 27, Aug. 23, 1834; Warren to F. P. Blair, April 21, 1835, to Montgomery Blair, Feb. 8, 1836, P.
8. April 20, June 14, 1835.
9. Notebook in P.
10. Yale University form letter to Blair, Oct. 23, 1837.
11. J. D. B. Hooper to Blair, June 21, 1839.
12. Henry to Frank Blair, Nov. 25, 1842, Joseph Henry Personal Papers, Smithsonian Institution Archives.
13. James to Blair, Jan. 4, 1831, April 23, May 9, June 4, 1832, March 8, Aug. 25, 1834, Jan. 18, Nov. 9, 1835, John D. Blair to Blair, Nov. 5, 1839, July 17, 1843, Gratz to Blair, Feb. 7, 1839, and many others.

Chapter 8. *The Changing of the Guard*

1. *Globe*, Jan. 5, 8, 15, 19, 24, Feb. 24, July 9, 1835, Jan. 26, 1836.
2. Jan 31, Feb 4, 7, 23, 28, 1835.
3. June 16, 1835.
4. Both quotations cited in *Globe*, Jan 5, 16, 1835.
5. Ibid., May 2, 1835.
6. July 28, Aug. 17, Sept. 11, Dec. 22, 1835, Jan. 2, 1836; quotation, Sept. 11, 1835.
7. *Globe*, March 19, 1836.
8. Ibid., May 28, 1836.
9. Sept. 4, 1835.
10. Schlesinger, *Age of Jackson*, 190–191, 232.
11. June 10, 20, 1836.
12. *Globe*, Nov. 28, 1836.
13. May 25, 1835.

14. Jan. 14, 18, March 2, 25, June 24, July 8, 1836.
15. July 10, Oct. 15, 1836.
16. Jesup to Blair, Aug. 6, 1836, P; exchange of letters between Jesup and Scott on June 17, 1836, Scott to Jesup, June 16, 1836, Jesup to Blair, Sept. 3, 1836—all printed in *Globe*, Sept. 26, 1836; also *Globe*, July 29, Aug. 4, 1836.
17. Sept. 19, 27, 29, 1836.
18. Ritchie to Blair, Dec. 9, 1836.
19. Jan. 20, 1837.
20. March 6, 1837.
21. James D. Richardson (ed.), *Messages and Papers of the Presidents*, III, 318.
22. Feb. 8, 1839, Bassett, VI, 3–4.
23. Benson, *The Concept of Jacksonian Democracy: New York as a Test Case* (1961); Hammond, *Banks and Politics*.
24. "Money and Party in Jacksonian America: A Quantitative Look at New York City's Men of Quality," *Political Science Quarterly*, LXXXII (1967), 235–252.
25. *The Birth of Mass Political Parties* (1971).
26. McCormick, *The Second American Party System: Party Formation in the Jacksonian Era* (1966); Van Deusen, *The Jacksonian Era, 1828–1848* (1959).
27. *The American Political Tradition and the Men Who Made It* (1948), 45–68.
28. *Andrew Jackson: Symbol for an Age* (1955).
29. *The Election of Andrew Jackson* (1963).
30. "Who Were the Southern Whigs?" *American Historical Review*, LIX (1954), 335–345.
31. *The Jacksonian Economy* (1969).
32. Pessen (ed.), *New Perspectives on Jacksonian Parties and Politics* (1969), *The Many-Faceted Jacksonian Era* (1977); Pessen, *Jacksonian America* (1969).

Chapter 9. Van Buren and the Jacksonian Aftermath

1. For example, Hofstadter, *American Political Tradition*, 45–68, and McCormick, *Second American Party System*.
2. *Jacksonian Persuasion*.
3. Hammond, *Banks and Politics*, 325, 533–534.
4. Hammond, "Jackson, Biddle, and the Bank of the United States," *Journal of Economic History*, *VII* (May 1947), reprinted in George R. Taylor (ed.), *Jackson versus Biddle* (1949), 66.
5. Govan, *Biddle*, 329–357, 368 ff.
6. David Kinley, *The Independent Treasury of the United States* (1863).
7. Maxcy to Lawrence, March 29, 1837, Benton MSS, Missouri Historical Society, St. Louis.

8. Leggett to Blair, April 25, 1837.
9. April 5, 1837, Bassett, V, 474–475.
10. April 18, 1837, Bassett V, 475–476.
11. May 11, 1837, Bassett, V, 481–482.
12. Sept. 6, 1837, Bassett, V, 508–509.
13. Blair to Jackson, Sept. 9, 1837, Bassett, V, 509–510.
14. Cited by Charles Wiltse, *John C. Calhoun: Nullifier* (1949), 351.
15. Bassett, V, 514.
16. Oct. 13, 1837, Bassett, V, 515–516.
17. Feb. 11, March 20, 1838, Bassett, V, 537–539.
18. Jackson to Blair, March 26, 1838, Bassett, V, 545–546.
19. April 17, 1838, Bassett, V, 550.
20. Blair to Bancroft, Dec. 11, 1837, Jan. 9, 29, March 9, 1838, Bancroft MSS, Harvard University Library; Blair to Jackson, Feb. 8, 1839, Bassett, VI, 3–4.
21. *Globe*, Jan. 5, 31, Feb. 2, 1837.
22. June 4, 1838.
23. Jackson to Blair, April 20, 1839, VBMSS.

Chapter 10. Defeat

1. *Globe*, Feb. 1, 1839.
2. Cited by Freeman Cleaves, *Old Tippecanoe: William Henry Harrison and His Time* (1939), 317–318. A good source for this election campaign is Robert Gunderson, *The Log Cabin Campaign* (1957), but even better is an unpublished M.S. thesis by James T. Emmerson, "The Campaign of 1840 as Seen Through the Political Press" (Iowa State University, 1963).
3. Biddle to Herman Cope, Aug. 11, 1835, cited by Schlesinger, *Age of Jackson*, 211.
4. Gunderson, 74.
5. *Niles' Register*, LVIII (May 9, 1840), 149–150.
6. Ibid., 152–159; Gunderson, 1–6; Emmerson, 24–25.
7. May 9, 1840.
8. Gunderson, 134, 226, 234; Emmerson, 41.
9. *Globe*, Jan. 16, Feb. 18, 26, March 4, April 10, May 28, July 1, 7, Aug. 14, 17, 18, 28, 1840; Emmerson, 52.
10. Oct. 10, 12, 1840.
11. April 18, May 28, 1840.
12. Jan. 8, Feb. 22, March 30, June 12, 1840; Emmerson, 126.
13. *National Intelligencer*, May 4, 6, June 18, 30, 1840; Emmerson, 126–127.
14. June 24, July 10, Aug. 6, 12, 13, Oct. 23, 1840; Emmerson, 127.
15. *Globe*, June 17, 19, 23, 24, July 17, Aug. 1, Sept. 12, Oct. 21, 1840; C.G., VIII, 460–462.
16. *Globe*, July 17, 19, 23, 24, 25, 26, 1840; Emmerson, 131.
17. *Intelligencer*, June 24, Sept. 12, 1840; Emmerson, 132.
18. *Globe*, June 25, 1840.

19. *Niles' Register*, LVIII (June 27, 1840), 266; (Sept. 19, 1840), 42–43; (Oct. 3, 1840), 71; Emmerson, 91–92.
20. *Globe*, Jan. 25, Feb. 1, 17, 28, 1840; *Intelligencer*, Jan. 21, 1840; Emmerson, 138–141.
21. *Globe*, July 8, 20, Oct. 17, 1840; Emmerson, 64; David Crockett, *The Life of Martin Van Buren* (1835), 13, 29, 57–59, 80–81.
22. *Regal Splendor* pamphlet, 1–6, 19, 21, 22, 24; Emmerson, 67–73.
23. *Globe*, Aug. 15, Sept. 7, 8, 10, 23, 29, 1840.
24. Jackson to Van Buren, Nov. 24, 1840, Bassett, VI, 84.
25. Oliver Carlson, *The Man Who Made News, James Gordon Bennett* (1942), 212–213, cited by Emmerson, 108.
26. *Globe*, Aug. 13, 20, 29, Oct. 23, 24, 26, 27, 28; Gunderson, 249; Emmerson, 152–154.
27. *Washington Evening Star*, Sept. 14, 1906, sketch of Elizabeth Blair Lee at time of her death. Copy in BLC. She and her father were in New York City when the final verdict was announced, but this often-told family story is probably true. Van Buren's defeat was certain several days earlier.
28. Blair to Van Buren, Nov. 8, 1840; *Globe*, Nov. 16, 1840.
29. Numerous letters in P and BLC.
30. July 8, 1840.
31. Philipson, *Rebecca Gratz*, 285; Lee to Sarah G. Moses, Aug. 14, 1840, P.

Chapter 11. The Maverick

1. Nov. 16, 1840.
2. *Globe*, March 8, 15, 1841.
3. Ibid., Aug. 16, 1841; *CG*, X (1841, special sess.), 355.
4. *Globe*, May 1, 4, 18, 1843.
5. Ibid., April 28, May 10, 1843.
6. Ibid., May 23, 1843.
7. Ibid., June 16, Aug. 14, 24, Nov. 7, 1843, Nov. 17, 1842; Rives to Kendall, Dec. 21, 1842, and thirty-one other letters on the subject in P and VBMSS, 1842–1843.
8. Jan. 8, 15, Feb. 5, 14, 1844.
9. Letter printed in *Globe*, March 20, 1844; Blair to Van Buren, March 18, 1844, VBMSS.
10. Thomas Hart Benton, *Thirty Years' View*, II (1856), 581–596.
11. *Globe*, Feb. 14, 17, 28, March 6, 1844.
12. March 18, 1844.
13. Walker to Blair, April 13, 1844.
14. *Congressional Documents*, no. 444, pp. 48–49; Calhoun to J. R. Matthews, July 2, May 9, 1844, Misc. Calhoun MSS, LC.
15. *Globe*, April 27, 29, 1844.
16. May 30, 1844.
17. *Globe*, April 29, 1844; *CG*, XIII (1843–44), Appendix, 474–486.
18. May 30, 1844.

19. May 29, 31, 1844.

20. June 7, 1844.

21. Jackson to Blair, June 25, 1844, Jackson MSS, LC, 112; Blair to Jackson, June 29, July 7, 1844, Bassett, VI, 298–299.

22. Jackson to Blair, Aug. 15, 1844, Bassett, VI, 313–314; *Globe*, Aug. 5, 1844.

23. Tyler to Jackson, Aug. 18, 1844, Jackson to Blair, Aug. 29, 1844, Bassett, VI, 315, 316–318; Blair to Jackson, Sept. 9, 1844, Jackson MSS, LC, 112.

24. *Globe*, Aug. 9, 24, 1844.

25. March 29, Sept. 18, 1844.

26. *Globe*, Sept. 23, 26, 28, Oct. 1, 29, 1844.

27. Sept. 27, Oct. 10, 1844.

28. *Globe*, Aug. 19, Oct. 1, 24, Nov. 24, 1844; Blair to Jackson, Oct. 27, 1844, Bassett, VI, 377–378.

29. Jackson to Donelson, Dec. 11, 1844, Jackson to Blair, Dec. 14, 21, 1844, Jan. 1, 3, 20, March 10, 1845, Blair to Jackson, Dec. 22, 25, 1844, Jan. 3, Feb. 28, 1845—all Bassett VI, 338, 342, 346–355; Benton to Donelson, Jan. 10, 1845, Donelson MSS, LC.

30. Tappan and Blair letters to *New York Evening Post*, July 21, 1848. Polk denied this (Polk to George Bancroft, Sept. 9, 1848, Bancroft MSS, Harvard University Library), while Haywood refused to be involved in the public controversy (Haywood to Blair, May 29, 1848, P).

31. Cf. Charles G. Sellers, *James K. Polk, Jacksonian* (1957), 249, 280, 293–294, 309–310, 366; Allan Nevins (ed.), *Polk, The Diary of a President*, 78–79. Polk to Jackson, March 26, 1845, Bassett, VI, 389–390.

32. Blair to Van Buren, Feb. 22, April 11, 1845, to John Van Buren, March 29, 1845, VBMSS.

33. Benton, *Thirty Years' View*, I (1854), 651; Blair pamphlet, *A Voice from the Grave of Jackson* (1856), BLC; Rives to Blair, sometime in 1842, from New York.

34. O'Sullivan to Van Buren, April 5, 1845, VBMSS.

35. Blair to Buchanan, June 2, 1845, Buchanan MSS, PaHS; Blair to Van Buren, April 21, 1845, Rives to Van Buren, April 12, 1845, VBMSS.

Chapter 12. The Planter

1. Gratz to Blair, April 27, 1845; O'Sullivan to Van Buren, April 5, 1845, VBMSS.

2. Crittenden to Blair, May 23, 1845; W. A. Harris to Calhoun, July 11, 1845, *Annual Report of the American Historical Association* (1899), II, 1038–1039.

3. Washington Topham, "The Old *Globe* Office and the Publishers," *Records of the Columbia Historical Society*, XXXV and XXXVI (Nov. 17, 1831), 124–132; *National Intelligencer*, Dec. 1, 1845; Blair to Van Buren, Feb. 9, 1845, VBMSS.

4. Blair to Rives, May 24, 1847, March 28, 1849, BRLC; Blair to Van

Buren, Oct. 16, 1849, VBMSS; statements of Blair–Rives financial transactions, LC; numerous letters between Blair and Franklin A. Dick, BLC and P.

5. Rives to Blair, March 31, 1853; Topham, "Globe Office."
6. Work schedule, P.
7. Blair to Rives, undated, BRLC; Frank to Blair, Nov. 25, 1847, Aug. 3, 1849, Lizzie to Phil, May 2, 1846, Sept. 15, 1851.
8. Lizzie to Phil, Jan. 31, 1864.
9. Nov. 6, 1847, BLC.
10. Martin, Jr., to Van Buren, Feb. 3, 1848.
11. Van Buren to Blair, Feb. 17, 1848, BLC.
12. Lizzie to Phil, Aug. 14, 1846, Blair to Lizzie, Sept. 9, 1846; Blair to Rives, Sept. 19, 1846, BRLC.
13. James to Blair, Sept. 22, 1845, P.
14. MS of Douglas speech in P.
15. Jackson to W. B. Lewis, Feb. 13, March 3, March 22, 1842, Jackson–Lewis MSS, NYPL.
16. Jackson, Jr., to Blair and Rives, June 3, Aug. 19, 1847, April 20, 1849, Blair to W. B. Lewis, March 20, April 9, 1855, Jackson, Jr., to Rives, Feb. 11, 27, 1856, Lewis to Rives, March 31, 1856—all BRLC.

Chapter 13. The Clan

1. Blair to Van Buren, Nov. 24, 1851; Lizzie to Phil, Oct. 7, 21, Nov. 3, 27, Dec. 16, 1851.
2. Numerous undated eloquent and passionate letters. The Jan. 4, 1843, temporary-breakup letter is the only one dated.
3. Quoted in Lizzie to Phil, undated but received April 20, 1843.
4. Lee, "Memo from Memory," Nov. 5, 1846; Lizzie to Phil, Nov. 16, 1846.
5. Lizzie to Phil, Oct. 31, Nov. 13, Dec. 2, 13, 19, 1855.
6. Philipson, *Rebecca Gratz*, 418.
7. Lizzie to Phil, Oct. 16, 17, 18, 20, 24, 26, Nov. 9, 1843.
8. Oct. 24, 1843.
9. James to Mrs. F. P. Blair, Jan. 16, 1844.
10. James to Mary Blair, March 31, 1850; James to Blair, April 10, 1849, June 30, Aug. 31, 1850, BLC; Blair to Van Buren, April 27, 1850; James to Blair, July 1, 1850, Lizzie to Phil, Sept. 8, 12, 1850.
11. Frank to Blair, July 26, 1852, year not stated. Lizzie to Phil, Feb. 2, 1852.
12. Lizzie to Phil, Sept. 9, 1851.
13. Blair to James, June 6, 1851, James to Blair, Nov. 15, 1852, BLC.
14. Montgomery to Minna, Jan. 26, 1854; returned to him by Lizzie in 1875.
15. Lizzie to Phil, May 26, 1854, Montgomery to Blair, April 9, 1854; Blair to Mary, June 20, 1854, Thomas Sidney Jesup MSS, LC.
16. Blair to Van Buren, July 7, 1847; Frank to Blair, April 10, 1846.
17. Blair to Frank, April 20, 1851, BLC.
18. Aug. 15, 1852.

Chapter 14. The Free-Soiler

1. Lizzie to Phil, May 1, July 24; Smith, *Benton*, 207–214.
2. Blair to Van Buren, Dec. 26, 1846, March 6, 1847, BLC; Smith, 214–224.
3. Smith, 225–227; Blair to Van Buren, Jan. 23, 1847.
4. Blair to Van Buren, Aug. 25, 1847; Nevins, *Polk Diary*, 201–202.
5. Rives to Van Buren, May 12, 1847.
6. George R. Graham & Co. to Blair, Nov. 15, 1847. Pamphlet, LC.
7. Dec. 7, 1847.
8. Feb. 2, 1848.
9. Frank to Blair, April 22, 1848, VBMSS; Van Buren to Blair, April 8, 1848.
10. Blair to Van Buren, June 2, 1848.
11. Ibid., June 26, 1848.
12. Blair to Montgomery, Aug. 7, 1848, BLC; to Van Buren, Aug. 13, 1848.
13. Blair to Van Buren, Aug. 13, 1848.
14. Blair to Montgomery, Aug. 29, 1848, BLC; to Van Buren, Aug. 9, 20, 1848.
15. Blair to Van Buren, Nov. 30, 1848.
16. Houston, "To my constituents," MS copy in Blair's handwriting, P.
17. Aug. 8, 1849.
18. Part of letter from Clay to John Botts, Dec. 15, 1849, P.

Chapter 15. Hope and Frustration

1. Jan. 22, 1850.
2. Blair to Van Buren, Jan. 29, 1850.
3. Feb. 9, 1850, BLC.
4. *CG*, XIX (1850), 355–356, 712.
5. Blair to Van Buren, July 15, 1850.
6. Blair to Van Buren, July 16, 20, Aug. 1, 1850; Lizzie to Phil, Aug. 1, 1850.
7. Blair to Van Buren, Sept. 30, 1850; Lizzie to Phil, Oct. 9, 1850.
8. Lizzie to Phil, Oct. 7, 9, 11, 14, 1850; Blair to Van Buren, Oct. 12, 14, 15, 1850.
9. Blair to Van Buren, Dec. 26, 1850.
10. Ibid., Feb. 6, 1851.
11. Feb. 25, 1851.
12. Blair to Van Buren, Sept. 14, 1851; Lizzie to Phil, Sept. 6, 7, 17; 22, Oct. 1, 7, 1851.
13. Lizzie to Phil, Sept. 18, 22, Nov. 3, Dec. 2, 1851.
14. Blair to Van Buren, Dec. 11, 21, 1851; Van Buren to Blair, Dec. 15, 1851, BLC; Benton to Van Buren, Jan. 11, 1852.
15. Lizzie to Phil, Jan. 2, 29, 30, 1852; Blair to Van Buren, Jan. 2, 9, 11, 18, 1852.
16. Blair to Van Buren, Jan. 18, 1852; Van Buren to Blair, Jan. 26, 1852, BLC.

17. Blair to John Van Buren, Jan. 23, Feb. 18, 1852, VBMSS; John Van Buren to Blair, Feb. 28, 1852; Blair to John Van Buren, March 2, 1852; VBMSS; Blair to Martin Van Buren, March 6, 1852.
18. Blair to Van Buren, Aug. 16, 1852, Sept. 30, 1852, Oct. 18, 1852; Pamphlet, P.
19. Blair to Rives, Nov. 6, 1852, BRLC.
20. Copy of Blair to Pierce sent to Van Buren Nov. 25, 1852; Blair to Van Buren, Dec. 18, 27, 29, 1852, Feb. 24, 1853, VBMSS; recommendations of Montgomery to Pierce from the Missouri secretary of state, John M. Richardson, Jan. 19, 1853, and Thomas L. Price, Feb. 8, 1853, BLC; Van Buren to Blair, Dec. 22, 1852, BLC.
21. Benton to Montgomery Blair, April 30, 1853, BLC.
22. Blair to Van Buren, July 17, 1854.

Chapter 16. The Republican

1. Lizzie to Phil, May 25, 27, 29, June 3, 10, 15, 18, 24, 1854.
2. July 22, 1854.
3. July 16, 1855; Lizzie to Phil, Oct. 27, 1855.
4. May 2, 1856.
5. Blair, draft of unaddressed letter, Sept. 1855, Blair to Bedford Brown, Oct. 30, 1855, Lizzie to Phil, Nov. 17, 30, 1855; Blair to Van Buren, Jan. 25, 1856.
6. Blair pamphlet, BLC.
7. Feb. 13, 1856.
8. *CG*, XXXI (34th Cong., 1st sess., 1855–1856), Appendix, 1070–1076.
9. Cf. David H. Donald, *Charles Sumner and the Coming of the Civil War* (1967), 329–333.
10. Lizzie to Phil, May 22, 23, 1856.
11. Ibid., May 26, 1856.
12. Ibid., June 2, 4, 7, 14, 1856; Henry Gilpin to Van Buren, July 17, 1856, VBMSS.
13. Halstead, *Trimmers, Trucklers, & Temporizers* (1861), 92, 102.
14. Lizzie to Eliza Blair, June 26, to Phil, June 27, 28, 1856.
15. Blair to Van Buren, Sept. 22, 1856.
16. *New York Evening Post*, Sept. 20, 1856; also pamphlet, P.
17. Rives to Blair, Sept. 22, 1856; see also Blair to Rives, Sept. 23, 1856, BRLC.
18. Cited by Avery Craven, *The Coming of the Civil War* (1957 edition), 378.
19. *Jefferson Enquirer* (Jefferson City, Mo.), Nov. 8, 1856; Smith, *Benton*, 313–316.
20. Catherine C. Phillips, *Jessie Benton Frémont* (1935), 214.
21. Blair to Van Buren, Dec. 24, 1856. For evidence supporting generalizations about Buchanan, see Elbert B. Smith, *The Presidency of James Buchanan* (1975).
22. Cited by Craven, 380.

Chapter 17. Cold War: North and South

1. Aaron V. Brown to Mrs. James K. Polk, Jan. 14, 1844, Polk MSS, LC.
2. Cited by Allan Nevins, *The Emergence of Lincoln* (1950), I, 85.
3. Montgomery Blair address to U.S. Supreme Court, Dec. 15, 1856, pamphlet, copy in BLC. Cf. Don E. Fehrenbacher, *The Dred Scott Case* (1978), 285–309.
4. Burritt to Blair, May 21, 1858.
5. Lizzie to Phil, April 2, 1857.
6. Lizzie to Phil, April 25, 28, May 8, 14, 21; Blair to Montgomery, May 29, 1857, BLC.
7. Lizzie to Phil, April 16, May 2, 1857.
8. Feb. 4, 1858, copy in BLC.
9. Lizzie to Phil, Aug. 23, 1858.
10. *CG*, XXX (1857–1858), 286–298.
11. Ibid., 1282–1294; Blair to Van Buren, April 2, 1858.
12. Blair to Van Buren, April 2, 11, 12, 1856; Lizzie to Phil, April 4, 5, 7, 13, 1856.
13. Jones, *Colonel Benton and His Contemporaries*, May 17, 1858, pamphlet in VBMSS.
14. *New York Tribune*, May 25, 1858; John Bigelow to Blair, undated; Blair to Van Buren, April 12, 1858.
15. Lizzie to Phil, Aug. 28, 1858.
16. Pamphlet, LC; Lizzie to Phil, Feb. 2, 1859.
17. Frank to Blair, undated but obviously in early 1859, BLC; Frank to Lincoln, Oct. 18, 1859, Lincoln MSS, LC.
18. Frank to Montgomery, Oct. 20, 1859, BLC.
19. Pamphlet on microcard (Louisville: Lost Cause Press, 1961).

Chapter 18. Triumph and Vindication

1. Aug. 2, BLC.
2. Oct. 10, 1859.
3. BLC.
4. Lizzie to Phil, March 28, 1860.
5. Blair to Crittenden, Feb. 16, 1860, cited by Mrs. Chapman Coleman, *The Life of John J. Crittenden* (1871), II, 186.
6. Lizzie to Phil, Sept. 29, 1860; MS copy of speech, BLC.
7. Dwight Dumond (ed.), *Southern Editorials on Secession* (1931), 315–316.
8. Basler, IV, 162–163; William E. Barringer, *A House Dividing: Lincoln as President* (1945), 212.
9. Blair to Frank, Nov. 22, 1860, BLC.

Chapter 19. In the Midst of a Revolution

1. Blair to Frank, Jan. 2, 1861, BLC; Montgomery to Lincoln, Dec. 8, 1860, LMSS.
2. Oct. 27, 1860, LMSS.

3. Dec. 6, 1860, Jan. 5, 1861, LMSS.
4. LMSS.
5. Burton J. Hendrick, *Lincoln's War Cabinet* (1946), 118–123.
6. Scott's "Views," *National Intelligencer*, Jan. 18, 1861; Philip S. Klein, *President James Buchanan* (1962), 368–402; Smith, *Buchanan*, 167–187.
7. Blair to Montgomery, March 12, 1861, enclosed in Montgomery to Lincoln, same date, LMSS.
8. Howard K. Beale (ed.), *Diary of Gideon Welles* (1960), I, 13, hereafter cited as *Welles*.
9. March 15, 1861, LMSS.
10. Hendrick, 170–171.
11. Ibid.
12. Quoted by John G. Nicolay and John Hay, *Abraham Lincoln: A History* (1890), III, 399, 413; Hendrick, 173.
13. Nicolay and Hay, III, 389–433.
14. *Welles*, I, 32–33, II, 248–249; Hendrick, 183; Nicolay and Hay, IV, 32.
15. *Welles*, I, 22–31; Hendrick, 176–182.
16. Quoted by Nicolay and Hay, IV, 32; cf. Hendrick, 183–185.
17. Basler, IV, 350–351.
18. Nicolay and Hay, IV, 98–99; Montgomery Blair to William Cullen Bryant, Aug. 5, 1866, in F. P. Blair's handwriting, BLC.

Chapter 20. The Warriors

1. Lizzie to Phil, Sept. 3, Nov. 26, 27, 1860.
2. Ibid., Oct. 2, Nov. 16, 23, 1860.
3. F. E. Spinner to Samuel P. Lee, Dec. 3, 1865, recounting these conversations, copy in P.
4. Twenty-two-page summary of Lee's career by his son, Blair Lee, pages 8–12; Robert S. West, Jr., *Mr. Lincoln's Navy* (1957), 178–182, pays no compliments but relates the same facts.
5. Blair Lee's summary, 13–14.
6. Lizzie to Phil, July 6, 1864, and numerous other family letters.
7. Lizzie to Phil, Jan. 22, 1864.
8. *Official Records of the Union and Confederate Navies in the War of the Rebellion*, series I, vol. X (1900), 271–273.
9. West, 291–295; Lizzie to Phil, Dec. 31, 1864.
10. Lizzie to Phil, Sept. 30, 1864.
11. Blair to Sumner, Jan. 29, June 6, 29, 1865, Sumner MSS, Harvard.
12. Franklin A. Dick to Blair, enclosing list of his debtors and amounts loaned in St. Louis, Oct. 31, Nov. 1, 1860; Dick to Blair, enclosing list of Frank's debts, Dec. 23, 1860; Frank to Blair, undated, and Dec. 23, 1860—all in BLC.
13. William E. Smith, *The Francis Preston Blair Family in Politics* (1933), II, 19–52, for the Missouri struggle. Professor Smith apparently had no access to the Blair—Lee Papers at Princeton, and his work antedates newer interpretations of Jacksonian Democracy, the Civil War, and Recon-

struction, but his chapters on Missouri politics are excellent. A southern version is Ralph R. Rea, *Sterling Price, the Lee of the West* (1959), 33–45.

14. Bruce Catton, *Terrible Swift Sword* (1963), 13–22.
15. BLC.
16. MS copy in her handwriting, LMSS.
17. Smith, II, 69; Allan Nevins, *Frémont: The West's Greatest Adventurer* (1928), II, 577.
19. Bruce Catton, *Grant Moves South* (1960); Basler, IV, 506, 517.
20. John M. Schofield, *Forty-Six Years in the Army* (1879), 48.
21. LMSS; copy in P.
22. LMSS.
23. Conversation recorded in John Hay's diary and cited in Nicolay and Hay, *Lincoln*, IV, 414–415; for their version of entire incident, 407–439. See also James G. Randall, *Lincoln the President* (1945–1955), II, 15–25.
24. Nevins, II, 585–587.
25. Ibid., 587–588.
26. Lizzie to Phil, Sept. 17, 1861; Montgomery to W. O. Bartlett, Sept. 26, 1861, marked "not sent" on envelope, BLC.
27. Lincoln to Jessie Frémont, Sept. 12, 1861, Basler, IV, 519.
28. Sept. 14, 1861, LMSS.
29. Telegram, Sept. 19, letter, Sept. 20, 1861, BLC.
30. MS copy in P.
31. Blair to Lorenzo Thomas, Sept. 26, 1861, copy in P; Blair specifications against Frémont, LMSS.
32. Frank to Blair, two undated letters in P.
33. Frank to Montgomery, Sept. 26, 1861, BLC; Oct. 1, 1861, LMSS; Montgomery to Blair, Sept. 26, 1861, P.
34. Cameron to Lincoln, Oct. 14, 1861, LMSS; Randall, II, 17–18, 25–26, 34.
35. Smith, *Blair Family*, II, 74–75.
36. Frank to Lincoln, Dec. 5, 1861, LMSS; Frank to Montgomery, Sept. 17, Dec. 6, 1862, BLC.
37. Ulysses S. Grant, *Personal Memoirs of U.S. Grant*, I, 573–574; *The War of the Rebellion: A Compilation of Official Records of the Union & Confederate Armies* (1893), series I, part I, 655; Frank to Montgomery, Jan. 6, 1863, BLC; Smith, II, 148–155; Nicolay and Hay, VII, 133–134.
38. Smith, II, 158–162.
39. Ibid., 170; Sherman to Frank, Oct. 16, 1863, BLC.
40. Smith, II, 180–182.
41. Nov. 10, 1864, BLC.

Chapter 21. To Win a War

1. Blair's achievements for the postal service taken from Madison Davis, "The Public Career of Montgomery Blair, Particularly With Reference To His Services as Postmaster General of the United States," *Records of the Colum-*

bia Historical Society, XIII (1910). Cf. Smith, *Blair Family,* II, 90–
111.

2. Kendall to Montgomery Blair, March 8, 1861, BLC; Lizzie to Phil, April 6, 1851.

3. Brief, undated, in Blair's handwriting; undated letter marked "Christmas," BLC.

4. *Recollections of Abraham Lincoln* (1911), 205.

5. Lizzie to Phil, July 11, 1861, April 20, 1865.

6. *Welles,* I, 205; Hendrick, *Lincoln's Cabinet,* 219–225, 237–242.

7. Randall, *Lincoln,* II, 37–49; Hendrick, 199–212.

8. Montgomery Blair, with P.S. by his father to John Andrew, Oct. 2, 1861, Andrew MSS, Harvard; Montgomery to Lincoln, Nov. 21, 1861; Blair to Montgomery, May 31, 1861, BLC.

9. Blair to unknown addressee, BLC; numerous Blair letters to various border-state leaders urging voluntary state emancipation with compensation, BLC and P; Nicolay and Hay, VI, 390 ff.

10. Blair brief, BLC; Blair to Montgomery, Nov. 16, 1861, Blair to Lincoln, Nov. 16, 1861, both in LMSS; E. O. Crosby to Blair, July 21, 1861; Ambrose Thompson to Blair, April 13, 1863; *Welles,* I, 123, 151–152.

11. Hendrick, 349–356; Nicolay and Hay, VI, 161–163; Montgomery Blair to Lincoln, July 23, 1862, LMSS.

12. Benjamin Quarles, *Lincoln and the Negro* (1962), 117–123; cf. John Hope Franklin, *The Emancipation Proclamation* (1965).

13. Pamphlet copy of Cleveland speech, BLC.

14. *Extracts of Letters Written to My Wife During the War of the Rebellion,* p. 28, McClellan MSS, LC.

15. Blair to McClellan, April 12, 1862, cited by Hendrick, 296; Blair to Montgomery, Nov. 7, 1862, BLC.

16. *Welles,* I, 104–105; William S. Myers, *General George Brinton McClellan* (1934), 298, 396.

17. *Welles,* I, 94–96, 104–105, 124–125; Hendrick, 306–316; Randall, II, 112–113.

18. Basler, V, 474; Hendrick, 390–392.

19. Blair to Lincoln, Dec. 18, 1862, LMSS; Hendrick, 390–392.

20. Douglas S. Freeman, *Lee* (1961 abridgement), 278.

21. Basler, VI, 78–79; *Welles,* I, 229–230.

22. Blair to Lincoln, May 17, 1863, LMSS.

Chapter 22. To Serve a President

1. Montgomery Blair, "Letter to the Meeting Held at the Cooper Institute, New York, March 6, 1862"; Smith to Montgomery Blair, April 5, 1862. Printed versions of both letters, BLC. Blair's letter also published in *Comments on the Policy Inaugurated by the President in a Letter and Two Speeches* (1863).

2. *Welles,* I, 196–197, 203.

3. Pamphlet, LC; Hendrick, *Lincoln's Cabinet*, 396–399.

4. Pamphlet, BLC. Rush R. Sloan to Montgomery, Jan. 28, 1864, reported that the circulation of this speech in Ohio and Indiana would exceed that of any speech since 1860.

5. Nicolay and Hay, IX, 30.

6. Knox, "Brief" pamphlet, BLC.

7. Basler, VI, 554–555; original, BLC.

8. Lizzie to Phil, Jan. 9, 1864, and almost daily for next few months.

9. R. J. Howard to Montgomery Blair, Sept. 24, 1864, and other letters from St. Louis, complaining of the Chase patronage policies, BLC.

10. Hendrick, 393–421; Nicolay and Hay, 79 ff.

11. Hendrick, 369–370; the unhappy quest of Chase and Kate for the presidency is best told by Thomas G. and Marva R. Belden, *So Fell the Angels* (1956).

12. *CG* (38th Cong., 1st sess.), Appendix, 46–51; Smith, *Blair Family*, II, 257–258; Hendrick, 422–434.

13. *CG* (38th Cong., 1st sess.), part 2, 1827–1832; Hendrick, 427–434.

14. Lizzie to Phil, April 21, 23, 24, 1864.

15. Riddle's account in clippings from his own reminiscences and from *New York Daily Tribune*, Oct. 22, 1886; NYPL; Hendrick, 430–434; Nicolay and Hay, IX, 79–81.

16. June 6, 1864, Samuel Simmons to Frank, Jan. 7, 1864, BLC.

17. Montgomery Blair to Lincoln, May 6, 1864, BLC; Nicolay and Hay, VI, 481–482.

18. The convention and the circumstances surrounding it are covered in great detail by William F. Zornow, *Lincoln and the Party Divided* (1954), 85–100. Cf. *Welles*, II, 173–174. Welles was certain the convention criticisms were aimed only at Seward.

19. Lizzie to Phil, July 16, 1864; *National Intelligencer*, Oct. 5, 1864; Nicolay and Hay, IX, 247–249; Zornow, 126; Smith, II, 280–281.

20. Myers, *McClellan*, 444–445; Zornow, 144–145.

21. Montgomery Blair to R. A. Sloan, July 21, 1864, to Benjamin F. Butler, Aug. 9, 1864; BLC; *Welles*, II, 84; Nicolay and Hay, IX, 333–342.

22. Blair to Montgomery, "Monday," 1864, BLC; Lizzie to Phil, Sept. 24, 1864; Blair to Lincoln, Sept. 5, 1864, BLC.

23. Zornow, 146–147.

24. Lincoln note, BLC; *Welles*, II, 156–159.

25. Frank to Blair, Sept. 30, 1864.

26. Copy of speech, and numerous letters answering the criticisms being made against Lincoln for dismissing Montgomery; also Montgomery's letters to Minna from different points of his campaign tour, BLC.

27. Petition for Montgomery from Maryland citizens (6 pages), Edward Everett to Lincoln, Nov. 22, 1864, Blair to Lincoln, Oct. 20, 1864— all in BLC; Blair to John Andrew, Nov. 17, 1864, Andrew MSS, Harvard.

28. Copy in BLC.

Chapter 23. The Home Front

1. Lizzie to Phil, March 11, April 12, 13, 14, 15, 17, 1862. The family information in this chapter, unless otherwise indicated, comes exclusively from Lizzie's letters, which are so numerous that listing them all is unnecessary.
2. Betty to Blair, Jan. 25 [1865].
3. Blair to John Andrew, Sept. 10, 1862, Andrew MSS, Harvard.
4. Ibid., May 18, 1861, Andrew MSS.
5. Lizzie to Phil, April 18, 23, 1862, Sept. 16, 1864.
6. Nelly Lee to Phil, Dec. 30, 1863, P; Lizzie to Phil, April 11, 1864, Aug. 20, 1863.
7. To Phil, March 30, 1862.
8. Ibid., April 9, 1864.
9. Cited by Hans Trefousse, *The Radical Republicans* (1968), 242.
10. Lizzie to Phil, July 16, 17, 27, 30, 1864.
11. Ibid., Aug. 9, 1864, Cameron to Blair, July 25, Sept. 17, 1864, Blair to Phil, Aug. 14, 1864.
12. Lizzie to Phil, Feb. 13, April 10, 13, 1864.
13. Ibid., May 9, July 18, 27, Aug. 9, Sept. 16, 1864.

Chapter 24. Peace

1. Blair to Lincoln, July 21, 1864, LMSS; Greeley to Blair, Dec. 1, 1864.
2. Dec. 15, 1864; copy in BLC.
3. Greeley MSS, Ford Collection, NYPL.
4. Lizzie to Phil, Dec. 27, 28, 1864; M. N. Falls to Blair, Dec. 28, 1864, James A. Seddon to Blair, Dec. 31, 1864, Blair memorandum written later about his mission, BLC; Nicolay and Hay, IX, 94–125, tell the entire story; various newspaper clippings in NYPL.
5. Memorandum of the conversations with Davis dictated by Blair to Montgomery on Jan. 18, 1865, BLC; copy of Blair suggestions to Davis in LMSS; Blair to Greeley, Jan. 18, 1864, Greeley MSS, NYPL.
6. Lizzie to Phil, Jan. 16, 1865.
7. Nicolay and Hay, IX, 111–125; Blair to Lincoln, Feb. 8, 1865, LMSS.
8. Lizzie to Phil, March 7, 27, 30, 1865.
9. Ibid., April 3, 14 (continued on 15), 1865.
10. Ibid., April 17, 19, 20, 21, 26, 28, 30, May 1, 3, 12, 22, 1865.
11. Ibid., April 15, 1865.
12. Ibid., May 10, 24, 25, 1865 .
13. Eveline M. Alexander to Phil, June 1, 1865, Dr. John F. Clary to Phillips Lee, June 3, 1865, Lizzie to Phil, June 9, 13, 26, 1865.

Chapter 25. The Quality of Mercy

1. Blair memorandum, Jan. 24, 1865, LMSS; A. G. Brown to Blair, Feb. 20, 1865, William E. Ware to Montgomery Blair, Feb. 15, 1865, BLC.
2. Dodge to Mrs. Blair, Jan. 13, 1862; P. Montgomery Blair to Stanton,

Jan. 18, 1862, BLC; A. P. Crittenden to Blair, July 22, 1862, Rives to Blair, Jan. 1, 30, March 9, Aug. 11, 1863, P; Krumsick to Frank Blair, Feb. 21, 1863, BLC; *Welles*, I, 406.

3. Gwinn to Montgomery Blair, Aug. 18, 1864, BLC; Basler, VII, 522.

4. Pleasanton to Blair, Aug. 23, 1864, July 18, 1865, A. E. Church to Blair, Sept. 3, 1864, Major Morris Miller to Blair, Aug. 15, 1864, Aug. 17, 18, Oct. 27, 1865.

5. Gratz to Blair, Aug. 29, 1863, P; Mrs. Critcher to Blair, Oct. 6, 1863, LMSS; Blair to Lincoln, April 14, 1864, Mrs. Waring to Blair, Sept. 11, 1864, Blair to Lincoln, Sept. 14, 1864, LMSS; Basler, VII, 491.

6. Bovic to Blair, May 4, 1863, March 5, Oct. 5, 1864, P; Jan. 28, 1865, BLC.

7. Andrew and Mrs. Comstock to Blair, Feb. 7, 17, 1865; *Maryland Gen. Assembly Documents (House)*, 1866, part 2, p. 9.

8. Mary F. Jackson to Blair, Nov. 14, 1864, Mary Alexander to Blair, Nov. 28, 1864.

9. Sallie H. Wooley to Stanton, Sept. 30, 1864, Thomas P. Chifelli to Blair, Jan. 26, 1865, Lillie Chifelli to Montgomery Blair, Feb. 8, 1865, Sallie H. Wooley to Lincoln, Feb. 1865, Robert W. Wooley to Montgomery Blair, July 17, 1865, Sam H. Wooley to Montgomery Blair, Oct. 2, 1865— all in BLC.

10. Mrs. Ewell to Blair, March 16, 1865, Thomas Gannt to Blair, March 15, 16, 1865, Mrs. Ewell to Montgomery Blair, April 4, 1864, P; and May 3, 1865, BLC; Gen. Ewell to Montgomery Blair, May 13, 1865, BLC; Lizzie to Phil, June 20, July 21, 1865.

11. Varina Davis to Montgomery Blair, June 6, 1865, BLC; to Francis P. Blair, June 23, 1865, P, and July 10, Sept. 26, Andrew Johnson MSS, LC; Blair to Andrew Johnson, Sept. 6, 1865, BLC; Jeff Howell to Montgomery Blair, June 20, 1865, BLC.

12. William W. Boyce to Blair, Aug. 15, 1865, Payne to Blair, July 21, 1865; Johnston to Blair, Aug. 3, 1865.

13. Frank Blair quoted in Jefferson City, Mo., *People's Weekly Tribune*, June 13, 1866.

14. Blair's views on reconstruction were supported for decades by popular works like those of William A. Dunning, *Reconstruction, Political and Economic, 1865–1877* (1907), and the books on individual states by his students like Walter L. Fleming, *Civil War and Reconstruction in Alabama* (1905), and Joseph G. de Roulhac Hamilton, *Reconstruction in North Carolina* (1914). Perhaps the most extreme history in this vein was Claude Bowers, *The Tragic Era* (1929). This sad story of white suffering at the hands of vindictive blacks, carpetbaggers, and scalawags was further disseminated in countless novels and motion pictures. More recent historians who have shown how thoroughly exaggerated this tale of woe really was include Kenneth Stampp, *The Era of Reconstruction, 1865–1877* (1965); John H. Franklin, *Reconstruction: After the Civil War* (1961); W. R. Brock, *An American Crisis: Congress and Reconstruction, 1865–1867* (1963);

and numerous others. The older economic thesis of Howard Beale, *The Critical Year: A Study of Andrew Johnson and Reconstruction* (1930), has been effectively refuted by Robert P. Sharkey, *Money, Class and Party: An Economic Study of Civil War and Reconstruction* (1959). Excellent anthologies that present the opposing interpretations side by side are Edwin Rozwenc (ed.), *Reconstruction in the South* (1972), and Seth M. Scheiner, *Reconstruction, A Tragic Era* (1968). My own revisionist viewpoints are derived from the books by Dunning and his students, who present a wealth of facts and information entirely at variance with their own conclusions.

Chapter 26. Reconstruction

1. Cited by Trefousse, *Radical Republicans*, 307–308.
2. Blair to Johnson, July 28, 1865, BLC; Aug. 1, 1865, March 18, 1866, Johnson MSS, LC; numerous drafts of letters and speeches in P and BLC.
3. Sept. 27 (year omitted), BLC.
4. See essays by Thomas C. Cochran, Stanley Coben, and LaWanda and John H. Cox in Charles Crowe (ed.), *The Age of Civil War and Reconstruction* (1966 edition), 281–304, 358–376; also Sharkey, *Money, Class, and Party*, and Brock, *American Crisis*.
5. Montgomery Blair's speech, pamphlets in LC; Smith, *Blair Family*, II, 339–343.
6. March 18, 1866, Johnson MSS.
7. This is argued and documented effectively by Eric L. McKitrick, *Andrew Johnson and Reconstruction* (1960).
8. James McPherson, *The Struggle for Equality* (1964), excerpt reprinted in Crowe, 396–410.
9. Notably Beale, *The Critical Year*.
10. Samuel L. M. Barlow to Montgomery Blair, July 19, 1865, Johnson MSS; Montgomery Blair to Johnson, Sept. 12, Nov. 21, 1865, enclosing letters from Barlow, Sept. 11, 1865, and John Cochrane, Nov. 19, 1865, Johnson MSS; Samuel J. Tilden to Montgomery Blair, March 10, 1866, BLC; George T. McJimsey, *Genteel Partisan: Manton Marble, 1834–1917* (1971), 63–75; F. P. Blair to Johnson, Sept. 7, 1867, Johnson MSS.
11. Blair to Johnson, July 28, 1865, BLC; Blair to Montgomery, June 22, 1865, Johnson MSS.
12. McPherson in Crowe, 407–408.
13. Frank to Blair, Nov. 10, 1865, June 19, 22, July 9, 1866; *Jefferson City People's Weekly Tribune*, May 22, 1865; Derringer to Blair, Aug. 29, Sept. 1, 1866.
14. Montgomery to Minna, Sept. 28, Oct. 9, 1866, BLC; *Welles*, II, 613.
15. Blair to Bryant, Aug. 5, 1866, BLC; rough draft of speech, P; B. Gratz Brown told several people that Blair advocated women's suffrage; see Mrs. George D. Hall to Blair, May 22, 1866.
16. McKitrick, 457–459.
17. Blair to Johnson, Feb. 24, 1867, Johnson MSS.
18. *Welles*, III, 70–71; Frank to Johnson, March 3, 1867, Johnson MSS;

orders to Frank from Johnson and the secretary of the interior, Dec. 25, 1866, Frank to John D. Perry, Jan. 24, 1867, Lizzie to Phil, Dec. 20, 1866.

19. Henry Clay Dean to Montgomery Blair, April 7, 1867, Edwin H. Webster to Montgomery, April 30, 1867, Montgomery to Simpson, May 1, 1867, Simpson to Montgomery, May 16, June 5, 26, Dec. 30, 1867—all BLC.

Chapter 27. The Candidate

1. Montgomery to Minna, Aug. 9, 1867, BLC.
2. *Welles*, I, 533–534; Blair to Johnson, May 13, Aug. 16, 1866, Johnson MSS, LC.
3. Blair to Montgomery, May 26, 1866; *Welles*, II, 243, 504–505, 512–514, 569, 578.
4. Blair to Minna, July 26, 1867, Frank to Montgomery, Dec. 10, 1867, BLC.
5. Blair to Montgomery, Nov. 2, 1867.
6. MSS drafts; Blair to Frank, May 20, 1868, BLC; Smith, *Blair Family*, II, 396–397. The senior Blair's draft closed with a blast at those who would take the vote away from whites and give it to blacks.
7. Smith, II, 408–409.
8. Ibid., 406–407.
9. Ibid., 409–413.
10. For example, see pamphlet of Frank Blair's speech at Indianapolis, Sept. 24, 1868, BLC.
11. Smith, II, 414–420.
12. *The Statistical History of the United States* (1976), 1071–1073, 1076, 1080.
13. Collection of newspaper clippings, Blair MSS, NYPL.

Chapter 28. The Last Hurrah

1. Lizzie to Phil, Sept. 10, 1868, May 12, 17, 19, 20, 1869; Minna to Mrs. A. H. Lowery, sometime in 1870, BLC.
2. Lizzie to Phil, Jan. 20, 1867.
3. Ibid., March 31, April 6, 22, 1869, Feb. 16, March 22, 1872.
4. Pamphlet, BLC.
5. MS copy, BLC.
6. Lizzie to Phil, April 10, 1869; Frank to Blair, enclosing his own letter to Betty, March 14, 1869; Betty to Blair, enclosing her letter to Mrs. F. A. Dick, Nov. 11, 1869.
7. Frank to Montgomery, Nov. 11, 17, 1870, BLC; *Missouri Republican*, Jan. 22, 1871; *People's Weekly Tribune*, Nov. 8, 1871.
8. Frank to Montgomery, Jan. 1, 1871, P; Lizzie to Phil, Jan. 14, 24, 27, Feb. 1, 7, 30, Aug. 17, 1871, Blair to Phil, March 18, 1871.
9. Lizzie to Phil, April 3, 27, May 3, 1871, Jan. 27, Feb. 15, 19, 20, 22, 1872.

10. MSS copy in P; Lizzie to Phil, March 30, 1871.
11. Lizzie to Phil, Feb. 20, 26, April 29, 1871.
12. Ibid., March 30, April 10, June 18, 1871, March 19, 1872.
13. Montgomery to Minna, Sept. 8, 1869, BLC.
14. For the overall story of the decline of radicalism see Trefousse, *Radical Republicans*, 436–470.
15. Cited by Paul H. Buck, *The Road to Reunion* (1937), 92.
16. Lizzie to Phil, May 4, 1872.
17. Ibid. For the overall presidential campaign, see Buck, 72–95; Dunning, *Reconstruction*, 90–102; Earl D. Ross, *The Liberal Republican Movement* (1919).
18. Lizzie to Phil, May 8, 1872; numerous letters in P and BLC.
19. Lizzie to Phil, June 5, 9, 23, 29, July 12, 20, Nov. 4, 13, 1872.
20. Ibid., April 8, Aug. 8, 1872.
21. Frank to Montgomery, Sept. 25, probably 1872, June 9, Oct. 16, Nov. 3, 21, Dec. 1, 1873, June 1, 1874, BLC; to Blair, Nov. 19, Dec. 24, 1873.
22. April 23, BLC.
23. Clipping from unidentified Rochester, N.Y., newspaper, BLC.

Chapter 29. Twilight

1. Montgomery to Minna, Sept. 16, 17, 23, 25, one undated, 1874, BLC.
2. Lizzie to Phil, Nov. 24, 1872.
3. Frank to Montgomery, Dec. 6 [1874].
4. Lizzie to Preston, May 29, 1873, Apo to Blair, Oct. 9, 1873; Frank to Montgomery, March 24, 1874, Apo to Lizzie, May 9, 1875, Lizzie to Apo, May 11, 1875, BLC.
5. Sherman to Montgomery Blair, May 27, 1875; *Chicago Times*, July 12, 1875, cited by Smith, *Blair Family*, II, 461; *Louisville Courier Journal*, July 10, 1875; *New York Evening Mail*, July 10, 1875; *New York Times*, July 10, 1875; *Boston Transcript*, July 10, 1875; Philadelphia *Inquirer*, July 10, 1875.
6. Smith, II, 464.
7. W. Perkins to Montgomery Blair, Oct. 27, 1876, BLC; *New York Times*, Oct. 20, 1876; *Philadelphia Gazette*, Oct. 20, 1876.
8. Eliza to Apo, Jan. 8, 1877, BLC.
9. Wills and codicils, BLC.

Index